# THE RAVEN
## A BIOGRAPHY OF
## SAM HOUSTON

BY

MARQUIS JAMES

*American Statesmen Series*

GENERAL EDITOR
### ARTHUR M. SCHLESINGER, JR.
ALBERT SCHWEITZER PROFESSOR OF THE HUMANITIES
THE CITY UNIVERSITY OF NEW YORK

CHELSEA HOUSE
NEW YORK 1983

This edition is an edited reprint of the 1968 edition by
THE BOBBS-MERRILL COMPANY

Copyright © 1983 by Chelsea House Publishers
All rights reserved
Printed and bound in the United States of America

ISBN: 0-87754-408-5

# BLAZING THE WAY
### Arthur M. Schlesinger, jr.

THE ORIGINAL AMERICAN STATESMEN SERIES
consisted of thirty-four titles published between
1882 and 1916. Handsomely printed and widely read, the Series made a notable contribution
to the popular appreciation of American history. Its creator was John Torrey Morse, Jr.,
born in Boston in 1840, graduated from Harvard
in 1860 and for nearly twenty restless years
thereafter a Boston lawyer. In his thirties he
had begun to dabble in writing and editing; and
about 1880, reading a volume in John Morley's
English Men of Letters Series, he was seized by
the idea of a comparable set of compact, lucid
and authoritative lives of American statesmen.

It was an unfashionable thought. The celebrated New York publisher Henry Holt turned
the project down, telling Morse, "Who ever
wants to read American history?" Houghton,
Mifflin in Boston proved more receptive, and
Morse plunged ahead. His intention was that
the American Statesmen Series, when com-

plete, "should present such a picture of the development of the country that the reader who had faithfully read all the volumes would have a full and fair view of the history of the United States told through the medium of the efforts of the men who had shaped our national career. The actors were to develop the drama."

In choosing his authors, Morse relied heavily on the counsel of his cousin Henry Cabot Lodge. Between them, they enlisted an impressive array of talent. Henry Adams, William Graham Sumner, Moses Coit Tyler, Hermann von Holst, Moorfield Storey and Albert Bushnell Hart were all in their early forties when their volumes were published; Lodge, E. M. Shepard and Andrew C. McLaughlin in their thirties; Theodore Roosevelt in his twenties. Lodge took on Washington, Hamilton and Webster, and Morse himself wrote five volumes. He offered the authors a choice of $500 flat or a royalty of 12.5¢ on each volume sold. Most, luckily for themselves, chose the royalties.

Like many editors, Morse found the experience exasperating. "How I waded among the fragments of broken engagements, shattered pledges! I never really knew when I could count upon getting anything from anybody." Carl Schurz infuriated him by sending in a two-volume life of Henry Clay on a take-it-or-leave-it basis. Morse, who had confined Jefferson,

John Adams, Webster and Calhoun to single volumes, was tempted to leave it. But Schurz threatened to publish his work simultaneously if Morse commissioned another life of Clay for the Series; so Morse reluctantly surrendered.

When a former Confederate colonel, Allan B. Magruder, offered to do John Marshall, Morse, hoping for "a good Virginia atmosphere," gave him a chance. The volume turned out to have been borrowed in embarrassing measure from Henry Flanders's *Lives and Times of the Chief Justices.* For this reason, Magruder's *Marshall* is not included in the Chelsea House reissue of the Series; Albert J. Beveridge's famous biography appears in its stead. Other classic biographies will replace occasional Series volumes: John Marshall's *Life of George Washington* in place of Morse's biography; essays on John Adams by John Quincy Adams and Charles Francis Adams, also substituting for a Morse volume; and Henry Adams's *Life of Albert Gallatin* instead of the Series volume by John Austin Stevens.

"I think that only one real blunder was made," Morse recalled in 1931, "and that was in allotting [John] Randolph to Henry Adams." Half a century earlier, however, Morse had professed himself pleased with Adams's *Randolph.* Adams, responding with characteristic self-deprecation, thought the "acidity" of his account "much too decided" but blamed the "excess of acid" on the acidulous subject. The book was indeed hostile but nonetheless stylish. Adams also wrote a life of Aaron Burr, presumably for the Series. But Morse thought Burr no statesman, and on his advice, to Adams's extreme irritation, Henry Houghton of Houghton, Mifflin rejected the manuscript. "Not bad that for a damned bookseller!" said Adams. "He should live for a while at Washington and know our *real* statesmen." Adams eventually destroyed the work, and a fascinating book was lost to history.

The definition of who was or was not a "statesman" caused recurrent problems. Lodge told Morse one day that their young friend Theodore Roosevelt wanted to do Gouverneur Morris. "But, Cabot," Morse said, "you surely don't expect Morris to be in the Series! He doesn't belong there." Lodge replied, "Theodore . . . *needs the money,*" and Morse relented. No one objected to Thomas Hart Benton, Roosevelt's other contribution to the Series. Roosevelt turned out the biography in an astonishing four months while punching cows and chasing horse thieves in the Badlands. Begging Lodge to send more material from Boston, he wrote that he had been "mainly evolving [Benton] from my inner consciousness; but when he leaves the Senate in 1850 I have nothing whatever to go by. .... I hesitate to give him a wholly fictitious date of death and to invent all the work of his later years." In fact, T.R. had done more research than he pretended; and for all its defects, his *Benton* has valuable qualities of vitality and sympathy.

Morse, who would chat to Lodge about "the aristocratic upper crust in which you & I are imbedded," had a fastidious sense of language. Many years later, in the age of Warren G. Harding, he recommended to Lodge that the new President find someone "who can clothe for him his 'ideas' in the language customarily used by educated men." At dinner in a Boston club, a guest commented on the dilemma of the French ambassador who could not speak English. "Neither can Mr. Harding," Morse said. But if patrician prejudice improved Morse's literary taste, it also impaired his political understanding. He was not altogether kidding when he wrote Lodge as the Series was getting under way, "Let the Jeffersonians & the Jacksonians beware! I will poison the popular mind!!"

Still, for all its fidelity to establishment values, the American Statesmen Series had distinct virtues. The authors were mostly from outside the academy, and they wrote with the confidence of men of affairs. Their books are generally crisp, intelligent, spirited and read-able. The Series has long been in demand in secondhand bookstores. Most of its volumes are eminently worth republication today, on their merits as well as for the vigorous expression they give to an influential view of the American past.

Born during the Presidency of Martin Van Buren, John Torrey Morse, Jr., died shortly after the second inauguration of Franklin D. Roosevelt in 1937. A few years before his death he could claim with considerable justice that his Series had done "a little something in blazing the way" for the revival of American historical writing in the years to come.

*New York*
*May, 1980*

# BOOK ONE

## ROMANCE

"Two classes of people pursued
Sam Houston all his life—
artists and women."
　　—Miss Anne Hanna, a
　　belle of Old Nashville.

# THE RAVEN

## CHAPTER I

## ". . . One Sword, $15"

### 1

The vessel seemed off her course, and the crew grumbled about its work while a troubled landsman paced the quarter-deck. The Captain was below in irons, the passengers on their knees in the waist thanking God that matters were no worse—which easily might have been. But for a chance discovery and a bold plan carried boldly through, who could say what should have been their fate at the hands of the wicked mariner to whom they had entrusted their lives and their fortunes?

The fortunes were at the root of the trouble. At Belfast too many kegs of gold sovereigns had gone on board under the meditative eye of the Master. It was uncommon for emigrants to be so well fixed. Half-seas-over the situation got the best of the Skipper. But his buccaneering plot was found out, and the passengers overwhelmed the ringleaders and took charge of the ship. One of their number said he understood enough navigation to bring her into Philadelphia.

That had happened eight days ago, and a landfall was overdue. But prayer fortified the voyagers' spirits, and surely enough, before the day was out, a seaman cried, "Land ho!" and the South River capes spread into view.

When the ship came to berth a thick-set man in middle life, with silver buckles on his shoes, stepped ashore with his mother, his wife and six children.  The family of "John Houston, Gent.," descendants of baronets, whose ancestors were in the company of Scottish archers that led the way for Jeanne d'Arc from Orleans to Reims, stood on the wharf and saw their keg of sovereigns safely on the soil of the New World, in the year 1730.[1]

2

Twenty-four years later Gentleman John could have looked back on a span of life extraordinary for its success at colonial endeavor.  He had tarried in Pennsylvania long enough to marry off young John, his son, and two daughters.  Then the tide of Scotch-Irish immigration streaming southward had swept him up and set him down in the upper Valley of Virginia among the Stuarts and the McCorkles, the Paxtons, Davidsons, Montgomerys, McCormicks and McClungs.  He had become one of the first citizens of the new Presbyterian commonwealth beyond the Blue Ridge, at which the Episcopalian aristocracy of the Tidewater was beginning to cease to tilt its nose.  His lands were extensive and he had been among the first to import negroes across the mountains—not without a twitch of his non-conformist conscience in the beginning, perhaps, for until then the rougher tasks had been undertaken by indentured white servants who were slaves but temporarily.  He had built roads that exist to this day and a stone church in which Valley folk still worship.  He had administered the King's justice as a magistrate and fought the French and the Indians.

At the age of sixty-five, rich and honored, he continued the pioneer.  He was clearing a new field, and when something went wrong, Squire John stepped under a tree that was afire to give an order.  A great limb fell, pinning him to the earth. When his servants reached him John Houston, Gentleman, the founder of an American family, was dead.

## 3

Squire John's son, Robert, had married one of the well-to-do Davidson girls and established himself on the Timber Ridge Plantation.  There Robert built a fine house (though aristocratic Tidewater would not have thought it much), with a two-story gallery supported by square columns.  He could sit on his gallery and look down the rows of locust and maple trees he had planted along the driveway that joined the main road to Lexington.  He could extend his field of vision for a long way down the Valley, and much of what he saw he owned.

The Valley had prospered and begun to lose some of the rawness and severity that irritated the Tidewater.  It built better houses and made a beginning at the art of living according to what was already a Virginia tradition.  But on the whole Tidewater remained unimpressed and was disposed to regard the Valley as a barbarous region where gentlemen worked with their hands and a man might be put in jail for skipping church service.

Tidewater's criticisms do not appear to have disturbed Robert Houston, who was not the kind to borrow trouble. When his work was caught up, he could enjoy his breeze-swept gallery or a court-day excursion to Lexington, the county-seat, seven miles away, to hear the news.  Perhaps he heard, and passed an opinion on the fact, that William Gray had been presented to the grand jury for driving a wagon on Sunday, and that Charles Given was complaining to the authorities that his left ear had been bitten off by Francis McDonald.

Yes, the court-house was the place to go for the news: Judith Ryley accused of killing her bastard child. . . . Nat, an Indian boy, complains that he is held in slavery by the rich Widow Greenlee. . . . John Moore presented for staying away from public worship. . . . Elizabeth Berry sentenced to receive twenty-five lashes on the bare back for stealing a shirt of Margaret McCassell. . . . Malcomb McCown indicted for the murder of Cornstalk and three other Indians;

no prosecution. Malcomb McCown suspected of stealing a horse; to jail without bail. . . . Sam Jack presented for saying "God damn the Army to hell."[2]

General Washington's Army was the one Sam Jack had in mind. This made the transgression a grievous one, offending the Deity and the cause of freedom as well. Upper-crust Tidewater had its share of Tories, but the Valley was for "independency" almost to a man. Mr. Jack was fined fifty pounds and sentenced to spend twenty-four hours in jail, which Robert Houston doubtless felt was no less than he deserved. For Robert was a rebel—and had a boy in the war.

### 4

Samuel Houston, the son of Robert, liked the military life and came home a captain in Morgan's Rifle Brigade, the most celebrated corps in the Continental Army. When his father died, Captain Houston got the Timber Ridge place. He married Elizabeth, a daughter of Squire John Paxton, one of Rockbridge County's richest men. The new mistress of Timber Ridge was tall and handsome. She was counted a lady—almost in the Tidewater manner.

The war had brought wonderful changes to the Colonies, and some of these had reached the sheltered Valley. Captain Houston, for one, had traveled and learned to prefer the easy life and cavalier tone of the seaboard. With his inheritance, and a rich wife, he felt in a position to order his life to conform to his new ideas. He decided to embrace the profession of arms as a career. It was a gentleman's occupation.

Consequently the Captain remained in the military establishment, the State establishment, with appointment as brigadier inspector, which was the utmost Virginia could do toward providing professional standing for an officer of militia. But it suited Captain Houston, who gravely pursued his uneventful rounds for twenty-three years—which is a long time to sustain an illusion.

## 5

Ten of these years had gone by when one day the Captain rode home in haste. It was late February and the last ascending curve of the Plank Road from Lexington lifted the rangy outlines of the homestead on the hill against a sunless background of sky and valley. On the maple and locust trees a few buds put forth their points shyly as if committing an indiscretion. The Captain crossed the two-story gallery, turned the small, burnished, brass door-knob and stepped briskly within.

All was well and he had arrived in time—in good time, for not until the second day of March, in 1793, was the baby born. It was the fifth that had blessed the union of Samuel and Elizabeth Houston and, like the others, a boy. Captain Houston gave his own name, Samuel, to the little fellow and posted away again, the hoofs of his saddle horse drumming on the great puncheons of the Plank Road an axiom of the trade of arms. It is hard for a soldier to have any home life.

The black nurse girl, Peggy, took charge of Sam, which enabled Mistress to resume supervision of the plantation sooner than otherwise.

## 6

When Sam was three his brother William was born. A year later a baby sister came. That was an event. Six boys and then a girl. They named her Mary. She was Sam's favorite, and grew up to be a great belle who lived bravely and died tragically. When Sam was five there was another girl— Isabelle. Two years after that, in 1800, the turn of the century brought Elizabeth Paxton her ninth child, christened Eliza Ann. In 1803 instead of another baby, the household at Timber Ridge was thrilled by the Louisiana Purchase and Papa's promotion to major. Then, presently, a war with Spain was spoken of.

Sam Houston had attained his eleventh year, one of six brothers and three sisters who rode horseback, swam in Mill Creek, hunted in the woods, and as Sam afterward recalled, slew Redcoats and Redskins impartially, with father's second best sword.  The cream of juvenile society in the Valley was theirs.  They visited at Cousin Matthew Houston's, near High Bridge, which is now called Natural Bridge.  Cousin Matthew's house was then as now a show place of the region, reckoned as grand, indeed, as Mr. Jefferson's Monticello and, unlike Monticello, maintained without bankrupting its proprietor.  They visited at Cousin Samuel Houston's, saw his wheat-cutting machine and heard the inventor discourse on the Greek and Latin classics.  Cousin Samuel expected to make a fortune with his reapers.  He might have done so had not Cyrus Mc-Cormick, the son of another Rockbridge County planter, who was always tinkering at his father's forge, fashioned a better machine for cutting wheat.

Sam and his brothers and sisters went to church every Sunday—the stone Timber Ridge Church, a hundred yards from the homestead, a monument to the pious initiative of their great grandfather and to the women who had brought sand for the mortar in their saddle-bags from South River. They went to school in a building of logs that stood a short distance from the church.  Major Houston had donated forty acres of land and with a few neighbors started the school.

Sam was a poor student and a truant.  He preferred his father's library to the classroom, and was often stretched with a book before the white five-foot-high mantel that lent brightness and charm to the somber walnut-paneled living-room at Timber Ridge.[3]  The book might have been Brook's *Gazetteer* or one of the eight volumes of Rollin's *Ancient History*.  And not improbably, in his explorations of the family copy of Morse's *Geography*, the boy's fingers wandered over a nebulous representation of "Téjas"—for the Spanish war talk had touched the routine of life at Timber Ridge.

Expresses from the West indicated that Kentucky and

Tennessee accepted the early coming of hostilities as one of the few certainties of life on a frontier. The Virginia militia was stirred. Never had the Major been busier with his inspections. The gravity of matters left little time for personal affairs. Perhaps this was a relief, for the Major's personal affairs were not a pleasant topic to consider. Timber Ridge was feeling the effect of a military career. The cash accumulations of two thrifty generations had been spent. A sizable inheritance from Mrs. Houston's father was gone. Slaves had been sold off, and then land—a parcel here and a parcel there, and some lots in Lexington. But with a war on the horizon a soldier puts selfish thoughts aside. Timber Ridge was still a valuable property and sufficient, with economies, to keep the family until the public crisis was over.

This crisis hinged—and with it Major Houston's expectations of a call to the field of honor—somewhat on the outcome of the designs of Aaron Burr, although no one knew, or has since found out, what those designs were. Colonel Burr had a way of keeping his projects flexible. They seemed to comprehend anything from a colonization scheme in the Spanish province of Téjas, to the seizure of New Orleans, the alienation of the Mississippi Valley, the conquest of Mexico and the coronation of Aaron I as emperor of the Southwest against a twinkling background of orders of nobility and star and garters. One paid his money and took his choice.

In any event, a part of the program was war with Spain, which the West was hot for, and therefore hot for the Burr business under the notion that it was somehow an instrument for hastening the humiliation of the dons and snatching a slice of territory in the bargain. Ohio and Kentucky were delirious with patriotic intentions. In Tennessee a lean backwoods lawyer named Andrew Jackson awaited a signal to rally two thousand frontiersmen and swarm southwestward. Western Virginia was on the qui vive.

In the summer of 1806 the flatboat flotilla that was to convey Burr and the vanguard of his "colonists" to their adventure was loading on the Ohio and on the Cumberland. Young Samuel Swartwout, of New York, rode through Virginia bound for the tropical Sabine. In his saddle-bag was a cipher message signed by Aaron Burr. That message got young Mr. Swartwout in jail and helped to encourage Mr. Jefferson's zeal to hang Mr. Burr. Consequently, no colonization of the Washita, no Emperor Aaron, or star and garters, or war with Spain. A little sheepishly the taken-in West turned to other forms of entertainment. The experience was also a lesson to young Mr. Swartwout.

7

Sam Houston was thirteen years old when the Burr bubble burst, and the Major, his father, was left free to resume the interrupted consideration of his personal affairs. There was much to consider. Timber Ridge was bankrupt. The Major was past fifty, and his health had begun to fail. A reckoning was on the way.

The old militiaman met the crisis with soldier-like poise. He made a plan. He would resign his commission and leave Virginia which had set the stamp of failure on his affairs. He and his would remove to Tennessee, a new country shimmering with the prospects that far fields almost infallibly display before the impaired in fortune.

The West tugged like a magnet. On the seaboard from Maine to Georgia waves of men were on the move. Few had rolled farther, or gathered as much moss with each roll, than a certain Connecticut Yankee, as astute as he was restless. Moses Austin had tried Pennsylvania and Virginia. Now he was in Missouri working lead mines in a wilderness, and listening with a shrewd squint to the tales trappers and traders brought from beyond the Sabine. Already Moses Austin's roving eye was on Texas. With him was a son named Stephen, born in Virginia the same year Sam Houston was.

The reckoning that was on the way never quite overtook

Major Houston. In September of 1806 he sold for a thousand pounds what was left of the Timber Ridge plantation. The Major was ill, but duty called and he rode away on his last tour of military inspections, dying at Dennis Callighan's friendly tavern house on the New Road to Kentucky. A large turnout of Valley gentility saw him buried in the High Bridge churchyard, near the elaborate mansion of Cousin Matthew.

"One sword," noted the executors in their appraisal of the estate, "one sword, $15. . . .

"One Negro Woman named Peggy aged 27 years $166.66 One Negro Woman named Lucy aged 17 years 250 One negro boy Jerry 13 years 250 One negro Boy a child named Andrew 2 years 40 one do a Boy named David 10 months 20 one iron grey mare 90 . . . One Riding Chair and Harness 55 . . . One red cow 10 . . . One womans sadle bridle and martingale 20 one mans sadle Plated stirup 17 . . . One card table $6.50 three tea boards $3 One bottle case & contents 4 . . . One umbrella $2 . . . One pistol 50 . . . 2 turkey counterpins $7. Nine sheets $.50 . . . Morse's Geography 2 vol 6.50 . . . Sundry bonds and notes amounting to 1468.20" and other items sufficient to fill two sheets of foolscap and foot up to $3,659.86.[4]

Riding chair, card table, tea boards, wine set, bed linen, eight saddles—relics of a Virginia gentleman who had seen better days. Still, thirty-six hundred dollars was no trifling inheritance. But debts took a large part of this residue.

## 8

Fearing he might not live to conduct his family to the promised land, the Major had taken steps to outwit the hand of death. In the closing weeks of his life he had opened negotiations for a grant of land in East Tennessee, and had inserted in his will a clause directing his executors to set aside "as much as they may actually find nessery . . . to Enable . . . [the family] to move with convenience." Two-thirds of what was left "is to be applied to purchase land . . . and such articles as may be needful" for the family's "support until they can be otherwise provided for." The remaining third was "to be at the disposal of my wife" with the injunction that having made the move "shee is to apply as much of the property of horses and other things which they will require in Moving to the purchase of [additional] Lands, [which] shal be divided at the deceas of my wife . . . in the following manner, to my son John two shares and to my other children one share each."

Western land. Sell the horses, the wagons that took you— and buy more land and be rich. Major Houston had imbibed the spirit of his age. Almost his last purchase had been a new "waggon with chain and gears compleat for five horses [$] 174." Fourteen-year-old Sam (calculated the Major) should ride in this wagon and have for his own a tenth part of the greater legacy that lay where the rainbow dipped in the southwestern sky.

# CHAPTER II

## DEER TRACKS AND TAPE

### 1

IN THE spring of 1807 a Virginia widow more accustomed to her own riding chair than an immigrant wagon, however new, took her place behind a five-horse team. The five-horse team, followed by a four-horse team and an older wagon, moved out on the road from Lexington that threaded the green Allegheny passes and descended into the wilderness of Tennessee. The widow was in her fiftieth year. Her hair was iron gray. Her tall form had grown matronly from bearing the nine children who shared the two wagons with the remainder of the worldly possessions of this reduced gentlewoman.

In three weeks the little procession passed through the collection of log houses known as Knoxville, the village capital of Tennessee. They forded a river and continued southwestward over an old Indian trace. Fifteen miles farther, they forded a creek by a grist mill that stood inside a stockade. Climbing the steep bank on the farther side, the travel-stained outfit creaked into the midst of another collection of houses, strung along either side of the trace. This collection was smaller and ruder than the one called Knoxville. Logs were unsquared and windows hung with shutters that would turn an arrow or stop a musket ball. This was Maryville, the seat of government of Blount County.

The ten miles beyond Maryville were the worst of the trip. The country got wilder and rougher. The trace was a poor excuse for a road. More streams to ford and steep banks

13

dense with underbrush to worry the wagons up and down. Up the Baker's Creek Valley and then up a branch stream that tumbled down from the hills, they worked their way over no road at all until the Big Smoky Mountains rose into view. Their journey was ended. Elizabeth Houston had fulfilled the dying wish of her husband. On the Baker's Creek branch she patented four hundred and nineteen acres that had been his personal selection.

Sam Houston seldom spoke of his father, whom he remembered "only for one passion, a military life." But his mother was "a heroine . . . an extraordinary woman . . . gifted with intellectual and moral qualities, which elevated her . . . above most of her sex. Her life shone with purity and benevolence, and yet she was nerved with a stern fortitude which never gave way in the midst of the wild scenes that chequered the history of the frontier settler."[1]

## 2

East Tennessee was filling up rapidly, but the arrival of the widow and her band was probably something of an event because of the local prestige of the Houston name. James and John Houston, cousins of the Major, had come out directly from the Army at the close of the Revolutionary War. There was no such place as Tennessee then. The country was a part of North Carolina. Reverend Samuel Houston, Greek scholar and unsuccessful inventor, had been there off and on. He had joined picturesque John Sevier and his resolute wife, Bonny Kate, in founding the State of Franklin. Though stonily ignored by the other commonwealths of our Federal Union, the State of Franklin for three stirring years maintained behind the long hunting rifles of its sponsors a sovereignty that paved the way for the creation of Tennessee.

When this was accomplished Blount County sent James Houston to the Legislature. Jim Houston of Jim Houston's Fort was a power in those clearings. Jim Houston's Fort—

Houston Blockhouse on old maps—was on Nine Mile Creek five miles from the spot Elizabeth Houston picked for the site of her homestead. As likely as not, Mrs. Houston and her flock put up at Cousin Jim's while the new home was being built, and there young Sam got a foreshadow of the life in store for him.

At Cousin Jim's the boy would have found himself behind a stockade enclosing the Houston residence, slave quarters and outbuildings. Jim Houston's Fort had turned back more than one Indian attack, but the last good fight had been nineteen years ago, with no serious scare for ten years. In that time a restless Paxton, Elizabeth's blood cousin, had made his way to Tennessee, and he and a Houston had married into the same family there. The blockhouse families were all intermarrying. Montgomery, Wallace, McClung, Stuart and other Rockbridge County names gave a feeling of familiarity to the countryside.

The adventure touched Sam Houston's passion for the heroic. Forty years later the recollection of it moved him to complain that American authors need not turn for inspiration to "European castles and their crazy knights and lady loves," but should "set themselves to work to glean the unwritten legends of heroism and adventure which the old men would tell them who are now smoking their pipes around the rooftrees of Kentucky and Tennessee."

But for Sam the romantic part of the migration ended when the new house on the Baker's Creek branch was finished and the family moved in and began to clear the farm. Of Elizabeth Houston's six sons, Sam seemed to take after his father the most in one respect: his talents did not incline to agriculture. Frontier farming was an occupation involving much commonplace labor in order to eat not any too well. Sam perceived flaws in this scheme. Nor did he share the frontier's opinion of contempt for the Indians, who got along comfortably by hunting and fishing, and when let alone by the whites, seemed to have a good enough time.

To what extent Sam's ideas were influenced by a book he was reading one can only guess. The book was Alexander Pope's translation of the *Iliad*. But there is no guesswork in the assertion that Sam's views were not accepted by the other members of the household. They went to work on the new four hundred acres. From the start they prospered better than most settlers. They bought slaves. They acquired an interest in a general store in Maryville. They enlarged the family residence.

The house stood near a cool mountain spring on a shelf of land sloping away in three directions, before which lay a magnificent sweep of mountain scenery. When he grew up and got into politics, Sam used to speak of his boyhood Tennessee home as a cabin, but the neighbors thought it a fine house, for it had an up-stairs, which in that day was a mark of splendor.[2]

By the terms of Major Houston's will, the Tennessee venture was a joint undertaking in which Sam originally enjoyed a ten per cent. interest. A few years after the family's arrival Paxton, the eldest boy, died. Death also took Isabelle. Sam's share was then one-eighth, and affairs were prospering. The value of his holding increased with the rest. This was because everybody worked—but Sam.

He was a likable culprit, though, and the handsomest of Elizabeth Houston's sons—fair and tall, with wavy chestnut hair and friendly blue eyes that looked from a head full of droll humor and long words he saw in books; in fact, a hard boy to scold. He would disappear for days—usually with a book, but the stories that came drifting back were often difficult to reconcile with the pursuit of literature. There were reproofs from Mother which Sam took with his tongue in his cheek, but the bossing by his brothers stirred him to rebellion.

At length it was conceded that Sam was not cut out to be a planter, and so he was placed behind the counter of the store in Maryville. Here Brother James also acquired his early merchandising experience and lived to become a successful shopkeeper in Nashville. But Sam gave promise of no such satisfactory future. His lapses increased, and he got the name of a wayward boy.

## 3

The conquest of the wilderness was not without its frivolities. At the taverns and ordinaries the bloods rolled dice and played with dirty cards. No cock-fight, wedding, log-rolling, dance or funeral was complete without whisky. There was a startling number of illegitimate children—if one included Indian and negro half-breeds, which one did not, of course. There were two kinds of liquor. "Whisky" was the native distillation of the native corn, price thirty-five cents a gallon. "Red whisky" came from the western, or "whisky," counties of Pennsylvania; this was the refreshment of the quality. To kill an Indian was a public-spirited act; to swindle one, the exercise of common sense.

The beau ideal of this frontier was Andrew Jackson. He had been a United States senator, a militia general and a judge. He had killed a man in a duel. He gave the old-timers smoking under the rooftrees plenty to talk about. A contemporary anecdote, somewhat apocryphal but not so much so as to give a false idea of the man or of his times, has Jackson holding court in a log house when a drunken bad man armed with a club, a knife and a gun started a row and defied the sheriff to arrest him. "This court is adjourned for ten minutes," said Judge Jackson, drawing a pistol. He collared the disturber in less time than that.

Reverend Peter Cartwright approached his ecclesiastical responsibilities with no less élan. "They came drunk," he wrote, "and armed with dirks, clubs, knives, and horsewhips, and swore they would break up the meeting. . . . I advanced toward them. . . . One of them made a pass at my head with his whip, but I closed in with him, and jerked him off his seat. A regular scuffle ensued. . . . I threw my prisoner down, and held him fast. . . . An old and drunken magistrate came up to me, and ordered me to let my prisoner go. I told him I should not. He swore if I did not he would knock me down. I told him to crack away. . . . The drunken justice made a pass at me; but I parried the stroke, and seized him by the collar and the hair of the head . . . brought him to the ground and jumped on him. . . . The mob then rushed to the scene; they knocked down several preachers and others. . . . The ringleader . . . made three passes at me. . . . It seemed at that moment I had not power to resist temptation, and I struck a sudden blow in the burr of the ear."[3]

Still, for a dreaming boy with a passion for pagan poetry, this life lacked something.

## 4

Sam Houston liked a good time as well as the next one, but after all that has been said on this subject he does not seem to have made the most of his early opportunities. Sixty years later a proud Tennessee grandmother said in her fireside reminiscences that he had no "small or mean vices." Sam himself allays our worst fears with the grave assurance that his youth "was wild and impetuous, but it was spotted by no crime."[4]

The family, however, expected more of Sam than this and was supported by an authority that spoke from the grave. "I give and bequaith," Major Houston had written in his will, "unto my son John my sword . . . and my appeuril." John also received a riding horse and two shares in the Tennessee venture to one share apiece for Sam and the other children. But John was to earn that horse and extra share. "He is to pay strict attention to my family and Endeavor to see them raised and treated with Justice. My executors are to be the gardians of my children until they shal arive at lawful age and I would recommend that they put my sons to such trades

as may seem most beneficial—and I d[...]
tors . . . my wife Elizabeth and my s[...]

Something more than moral suasio[...]
force these stipulations. "If any dispu[...]
the Executing of the above . . . the court [...]
wherein the majority of the legatees shal reside shal have po[...]
to appoint five men who shal put a construction on the
same . . . which shal be the final decision." But Sam saw
a simpler way. One morning he did not show up for work
at the store.

Weeks passed, and there was a great search and stir.
Finally the family heard that its black sheep had crossed the
Tennessee River into the Indian country and was living with
the Cherokees. James and John went to bring him back.
They were directed to the wigwam of the chief.

Chief Oo-loo-te-ka's personal seat and the council house of
his band were on an island that parts the current of the Tennessee where the yellow Hiwassee boils into it from the Big
Smokies. The brothers paddled up to find the runaway lying
under a tree, scanning lines of the *Iliad*. He was invited to return home. Sam relates that he stood "straight as an Indian,"
and (with a creditable touch of Cherokee imagery for a be-
ginner) replied that he "preferred measuring deer tracks to
tape" and "the wild liberty of the Red Men better than the
tyranny of his own brothers." He begged to be excused from
saying more as "a translation from the Greek" claimed his
interest and he desired to "read it in peace." He got his wish.

5

But when the brothers left they thought that Sam would
follow them home. Sam did follow, though not for more than
a year. His mother and sisters were scandalized by his wild
appearance. They made him a new suit of clothes, but this
outward sign of respectability had slight influence on the
deportment of the prodigal. "Ordered . . ." runs the record

# THE RAVEN

Blount County Court under date of September 29, 1810, that John B. Cusack be fined Ten Dollars & Samuel Houston five Dollars for . . . disorderly riotously wantonly with an Assembly of Militia Annoying the Court with the noise of a Drum and with force preventing the Sheriff and Officer of the Court in the discharge of his duty . . . against the peace and dignity of the State."[5]

This is the earliest public notice of the military prowess of a man whose sword was to alter the destiny of a continent. The occasion was a muster of the Mounted Gunmen, the local militia company of which John B. Cusack (or Cusick) was captain. At these musters there was always whisky on tap and a good deal of horse-play at the finish. Neither Captain Cusack nor Drummer Houston paid his fine, however, and at the next term of court the penalties were remitted. Drummer Houston was not on hand to receive this absolution. He had disappeared again and did not return until after another year's absence. On this occasion Mother provided a suit of homespun as before and Sam promised to stay. Very shortly, however, he fell out with his brothers and was off for his third year with the Indians.

Chief Oo-loo-te-ka adopted Sam as a son and christened him Co-lon-neh—The Raven. The name was a revered one, with associations in Cherokee mythology. It was borne also by a neighboring chieftain who sat with Oo-loo-te-ka on the National Council of the Cherokee Nation. Sam liked the change—a new name and a new life; new sights, new sounds, new occupations, new ideas communicated by a new language with which he became daily more familiar. The young braves taught him the green corn dance, the hoop and pole game and the ball play.

The Indian ball play is the father of lacrosse. It was the national pastime of the Cherokees and had a religious significance proceeding from the nebula of tribal mythology dealing with the days when only animals inhabited the earth. From the lips of the shamans, or priests, The Raven heard the sacred lyrics of the first ball play, which was between the birds, led by an eagle, and the beasts, led by a bear. The birds won a spirited contest through the dexterity of the flying squirrel and of the bat, whose services had been rejected by the animals. The history of that game is a long one, wonderful with detail and allusion to the meshwork of myth that forms the background of Cherokee theology. It opened the door to the Cherokee spirit world, where Sam perceived the existence of more and quite as extraordinary gods as dwelled on Olympus. Behind the fantastic conception lay a range of thought and imagination frequently as lofty as that of Greek invention, though the simple imagery of the shamans exhibited few of the ornaments of style so treasured by Mr. Pope.

Sam preferred these diversions to those of the gilded youth on the civilized side of the Tennessee. He reveled in the wealth of legend with which Cherokee life abounded. The earth and the air, the trees and the streams were peopled by the supernatural, all with their curious histories. In the evenings Sam sat about the fires where the long pipe was passed, filling his mind with the maxims of the headmen and the picturesque idioms of the Indian speech, which time never eradicated from his vocabulary.

Oo-loo-te-ka was the head of a contented following of nearly three hundred Cherokees—a large constituency, Indian bands having been much smaller than most white people suppose. They lived by hunting and by fishing and on corn cultivated by their women. Oo-loo-te-ka was about forty-five years old. He was not a warlike chieftain. His name means He-Puts-the-Drum-Away. He had more brains than most local chiefs but, at this time of life, little ambition. Membership on the National Council was a genuine distinction, but Oo-loo-te-ka found the journey to the grand council house in Georgia too great an exertion to draw him very often from the comforts of his island home, his squaws, and the affairs of his own band which he administered with more than ordinary skill. Some of Oo-loo-te-ka's success, however, must be attributed to his brother-in-law and headman, John Rogers, who was part Scot. Headman Rogers had two wives and many children, including two boys named, singularly enough, John and James. They were The Raven's fast friends.

Such were the unconscious preceptors of an imaginative boy who had forsaken a disorderly civilization to find tranquillity in the camps of decorous barbarians. These years were a permanent influence on Sam Houston's life. They left him with an attachment for the wilderness, a deep interior preference for deer tracks to tape, and a faith in primitive fellowships that one day was to break the impact of a world tumbling about his ears, and whip him into the desperate improvisation of the Texas epic.

"It was the moulding period of life," he wrote, "when the heart, just charmed into the feverish hopes and dreams of youth, looks wistfully around on all things for light and beauty—'when every idea of gratification fires the blood and flashes on the fancy—when the heart is vacant to every fresh form of delight, and has no rival engagements to draw it from the importunities of a new desire.' The poets of Europe, fancying such scenes, have borrowed their sweetest images from the wild idolatry of the Indian maiden."[6]

The Raven knew the warm touch of delights that captivated these worshipers from afar. But the hearts of the wild idolatrous maidens were not to be possessed without assistance from the gods, who must be petitioned in proper form. In the first place it was necessary to dispose of any possible rival. "Now your soul fades away. Your spirit shall grow less and less and dwindle away, never to reappear." If the gods were willing to accommodate in this matter the next step was to influence the girl. "Let her be completely veiled in loneliness. O Black Spider, may you hold her soul in your web, so that she may never escape its meshes." Then the final declaration to the desired one thus involved. "Your soul has come into the very center of my soul, never to turn away."[7]

This was the way of the school in which Sam Houston

learned to practise the arts of courtship, "wandering," he wrote, "along the banks of streams, side by side with some Indian maiden, sheltered by the deep woods . . . making love and reading Homer's *Iliad*." Enchanted island.

Thirty-seven years later a man to whom few illusions remained lingered over the memories of his youth in a Pan's garden. "Houston," he said, speaking of himself in the third person, as he frequently did, which is another Indian trait, "Houston has seen nearly all in life there is to live for and yet he has been heard to say that when he looks back over the waste . . . there's nothing half so sweet to remember as this sojourn he made among the untutored children of the forest."[3]

# CHAPTER III

## White Pantaloons and Waistcoats

### 1

Sam acknowledged the hospitality of the island by occasional trips to Maryville and to Kingston to buy powder and shot and "little articles of taste or utility" for his Indian friends and sweethearts. Purchasing on credit, at the end of three years he owed a hundred dollars. In the spring of 1812 The Raven left the wigwam of Oo-loo-te-ka to pay the fiddler.

It was not an easy thing in normal times for a youth of nineteen with an attitude of reserve toward labor to lay hands on a hundred dollars. In the spring of 1812 times were abnormal, which made it still more difficult. The air was full of war talk. Now it was England the West wanted to fight. The East was against it, and this made the West more bloodthirsty than ever. The Mounted Gunmen were mustering often. Sam's brother, Robert, had joined the Regular Army.

Sam loafed about Maryville and made known his need of employment. Maryville contained forty families now and was a place of importance. Two stage routes crossed there: one from the Carolinas to Nashville, and one from Georgia to Knoxville. The horses were changed at Russell's Inn. They were shod at Samuel Houston's blacksmith shop which stood at the fork of the roads. Mr. Houston's residence was in front of his shop. The firm of Love & Toole made saddles, but the partners had their individual enterprises. Sam Love built beaver hats for gentlemen, such as Jim Houston, of Jim Houston's Fort, and Reverend Mark Moore,

24

head teacher at the Academy. William Toole had a tan-yard on the edge of town. There were four general stores. The largest building in the town was the court-house where John Houston was clerk of the court. Back of the court-house was the jail and a pair of stocks. Across Pistol Creek was John Craig's grist mill.

Sam probably could have found work had he been willing to take anything. Brother James was clerking in the store his mother was interested in. But Sam was discriminating— and entertaining as well. What Sam Houston would do next was occasion for a great deal of spoofing, but Sam did not mind. It was a form of advertising. Presently Sam announced that he would open a private school.

## 2

This was the best joke in a long while. Sam tolerated a good many pleasantries about his "degree" from the "Indian University," and enjoyed himself thoroughly. True, Sam's formal schooling amounted to little. He had taken slight advantage of the excellent opportunities that Major Houston had provided for his children; but he read every book within his reach; he had spelled down half of Blount County; he could recite from memory the best part of all twenty-four books of the *Iliad*. These claims to scholarship Maryville did not take lightly. Moreover, before carrying Homer off among the Indians, there had been a term at Porter Academy.

Porter Academy—or, rather, "The Academy," since it was the only one in that part of the country—occupied a two-story log house in a meadow just off Main Street. There were about twenty students. Classes were kept the year round with one three-week vacation in the spring and another in the fall. The summer hours were from eight to twelve in the fore-noon and from two to five-thirty in the afternoon. During the winter when the light was poorer the hours were from nine to twelve and from one to four. "No student," said the regulations of Sam Houston's day, "shall get drunk, or be admitted to play at cards or other games of hazard. . . . No student shall use profane, irreverent or obscene language or be guilty of conduct tending thereunto. . . . No student shall attend a horse race, a ball, or other frolicking assembly. . . . No student shall be guilty of fighting."[1]

Sam had left the Academy under a cloud. He said this was because he insisted on being taught Latin and Greek classics in the original. The implication that this was beyond the depth of the Academy's faculty is not supported by the minutes of the Board of Trustees, of which James and Robert Houston were members. These mention "the Latin and Greek languages" as a part of "the course of academical study," and give the names of the students passing examinations in the same. Sam Houston's name is not on the list.

Sam obtained quarters for his school, and gave out the tuition rate as eight dollars for the term. This was a stiffer price by two dollars than any other teacher had charged for a primary or "English" school. The Academy charged only fifteen dollars a year. Sam stipulated that one-third of the eight dollars should be paid in cash, one-third in corn at thirty-three and one-third cents a bushel and one-third in calico "of variegated colors," from which the professor was to have his shirts made.

Although few pupils applied, Sam opened his classes after corn-planting in May of 1812. Except for the wheat harvest in July, there would be nothing to take the pupils from their studies until corn-gathering in November. After that school was impossible anyhow; it would be too cold to open the "windows" for light. The schoolhouse was in a clearing on John McCulloch's farm five miles east of Maryville. An oak tree had been spared to shade a spring of drinking water.[2] On one side and at one end of the room a log had been omitted from the walls. These apertures answered for windows. They were equipped with shutters which, in daytime, were opened downward on the inside, forming shelves that served as desks.

Sam's school caught the air of success.  The split log benches were filled, and applicants were turned away.  Years afterward, while swapping yarns on a steamboat crossing Galveston Bay, an old army comrade reminded General Houston that he had been the governor of one state, a United States senator from another, the commander-in-chief of an Army and the president of a Republic.  Which office had afforded him the greatest pride?

"Well, Burke," replied Sam Houston, "when a young man in Tennessee I kept a country school, being then about eighteen years of age, and a tall, strapping fellow.  At noon after the luncheon, which I and my pupils ate together out of our baskets, I would go into the woods and cut me a 'sour wood' stick, trim it carefully in circular spirals and thrust one half of it into the fire, which would turn it blue, leaving the other half white.  With this emblem of ornament and authority in my hand, dressed in a hunting-shirt of flowered calico, a long queue down my back, and the sense of authority over my pupils, I experienced a higher feeling of dignity and self-satisfaction than from any office or honor which I have since held."[3]

When corn-gathering and cold weather put an end to Sam Houston's school, the professor's debts were paid and he returned to Maryville with money in his pocket.

## 3

It had been an eventful six months.  At sundown on the twelfth day of June, 1812, little Billy Phillips, an old racehorse jockey from Nashville, swung into his saddle in front of the War Department in Washington and was off "like Greased Lightenin' . . . his horse's tail and his own long hair streaming in the wind."  The President's courier reached Knoxville to find that Governor Blount had gone to Nashville.  But Maryville got the news.  The West had its war.

Billy clattered into Nashville at seven in the evening of June twenty-first and placed a copy of the war message in the hands of the Governor. In nine days to the hour, he had ridden eight hundred and sixty miles over primitive roads and a chain of mountains. Tennessee had convulsions. The Governor summoned volunteers. "Those having no rifles of their own . . . will be furnished by the State to the extent of the supply on hand. . . . Each volunteer, including Company officers, is entitled to a powder horn full of the best Eagle powder, one dozen new sharp flints and lead enough to mould 100 bullets that fit his rifle. . . . It is desired to avoid the use of smooth-bore muskets as much as possible. They . . . do not carry straight. They may be good enough for Regular soldiers but not the Citizen Volunteers of Tennessee. Uniform clothing being desirable . . . the Major General advises . . . dark-blue or nut-brown homespun. . . . Buckskin hunting shirts and leggins also may be worn. . . . Men who have them may, upon parade, wear white pantaloons and waist-coats."

The force was raised in two "divisions"—those of West and of East Tennessee. The West Tennesseeans, under Major General Jackson, formed the corps d'élite. They rushed to meet the foe at Natchez, but not until the commanding general had written a proclamation. "There is not one individual among the Volunteers who would not prefer perishing on the field of battle . . . than to return . . . covered with shame, ignominy and disgrace! Perish our friends—perish our wives—perish our CHILDREN . . . nay, perish . . . every earthly consideration! But let the honor and the fame of the Volunteer Soldier be untarnished."

Captain Cusack's Mounted Gunmen flew the colors and were mobilized with the eastern division, but no such prospects of glory awaited these defenders.

Sam Houston had taken in all this from his classroom. No dark-blue or nut-brown homespun regalia for him; no flask of Eagle powder. Sam continued to work off his debts. It was just as well. There was glory that winter for none of the Tennessee troops. At Natchez no foe turned up.

In the fall Sam returned to Porter Academy as a student, but Sam never had much luck at the Academy. This time it was mathematics. He said he found geometry so "uninspiring" that he could not bring himself to solve the first problem in the book. Dr. Isaac Anderson, the new head teacher, does not mention geometry, but says Sam Houston was the most provoking student he ever had. "I often determined to lick him, but he would come up with such a pretty dish of excuses I could not do it."[4]

Tennessee war news continued unencouraging. But Sam had his fill of school. Besides, his money had run out. On the twenty-fourth of March, 1813, he and a small boy named Willoughby Williams stood on a corner in Maryville watching a recruiting demonstration. Sam had watched many such, but this was a Regular Army party—smooth-bore muskets, possibly, but white pantaloons and waistcoats for every man. The drums were rolled, the colors paraded and the sergeant made a talk. When he finished Sam Houston stepped up and took a silver dollar from the drumhead. That was the token of entry into the military service.

As the recruit had barely passed his twentieth birthday, his mother's consent was necessary for his enlistment. She gave it and, at the same time, slipped on Sam's finger a plain gold ring—a talisman for the young soldier about to face the world. On the inside of the ring was engraved a single word epitomizing the creed that Elizabeth Houston said must for ever shine in the conduct of her son.

Before he left home Sam received from his mother another gift, and a most practical one considering the state of the western depots of the Army. "My son, take this musket and never disgrace it: for remember, I had rather all my sons should fill one honorable grave than that one of them should turn his back to save his life. Go, and remember, too, that while the door of my cabin is open to brave men, it is eternally shut against cowards."[5]

This quotation was set down by her son in later years. It

is possible that Elizabeth Houston said it that way; possible also that Sam may have touched up her remarks with a few ennobling phrases of his own. But when one considers the temper of the motto in the ring—and Sam Houston had that ring on when he died—the feeling grows that the words were his mother's.

There was the usual feeling between the Regular and the volunteer troops, and before he joined his regiment Sam heard from the home-folk on this subject. With the galling inactivity of the East Tennessee militia and the bootless Natchez expedition in mind, Sam retorted that Blount County should "hear of *me*" before the war was over.

He marched off to the encampment of the 7th Infantry at Knoxville. In thirty days he was drill sergeant. In four months he was commissioned an ensign and transferred to the 39th Infantry. After a year of careful preparation, the 39th Regiment took the field. Not, however, to fight the British. At the last moment it was diverted against a strong tribe of Creek Indians who had gone over to the English. But the Cherokees whose hospitality Houston had enjoyed for three years were loyal. A band of their warriors—John and James Rogers among them—went ahead as scouts when the 39th Infantry marched into the wilderness of the Creek country.

### 4

The Creeks owned much of the land that is now Alabama. It had been guaranteed to them by a treaty which the whites had violated. This state of affairs was turned to the advantage of the British by Tecumseh, probably the most gifted of North American Indians, and a brigadier-general in the British Army. Tecumseh went south and stirred up a clan of the Creeks. The crimson war club, or Red Stick, was hung in the squares of their encampments, the British supplied arms and the braves rose under the half-breed, Bill Weathersford. Settlers fled to stockades. In August of 1813 Weathersford fell upon one of these and scalped four hundred of the occupants.

With twenty-five hundred Tennessee militia, Andrew Jackson went after Weathersford. He won the first two battles. The next two were draws because a good part of Jackson's army ran away. Weathersford remained in the field with a thousand Red Sticks. Jackson was in camp at Fort Strother with a rabble of mutinous militiamen. Five thousand more militia had been ordered out, but what pleased Jackson most was the unexpected news that the 39th Regular Infantry was on the way to join him. "I am truly happy," he wrote in a confidential letter. "The Regulars will give strength to my arm and quell mutiny."

Ensign Sam Houston was leading a platoon when the 39th Infantry, three hundred and sixty strong, marched into Fort Strother on February 6, 1814. The Regulars' presence restored the fortunes of the campaign. Their first job dealt with mutiny, and gave Ensign Houston his first close view of the man whose star he was to follow so long and so far.

The morning had dawned cold and rainy and Private John Woods, having been on guard all night, obtained permission to leave his post and get something to eat. John was a quick-tempered boy of seventeen who had been in the militia a month. He was in his tent eating when the officer of the day came by, and ordered the occupants to remove the scraps of their meal from the ground. Woods refused and couched his refusal in quite unmilitary terms. The officer ordered him arrested. Woods primed his gun and threatened to use it on the first man to touch him. Jackson heard the commotion.

"Which is the rascal? Shoot him!" he shouted, rushing from his tent.

Woods submitted to arrest and was confined in irons in the camp of the Regulars, but no one took the incident seriously. At worst it would mean drumming another man out of camp. Insubordination had been no novelty with the Tennessee militia.

John Woods was tried for mutiny and sentenced to be shot. For two nights Jackson paced his tent without closing his eyes. Then he mounted his horse and rode out of earshot of musketry. The army was formed in hollow square. A scared backwoods Tennesssee boy faced a squad of Regulars with their smooth-bore rifles of .70 caliber primed and cocked. An officer dropped his sword, and the professional soldiers did their duty.

The effect on the army was described, by one who was there, as "salutary."

## 5

Forty hours later the army was on the march. Weathersford was waiting. He had put the finishing touches to his entrenchment at To-ho-pe-ka, or the Horseshoe, a bend in the Tallapoosa River, fifty-five miles south of Fort Strother. It took Jackson ten days to beat through the wilderness that far. He arrived on March 26, 1814, with two thousand men.

The Horseshoe enclosed one hundred acres, furrowed by gullies and covered with small timber and brush. Weathersford had improved this natural situation with a log breastworks across the neck of the peninsula. At the end of the peninsula, he had tied a fleet of canoes to insure his retreat should the breastworks be overrun.

Jackson surrounded the peninsula. Cherokee scouts swam the river and carried off Weathersford's canoes. A thousand men were drawn up on the land side to storm the breastworks. Interpreters were sent to tell the Creeks to send their non-combatants across the river. At ten o'clock on the morning of March twenty-seventh, Jackson's two little cannon began to whang away at the breastworks at eighty yards. The round shot sank harmlessly in the spongy green logs, and Creek sharpshooters picked off the artillerymen at the guns.

The infantry attack was delayed until the Indian women and children were conveyed to places of safety. This was completed at twelve-thirty o'clock. The Red Sticks signaled that they were ready. Jackson was ready. The drums beat the long roll, and the infantry charged.

The Regulars reached the ramparts first. Major Lemuel P. Montgomery scaled them and toppled back dead, but his name survives in the capital city of Alabama. Ensign Sam Houston was the next man on the works. Waving his sword he leaped down among the Red Sticks on the other side. The platoon scrambled after its leader. The first men over found him, covered with blood, beating off a ring of Indians with his sword.

The ramparts were taken. Ensign Houston tried to pull out an arrow that was sticking in his thigh, but it would not come. He asked a lieutenant who was fighting near by to remove it. The officer gave a pull, but the arrow was a barbed one and held fast. The lieutenant said to go to a surgeon. Infuriated by pain, Houston brandished his sword and commanded the lieutenant to pull with all his strength. The officer braced himself and yanked the arrow out, but made such a gash that Houston limped away to find the surgeons. They plugged up the wound, and Houston was lying on the ground to steady himself when Jackson rode by. He inquired about Houston's injury and ordered him not to return to the battle. Houston later said he might have obeyed if he had not recalled his boast that Maryville should hear of him before he got back.

## 6

When their fortification was overrun, the Creeks split into bands and retreated into undergrowth which made ideal Indian fighting ground. Twenty small battles raged at once, each a confusion of arrows, balls, spears, tomahawks and knives. The Red Sticks fought with the impersonal courage that is a part of the Indian culture. If the battle had started off badly, no matter. The Great Spirit was testing the faith of his children. He would intervene and give them victory.

The medicine-men had said so. The signal would be a cloud in the heavens.

So Weathersford's men fought on—beneath a cloudless sky that spanned the bloody hundred acres. "Not a warrior," Sam Houston related, "offered to surrender, even while the sword was at his breast." Band after band was surrounded and slain to a man. Medicine-men moved among those who held out, impassively scanning the heavens.

In the middle of the afternoon Jackson suspended hostilities and sent an interpreter to say that all who surrendered should be spared. During this lull in the action a small cloud appeared. The medicine-men redoubled their incantations and the warriors renewed the fight with fanatic fury. The result, said Houston, was "slaughter." The signal in the heavens brought a quiet spring shower, but no deliverance to the brave. By evening resistance was at an end, except for a band entrenched in a covered redoubt at the bottom of a ravine. Jackson offered them life if they would give up, but they declined it. The General called for volunteers to storm the stronghold. For a moment no officer stepped out. Then Ensign Houston, calling to his men to follow, advanced down the ravine.

When the men hesitated the wounded Ensign seized a musket from one of them and ordered a charge. The only chance of success was to rush the port-holes which bristled with arrows and rifle barrels. Houston plunged on, and when five yards from the redoubt stopped and leveled his piece. He received a volley from the port-holes. One ball shattered his right arm. Another smashed his right shoulder. His musket fell to the ground and his command took cover. The rash boy officer tried to rally his men; they failed him, and alone he climbed back up the ravine under fire and collapsed when he reached the top.

Jackson reduced the redoubt by setting fire to it with flaming arrows. The Creek insurrection was over, and the British were without military representation in the South.

# CHAPTER IV

## Mr. Calhoun Rebukes

### 1

They carried Ensign Houston to the clearing where the surgeons were busy by the light of a semicircular brush fire. A canteen of whisky was thrust in his hands, and the wounded boy was told to take a pull. A pair of muscular orderlies took hold of him, and the doctors went to work. They redressed the lacerated thigh and splinted the broken arm. They tried to fish the ball from the smashed shoulder, but gave up the job; it did not seem that the Ensign could live until morning anyhow. He had bled too much.

Sam was laid on the wet ground for the night. It occurred to him that he had done enough for the home-folk to hear of it. He tried to recall just what he had done, but things grew dimmer and calmer and he went to sleep.

In the morning Sam, too weak to walk, was lifted on to a litter made of saplings and started on a journey through the wilderness to Fort Williams sixty miles away. How he survived the trip, Houston himself said he never knew. The other wounded officers were taken to Fort Jackson and well cared for, but through an oversight, or because his condition would not admit of removal, Sam was left at Fort Williams under the care of two sympathetic militia officers of no medical experience. They finally sent him to a crude field hospital maintained by the volunteer troops of East Tennessee.

When the East Tennesseeans started home to be demobilized, they carried the abandoned Ensign on a horse litter.

35

He was delirious part of the time, his food was of the coarsest description, and he lacked the simplest medicines. In May of 1814, nearly two months after the battle, he reached his mother's home. Mrs. Houston recognized her son only by the "wonted expression" in his eyes.

At the house on the hillside Sam began to mend and presently traveled to Knoxville to see a doctor. The journey exhausted him completely. The doctor, a Scotchman, said that since Sam could live only a few days, it would be needless to run up a bill. Houston installed himself in lodgings, and two weeks later revisited the doctor, who then took the case. After a couple of months, the convalescent was able to set out on horseback for Washington, thinking to benefit by the change of scene. Besides, he had never been to Washington.

The British started for Washington about the same time and got there first. Houston saw only the ashes of the Capitol and of the President's house. Beholding "the ruins that *heroic* people had worked" Sam said his "blood boiled" and caused him "the keenest pangs" to think that he "should be disabled at such a moment." His wounds began troubling him again, so he posted over the Blue Ridge to rest at the homes of his relations in the Valley of Virginia.

Early in 1815 Sam rejoined his regiment in Tennessee, there receiving the glorious news of the battle of New Orleans. "People here are much gratified at the restoration of peace," he wrote to his cousin, Robert McEwen. "The officers of the army," however, "would as soon the war continued." But Sam was "willing to sacrifice my wish to the welfare of the Republic." The sacrifice might be a real one. Sam was afraid peace should leave him without an occupation. If so, he would go to Knoxville "for it will be proper for me to pursue some course for a livelihood which will not be laborious as my wounds are not near well, and I suppose it will be impracticable for a disbanded officer to marry for the[y] will be regarded as cloathes out of fashion . . . but I will not despond before I am disappointed and I suppose that will be some time for I will not court any of the Dear Girles before I make a fortune and if I come no better speed than I have done heretofore it will take some time."[1]

The young veteran's misgivings concerning peace proved baseless. The 39th Regiment was discontinued in post-war reduction of the Army, but Ensign Houston was promoted to second lieutenant and transferred to the 1st Infantry, garrisoned at New Orleans. At Nashville he equipped himself for active duty.

A promenade in the public square brought the new lieutenant to the notice of two elegantly attired young ladies. They were the Misses Kent, top-notch quality from Virginia, but Sam had not been introduced. Nevertheless, he touched his shako.

"Who was that handsome officer?" whispered one of the girls.

Sam turned and saluted the sisters with an elaborate bow. "Lieutenant Houston, United States Army, ladies, at your service," he said, and strolled on.[2]

## 2

Sam was delighted with the prospects of the New Orleans assignment. With two youthful companions he bought a skiff and embarked by way of the "three rivers," as the saying was—the Cumberland, the Ohio and the Mississippi. The first two thousand miles of the circuitous journey proved devoid of adventure, however, and Sam spent most of his time reading some books he had brought along, including Shakespeare, Akenside's poems, *Robinson Crusoe, The Pilgrim's Progress, The Vicar of Wakefield* and a Bible that his mother had given him. Rounding the point of a bluff above Natchez, the young travelers saw what looked like a great raft afire in the middle of the river. It was a steamboat, the first the adventurers ever had seen. They sold their skiff and took passage to New Orleans on the steamboat.

New Orleans came up to expectations. Saturday parade in the Place d'Armes was followed by a promenade of the fashionable along the willow bordered walks beyond the dismantled ramparts. At the Hotel du Trèmoulet in the Rue St. Pierre, the Bourbonists held forth in high feather, while two threadbare generals of Napoleon sipped their four-o'clock coffee and cognac at the Café des Refugies, and plotted with the retired pirate, Dominique You, to bring the Emperor thither from the Rock. In the cool of the evening, Spaniards strummed guitars among the palms of the Place Congo. Nights were gallant and gay: the twice-weekly masked ball at the French theater in the Rue St. Philippe . . . the quadroon ball which began at midnight a square away . . . a peal of laughter from a shuttered house . . . the silvery cathedral bells. The old Creole town was not the place to ignore a big good-looking boy with a locker full of white pantaloons.

This was too pleasant to last. The Army doctors looked at Sam's To-ho-pe-ka shoulder, and said that the ball in there would have to come out. It was removed, but Sam nearly died as a result of the operation, which lamed him for life. The shoulder never healed.

During a winter of suffering in the damp French-built barracks by the river, the invalid got a taste of the dismal bickerings that seem inseparable from peace-time Army life. Lieutenant Houston wrote to the Secretary of War in February of 1816:

"Mr. Crawford, Sir, I address you in consequence of an error in my last promotion, which was to a 2d Lieut in the 39th Regt of Infy. My promotion is dated the 20th of May 1814 and the vacancy which I filled occur'd on the 27th of March 1814, [when] the deaths of Lieuts Somerville and Moulton gave me promotion and I hope you will not conceive me intruding when I am contending for the rank which I am entitled to. . . . For a proper knowledge of my conduct . . . I refer you to Major Genl Jackson under whose eye I was

amongst the first to charge over the enemies Breast-work. . . . My reasons for not referring you to my former Col Williams are He has ever been inimical to me, since I have joined this Regiment he has written letters to officers cal-culated to prejudice them against me. . . . Your Hble Servt
"SAM HOUSTON,
"Lt 1st Regt Infantry."[3]

The interest that Jackson had taken in the wounded Ensign appears to have been the cause of Colonel Williams's aversion. Sam was disgusted and thought of leaving the Army as soon as his wounds were well. But his health showed no improvement, and in the spring he was sent by sea to New York for further treatment. After several weeks there, he began to feel better and went to East Tennessee on furlough to visit his family. He was not home long, but there was time enough to fall in love before orders came to report at Nashville for duty at the headquarters of the Southern Division of the Army.

Jackson commanded the Southern Division. He had been a major-general in the Regular establishment since To-ho-pe-ka. This made a difference in Army life for Lieutenant Houston. The East Tennessee love-affair also made a differ-ence. But surveying matters from the perspective of Nash-ville, Sam seems to have regained his grip on his earlier resolution concerning matrimony. True, he was in rather deeply—so deeply that he felt the need of help in extricating himself. He asked a boyhood friend in Knoxville to call on the young lady and see what could be done. This ambassador mismanaged his mission:

"Sam, perhaps I ventured too far after hearing from you . . . respecting the affair between yourself and M——. . . . Things stand in a remarkably unpleasant sit-uation with respect to you & the queen of 'gildhall' Her friends perhaps have led her into error and one too for which she will not soon pardon herself but she has thrown W M—— sky high and is ready any moment to join her fate to

Sam's. . . . Why should you not realize the golden days that await an union with the Princess of E. T.? When you cease to love her your heart will become vitrified & a marriage with any other person will be for *convenience* and not for *happiness*. . . . Here she is . . . ready to leave mother home friends and every thing dear to her, and forsake them all, and go with you to earth's remotest bounds. . . . I know & you know that J. Beene is your friend & if I were to advise you it would be to speedily marry M——— by moonshine or any other way the most handy. . . . *Weigh well the verdict you are about to pronounce*. . . .

> "Yours Sentimentally,
> "JESSE BEENE."[4]

How the Lieutenant wiggled out of the dilemma does not appear, but the files of the War Department indicate a mood for special duty. Houston solicited a transfer, which Jackson endorsed, and the Lieutenant took off his uniform and unobstrusively left Nashville.

### 3

In beaded buckskins, Co-lon-neh crossed the boundary into the Indian country and took the trail toward the island home of Oo-loo-te-ka: The Raven had returned to his brothers. The Indians received him without suspicion, which, in view of the strained relations existing between the United States and the Cherokee Nation, was more than they would have done for almost any one else bearing the credentials of a subagent of the Indian Bureau.

The trouble arose from the treaty of 1816, signed the year before. By this instrument a group of Cherokee chiefs had ceded to the United States one million three hundred thousand acres of the Cherokee Nation in eastern Tennesse in exchange for territory west of the Mississippi for which the whites had no use. The individual tribesmen, and many of the chiefs, not having been consulted, sought to repudiate the action of the signers. The Tennessee mountains were the only home they had ever known. Their cornfields were there; their gods dwelt in those skies. This land had been guaranteed to them "for ever" by the United States Government. They declined to move. The treaty-making chiefs could do nothing about it.

In the eyes of the United States this was impertinence. "Unprincipled" was what Governor McMinn, of Tennessee, called these Indians, repudiating the pledged word of their own leaders—whom the United States had so carefully bribed. They were "a Set of the most Finished Tyrants that ever lived in a land of liberty."[5]

The frontier took alarm and demanded "firm" measures. But this fell out at an awkward time for the military. The Commanding General of the Southern Division was occupied with plans for another Indian war. The disrespectful attitude of the Georgia Seminoles afforded a pretext for seizing Florida, and so Jackson wanted no distractions at home. The olive branch and not the sword must be carried among the Cherokees. When Lieutenant Houston applied for an Indian assignment, Jackson wrote a strong endorsement to the application. Houston "has my entire confidence," the Secretary of War was informed.

The new Indian agent began his labors well. He appeared among the nettled tribesmen, speaking their language and living their life. His first acts were to make good some of the government's defaulted promises. It was winter, and Houston requisitioned blankets and distributed them. He got kettles for the women, traps for the hunters and, as proof of his confidence in the honor of his Indian brothers, rifles for the braves. Then it was time to sit by a council fire and speak of the unfortunate treaty of 1816.

Sam Houston approached the whole situation from his knowledge of the Indian's character and of the pattern of his mind. The first consideration concerned the sacredness of treaties. A "paper talk" had been made. Rightly or wrongly certain chiefs had signed it. Houston was on strong ground there. Contrary to centuries of propaganda that has crystallized into a fixed idea, Indians were usually more faithful to their word than the frontiersmen with whom they came in contact.

Yet, a difficulty confronted the negotiator of which the white officials probably knew nothing. Irrespective of the treaty, a grave consideration interposed against the emigration. The Cherokees were to go West, and West in the Cherokee religion had a sinister connotation. The West was the Darkening Land, abode of the Black Man, the god of evil, and his myriad of ill-intentioned black godlings. The Cherokees had no wish to turn their backs on the East, the Sun Land, residence of the Red Man and his good under-gods. In all the legends the Cherokee people knew, the West symbolized darkness, death and defeat.

Nevertheless, Lieutenant Houston convinced the Cherokees that they would be better off beyond the Father of Waters where the white man should never intrude. Oo-loo-te-ka and his band were the first to depart. The government generously equipped them for the journey. A party of three hundred and forty-one, including one hundred and nine warriors "each armed with a good new rifle," embarked on well-provisioned flatboats. This "dazzling" display was paraded before the Indians who still hesitated. The moral effect was tremendous.

Oo-loo-te-ka's name was also signed to a propaganda letter enumerating the benefits the Indians should derive from emigration to this Eden on the Arkansas. "You must not think by removing we shall return to the savage life. You have taught us to be Herdsmen and cultivators. . . . Our women will raise the cotton and the Indigo and spin and weave cloth to cloath our children. Numbers of our young people can read and write, they can read what we call the Preachers Book. . . . By intermarriages with our white brethren we are gradually becoming one people."[6]

Since Oo-loo-te-ka could not write and was opposed to Christianity and cross-marriages, the origin of this document is obscure, but Sam Houston may have inspired it. In any event, the Cherokees were off, the border rested easier and Sam returned to Nashville to receive the thanks of Governor McMinn, and promotion to first lieutenant.

4

Then something happened that threatened to upset everything. Ten years before, there had been a voluntary westward emigration of Cherokees under Tah-lhon-tusky, an older brother of Oo-loo-te-ka, and one of the great Cherokee leaders of the period. The vanguard of the new exodus was scarcely on its way when Tah-lhon-tusky appeared in Knoxville. His look was troubled.

The West, indeed, was the Darkening Land. There were the Osages to fight; but Tah-lhon-tusky said he could handle the Osages, if the government would attend to some other things. His western Cherokees had not received their share of the annuities the government paid into the treasury of the Cherokee Nation, as indemnity for ceded lands. Tah-lhon-tusky wished to secede from the central government of the Nation, located in Georgia, and wished the United States to recognize his independence. With a number of warriors and statesmen, he was on his way to lay the case before President Monroe.

Governor McMinn detained Tah-lhon-tusky with fair assurances, and sent letters to forewarn Washington of the impending complication. The venerable Indian made a deep impression on the Governor who endeavored to pass on to Secretary of War Calhoun some idea of Tah-lhon-tusky and his colleagues. "I hazard nothing that he is considered in the light of a king among his people." Next in rank of the delegation was Too-chee-la, a chieftain second in influence only to the great leader. There was also The Glass, "more celebrated for his upright deportment than . . . for his valor in war," but the military was represented by Captain Speers and Captain Lamore, who had fought with Jackson in 1812. The interpreter was James Rogers, nephew of Tah-lhon-tusky and a boyhood friend of Sam Houston. This selection seems to have been a happy one. James's father was now secretly in the pay of the United States. And Governor McMinn had provided still another safeguard. "Lieutenant Houston . . . by whose vigilance and address they will be most profited" would accompany these important travelers to the seat of the Great White Father.[7]

5

Lieutenant Houston had returned from his earlier mission to the Indian country in great distress from an inflammation of his shoulder wound. Nevertheless, he resumed his breech clout and blanket and, as The Raven, presented himself to his foster-uncle, the eminent Tah-lhon-tusky. The prestige that family ties have among Indians placed Sam Houston in a position of tactical importance to his government.

The delegation set out from Knoxville making a fine show—"the equal," wrote so watchful a critic as Governor McMinn, "in point of respectability of Character, of appearance and Dress to any other I have ever seen from any of the Indian Tribes." They traveled slowly. Tah-lhon-tusky was old, he had been little in the white man's country, and there was much to see. On the fifth day of February, 1818, the party arrived in Washington and was received by the Secretary of War. Mr. Calhoun had been coached in advance. He welcomed the visitors with the flawless Carolina courtesy that was to carry this statesman near, quite near, to the goal of his ultimate ambitions. After an exchange of amenities, the Secretary said that President Monroe was waiting to greet the delegation.

Tah-lhon-tusky and his people rose to depart. As they filed out the Secretary signed for Lieutenant Houston to remain. When the two were alone the mask of official politeness fell, and Mr. Calhoun abruptly demanded what an officer of the Army meant by appearing before the Secretary of War dressed as a savage.

Houston was somewhat stunned.  The diplomatic advantage of having an agent who could pass as Tah-lhon-tusky's kinsman, was evidently less important to Mr. Calhoun than the punctilio of military etiquette.

With the reprimand still galling his pride, Houston some days later received a second summons to the Secretary's office. Mr. Calhoun gravely informed the Lieutenant that he had been accused of complicity with slave smugglers.  Houston told his side of the story.  During his recent presence among the Cherokees in Tennessee, he had come across a band of slave smugglers carrying negroes from Florida and broken up its activities without asking for instructions.

Houston's story was so straightforward that the Secretary promised an investigation.  Houston vigorously assisted this inquiry.  He carried his case in person to President Monroe. It was disclosed that Houston had told the truth, and that the accusation had originated with members of Congress who were, to say the least, on friendly terms with the smugglers.

Houston cleared himself,—merely that.  There was no move to prosecute those whose guilt he had made plain; no move to investigate the crooked politicians who had undertaken to ruin an obscure Army officer; no expression of thanks to Houston; no regret for the false accusation.  Sam Houston went to his lodgings and wrote in a hand too hurried for punctuation:

"Washington City
"March 1st 1818

"Sir

"You will please accept this as my resignation to take effect from this date.        I have the honor
                    to be
                "Your Most Obt Servt
                "SAM HOUSTON
                "1st Lieut 1st Infy

"Genl D. Parker
"A & Ins Genl.
"W. City."[8]

With a certain impassioned dignity, the profession of arms was renounced by a young man of twenty-five, who had intended to follow that calling through life. Sam Houston had grown to like the Army. He was ill from wounds. Five years of somewhat distinguished, and certainly disinterested service, had been shabbily rewarded. Yet the regret with which he took his leave appears in the request for a memento, appended as a postscript to his resignation.

"I will thank you to give me my commission, which I am entitled to by my last promotion. Yours &c
                   "S. HOUSTON"

Tah-lhon-tusky and his followers had been in Washington all this time. They were showered with attention and sent away with promises, personal gifts and a consignment of seed corn for the tribe—apparently as pleased as if they had obtained all that they had come for. Governor McMinn hastened to congratulate the Secretary of War. "I am truly pleased to learn that the usual plan has been taken with the Chiefs . . . corrupt as it may appear," namely that of "purchasing their friendship."⁹

The ex-Lieutenant journeyed westward with Tah-lhon-tusky as far as the Hiwassee River in Tennessee. He wound up the affairs of his subagency and resigned that office also. Saying good-by to the last of his Cherokee friends who were leaving for the Arkansas, he turned his horse toward the distant metropolis of Nashville.

# CHAPTER V

## THE STEPS OF THE TEMPLE

### 1

WHEN Lieutenant Houston left the Army he was fashionably in debt, and to liquidate his obligations sold "everything" he could spare, "including some land." This seems to have been the end of his eighth interest in the Baker's Creek farm, which already had afforded an example of worldly possessions failing to comfort the possessor. The property was taken over by Brother James.[1] The consideration does not appear to have been much, although the land was valuable by now. At any rate, the sale of all his effects failed to bring Sam out of debt. Sam was no great business man, but he usually got what he wanted. If he tossed his patrimony to a hard-fisted brother for a pittance it was probably because the gesture was worth more to him than the money.

In Nashville he began to read law in the office of James Trimble. Judge Trimble had known Sam's people in Virginia. He outlined an eighteen-month course of reading. Sam sat down in the chair that Lemuel Montgomery had occupied, and opened the same books that that eager young man had put down in 1812 to go to war.

In six months the student astonished his preceptor by passing an examination for admission to the bar. He went to Lebanon, thirty miles east of Nashville, to practise. There he was befriended by Isaac Galladay, whose benevolences Houston never forgot. For a dollar a month Mr. Galladay provided the young lawyer with an office. As postmaster, Mr.

Galladay extended credit for postage—quite an item since it cost twenty-five cents to send a letter. As merchant, he furnished his young friend with a wardrobe, and in this detail Sam did not stint the generosity of his benefactor. He dressed fit to kill: bell-crowned beaver, plum colored coat, tight breeches and waistcoats that were studies.

The well-attired stranger was instantly popular. He was easy to remember—a perfectly proportioned, military figure considerably more than six feet tall, with a pleasant way, a pleasant word and a rich warm voice. Maidens were interested when he bowed over their hands, and the young ladies' mothers no less charmed by his careful courtesy. Men repeated his anecdotes and listened to his views on politics.

The barrister rode to Nashville often. Lebanon knew little of these journeys, except that they had an air of importance—which was enough. On the way Houston usually stopped off at the Hermitage. Governor McMinn also was a regular caller at General Jackson's residence. After one of his visits, the Executive drove back to Murfreesboro and announced the appointment of Sam Houston as adjutant-general of the state militia.

This made him Colonel Houston, and Sam was not the man to scorn a military title so essential to good standing. There were journeys to Murfreesboro, the state capital, to sweat over muddled records. It was tedious business, and so one day when John Rogers was announced, the Colonel cheerfully pitched aside his ink-spattered muster rolls to talk of old times.

The two friends had much to say. Times had changed since the days on Oo-loo-te-ka's island, where Sam had discovered love and John had discovered English from Sam's recitations of the *Iliad*. John's father was still headman of the tribe, and young John himself was coming on—Captain Rogers, he now subscribed himself, showing the effect of proximity to a superior culture.

John related the story of the Cherokees' odyssey. They had fulfilled their part of the treaty, but the government had not fulfilled its part. The generous gesture that had lured the Indians away peaceably was terminated when the government had the Indians where it wanted them. The lands on the Arkansas had been flagrantly misrepresented. The neighboring tribes were hostile. There Cherokees were harassed, hungry and homesick. The agent, Reuben Lewis, rather increased their hardships than otherwise. The West was the Darkening Land.

Oo-loo-te-ka was trying to make the best of his bargain. He had prevailed upon the agent to resign,[2] a statement which Sam must have thought incredible until John exhibited a copy of the resignation. This was all very well, but Oo-loo-te-ka had another idea in mind when he persuaded the agent to withdraw. He besought The Raven to return to his "father" and accept the vacancy.

Sam Houston was profoundly touched. He sensed an obligation unfulfilled. Already Sam had seen enough of another life to appreciate the wilderness and his early taste of its sweets. He wavered from the resolution that had fortified him against the loss of an Army career, and bidding John an affectionate good-by, wrote impulsively to Jackson. "Now, General, be candid. . . . I have some liking for such a situation! I don't know what is best, but permit me to ask you."[3]

Jackson did not lose a day in sending a three-page letter to Mr. Calhoun. "I . . . enclose you a letter from Col. Samuel Houston . . . formerly of the 39th and last of the first Regiment of U. States Infantry. I have recommended him to accept the appointment of Agent. I have done this more with a view to the interest of the U. States than his own. . . . In the capacity of agent he can draw to the Arkansas in a few years the whole strength of the Cherokee Nation now in the East of the Mississippi River."[4] In the light of contemporary Indian policy, better reasons for the appointment could not have been urged.

Mr. Calhoun made the appointment—but Houston's mood

had passed. He declined the post. A little later another opening was presented that was more in accord with his previous aims. With Jackson's endorsement, Sam Houston captured a nomination for prosecuting attorney, or attorney-general as they called it, of the Nashville district and was elected.

In Lebanon there was a great ceremony of leave-taking. The public square was filled. Houston stood on the steps of the little court-house and made a speech. Descending, he moved through the throng of well-wishers, shaking hands and bowing himself from Lebanon's small world which had known the man it honored in such warm fashion for less than a year.

**2**

General Jackson's presentable young friend proved so successful as a public prosecutor that he resigned in a year to reap the larger rewards of a private practise. He made a local reputation as a trial lawyer. His fellow officers in the state militia elected him their major-general. The ground of Tennessee was rising under Houston's feet, but this was of no avail in a matter that had been hanging fire in the War Department since the Major-General was a first lieutenant of Regulars. After resigning from the Army and from the Indian service, the final audit of his accounts showed a balance due from the government of one hundred and seventy dollars and nine cents. In his starving student days and later, Houston had vainly tried to collect this money, but could never surmount the complications which he attributed to the personal vindictiveness of the Secretary of War.

In 1822, when Houston's law practise was yielding a good income, the debt was paid by a draft on a Nashville bank. The bank offered to honor the draft at a discount of twenty-seven per cent., and Houston returned it to Mr. Calhoun. "I can see no reason for the conduct pursued by you . . . unless it is that I am the same man against whom you conceived so strong a prejudice in 1818. . . . Sir I could have forgotten the unprovoked injuries inflicted upon me if you were not disposed to continue them.   But your reiteration shall not be unregarded. . . . Your personal bad treatment, your official injustice . . . was to oblige a Senator—secure his interest and crush a sub agent. . . . All this will I remember as a man."[5]   Fair warning, Mr. Calhoun.

But where one man in Washington seemed to go out of his way to court the ill-will of Sam Houston a thousand in Tennessee were anxious to be his friends.   The young lawyer was well up in the Jackson political hierarchy in the state, and much in the company of the new Governor, William Carroll. Billy Carroll was Jackson's right-hand man in Tennessee. Just now he was experimenting with the political machine designed to help the General capture the presidency in 1824. Carroll's manipulations mark the dawn of modern politics, and various chores were delegated to Houston who did them well.   In 1823 the new helper had qualified himself for promotion.   A nod from Jackson and Sam was nominated for Congress.   The election that followed was somewhat in the nature of a try-out for the Carroll machine.   The performance was satisfactory.   Having no opposition, Houston received every vote cast.

### 3

Five years after Sam Houston had left Washington a disillusioned ex-lieutenant without occupation or prospects, he returned a major-general, a congressman-elect and a protégé of the most popular man in the country.   He strolled along Pennsylvania Avenue rather pleased with himself except in one particular: he did not care for the hat he was wearing.   But this upsetting circumstance did not endure for long.   He ran across Edward George Washington Butler, an old Tennessee friend, who knew Washington.   Where was the best place to buy a narrow-brimmed beaver?

The two visited shop after shop until Sam found the right hat.   He put it on and asked his friend to walk to the Capitol.

They crossed the sheep meadow that surrounded the government house, and ascended the broad white steps. Sam made his way to the colonnaded hall of Representatives and roamed through the empty chamber. Finally he selected the seat he wanted for his own.

"Now, Butler," he remarked, "I am a member of Congress. I will show Mr. Calhoun that I have not forgotten his insult to a poor lieutenant."[6]

The dome of the new Capitol under which Representative Houston confided this inkling of his aspirations was smaller than the one that is there now, but otherwise the plan of Washington was "colossal," as the visiting Duke of Saxe-Weimar expressed it, "and will hardly ever be executed. It could contain a population of one million, whilst it is said at present to have but 13,000." Public buildings were miles apart. When one had to walk through the mud from one to another, the metropolitan idea seemed like carrying optimism too far, and there was talk of moving the seat of government to Wheeling, Virginia.

But congressmen need not walk to the sociable tavern which advertised "a post coach and four horses . . . kept for the conveyance of Members to and from the Capitol . . . by the public's obedient servant WILLIAM O'NEALE." A night's lodging at Major O'Neale's cost twenty-five cents, fire and candle extra. Meals were a dollar a day, bitters and brandy twelve and a half cents, toddy a quarter.

The élite of southern officialdom held forth at O'Neale's. Jackson stayed there, and for five winters it had been the home of John H. Eaton, Jackson lieutenant and the senior senator from Tennessee. The junior senator was Jackson himself. He had been elected on short notice. The distinction was unsought and unwelcome, but necessary to keep the seat from unfriendly hands.

Taking his place in Congress under the eye of the Master gave Sam Houston entrée to the inner circle at O'Neale's where the great and the aspiring discussed matters in a close atmosphere of tobacco juice and Monongahela toddies. A young man could have found no better school of applied politics, although it did not leave Houston much time to use the personally selected seat on the floor of the House. In fact, trace of his presence in the House is practically limited to the yeas and nays. This voting record is a simple duplication of the views of the Master, including support of the proposal to place frying-pans on the free list—a concession in the Tariff Bill designed to captivate the frontier.

Socially the Congressman had a good time. He kept late hours and cruised in interesting company. One evening Representative Daniel Webster and Junius Brutus Booth took advantage of an afflorescent tavern fellowship to rally Sam on the style of his oratory. Mr. Webster professed chagrin that the Tennesseean should prefer the manner of Booth, while the tragedian affected disappointment because so promising a pupil had selected for his model the gentleman from Massachusetts. Both were unjust to their young friend. Sam did not make many speeches, and those he did make were quite succinct for an era when to be a great orator was to be a great man.

As a matter of course Sam made the acquaintance of Margaret O'Neale, the innkeeper's daughter. Peg was good-looking, and the camaraderie of the big tavern house did not diminish her charms. To be quite accurate, Peg was now Mrs. John Timberlake, but John Timberlake was not much in evidence, being a purser in the Navy who went on long voyages. The sailor's wife consoled herself with the society of her father's clientele. The name mentioned most frequently was that of Senator John Henry Eaton, of Tennessee. He was rich and a widower.

4

The winter passed agreeably enough for Representative Houston. "Jackson is gaining every day," he wrote in February of 1824, "and will be the next president."[7] And so it seemed when the votes were counted that November. Jackson carried eleven states. John Quincy Adams carried seven states. Three went to Crawford of Georgia and three to the Speaker of the House, Mr. Clay. But there was no majority in the electoral college, and it devolved upon the House of Representatives to break the deadlock.

This would take place in February. Meantime, Washington seethed with electioneering. When all was said, it was Mr. Clay who would name the next president of the United States. Sam Houston was in the midst of that boiling activity. He boldly bid for the support of Clay. "What a splendid administration it would make," he told the Speaker's friend, Sloane, of Ohio, "with Old Hickory as President and Mr. Clay as Secretary of State."[8]

The trend of affairs was not encouraging to the Jackson forces. Their patron was of slight assistance, turning not a hand to win the favor of Mr. Clay. "The members are as the *tomb*," wrote Houston as the weeks dragged on and the rumor grew that Clay would swing his strength to Adams. The Jackson people still had strong hopes, though, and in the last days of the canvass Houston was grimly "confident . . . that Jackson will succeed. . . . This you will at least suppose is my honest opinion as an expression of an opinion at this time can answer no purpose!"[9]

But Jackson did not succeed. In a dramatic scene, which surprised seasoned politicians who expected a long battle, Adams won easily on the first ballot.

Old Hickory took it more calmly than many of his followers and paid the President-Elect a stiff courtesy call. And then Mr. Clay was made Secretary of State. This was too much. The virtuous Jacksonians recovered their tongues and cried, "Corrupt bargain!"

Meantime John C. Calhoun had slipped into the vice-presidency. All in all, the campaign of 1824 represented a reverse to a tall young man with a tall hat and similar ambitions.

## 5

But Sam still had an iron in the fire. On his way to Washington the autumn previous, he had thought of stopping off en route and resuming his journey with a bride. But "to have married on my way here would not have answered a good purpose. My errand here is to attend to . . . business . . . and not to 'spend honeymoons.' *Everything in due season!*"[10]

Through the stresses of a winter that had seen the lapse of many loyalties, the ardent hope persevered in the breast of Sam Houston. On the eve of the fatal balloting in the House chamber, he wrote to a friend who stood in need of consolation. "I regret that you have been unsuccessful in love affairs. But you have taken the best course possible to be extricated, by taking a new chase! For my *single self* I do not know the sweets of Matrimony, but in March or Apl. Next I will; unless something takes place not to be expected or wished for."[11]

The unexpected and unwished for somehow interposed. March and April came. Houston went home and was reelected to Congress, but he returned to Washington still a stranger to the sweets of matrimony.

## 6

There was work to do. Discreet preliminaries for the Jackson campaign of 1828 were under way. Sam Houston was a freer agent than heretofore, because Jackson was not at his side. The old leader had drawn a long breath and retired from the Senate to the agreeable shades of the Hermitage.

Jackson's going gave Houston a chance to develop as a legislator rather than a lobbyist. He began to show his head above the level of the Congressional pack. He had his miniature painted and went about in society. The new chase theory, possibly; at any rate, the miniature is said to have changed hands rather often. He crossed the river to call on Mary

Custis, the daughter of George Washington Custis, great-granddaughter of Martha Washington and heiress to the mansion of Arlington. Representative Houston was the chairman of the Congressional Board of Visitors of the United States Military Academy. The annual inspections of this august body were a great event at the institution on the Highlands of the Hudson where a shy third-classman was writing letters to the same Mary Custis. The young lady was so indifferent to the claims of fame as to prefer this quiet youth who did not drink or smoke, and eventually to marry Second Lieutenant Robert E. Lee, Corps of Engineers.

Still, it was as one of Andrew Jackson's young men that Sam Houston owed his surest claim to contemporary notice. He was one of the trio that Jackson dubbed his "literary bureau," from the amount of writing they did to keep the General's candidacy before the country. The other two were Senator Eaton and Judge Jacob C. Isacks, of Winchester, Tennessee. They enjoyed themselves and contributed to a great many newspapers. Sometimes the same man, using different names, would carry on both sides of a controversy.

Sam Houston is believed also to have written "*A Civil and Military History of Andrew Jackson,* by an American Army Officer," which in 1825 took its place in the current flood of Jackson literature. It is better and briefer than "*The Life of Andrew Jackson,* by John Henry Eaton, Senator of the United States," which the author was now enlarging to include such details of the Florida campaign as he thought proper. The two authors were jealous of each other; Houston's rapid rise had irritated many older men. His work suited Jackson, though, and, in the second campaign, he was one of the responsible circle upon whom devolved the ticklish duty of curbing the Master's temper. Once Houston declined to deliver a letter that Jackson addressed to Mr. Southard, the Secretary of Navy, saying the language was too strong. Jackson recast the communication. It got out that Houston could "handle" Jackson, an accomplishment claimed for few men.

Henry Clay was the bête noire of the Jackson following and the most active in countermining the Jackson moves for 1828. With the Southard matter still in delicate balance, Houston received from the Hermitage an allusion to the Secretary of State. "I have lately got an intimation of some of his secrete movements; which, if I can reach with positive & responsible proof, I will wield to his political, & perhaps, to his actual Destruction—he is certainly the bases[t], meanest scoundrel that ever disgraced the image of his god—nothing too mean or low for him to condescend to to secretly carry his cowardly & base *slander* into effect; even the aged and Virtuous female is not free from his secrete combinations of base slander—*but enough—you know me* . . . retributive *justice will visit him and his pander[er]s heads.*"[12] The campaign was warming up.

Sam Houston did know his patron. He knew that he kept in order the pistols with which he had killed one man for slandering Mrs. Jackson. But the thought of shooting one-self into the presidency had so little besides novelty to recommend it, that Jackson's advisers were cold to the idea. Moreover, Mr. Clay had just put a bullet through the coat-tails of Jackson's friend, John Randolph, of Virginia.

The opposition continued its assaults on the character of "Aunt Rachel," as Sam Houston affectionately called the wife of his patron. These reached a climax when the unintentional irregularity of the General's marriage was made the subject of a contemptible allusion by Adams's organ, the *National Journal*. Duff Green replied in his *United States Telegraph* with tales of Mr. Adams's private life that were the product of an equally creative imagination. Pleased as Punch, Green wrote to Jackson of what had been done. "Let her [Mrs. Jackson] rejoice—her vindication is complete. . . . The whole Adams corps was thrown into consternation."

This was not the kind of vindication Jackson wished. He told Green to be truthful. "Female character should never be introduced by my friends unless attack should continue . . , on Mrs. J. and then only by way *of Just retaliation upon the known* GUILTY. . . . *I never war against females* & it is only the base & cowardly that do." Whereupon, each side having had its moment, the petticoats were nervously restored to the comparative privacy of the whispering gallery.

7

The theater of our national affairs did not remain an Eveless Eden long enough to become a bore. The choice of her father's tavern house as a Jackson stamping-ground placed Peggy O'Neale in a position to enlarge the scope of her already comprehensive acquaintance. She charmed the old General. She won the heart of Aunt Rachel, and was not unattractive to the critical eye of an elegant widower who was assisting the Jackson fortunes in New York—Mr. Martin Van Buren.

But General Jackson's health was the important thing now. The candidate was ailing and had openly declared for a single term. This made the selection of a vice-president a matter of especial interest, since it was Jackson's plan to promote his vice-president in 1832. There were two candidates for vice-president between whose claims the Jackson leaders themselves were divided. Ostensibly the General was neutral, but the world knew he had not abandoned his old friendship for John C. Calhoun. As Secretary of War, Mr. Calhoun was understood to have supported Jackson in his Florida campaign. The General could not forget such an act of accommodation. On the other hand, he did nothing to check his supporters who were booming Governor DeWitt Clinton, of New York.

Sam Houston was for Clinton, naturally. Eaton was for Clinton; so were Martin Van Buren and the other New Yorkers in the Jackson camp, including Samuel Swartwout, one-time dispatch rider for Aaron Burr. Major William B. Lewis, Jackson's personal man Friday and inseparable companion, also cast his lot with the easterner. Still, the anti-Calhoun wing failed to gain much ground. The Clinton people were getting uneasy when Sam Houston laid his hands on a letter that revived their hopes.

This communication was written in 1818 by President Monroe to the Secretary of War, Mr. Calhoun. It made clear that Calhoun did not approve of General Jackson's high-handed invasion of Florida. There were phases of the Florida campaign, concerning which Jackson said as little as possible, except to intimate that he had merely taken the steps necessary for the ends desired by the administration. Perceiving a chance to ride into the presidency on the tail of Jackson's kite, Mr. Calhoun had done nothing to damage this impression.

Sam Houston is said to have kept this letter under cover for a year, presumably awaiting the right moment to present it at the Hermitage. This came early in 1827. The effect was "like electricity," as Duff Green might have said. "It smelled so much of deception," wrote Jackson, "that my hair stood on end for an hour." Calhoun had been playing him false all these years. There was a great stir, but Calhoun and his supporters kept it under cover. Calhoun protested that the letter had been stolen, and the real villain was made out to be Mr. Monroe. But Jackson was not ungrateful to Sam Houston for his interest.

The national campaign thundered on its way. In the midst of it, Houston was elected governor of Tennessee which transferred his activities from O'Neale's tavern to scenes less remote from the Hermitage. In this favored position, he continued to fight Calhoun. There was a plan to induce William H. Crawford, who was also in the Monroe Cabinet, to confirm Sam Houston's disclosure of Calhoun's attitude on Florida, but before it could be executed Governor Clinton died, rendering the Calhoun opposition leaderless. An attempt to rally about Martin Van Buren was unrealized. Mr. Calhoun was nominated and elected with the Jackson landslide.

But the anti-Calhounists were not ignored. Mr. Van Buren was to be Secretary of State. John H. Eaton was to be Secretary of War. And as Andrew Jackson's friend and personal confidant, the handsome young Governor of Tennessee found himself with his feet on the steps of the temple.

## 8

In the closing weeks of the campaign, the O'Neale tavern was a gay as well as a busy place. Upon this scene intruded a messenger from the Navy Department to say that Purser Timberlake was dead. He had cut his throat while on a Mediterranean cruise. No official explanation of the act was offered, but Washington gossip found a motive in his wife's affair with the Senator from Tennessee, although actually the Purser's depression appears to have been caused by a shortage in the accounts of his ship, the celebrated *Constitution*.

The public mind honored the deceased with a racy if transient notice of obituary, and lost him in the rush of the campaign. Within a few weeks the incident was so completely submerged that polite Washington would have been surprised to know that Senator Eaton privately had confessed "many an anxious and distressed moment" on account of it. For polite Washington mistakenly assumed the Purser's passing to have simplified matters for the Senator, who had already shown substantial proofs of his good-will toward the O'Neales. In fact the O'Neale tavern, though it sometimes still went by its old name, was now properly Gadsby's Hotel. When the Major, Peg's father, encountered money troubles Eaton had bought the inn to help him out, selling it to Gadsby.

The death of Mr. Timberlake did not simplify matters for Senator Eaton. It complicated them. The complication arose, the Senator wrote in great confidence, from an impulse to marry Peg and "snatch her from that injustice" done her name by "the City gossipers who attend to everybody's reputation . . . to the neglect of their own." That is what the Senator wrote. It is not what he meant, as the complete text of his letter, written during one of those "distressed" moments, shows. The Senator wished to avoid a marriage and after ransacking his wits for a way out, he finally went to Jackson with the plea that there would be "talk" that would work to the injury of the new administration, of which Eaton was to be a part. The Senator confessed that it took time to acquire courage to face Jackson in an effort to obtain his sanction to a "postponement" of the wedding on such grounds.[13]

The interview took place at the Hermitage. Major Eaton assured the President-Elect that Peg's "own merits" as well as "considerations of honor" would impel him "at a *proper time* [italics Eaton's] . . . to tender her the offer" of marriage. Even then there would be consequences. "The impossibility of escaping detraction and slander was too well credenced to me," the Senator went on, "in the abuse of those more meritorious and deserving that [than] I ever could hope to be."[14]

Eaton's uncertainty as to Jackson's attitude was well founded. Old Hickory would hear of no delay. The nervous allusion to the manufactured scandal over Jackson's own marriage availed as little as one less upset in mind than Senator Eaton might have expected. Jackson ordered Eaton to marry Peg at once, and the gossips be damned.

The involuntary suitor returned to Washington. He saw Peg and a wedding was spoken of to take place, somewhat vaguely, "after the adjournment." Senator Eaton then would be a Cabinet officer—and anything might happen. But no sooner had this improvisation been arranged than Eaton received by the hand of Judge Isacks, late of the literary bureau, a letter from Jackson telling Eaton to marry Peg "forthwith" or "change your residence." Eaton wrote a labored epistle of "gratitude." "Your admonition shall be regarded. . . . In the first week of January . . . an honorable discharge of duty to myself and to her shall be met, and more than this . . . I rendered a happy and contented man."[15]

The announcement of the betrothal bowled over Washington, which, in its agitation, passed Major Eaton on to posterity adorned with a reputation for undiscriminating gallantry that is undeserved.

In Albany, New York, Mr. Van Buren read the tidings in a New Year's note from a congressman friend in the capital. "May you live a thousand years and always have . . . a thousand sweethearts—and not one applicant for office. . . . La Belle Hortense thinks she would like to live in the *palace again.* . . . She will be here in February. . . . Poor Eaton is to be married tonight to Mrs. T——! There is a vulgar saying of some vulgar man, I believe Swift, on such unions— about using a certain household——[sic] and then putting it on one's head. The last sentence prevents me signing my name."[16] This delicacy has deprived the world of an autograph—and he wrote a lovely hand—of Mr. Churchill C. Cambreleng, than whom none was more au courant with the smart talk of the Washington haute monde.

Poor Eaton, indeed! General Jackson had laid the foundation for his house of cards. Its collapse flung careers about like autumn leaves.

# CHAPTER VI

## Six Feet Six

### 1

"PRESENT me," Andrew Jackson wrote to Representative Houston in November of 1826, "to Mr. John Randolph——"

Mr. Randolph was wearing a new coat now, the gift of Henry Clay as reparation for the damage the Secretary had done to the Senator's wardrobe with a bullet. But surely this was unknown to Jackson, already sufficiently chagrined over Randolph's poor marksmanship.

"Present me to Mr. John Randolph. . . . You may suggest a desire I have of obtaining a good filly got by Sir Archey and a full bred by the dam side. If he has a filly of this description . . . that he can sell for $300 or under . . . and you will bring her out I will be prompt in remitting him the amount." And when that was done: "Capt. A. J. Donelson who has engaged my stud colts desires me to say to you if a faithfull keeper of horses can be got he will give them good wages, a freeman of colour, from one hundred to one hundred and fifty of standing wages . . . besides other privileges."[1]

More august personages than Representative Houston would have flown to perform services such as these. Their asking bore the stamp of the old General's affection, and every one knew how far Andrew Jackson would go for a friend. Sam Houston possessed a nature sufficiently warm to be drawn to a man like that, and his reciprocation sometimes colored his official conduct.

Early in 1826 the postmastership of Nashville fell vacant. Jackson had a candidate, and Clay had one—in the person of John P. Erwin, editor of the Nashville *Banner and Whig*. Naturally, the Clay man must be headed off. "Attend to this business,"[2] Jackson wrote Houston, and the Nashville post-mastership became a national issue. Houston did his best. He fought Erwin at every turn, writing the President that the Clay candidate was "not a man of fair and upright moral character," and accusing him on the floor of the House of "a want of integrity." Yet Erwin got the place, and Houston was warned to look out; whereupon he took up pistol practise on the outskirts of the capital.

**2**

This seemed a prudent thing to do. Houston was already involved in an affair of honor with a Tennesseean named Gibbs, and a duel seemed so likely that he had written a letter to be published "should I perish." "My firm and undeviating attachment to Genl Jackson has caused me all the enemies I have, and I glory in the firmness of my attachment. . . . I will die proud in the assurance that I deserve, and possess his perfect confidence."[3]

The affair with Gibbs did not come off, but on his return to Nashville, Houston received a note from Postmaster Erwin asking about the aspersions attributed to him. Houston stood by what he had said, which could only be construed as an invitation to fight. Nashville was Jackson-Houston ground, and Mr. Erwin had trouble finding a messenger to deliver his challenge, until Colonel John Smith T., as he called himself, a professional duelist from Missouri, alighted from a westbound stage. Houston named Colonel McGregor, of Nashville, as his second. With most of Nashville looking on Smith T. confronted McGregor in the public square.

"I have a communication from Colonel Erwin to General Houston, which I now hand you, sir," said the challenger's representative.

"General Houston can receive no communication from your hands because you are not a citizen of this state," McGregor replied.

Smith T. went away, and Houston and his friends were gathered in front of the Nashville Inn when Smith returned with General William A. White, a lawyer and veteran of the battle of New Orleans. Instead of seeking McGregor, Smith handed Erwin's message directly to Houston.

"Colonel," said White triumphantly to Smith, "I reckon he will not deny having received it."

Houston turned on his heel.

"I have not received it," he exclaimed, "I do not know its contents. I will not open it, but will refer its contents to Colonel McGregor. But I will receive one from you, General White, with pleasure."

"I will receive one from you, General Houston."

"The saddle is on the other horse, General, and that is enough to be understood between gentlemen."

"If I call on you there will be no shuffling, I suppose."

"Try me, sir," said Sam Houston.[4]

But White had no idea of trying Houston. Days passed. Erwin evinced a disposition to transfer the controversy to the newspapers. Smith T. showed more spirit. He wrote to demand whether Houston's only reason for refusing to receive the challenge in the first instance was because Smith lived in another state. Houston replied that this was the only reason he had had at the time, but inquiry had given him ground for others, such as Smith's "reputed standing and character." To the amazement of every one, the Missouri bad man took a boat for the West.

This left White to hold the bag. "Knowing that a coward can not live except in disgrace and obscurity," he wrote a friend, "I did not hesitate as to my course." He challenged Houston on an academic point of honor which disavowed any feeling of personal animosity. Houston chose pistols at fifteen feet. As it had turned out, Houston was to meet the poorest shot of three possible opponents, but the short distance was a concession to White's indifferent skill. At fifteen feet any one stood a chance of hitting a man of Houston's size.

The date set for the meeting allowed the contestants a week in which to improve their marksmanship. Sam Houston went to the experienced Jackson for advice. Old Hickory told him to bite on a bullet when he drew. It would help his aim. Houston practised for a while on the grounds of the Hermitage and then retired to the farm of Sanford Duncan, near the Kentucky line, to polish off his training.

Sanford Duncan had two pups named Andrew Jackson and Thomas Benton because they always were fighting each other. Houston noticed that Andrew usually came out on top, and took this to be a good omen. On the night of September 21, 1826, the party that was to accompany Houston to the field slept at the Duncan house. At three-forty in the morning, Houston was awakened by a barking dog. It was Andrew, the pup. Sam arose without disturbing his friends, tiptoed into the kitchen and began to mold bullets. As the first ball fell from the mold, a game cock crowed. Houston picked up the bullet and marking it on one side for the dog, and on the other side for the rooster, resolved to use it in his first fire.

At sunup the two parties met in a pasture just over the line in Kentucky. The ground was paced off. The principals took their places.

"Gentlemen, are you ready?"

"Ready, sir."

"Ready, sir."

"*Fire!* One, two, three, four."

Houston drew quickly and fired. White sank to the ground, shot through the groin. The Houston group started toward the Tennessee line when White called weakly. Houston returned and knelt beside the wounded man.

"General, you have killed me," White said.

"I am very sorry," Houston replied. "But you know it was forced upon me."

"I know it, and forgive you."[5]

General White spent four months in bed. No one watched his progress closer or received assurances of his recovery with greater relief than Sam Houston. The Clay faction in Kentucky made use of the duel in an effort to embarrass Jackson. A Kentucky grand jury indicted Houston for assault, but there was no arrest and the presiding officer at a political meeting in Tennessee introduced Houston with a heroic allusion to the affair with White. Sam Houston silenced the applause, said he was opposed to dueling, and declined to be honored as a duelist. "Thank God," he concluded, "my adversary was injured no worse."[6]

## 3

Everything Sam Houston did redounded to the credit of his white-haired patron, who arranged another advancement for his protégé. William Carroll was retiring from the governorship, having served three consecutive terms, the limit permitted by the constitution.

Billy Carroll was an interesting man. At New Orleans he had been Old Hickory's second in command. In Tennessee his tall, fastidiously groomed figure was as well known as that of Jackson himself. He was rich and ruthless. One glance from his steel-blue eyes had made and unmade senators. Friendship, which was everything to Jackson, was nothing to Carroll in politics. The only office the dictator cared for personally was the governorship. This was his passion. Sam Houston became the candidate of the Jackson democracy to fill in as governor for one term, after which Carroll would be eligible to resume the reins. Another of General Jackson's young men, Mr. James K. Polk, was to take Houston's place in the House and carry on the good work at Washington.

But the governorship was not to be kept in Jackson's hands without a fight. A little revolt against the grenadier methods of the old leader encouraged the Whigs, who put up Newton Cannon, a strong man.

Houston made an unprecedented campaign. He had been preparing for it for years, under Jackson's coaching. He was the best mixer in Tennessee. Log-rollings, barn-raisings and barbecues were his forte. On election day he closed his canvass with a tour of the polling places in Nashville. "Mounted on a superb dapple-gray horse he appeared unannounced," one dazzled spectator recorded, ". . . the observed of all observers."

It is no wonder. Sam had dressed for his public: bell-crowned, black beaver hat, standing collar and patent-leather, military stock, ruffled shirt, black satin vest and "shining" black trousers, gathered at the waist with legs full "the same size from seat to ankle." In place of a coat the broad shoulders were loosely draped with a "gorgeous" Indian hunting shirt, encircled by a beaded red sash with a polished metal clasp. His silk socks were lavishly embroidered and his pumps set off by silver buckles.[7]

Judge Jo C. Guild has left a description of the man himself. "Houston stood six feet six inches in his socks, was of fine contour, a remarkably well proportioned man, and of commanding and gallant bearing; had a large, long head and face and his fine features were lit up by large eagle-looking eyes; possessed of a wonderful recollection of persons and names, a fine address and courtly manners and a magnetism approaching that of General Andrew Jackson. He enjoyed unbounded popularity among men and was a great favorite with the ladies."[8]

Six feet six—an entire school of southwestern tradition confirms it, but the descriptive list of the War Department, wanting in imagination, and by no means incapable of error, undertakes to whittle Sam Houston's stature down to six feet and two inches. Guild knew Houston well, and the nature of their relations protects the Judge against a charge of intentional flattery. But no escaping it, there was something about this man that made light of yardsticks.

A probability of similar exaggeration exists in the report

of the election-day attire, though it was doubtless bizarre enough. Sam Houston's clothes were usually equal to the rococo tastes of his generation, but he did not wear Indian shirts in Washington, and he did not wear them in Nashville when he danced with Miss Anne Hanna, who has enriched history with the observation that "two classes of people pursued Sam Houston all his life—artists and women."[9]

But Nashville was not composed exclusively of persons as discriminating as Miss Anne Hanna. Nashville was the backwoods capital of a backwoods state. Of its population of five thousand, one thousand were negro slaves. The town made a ragged pattern about a public square which crowned a noble bluff overlooking the steamboat landing. In the square stood the court-house, fenced by a hitch-rail. The Nashville Inn was on one side of the square and the City Hotel on another. These places of entertainment served the notable of two generations. The Inn with its imposing three-story colonnade was the headquarters of the Jackson democracy, while all the important Whigs hung up their saddle-bags at the City Hotel.

Sam Houston lived at the Inn. The vacant lot next door was reserved for cock-fights. Billiards was also a craze with the quality until the Legislature, which convened at seven o'clock in the morning, levied a tax of one thousand dollars a table on the wicked luxury. But not until later did this revolutionary body abolish the stocks, whipping-post and branding-iron for minor offenders, and the penalty of death without benefit of clergy for stealing a horse. The executioner's fee at a hanging was two dollars and fifty cents. Nashville's Clover Bottom race-track was one of the best known in the West. Patrons were carried thither in a yellow coach "fitted up in all the style of Philadelphia." Nine miles east of town was Jackson's Hermitage, the finest residence in Tennessee.

4

The returns were slow coming in. The City Hotel people were more than hopeful at first. In the strong Jackson terri-

tory of Middle and West Tennessee, Cannon ran surprisingly
well.   In East Tennessee Jackson was weak due to resentment
over the removal of the state capital from Knoxville.   The
Whigs needed only a small plurality from this territory to
overcome the slender lead Houston held in the sections where
Jackson was normally invincible.   East Tennessee, however, returned great majorities for its favorite son, Sam Houston, and
the final tally was 44,426 votes for him to 33,410 for Cannon.
It was a personal triumph rather than a victory for William
Carroll's machine.

The Governor-Elect lost no time in starting for Knoxville
on his dapple-gray horse to thank his friends in the East.
They gave him a banquet at the Widow Jackson's tavern "and
it is only necessary to say," remarked the Knoxville *Register*,
"that Mrs. Jackson had it in a stile suited to the occasion. . . .
The ladies generally of the town, and between fifty and sixty
gentlemen attended. . . . The ladies having withdrawn from
the table to other seats. . . . and the cloth being removed . . .
TOASTS were drunk."

The schedule called for thirteen of these, with incidental
music.   Glasses were drained to "Major-General Houston—
Distinguished in the social circle by the affability of his manners, in war by the intrepidity of his character, and in public
life, by the integrity of his course." (Music, *The Wounded
Hussar.)*   Others of the illustrious were remembered and the
formal program ended on a chivalrous note: "To the ladies—
by their sweet names we wave the sword on high, and swear
for them to live, for them to die."

But the evening was young.   Pryor Lea, Esquire, arose to
say that the ladies present had asked him to deliver "*for them
a* sentiment."   Congressman Lea turned to the guest of the
evening.   "I pledge you, General Houston, that the ladies will
not forget the brave."   Sam Houston was on his feet, glass in
hand.   "*The Fair of Tennessee*," he said.   "Their charms cannot
be surpassed by the valor of *her sons*."   There were forty-two
more toasts.  Spencer Jarnagin, Esquire, an alumnus of Porter

Academy at Maryville, had the last word. "Mrs. Jackson," he said. "May all festive boards have such a land lady."[10]

In the Governor's chair Sam Houston continued to improve his hold on popular favor. When Jackson was elected president, Tennessee became politically the most important state in the Union. This made the Governor of Tennessee, whoever he might be, a national figure. Sam Houston was equal to the occasion. Jackson's health gave an interesting drift to speculation. "J$^n$ . . . is wearing away rapidly," wrote Alfred Balch, who lived near the Hermitage. "Already J$^{ns}$ successor is as much spoken of as J$^{ns}$ late success." Then Aunt Rachel died. It seemed as if the old soldier could not survive this blow. He rallied, but was not the same man. Sam Houston may very well have reflected that the effacement of Mr. Calhoun might now do more than assuage an old resentment.

Houston's name took its place on the inevitable list of "possibilities." As a state executive he was independent and level-headed. He made no mistakes for adversaries to seize upon, and his growing prestige filled the stage. He cut away from the Carroll wing, and as his term drew near the close, showed no sign of preparing to relinquish the office in which he had entrenched himself. Jackson viewed this state of affairs with a strange complacency, and Billy Carroll was disturbed. From distant parts of the country the gaze of observers fell upon the rising figure in the West, idol of the politically consecrated populace of Tennessee. He seemed to be the Man of Destiny that many were looking for. The era had dawned that was to see three men from Tennessee attain the white "Castle" on Pennsylvania Avenue. Two of these were to step up from the Governor's chair. With Tennessee and Tennesseeans favored of the gods, one so disinclined to exaggeration as Judge Guild saw Sam Houston headed for the presidency.

The Governor appeared to want only one thing desirable for political advancement. Sam Houston was thirty-five years old. There had been too much toasting the ladies and too many tales of a variety the Governor's reputation for gallantry rendered inescapable. "I have as usual had 'a small blow up.' What the devil is the matter with the gals I cant say but there has been hell to pay and no pitch hot!"[11] The situation worried Houston's friends whose earnest counsel was to marry and settle down. Plenty of time for that, said Sam, who was credited with the ability to take his pick of the highly eligible damsels who beautified Mrs. James K. Polk's cotillions. But as a matter of fact the gallant Governor was deeply and miserably in love—a circumstance at length revealed to an anxious friend, Congressman John Marable, in a jocose note that sought to disguise the tenderness that was in the writer's heart. "May God bless you, and it may be that I will splice myself with a rib. Thine ever, SAM HOUSTON."[12]

Within a fortnight Colonel and Mrs. John Allen, of Gallatin, had the honor to announce the forthcoming marriage of their daughter, Eliza, to General Sam Houston. The Allens of Gallatin! The Governor's friends were overjoyed. The Carroll people pegged down the flaps of their tents and silently whetted their knives.

# CHAPTER VII

## SIC TRANSIT——

### 1

THE President-Elect gave the match his blessing and took the road to Washington. General Jackson had known Eliza Allen from babyhood. She was the eldest child of his old friend, John Allen, of Sumner County, the head of a family much of whose history is involved with the early annals of Middle Tennessee. Eliza's uncles, Robert and Campbell Allen, served under Jackson in the War of 1812, Robert commanding a regiment of volunteers. Later Robert went to Congress where he met Sam Houston. Representative Houston became an occasional guest of Colonel John Allen's plantation home in a bend of the Cumberland three miles south of Gallatin. The Allen house was a gay one at all times, and during the racing at the Gallatin track, in the days when Old Hickory himself was Tennessee's first patron of the turf, it was headquarters for General Jackson and his entourage.

Sam Houston enjoyed the hospitality of the big house and the lively society of the Cumberland Valley, celebrated beyond any region in Tennessee for its blue-grass. Colonel Allen liked his brother's pleasing young friend and made him welcome. In point of fact, the Colonel had a weakness for notables.

Eliza did not come in for a great deal of attention at first, being not more than thirteen years old—a thoughtful, self-contained little girl with large blue eyes and yellow hair. Seasons went by, Sam Houston dropping in at the Allen place as he passed and repassed between Tennessee and Washington, threading his way from backwoods obscurity to the threshold of national affairs.  One day he looked into Eliza's blue eyes and ceased to speak to her of childish things.

The Governor had not been the first to perceive that the blonde girl had grown up.  He had a rival.  But above all the women he had known Sam Houston desired Eliza, and meant to win her.

The Allen family found it impossible to be indifferent to a connection so agreeable, but Eliza was simply bewildered to find this grown man, who had been a sort of adult confidant and comrade, changed to the rôle of suitor.  Moreover, Eliza thought her heart no longer hers to give.

But Eliza's was an age of sheltered daughters.  There were family councils in the manor that sat on a knoll by the curving Cumberland: a confused and immature girl encircled by many elders who said many things no girl possibly could understand.

Still, the Governor had something in his favor aside from position, prospects and the family endorsement.  His manners were charming; his past was romantic and a little mysterious; he was handsome and there was fire in his wooing.  Did he not desert the splendid society of Nashville, did he not foresake grave matters of state in the critical days of Andrew Jackson's fight for the presidency to post all the way to Gallatin for an hour with his adored?  What other Tennessee girl of eighteen could say as much for the devotion of a suitor?

One such hour was somehow enchanted.  On an evening when the woods that bordered the Cumberland were aflame with the emotional colors of autumn, the enormous passion of Sam Houston's hot words went home.  The blonde girl was swept away.  An image melted from her mind, and Eliza Allen was persuaded that she loved this handsome giant, this devastating Man of Destiny.

No other woman by such womanly means, or by any means, has so strangely changed the face of American history.

## 2

At candle-light on the twenty-second day of January, 1829, Colonel Allen conducted his daughter down the great staircase to her place beside the Governor of Tennessee. Before a houseful of the socially eligible and Reverend William Hume, pastor to the Presbyterian aristocracy of Nashville, Eliza Allen and Sam Houston exchanged the wedding vows.

Next afternoon the Governor and his bride set out for Nashville on horseback, but the weather turned blustery and they stopped overnight at Locust Grove, the manor of Robert Martin on the Gallatin Pike, a short hour's ride from the capital. The day following they rode into town, were entertained for a few days at the residence of Houston's cousin, Robert McEwen, and then moved to the Nashville Inn. They went about little, which Mrs. McEwen attributed to a desire to be alone together; she had never seen a more affectionate couple.

Moreover, public affairs had intruded upon the honeymoon. The day before the wedding the *Banner and Whig* contained a three-line item to the effect that William Carroll would be a candidate for governor in the August election. Nine days later the *Banner and Whig* contained another three-line squib.

"We are requested to announce the present Governor of Tennessee, Honorable SAMUEL HOUSTON, is a candidate for reelection."

In campaign literature "Samuel" was an innovation. It is impossible, however, to ascertain whether the Governor was married as "Samuel" or as "Sam." The papers are missing from the yellowed file of licenses and returns for the year 1829, which a dark closet and a coverlet of dust shield from casual eyes in the old brick court-house at Gallatin. Therefore, one is unable to bring this detail of official evidence to bear upon the question whether, as stated in certain quarters at the time, Sam Houston married Eliza Allen to break with the past and prepare himself for the decorous atmosphere of higher estates that seemed to lie in the path of his star.

The contest for the governorship overshadowed every other topic in Tennessee. Sam Houston had dared to challenge the boss. The question on every lip was: Where will Jackson stand in the battle between his lieutenants?

A direct answer was not forthcoming, but the public could read the signs. The Houston people wore a confident air— never more so than when the question of Jackson's position was raised. The Carroll people seemed anxious to exclude the President's name from "local issues." The fact is that Jackson had decided to elect Sam Houston, and Houston had tacitly conveyed this to some of his friends.

Thus the two men marshaled and warily maneuvered their forces. Both were masters of the usual arts of political warfare: Carroll at his best in a room manipulating combinations, Houston at his best out-of-doors handling a crowd. But Carroll was no weakling, and odds against him meant strength to his arm. Besides, he was furiously angry, and felt himself tricked by a man he had "made."

The campaign opened at Cockrell's Spring on Saturday afternoon, the eleventh of April. Governor Houston and ex-Governor Carroll met on the stump, and the countryside was out to see the fun. Houston had hit upon a scheme to swell the attendance and possibly turn up some useful political information. He asked Colonel Willoughby Williams, the sheriff of Davidson County, in which Nashville is located, to muster a battalion of the militia at Cockrell's Spring. Williams was also to pass through the crowd during the flow of oratory and find out what the voters were saying.

When the meeting was over, the Sheriff and the Governor mounted their horses and rode from the muster ground, deep in conversation. Williams had good news. The crowd was for Houston. Near Nashville Houston stopped off at the residence of John Boyd. Williams returned to his command, leaving Houston, he said, "in high spirits."

Williams dismissed the militia but did not personally get back to Nashville until five days later—Thursday, April sixteenth.  He rode directly to the Nashville Inn.

"Have you heard the news?" inquired Dan Carter, the clerk.

"What news?" the Sheriff asked.

"General Houston and his wife have separated and she has gone to her father's house."[1]

## 3

Up-stairs Williams found the Governor alone with Dr. John Shelby.  Doctor Shelby was a Sumner County man, old enough to be Sam Houston's father.  He had known Eliza Allen all her life.  Houston looked very tired and very troubled.  He had little to say.  The separation had occurred, but the cause was something he would never disclose "to a living person."

Williams plead for a word of explanation.  He was an old friend, and loyal, but Sam shook his head.  The Sheriff withdrew leaving the Governor with Doctor Shelby.  Confidences are a part of a doctor's profession.

The Sheriff crossed the street to the court-house.  His office was filling with people, as were the other offices and the corridors.  Knots of men gathered in the square, every one asking what had come between the Governor and his wife.  Reports, hearsay, rumor; hints, whispers, insinuations.  The scandal-mongers were feeling their way.  Willoughby Williams passed from group to group, and enigmas began to fill his mind.

The thing was serious.  From the general drift Williams gathered that Sam Houston had "wronged" his bride.  There were no particulars, not one detail that any one knew.  But a lady's honor was concerned; if Houston did not furnish particulars, they would spring from the ground.

The Sheriff contrasted the mounting excitement of the crowd with the incomprehensible scene in Houston's apartment.

Willoughby Williams had never seen Sam so shaken before, and they had been boys together in East Tennessee. Together they had gone to the recruiting rally in 1813 when Houston joined the Army. Eighteen months later Willoughby had gone down the wilderness trail to meet the stretcher-bearers who were bringing the wounded Ensign home to die. Williams walked back to the inn to report on the temper of the crowd. His friend must talk, defend himself. The fortunes of the campaign might hinge upon it.

The Governor was with Doctor Shelby as before. He was greatly agitated and striving to control himself, but had revealed nothing.

Williams reported on the state of affairs outside. "I said to him, 'You must explain this sad occurrence to us, else you will sacrifice your friends and yourself.' He replied, 'I can make no explanation. I exonerate this lady [Eliza] freely, and I do not justify myself. I am a ruined man; will exile myself, and now ask you to take my resignation to the Secretary of State.'

"I replied, 'You must not think of it' when again he said, 'It is my fixed determination, and my enemies when I am gone will be too magnanimous to censure my friends.' "[2]

The resignation showed careful attention to penmanship. It had been written, written slowly, in Houston's round, readable script. The signature was in a bolder, quicker hand. Williams delivered it to "Genl William Hall"—as the superscription styled him—"Speaker of the Senate, Tennessee."

"Executive Office, Nashville, Tennessee 16 April 1829. "Sir,

"It has become my duty to resign the office of Chief Magistrate of the State, & to place in your hands the authority & responsibility, which on such an event, devolves on you by the provisions of the Constitution.

"In dissolving the political connexion which has so long, & in such a variety of form, existed between the people of Tennessee & myself, no private afflictions however deep or incurable, can forbid an expression of the grateful recollections so emenently due to the kind partialities of an indulgent public.—— From my earliest youth, whatever of talent was committed to my care, has been honestly cultivated & expended for the Common good; and at no period of a life, which certainly has been marked by a full portion of interesting events, have any views of private interest or private ambition been permitted to mingle in the higher duties of public trust.——In reviewing the past, I can only regret that my capacity for being useful was so unequal to the devotion of my heart, & it is one of the few remaining consolations of my life, that even had I been blessed with ability equal to my zeal, my country's generous support in every vicissitude of life has been more than equal to them both.

"That veneration for public opinion by which I have measured every act of my official life, has taught me to hold no delegated power which would not daily be renewed by my constituents, could the choice be daily submitted to a sensible expression of their Will;——and although shielded by a perfect consciousness of undiminished claim to the confidence & support of my fellow citizens, yet delicately circumstanced as I am, & by my own misfortunes more than by the fault or contrivance of anyone, overwhelmed by sudden calamities, it is certainly due myself & more respectful to the world, that I should retire from a position which, in the public judgment, I might seem to occupy by questionable authority.

"It yields me no small share of comfort so far as I am capable of taking comfort from any circumstance, that in resigning my Executive charge, I am placing it in the hands of one whose integrity & worth have long been tried; who understands & will pursue the true interests of the State; and who in the hour of success & in the trials of adversity has been the consistent & valued friend of that Great & Good man, now enjoying the triumph of his virtues in the conscious security of a nation's gratitude.

"Sam Houston"[3]

## 4

In his trial draft of this difficult letter Houston had written, "Overwhelmed by sudden calamities, *which from their nature preclude all investigation,*"[4] but was sufficiently rational to strike out the inhibitory clause. Powerless to "preclude investigation," he could nevertheless strive to confuse it by concealing the secret of the "private afflictions . . . deep . . . incurable," which "by my own misfortunes rather than by the fault or connivance of anyone," had precipitated the present extremities.

This resolution Sam Houston sustained through life, whatever the occasion, whatever the cost.

The news that the Governor and his bride had parted flew from tongue to tongue in Nashville, from county to county in the important state of Tennessee. William Carroll's steamboats bore the intelligence down the Cumberland. Pony expresses posted over the mountains to Richmond, Washington and the East. Then came the thunderclap of the resignation by a sensational, enigmatical, vaguely self-accusative letter which concealed more than it disclosed.

Rumors multiplied, but after three weeks the responsible *Niles' Register*, of Baltimore, could vouch for no dependable "information as to the allusions made in the . . . letter [of resignation]—which while it shows a deeply wounded spirit, manifests a lofty patriotism." The Richmond *Inquirer* discovered "rumors about Gen. Houston . . . too unpleasant . . . to be repeated. They relate to his domestic misfortunes" and in consequence "he has not only left the governor's chair of Tennessee—but . . . the state . . . forever!" While these stories spread, the *Register* found "the public curiosity . . . much excited. The papers rather increase than dissolve the mystery, by saying that Gen. Houston has left Nashville and that his destination is the Cherokee Indians."

This uncertainty was more than Tennessee could bear. Rather than believe nothing, under the impulse of careful stimulation it believed the worst. The tongues of scandal hesitated at nothing. Tales of the marriage-bed were bawled from the roof-trees, and Sam Houston was burned in effigy before a howling crowd in the court-house yard at Gallatin. In Nashville there was a great running to cover. Friends of

yesterday, basking in the favor of a favored man, were among
the most punctual in their repudiation of the same man, in-
explicably ruined.

There was one who seemed to be in a position to obtain
an answer to the questions that were on every lip. The prerogatives of the cloth favored Dr. William Hume, who eleven
weeks before had joined the Governor of Tennessee and Eliza
Allen in marriage. He retained the confidence of both parties
to the controversy, and, moreover, his personal curiosity was
excited. He was one of the few admitted to the chamber where
Houston, in one of his rare allusions to the subject, said he endured "moments which few have felt and I trust none may ever
feel again."[5]  "I am sorry for him," the clergyman wrote in a
private letter after this visit, "and more sorry for the young
lady he has left." Doctor Hume also received the latest tidings
from Gallatin. Yet, "I know nothing that can be relied upon
as true. Tales in abundance . . . but which of the two is the
blame I know not."[6]

Doctor Hume's visit to the Nashville Inn was by invitation.
Sam Houston was not a member of a church. He was called a
worldly man, but he believed that "in the affairs of men . . .
there must be a conducting Providence." Trouble inspires more
reverent thoughts than preachers, but Sam Houston had
expressed this belief in Providence when his fortunes were on the
rise. "I am more satisfied of this fact when I . . . behold
the changes that have taken place with myself. But this advancement is not by the consent of all parties or persons. . . .
They smile at me, and seem kind, but like the rose there is a
thorn under it."[7]  The thorns were now tearing his flesh, and
Sam Houston asked Doctor Hume to administer the rite of
baptism.

The clergyman promised to take the matter under advisement. He consulted Obadiah Jennings, pastor of the First
Presbyterian Church, and together they surveyed the situation.
"The respectable connections of the lady in Sumner County
are much offended." So, taking it all in all, "Mr. Jennings and

myself, to whom he applied to be baptised . . . declined on good grounds, as we think, to comply with his wishes in relation to that ordinance."[8]

However, there remained those who were loyal and who believed in the integrity of the man from whom was withheld the consolation of the church. To their entreaties for one word or sign upon which to erect a defense, Sam Houston answered as before: whatever the price of silence, he was prepared to pay it. The suffering man's friends protested that the public could not be satisfied with scruples of conscience. Houston must explain.

"This is a painful, but it is a private affair," replied the ex-Governor. "I do not recognize the right of the public to interfere in it, and I shall treat the public just as if it had never happened."[9]

Houston's supporters pointed out that the "respectable connections" of Mrs. Houston were making the affair distinctly a public matter. The growls of the mob in the square could be heard from the windows of the Nashville Inn. Houston was told that the most important moment in life was at hand.

"Remember," said Sam Houston, "that whatever may be said by the lady or her friends, it is no part of the conduct of a gallant or a generous man to take up arms against a woman. If my character cannot stand the shock let me lose it."[10]

### 5

In the beginning the matter had worn an aspect of private retaliation directed by the Allen family against the man who had "wronged" their daughter. Particulars of the transgression were not forthcoming, but it was enough to understand that the Allens' white anger was real: this brilliant marriage, upon which a proud family had erected such hopes, a shambles after three months—an Allen woman, pale and trembling at the door of her father's house.

This feudal phase did not last long. The first stirrings of

rumor had been a windfall to the political camp of William Carroll. With the quickness of thought, the "vindication" of Eliza Allen assumed broader proportions, as twin swords in the hands of an enraged family and an embittered politician flashed and fell. Then came the effigy burning. No story was too base. Every fault, every weakness, Sam Houston had ever indulged was magnified into a grave crime, and the silence of the accused was proclaimed to confirm everything.

The news was two weeks reaching Washington. While it was on the way the President decided that the time had come to insure the reelection of Sam Houston as governor of Tennessee. He wrote a letter calculated to remove Carroll from the race and save his face with the offer of a diplomatic post in South America. "It is all that can be done for him."[11] Jackson made the offer,[12] but at that moment Sam Houston was on his way to a place of banishment more remote politically than the Amazon, and his rival declined with thanks the opportunity to represent his country abroad.[13] The triumphant Carroll was feeling comparatively mellow. "That fate of Houston," he wrote to Jackson, "must have surprised you. . . . His conduct, to say the least, was very strange and charity requires us to place it to the account of insanity. I have always looked upon him as a man of weak and unsettled mind . . . incapable of manfully meeting a reverse of fortune."[14]

After Doctor Hume had rendered his decision on the baptism, Sam Houston remained locked in his room. A letter phrased with the simplicity of despair indicates his thoughts. "I . . . do love Eliza. . . . That she is the only earthly object dear to me God will bear witness."[15] The Man of Destiny wished merely to be alone. In the public square outside the whipped-up tempest grew. It swept out of hands, and the mob cried out that Houston was afraid to show himself. Houston ignored it, and after a custom of the day supposed to represent the ultimate insult, he was "posted" as a coward.

The dazed man walked into the square. A few of the steadfast rallied about him, but no one approached to make the placarded denunciations good. If they had, Sam Houston, who was not a braggart, said that "the streets of Nashville would have flowed with blood."[16]

On the twenty-third of April, 1829, Sheriff Williams and Doctor Shelby emerged from the Nashville Inn. Between them walked a tall stranger who had spent the night burning letters in a room. A few others silently fell in behind. The procession descended the steep thoroughfare to the steamboat landing. With one companion the tall stranger boarded the packet, *Red Rover*. The name he gave his fellow voyagers has been forgotten.

"*Sic transit gloria mundi*," Doctor Hume wrote on the following day. "Oh, what a fall for a major general, a member of Congress and a Governor of so respectable a state as Tennessee!"[17]

## 6

Two men of the Allen family,[18] heavily armed and much excited, boarded the *Red Rover* at Clarksville. Houston met them and listened to their story that his unexplained departure had given rise to the rumor that he had been "goaded to madness and exile by detecting our sister in crime." The shoe was now on the other foot. Houston was asked to give his written denial to this accusation or to return "and prove it."

He declined to do either, but dropping his pretense of incognito, "in the presence of the captain and these well-known gentlemen," requested his callers to "publish in the Nashville papers that if any wretch ever dares to utter a word against the purity of Mrs. Houston I will come back and write the libel in his heart's blood." The Allens departed, and had the good sense, for the present, to refrain from giving the newspapers anything more to write about.

That evening Sam Houston patrolled the deck of the *Red Rover*, "reflecting on the bitter disappointment I had caused General Jackson and all my friends, and especially the blight and ruin of a pure and innocent woman who had entrusted her whole happiness to me. I was in an agony of despair and strongly tempted to leap overboard and end my worthless life. At that moment, however, an eagle swooped down near my head, and then, soaring aloft with wildest screams, was lost in the rays of the setting sun."

The incident caught the wonderfully sensitive imagination of Houston. "I knew then," he said simply, "that a great destiny waited for me in the West."[19]

# BOOK TWO

## Exile

"My son Gen<sup>l</sup> Houston or The
Raven has walked straight. His
path is not crooked. He is
beloved by all my people."

—Oo-loo-te-ka, Head Chief
of the Western Cherokees

# CHAPTER VIII

## A Wall to the East

### 1

THE ex-Governor and his traveling companion left the *Red Rover* at Cairo. Houston had resumed his incognito and was growing a beard he vowed never to cut. The two bought a flatboat and employed a flatboatman who had two big bear dogs. The dogs would be "company," Houston said. The raft was stocked for a long trip, a young free negro engaged and the four men and two dogs shoved off down the Mississippi.

The companion of Sam Houston's journey into exile is an indistinct figure. Nashville knew him as a roving Irishman with the dust of half Europe on his shoes, who had come temporarily to rest in Tennessee a few months back, charming his way into the select and convivial circle at the Nashville Inn bar. He signed himself H. Haralson, and not until he had gone did Nashville reflect on its meager knowledge of the attractive stranger. En route Houston told his new retainer that he had changed his mind about stopping among the Cherokees and was bound for the Rocky Mountains. This seemed to suit Mr. Haralson, to whom one destination was the same as another.

The travelers took it easily, delaying to fish and hunt in the cane-brakes, as the mood struck the head of the expedition. They avoided towns until reaching Memphis, a scraggling hamlet on the Chickasaw Bluffs, where Houston went ashore. He was recognized, and Nashville received a bulletin on his progress.　At Helena Sam Houston was introduced to James Bowie, of Texas.

The flatboat ascended the Arkansas River to Little Rock, seat of the territorial government and westernmost of American capitals.　There Houston discharged the flatboatman and wrote several letters.　"I will accept no situation under the Government, nor do I wish anything of you but a continuation of your friendship, and that arises from the proud consciousness that it is merited."[1]　This to the President of the United States.

Houston and his servant left Little Rock on horseback. Haralson stayed behind to bring the baggage to the head of navigation on the Arkansas.

Twenty miles from Little Rock was a collection of log houses called Louisburgh where the traveler put up at the residence of John Linton.　Like Houston, John Linton was a lawyer, a Virginian and a brooding exile.　He spoke Latin like a priest and flattered illiterate frontier magistrates with classical allusions.　Whisky helped to blunt memories of a romance connected with his early life and a term in an eastern penitentiary.

When Houston left Louisburgh Mr. Linton, in the performance of a simple courtesy of the frontier, mounted his horse Bucephalus, and escorted his guest one hundred and twenty miles to Fort Smith, the last outpost of civilized life and the principal base for whisky running in the Indian country.　Sam and John had enjoyed each other's society and were reluctant to part.　They camped in an abandoned hut on the edge of the settlement and stayed for a couple of days, to feast and roll the classics on their tongues.　When it came time for John to go, Sam said the occasion should be made memorable. After an exchange of ideas, "a sacrifice to Bacchus" was agreed upon.　The decision was to sacrifice the clothes they wore, and Sam's servant built a fine fire in the hut.

Sam opened the ceremony by shying his hat into the flames. When it was consumed the celebrants were, under the rules, entitled to a drink. John shied his hat in, which made them eligible for another swig. Sam's coat went next, then John's coat, and so on until Sam had nothing more to sacrifice. John stripped off his remaining garment—an undershirt. He threw it in, but almost immediately snatched it back, beat out the fire and started to put it on again. A storm of denunciation from Houston stopped him. John had repudiated a vow. He had angered Bacchus.

Tearing the undershirt from the astonished Linton, Houston dashed it on the sacrificial pyre. Then he turned to his companion to announce that, thanks to his presence of mind, the god had been appeased, but Lawyer Linton was not listening. He was asleep.

Whereupon, General Houston composed himself for a nap While he slept, the servant put a fresh outfit of clothing on his master and aroused him sufficiently to get him to mount his horse. The pair were miles beyond the Indian frontier before Houston appreciated what had happened. He declared it a great joke on Linton, a conclusion concurred in by nearly every one else, including Mrs. Linton, one helpmeet who understood a talented husband.[2]

## 2

A rough military road penetrated as far as Cantonment Gibson, but Houston took the old trail following the wild and winding Arkansas River Valley. This path was traveled mostly by Indians. White men used the military road or the snorting little steam packets that made four or five trips a year. The packets towed supplies for Cantonment Gibson and its redoubtable sutler, John Nicks. They carried stocks to the traders about the Three Forks and returned laden with pelts from the "magazins" of the interesting Chouteau brothers who lived in a wilderness because they liked it, and were the chief props in those parts of John Jacob Astor's American Fur Company.

A steamboat picked up Houston and carried him to the

clearing at Webber's Falls near where "Colonel" Walter, or Watt, Webber, a wealthy half-breed trading-post proprietor and official of the Cherokee Nation, had one of his places of business.    Cherokee runners outstripped the packet with news of the visitor's identity and a gathering of notables of the Nation was on hand at the Falls.

A stately old Indian advanced and embraced the traveler. "My son," said Oo-loo-te-ka, "eleven winters have passed since we met. . . . I have heard you were a great chief among your people. . . . I have heard that a dark cloud has fallen on the white path you were walking. . . . I am glad of it—it was done by the Great Spirit. . . . We are in trouble and the Great Spirit has sent you to us to give us counsel. . . . My wigwam is yours—my home is yours—my people are yours— rest with us."[3]

Oo-loo-te-ka conducted his son over a trail leading to the crest of a knoll that separated the Arkansas River from the Illinois.   Here the Chief had built his wigwam in a grove of sycamores and cottonwoods.   "Houston has often been heard to say," he wrote in later years, "that when he laid himself down to sleep that night, he felt like a weary wanderer returned at last to his father's house."[4]

### 3

Oo-loo-te-ka did not speak irreverently when he said that Providence had sent The Raven to help his adopted people. He-Puts-the-Drum-Away was an old man now, and a trifle stout. He felt the weight of his years and of his responsibilities. His ablest counselor, the fiery old Ta-kah-to-kuh, had recently died, leaving him alone to grapple with problems that seemed beyond his powers.

These difficulties had their origin in East Tennessee, the heart of the Cherokee homeland, where Oo-loo-te-ka was born. In his youth the Nation had been at peace.   Cherokees were neither nomadic nor warlike, as Indians go, and perhaps they were the most intelligent of all the North American tribes. Their formal relations with the white race began when they welcomed Oglethorpe and his respectable paupers to Georgia in 1733. With unaccustomed tact the British recognized the independence of the Cherokee Nation and received its ambassador at the Court of St. James's. This attention gained the Crown an American ally in 1775.

Oo-loo-te-ka was a boy of ten when his older brother, Tahlhon-tusky, took the war-path on the British side of the Revolution. At the close of the war, the United States negotiated separately with the Cherokees. The young white republic was in serious straits and needed peace on its frontier at almost any price. The price the Cherokees set was reasonable. They ceded a small amount of territory and their political status remained as before, the United States recognizing the sovereign character of the "Cherokee Nation of Indians." Boundaries were fixed to include most of what is now Middle and East Tennessee, the northeastern corner of Alabama, northern Georgia, a small bit of the western Carolinas and a pocket in south central Kentucky; with the provision that "if any citizen of the United States . . . shall attempt to settle on any of the [Cherokee] lands . . . or having already settled and will not remove from the same within six months after the ratification of this treaty, such person shall forfeit the protection of the United States, and the Indians may punish him or not as they please."

But when the white nation began to get on its feet, confident settlers overran the Cherokee border and usurped the Indians' lands. The Cherokees forebore exercising their right to punish whites "as they please," and conscientiously protested the invasion. Washington negotiated again; the Cherokees yielded, and a new boundary was fixed farther back in the woods.

Whites poured over the new boundary. A cry of protest again came from the wilderness, but all except the highest national authorities winked at the violation. The Cherokees began to put white intruders to death. The whites retaliated by pushing their blockhouses farther into the invaded territory. The Indians crossed the United States boundary and raided settlements. In 1788 Jim Houston's Fort in East Tennessee repulsed a foray with the loss of one white man who imprudently exposed himself above the stockade. A few weeks later the Cherokees killed Jim's son, Robert, along with seventeen other settlers who had ventured outside the confines of the fort to pick apples. This was the Apple Orchard Defeat famed in East Tennessee frontier history. Sam Houston had heard the story of it many times—from both sides.

The Cherokees appealed to the United States to help them stop hostilities. Secretary of War Knox said that the Indians were in the right and the whites in the wrong, but nothing was done.

4

More treaties, "final" cessions and "solemn" guarantees, and the Cherokees lost by each negotiation. The time came when the Indians could no longer fight to establish their rights, the whites having become the stronger party.

In 1809 Oo-loo-te-ka's brother, Tah-lhon-tusky, decided on a radical policy. With a few hundred followers, he crossed the Mississippi and, to be out of the white man's reach for ever, marched westward for thirty days through the uninhabited wilderness and constructed his lodges on the banks of the Arkansas. There he enjoyed a few years of comparative tranquillity.

But there was no tranquillity in the East. Settlers continued to invade the Indian domain. Agents of the Federal Government appeared among the chiefs and headmen, bribing, intimidating and distributing whisky. The treaty of 1816, by which they relinquished extensive holdings ,in Tennessee, Georgia and Alabama, was followed by the treaty of 1817, by which additional land in Tennessee was exchanged for territory in the West adjacent to that settled by Tah-lhon-tusky.

There was more than the usual resentment over the cession of 1817, and Lieutenant Sam Houston, First Infantry, played an important rôle in the program of duplicity that sent his foster-father on his way and temporarily mollified Tah-lhon-tusky, whose days of serenity in his self-sought western paradise were at an end.

In the West Oo-loo-te-ka tussled with one difficulty after another. An impoverishing warfare was kept up with the Osages. The hunting-grounds to the westward were disputed by the savage Pawnees and Comanches. The government had failed to run lines that would settle these questions. Its agents grew rich at their wards' expense. The American Fur Company interpreted treaties as it pleased. The Territory of Arkansas was organized, the Cherokee lands being included in the territorial domain and a white justice of the peace given authority over the sovereign tribesmen.

Tah-lhon-tusky died, and Oo-loo-te-ka was elected principal chief of the western Cherokees. The local whites clamored for the eviction of the Indians from Arkansas. Government agents pressed Oo-loo-te-ka to consent to another treaty and remove still farther west. The old Chief pondered the matter. What use to remove or to make paper talks when the white brother's word was never kept? Why not stay and settle the issue here?

Oo-loo-te-ka was assured that this move would be the last. The Cherokees would not be disturbed again. The United States would bind itself to give "the Cherokee Nation of Indians . . . a permanent home, and which shall, under the most solemn guarantee of the United States be and remain theirs forever . . . never, in all future time . . . embarrassed by having . . . placed over it the jurisdiction of a Territory or State." Oo-loo-te-ka's people were to get fifty thousand dollars indemnity cash down and two thousand dollars annually for three years. But still Oo-loo-te-ka hesitated. He sent The Black Fox to Washington to negotiate for the fulfillment of past treaties, but the white diplomats got around him and the Indian negotiator signed the **removal** treaty in May of 1828.

5

However embarrassed by the unauthorized action of The Black Fox, Oo-loo-te-ka accepted the compact as binding and prepared to fit the new situation into a scheme which he had been cautiously maturing.

The eastern Cherokees were in the throes of a controversy with the state of Georgia to prevent their deportation to the West. In the voluminous history of intercourse between the Indian and white races, nothing reflects so little credit upon the latter as the case of the Georgia Cherokees. Indifferent as the sentiment of the day was to the rights of an Indian, there was a popular outcry of sympathy for the Cherokees. This, however, did not hinder the Georgia Legislature, which annulled federal treaties and, in effect, licensed the murder of Indians.

Oo-loo-te-ka had lost much of his earlier naïveté. He accepted bribes without compunction when by doing so he was that much ahead. He thought his eastern brethren unwise not to follow his example. The whites would have their way anyhow. He sent James Rogers to the Old Nation with a message.

"I am now advanced in years & . . . have studied a great deal to find out a plan to save our people from wasting & destruction. . . . We are now to be settled beyond all the settlements of white people, and there is no reason to fear that the whites will ever penetrate beyond us in consequence of the grand prairie, unless they go beyond the Rocky Mountains. My plan is to have . . . our brothers of the old nation . . . remove to this country. . . . If they wish to become independent . . . now is the time and the only time. . . . Let us unite & be one people and make a wall to the east which shall be no more trodden down or ever passed by whites. . . . Thus may we plan for our posterity for ages to come & for the scattered remnants of other tribes. . . . Instead of being

remnants & scattered we should become the United Tribes of
America . . . [and] preserve the sinking race of native
Americans from extinction."[5]

This interesting appeal excited no enthusiasm among the
idealistic easterners. The ambassador was coldly received. He
was informed that the Cherokees had a right to keep their
Georgia homes and meant to keep them. Oo-loo-te-ka was
denounced as a deserter of the fatherland.

Envoy Rogers returned to the Arkansas Valley to find that
his wife, Susy, had eloped with the hired man.

# CHAPTER IX

## THE INDIAN THEATER

### 1

WITH an Irishman's impulse to tell somebody something, Mr. Haralson reported the postponement of Houston's Rocky Mountain expedition to the Secretary of War,[1] thus innocently sharpening the concern that Jackson already felt over his old lieutenant's presence in the West. Washington had not been without intimations of the imperialistic notions of Oo-loo-te-ka. In view of the reckless state of Houston's mind and his known attachment for the plotting Chieftain, Jackson took steps to learn something more of the ex-Governor's activities. But whatever measures he might take to contravene Sam Houston, the suspected conspirator, the staunch heart of Jackson ached for his friend. "Oh, what a reverse of fortune," he wrote to him. "Oh, how unstable are human affairs!"[2]

The arrangements Sam Houston made for his sojourn in the Cherokee country did seem rather elaborate for the simple seasonal stop-over mentioned to Mr. Haralson. He had destroyed his civilized clothes, changed his name and renounced the English tongue. As an instrument of the gods, The Raven, in breech clout and turkey feathers, was a more plausible figure than a general in broadcloth and a cravat. But irrespective of the political significance that might be read into the transformation of the man who six weeks before had been considered an aspirant for the presidency, it represented an essentially personal desire to shut another door against the past.

Runners carried the news of The Raven's return to the remotest creek within the bounds of the Cherokee Nation, West, as Oo-loo-te-ka called his domain. Barely had Sam Houston time to correct the superficial details of his reincarnation before visitors began to ascend the trail and fill the cluster of log huts that comprised the residence of Oo-loo-te-ka. From each of the seven clans came distinguished men: Big Canoe and Black Coat, Watt Webber, Little Tarrapin, Young Elder, Old Swimmer and many others, some with their squaws and children, perhaps recalling The Raven's popularity with such society.

Oo-loo-te-ka's means were equal to costly house parties. "His wigwam was large and comfortable, and he lived in patriarchal simplicity and abundance. He had ten or twelve servants, a large plantation, and not less than five hundred head of cattle. The wigwam of this aged chieftain was always open to visitors, and his bountiful board was always surrounded by welcome guests. He never slaughtered less than one beef a week, throughout the year, for his table—a tax on royalty, in a country, too, where no tithes are paid."[3]

During the week of the celebration of The Raven's homecoming many beeves were slaughtered—not that this mattered to the host, who had other affairs on his mind. Oo-loo-te-ka was concerned with the impression The Raven should make upon the tribal leaders, and on this score the chief must have been pleased with his son.

The Raven presented himself extravagantly arrayed in the raiment of the "blanket and rifle party" as old Ta-kah-to-kuh had christened the wing of the Nation that stood for the preservation of the ancient traditions. He had shaved his face except for a mustache and goatee. His chestnut hair was plaited in a long queue. He wore a white doeskin shirt, brilliantly worked with beads. Leggings of elaborately ornamented yellow leather extended to his thighs. On his head was sometimes a circlet of feathers, sometimes a turban of figured silk. Over his shoulders was negligently thrown a bright blanket, more decorative than needful in the soft June air.[4]

The tall and commanding figure of The Raven moved through a gallery of tall, commanding men, saluting the elders with deference, embracing the younger ones with whom he had hunted and played as a boy on Oo-loo-te-ka's island. He flattered his former sweethearts on their good looks, their pretty shawls and the aptitude of their children. The Cherokees were a lively and warm-hearted race, fond of colors and dearly loving a fête such as this. Groups laughed and sang and strolled about the shady grove on the bluff, the vivid reds and yellows of their garments flinging animated patterns against the foliage. An army of dogs bedeviled the negroes who did the cooking. Tethered horses switched flies and ate grass.

A note of gravity tempered the merrymaking. The fiesta was to dissolve into a meeting of the General Council of the Nation, before which serious matters would come for consideration. Already, while the young ones frolicked, the headmen of the seven clans sat apart in a circle and passed the ceremonial pipe. The Raven sat with them and heard politics discussed with little reserve. He listened attentively and said very little. Not even to Oo-loo-te-ka did he confide all that was passing in his mind.

**2**

There was much for The Raven to absorb and to reflect upon. If they were to stem the tide of adverse fortune which had run so perseveringly against them, the time had come for the Cherokees to formulate a national policy and to follow it. Oo-loo-te-ka's daring proposal to unite the western Indians and build a wall to the east was one suggestion. A dream of empire fetched from the resolute past made glorious by Pontiac and by Tecumseh! And why not? The Indian deserved to live. To preserve him by these means entailed a desperate hazard, but The Raven was in a desperate mood, with little to lose and forgetfulness to gain.

The success of this plan, or of any plan, required a degree of harmony in the tribal councils which did not exist. The Cherokees were divided, first, on their Osage war policy, and second, on a general question of culture—whether to study more carefully the white man's arts, or to discard them altogether in favor of a vigorous renaissance of the ways of the fathers.

The two issues were interwoven. The primary migration to the West under Oo-loo-te-ka's brother, Tah-lhon-tusky, had been for the stated purpose of evading the influences of civilization. His minister of war, Ta-kah-to-kuh was the soul of this policy. This snorting old reactionary had kept the Osage war going for years, and Indians who favored missionaries, schools or civilization in any particular were targets for his delicious satire.

When first Tah-lhon-tusky and then Ta-kah-to-kuh died, many Cherokees, freed from the influence of such strong personalities, began to reflect that the advantages of the Osage war were hard to discover. The war party, therefore, considered abandoning the cause against the Osages, preferring to make allies of them and, with the Creeks, the Choctaws, Shawnees and Delawares, swoop upon the Comanches and Pawnees, the wild plains Indians to the westward. The prize in the new war program was a portion of the western prairie, an excellent hunting-ground, which the United States had promised but had not delivered to the Cherokees. Oo-loo-te-ka opposed this projected tribal war as disastrous to his larger design of an Indian confederation.

On the question of culture, the old Chief had weighed the gains derived from civilization against the losses. The gains were cloth, gunpowder and some notions of agriculture. The losses were whisky and a tendency to forget the weapons and the ways by which the Cherokees had become one of the proudest of Indian peoples, to decline within living memory, dependent upon the white man, the author of all their woes. Despite his cross affixed to the policy letter written in 1817 by

Lieutenant Houston or some other white official connected with the diplomacy of the Cherokee exodus, Oo-loo-te-ka was no evangelist of civilization.

But the old gentleman possessed a great deal of tact. He had adopted the English name of John Jolly, which he used in his intercourse with white officials and with his pro-civilization brethren in Georgia. This concession worked two ways, however. An old-time Cherokee regarded his name as a part of his person, as much as his eyes or his teeth—consequently, the great respect for his pledged word or for treaties he had signed. His religion taught him that by calling maledictions upon his name, an enemy might injure him as surely as by shooting an arrow into his flesh. Indians got around this by giving themselves additional names that did not count with the gods. It may be for this reason that Powhatan and Pocahontas are known in history by assumed names.

He-Puts-the-Drum-Away was a shrewd old man, and his people profited by his shrewdness. He trimmed his sails on the civilization issue so as to satisfy the majority of his people and the United States Government as well. The Cherokees no longer painted their faces or wore the scalp-lock, but the personal example of their western leader, their isolation and the revival of the fall hunt, had a tendency which all the good works of the missionaries failed to overcome.

Yet there were gaps in the successes of Oo-loo-te-ka. Much had been staked on the treaty of 1828 wherein the United States had made such unambiguous pledges of fulfillment. The Cherokees had carried out their pledges and removed into the unorganized wilderness beyond the western border of Arkansas. But with the United States it was the old story of promises unredeemed: the indemnity had not been paid; boundaries delineating the Cherokees lands had not been run; rations to tide the people over until they could make a crop and organize their hunts had not been distributed. The United States agent was growing rich, and white settlers refused to vacate Indian lands.

The Cherokees felt baffled and bitter, and the dramatic appearance of The Raven seemed to them genuinely an act of Providence. There was a disposition to forget family differences and accept his leadership.

As the celebration at Oo-loo-te-ka's progressed, word of the arrival of Houston, the protector of oppressed Indians, spread among the other tribes. This interested the Indian agents, the white traders and squatters, the Army officers at Cantonment Gibson and the Governor of Arkansas. The trusted few who were in the secret endorsed the action of President Jackson, who had ordered a surveillance of Sam Houston's movements.

Consequently the session of the Grand Council that was to follow Oo-loo-te-ka's hospitality became a matter of more than local interest. Colonel Arbuckle, the Commandant at Cantonment Gibson, accepted Oo-loo-te-ka's invitation to attend. But nothing happened for all this anticipation. When the council met, The Raven did not even appear. He was, indeed, many miles away. Possibly for this reason, Colonel Arbuckle remained away and sent Captain Bonneville and Lieutenant Phillips of the garrison.

"My Young Friends," read the memorandum that Oo-loo-te-ka handed the officers, "I invited my son Governor Houston here to listen to what I had to say on this subject but my son had promised to attend a council of my Neighbors the Osages and could not come. I must do the best I can without him."[5]

For the rest, the council proved a tame affair, being merely a recital of tribal suffering due to the non-fulfillment of the treaty of 1828. Two bored junior officers retraced their way toward the dreary palisades of Gibson.

### 3

The Raven's withdrawal from the festival in his honor and his disappointing absence from the council had what one will recognize as the Houstonian touch. Much of the glamour that followed Sam Houston through life arose from the simple fact that he seldom stayed too long in one place.

What had happened now? To provide a suitable climax for Oo-loo-te-ka's entertainment was simply a matter of seizing an opportunity to do the right thing at the right moment.

Into Oo-loo-te-ka's garden party had ridden an Osage scout. Mounted on a pony whose rawhide bridle was innocent of the least decoration, he presented a striking contrast with the volatile Cherokees in their fête attire. His head was close-cropped, save for a bristling ridge that stood up like the crest of a helmet and a scalp-lock hanging behind; arms bare and body bare to the waist; breech clout, leggings and moccasins well-worn and without ornament. There were ladies present who had never seen an Osage scout before, but they had heard dark stories of what rakes they were—they and their half-breed Creole squaws.

With an economy of words the haughty newcomer identified himself as a courier of Auguste Chouteau, who sent his respects to John Jolly and a message to General Houston. Before the crowd could grasp it, The Raven and Mr. Haralson had ridden away with the arresting stranger.

They followed him into the heart of the Osage country, more than one hundred miles by horse-path up the wooded Arkansas and Six Bull River Valleys, where the hills left off, disclosing a "pleasant country—looks like park land." Here stood a large "white log house Piazza surrounded by trees." In front of the house ran a "beautiful clear river. Groups of Indian nymphs half naked on the banks." Visitors to the solitary estate were rare. "Old negro runs to open gate— mouth from ear to ear—Group of Indians round trees in court yard roasting venison—Horses tether[ed] near—negroes run to shake hand and take horses. Some have handkerchief around head—Half breed—squaws—negro girls running & giggling. Horses, dogs of all kinds—hens flying and cackling, wild turkeys, tamed geese. Piazza with Buffalo skin thrown over railing. [Powder] Horns with guns—rifles."[6]

Thus the discovery of the wilderness abode of Monsieur Chouteau as penciled on the spot by Washington Irving, who made its acquaintance three years later. At the gate, or somewhere along the trail, General Houston was met by Monsieur Chouteau, a dark-skinned man in linen riding breeches who spoke the faultless English of a well-educated foreigner.

Twenty years in the wilderness and on the plains had not altered the salon manners of Auguste Pierre Chouteau, who was then only forty-three. His father was one of the founders of the French outpost of St. Louis. The subsequent rise of the house of Chouteau to the dominating position in southwestern trade illustrates the truism that the Indian regarded the French as his natural friend and the English as his natural enemy. Auguste became the most influential man, white or red, beyond the frontier south of the Missouri River and west to Spanish territory. His ascendency over the Osage Indians was complete, and his influence with the other tribes stronger than that of any white man until Sam Houston came. He was one of the founders of the Santa Fé Trail. His alliance was sought and gained by John Jacob Astor. Monsieur Chouteau had one wife in St. Louis and two wives in the Osage country who presided over the domicile Mr. Irving dismissed as a "house formed of logs, a room at each end. An open hall with staircase in the center. Other rooms above. In the two rooms on ground floor two beds in each room, with curtains. Whitewashed log walls—tables of various kinds, Indian ornaments &c."

Mr. Irving was too new to the frontier to be sufficiently impressed. The residence of Auguste Chouteau was the most imposing one between the Missouri border and Santa Fé. Sam Houston enjoyed it there and returned often.

"Supper, venison stakes—roast beef, bread, cakes, coffee. Waited on by half breed sister of Mr. Chouteau's concubine—— Adjourn to another room, pass through open Hall in which Indians are seated on floor. They come into the

room—two bring chairs—the other seats himself on the floor
with knees to his chin—another Indian glares in at the window. . . . Dogs & cats of all kinds strolling about the Hall
or sleeping among harness at one end of the piazza. In these
establishments the world is turned upside down—the slave the
master, the master the slave. The master has the idea of
property, the latter the reality. The former owns, the latter
enjoys it. The former has to plan & scheme and guard &
economize—the latter . . . cares nothing how it comes or
how it goes."[7]

Mr. Irving was somewhat right about that, for Auguste
Chouteau had adopted a fashion of living that in ten years was
to send him to his grave practically a penniless man. A career
of profitable adventure had suddenly palled and Auguste had
surrendered to a passion for ease. Preferring life beyond the
frontier to other modes of living he had known, he built the
comfortable house on the Six Bull River for his Osage help-
meets, Rosalie and Masina. He brought out a carriage from
St. Louis. He built a race-track. He engaged a tutor for his
half-breed children, gave them his name and had them received
into the church by the Jesuit missionary to the tribe.

Nominal leadership is a bright toy, the delights of which
only the nurseries of civilization know. In three years the
unique domain that Auguste Chouteau had gathered into his
capable hands had begun to fall away. There was still time
to recoup by energetic action, but Monsieur Chouteau had no
thought of deserting his country seat for fields of energetic
action. He had seen enough of that for any ten men. He
might, however, send a chosen successor on the highroad under
a favored ægis. This fact seems to have given a practical cast
to his hospitable invitation to Houston.

4

Sam Houston spent several days at the big house by the
Six Bull, and the conversation of his host brightened the horizon of possibilities open to an ambitious man in the Indian
theater.

These pleasant discussions were interrupted, noted Mr. Haralson, by the arrival of "a parcel of the Osage Indians at Colonel Shouteau's." The Indians said that their agent was stealing their annuities, another instalment of which was due. "They had concluded," continued Haralson, "not to go to receive their annuity but hearing that some strangers were in the country (which was us) they came to see us. They insisted that Genl Houston . . . and myself go with them to the agency. We told them we would go and see what passed between them and their agent."[8]

The Osage Agency, in charge of John F. Hamtramck, was at the Three Forks, as they called the place where the Verdigris, Six Bull and Arkansas Rivers came together about fifty miles below Chouteau's establishment. The agency was a part of the nameless settlement that had grown up around the trading-post of the Creole, Joseph Bogy, who came to the Three Forks in 1807. The importance of the place had grown steadily and Sam Houston saw perhaps thirty log houses strung along a clearing by the Verdigris opposite a waterfall.

The settlement was important as a station of the American Fur Company, whence the trappers worked westward, laying their snares along the creeks and bartering for skins among the Indians. An Indian thus drawn into business relations with Mr. Astor was advanced equipment and supplies on credit at a net profit to the fur company of about one hundred per cent. When he brought in his catch at the end of the season he discharged this obligation in pelt currency at something near half the figure the hides would bring in the market. If, as often happened, the catch was insufficient to liquidate the account for supplies, an Indian would begin his second season with a debt over his head as an incentive to industry.

Trappers came to the village to deliver their skins, square their accounts and cultivate the amenities. There were soldiers off duty from Cantonment Gibson and an occasional white derelict who drifted in and then drifted out; also a few permanent residents who lived quietly respectable lives, like Nathaniel

Pryor, an honest old soldier who had been to the Pacific Ocean with Lewis and Clark, and had taken a squaw and settled down to ignore a civilization that had used him shabbily. Captain Pryor had tried trading but could not make it pay, lacking the finesse of Hugh Glenn and Colonel Hugh Love, prominent among the Anglo-Saxon contingent of Arkansas River merchants who had their establishments at the Three Forks. The largest trading store in the place was still owned by Auguste Chouteau, and managed by his half-brother, Paul. The Creek and the Osage tribal agencies contributed their personnel to the society of the community, which with its negro slaves, Indian mistresses and the mixed-breeds of various crossings, led a free-and-easy life facilitated by a patois of French, English, Osage, Creek and an occasional idiom from the Spanish.

Into this milieu rode Sam Houston, moved by a disposition of inquiry. The austere Osages were present in large numbers. The friendly house of Chouteau had early won their loyalty, mainly by keeping their exploitation within bounds. The Creole influence upon them became such that when the United States purchased Louisiana the Osage chief, Big Track, refused to recognize the change of sovereignty until the Chouteaus approved.

After that changes were rapid. The Cherokees and other tribes were thrust westward. Agents were appointed to administer the affairs of the Osages and to pay them for the lands they had relinquished. The Anglo-Saxons came and plundered, and the easy Creole régime developed a prevalence of murder, venereal disease, incest, drunkenness and starvation. Or such was the observation of a Presbyterian missionary who visited the tribe shortly before Sam Houston.[9]

Nevertheless, two generations of debauchery had failed to efface the singular native dignity of the race. With their magnificent copper-colored bodies two-thirds bare, the Osages sauntered about the agency with an air of impoverished noblemen in a world of affluent parvenus. For all that, they looked to the elegantly tricked-out white counselor of the Cherokees for protection, which was a strange pass of affairs for an Osage who had fought the Cherokees for twenty years and deferred to no white man on earth save a Chouteau.

The decline of the Creole leader's prestige was hastened by John Hamtramck, the agent, a strong-willed man who had been quick to take advantage of the retirement of Auguste. As Mr. Hamtramck controlled the tribal purse strings, his overtures proved more than some of the tribesmen could resist. Lately he had captured the friendship of the first Chief, White Hair. The body of the tribe, however, stood with the inactive Chouteau—and paid the penalty. Many were actually hungry when the appearance of Sam Houston gave them hope.

The coming of Houston created a problem for Mr. Hamtramck. He took counsel with his colleague, David Brearley, the agent of the Creeks, with Trader Hugh Love and others content with the status quo.

"At the last annuity Genl Houston was there," Paul Chouteau wrote to a cousin in Washington, Colonel Charles Gratoit of the Army. "Mr. Brannin [the blacksmith at the Three Forks] and Carble all called upon him and beged him if he could render them any aid to do so for they had despaired of receiving any from Mr. Hamtramck." From them Houston heard tales of outrages by hungry Indians against the stock and property of the white residents. It was charged that the agent had encouraged this sort of thing by joining the Osages on their hunts and stimulating their "Savage Propensities." "But . . ." continued Mr. Chouteau, "the Agent had a powerful inducement to this, he had become enamoured of a young woman, a relation to the principal chiefs and warriors." To advance his suit with this well-connected damsel Mr. Hamtramck had "lavished favors" upon her male relatives "and made offers of la[r]ge bounties but . . . failed of success."

During a hunt Mr. Hamtramck "bribe[d] a Warrior called the Iron, a brother to Bel Oiseau (Fine Bird), one of the principal chiefs of the Band, to accompany him to the lodge where the young woman slept. . . ." The writer's description of what followed left little to his correspondent's imagination. The young lady declined to be possessed in any such violent fashion, however, and after a furious scuffle she "repulsed" the ardent agent who "skulked from the lodge."

But a faint heart—— "After that failure he commenced negociation with White Hair for one of his Wives Whom he had not taken to bed, obtained her, and now keeps her publicly at the Agency. . . . His squaw is displayed on all public occasions loaded with wampum and decorated with trinkets and a Green Mantle Set off with Silver Lace. This is a great cause why the indians are dissatisfied. . . . They are suspicious enough to believe that their annuity is appropriated in part to purchase the finery that drapes Mr. Hamtramck's squaw."[10]

Sam Houston was suspicious also, but for the present confined himself to the formality of signing a petition to Colonel Arbuckle suggesting that Hamtramck be superseded as agent by Paul Chouteau.

## 5

From the Three Forks settlement Houston moved on to Cantonment Gibson, five or six miles away, where he remained for two weeks. By this time the curiosity of the whole region was excited. Officers' ladies stood guard at their cheerless windows for a glimpse of the romantic figure, envying, not for the first time in their lonely lives, plump and pleasing Sallie Nicks, the sutler's wife, who served the visitor with refreshments. Houston's actions were observed and his letters intercepted. Beyond the fact that he drank heavily, appeared to be getting on good terms with Colonel Arbuckle and seemed never to go to bed, little was learned.

Matthew Arbuckle was a good-natured bachelor in his fifties who liked his dram. An old frontier campaigner, he appreciated the boon of a caller and welcomed Houston with the courtesies due a former officer of the Regular service and a friend of the President.

The hospitality of Colonel Arbuckle was interrupted by another windfall for The Raven when the most "impressive" delegation of Indians ever seen on the Arkansas appeared unannounced at the cantonment gate. The "full council" of the Creek Nation, with clerk and interpreter, had come to request an audience with Colonel Arbuckle—and General Houston. The spokesman was Roly McIntosh, a son of the late Chief William McIntosh, of Georgia, who had kept his followers in hand during the War of 1812 and had joined Jackson in the campaign against the Alabama Creeks under the pro-British Weathersford. Roly McIntosh handed Arbuckle and Houston a document of nine pages.

"To General Andrew Jackson President of the United States Council Ground of the Western Creeks 22d June 1829

"The Chiefs, Headmen & Warriors of the Creek Nation . . . cannot overlook the unhappy situation in which they are placed, and deeply impressed with their misfortunes . . . Complain to a Man whose ears have always been open. . . .

"General Jackson knows the Circumstances under which we emigrated to this country; He heard the groans of the Mackintosh Party in the old Nation . . . and he told us to come to this country.—In War and in Peace we have always taken his Counsel; In coming to this Country an agent was given us. . . . That agent has not tried to make us happy.— He has done bad things toward us. . . . We will state the causes of our Sorrows.—

"1st Col Brearly has failed to pay us the bounty promised us by the Treaty and we have reason to believe that the money was placed in his Hands. . . .

"3d He has Connived at the introduction of spiritous liquors into Creek Nation. . . .

"4th He has speculated on the Necessities of the Indians through his Clerk by permitting him to sell flour to the Indians at the enormous price of $10 the barrell.

"5th Intoxication and disrespectful language to the Chiefs. . . ."

The complaints against Agent Brearley contained eleven specifications. Summing up, "the Chiefs feel Sensible that Col Brearly does not Regard them or their people in the light contemplated by the Government and that his Sole object is *speculation*." They asked the removal of Brearley, but did not want John Crowell, the eastern Creek agent, transferred west in Brearley's stead. They had heard that this was contemplated. But surely "Genl Jackson would not make us so unhappy. . . . He has not forgotten the Murder of Mackintosh.—He knows that his blood yet lies on the ground unburied. Mackintosh was a Warrior of Genl Jackson's.—The Genl told him he would protect him, but Jackson was far off— Col Crowell near at hand. He whispered to the enemies of Mackintosh—he pointed at him and he perished. . . . We hope Genl Jackson will not make us miserable and that he will keep this man from amongst us."[11]

"He whispered to the enemies of Mackintosh—he pointed at him and he perished"—written by an unhappy tribal scribe fumbling through the great haystack of English for words to express his meaning, rather than to contrive an effect of style. The Indian was a natural stylist. A scholarly Jesuit once wrote to Paris that the first orators of France would not despise some of the addresses he had heard from the lips of savage chieftains.

The apprehension of the western Creeks that Crowell might be foisted upon them had a basis. The eastern Creeks were doing their best to get Jackson to send Crowell away: "Father listen, we beseech you to hear us. Col Crowell has been the Agent for this nation a good many years . . . and there has been large sums of money appropriated to pay the Creek Nation [for ceded lands]. His Brother Thomas Crowell has been a Merchant during the whole time and from the various large sums of money we have received but a small proportion. . . . They have become immensely rich and we have become poor, although the agents accts. and vouchers may appear to the Genl Government to be fair and equitable. But

Father listen, you know that we do not understand keeping
accounts of such magnitude. . . . We cannot resist the belief
that He has defrauded the Creek Nation of large sums of money
and Father . . . we have lost all confidence in the agent and
his brother the Merchant and it can never be restored. . . .
Father listen to Your red Children, we wish you to remove
Coln. John Crowell from the office of I. A. of this Nation
and order Him and his brother from the confines of the Creek
Country."[12]

Having read the McIntosh memorial and witnessed its
signing, Houston cultivated the acquaintance of the distinguished Creeks who were present. The following day Roly
McIntosh placed the memorial in Houston's hands to send to
General Jackson, explaining that previous petitions entrusted
to official channels had not reached their destination. Houston
forwarded the document with a personal note saying that the
complaints deserved investigation. The President could then
determine what remedy would be necessary to restore the confidence of the Indians and quiet the angry feelings of the
different tribes toward each other.[13]

## 6

The closing lines of Houston's letter broached a matter
that disturbed Colonel Arbuckle. The question of peace was
in delicate balance. Arkansas was mobilizing militia. Events
seemed to move toward a general war, which the United States
must avert at all hazards. Houston was willing to assist,
writing to Secretary Eaton that the War Department's latest
gesture of sending troops to guard the Santa Fé Trail would be
a local and temporary remedy at best. The real trouble was a
war that had been going on for years among the various plains
tribes that were little known to white men. Houston suggested
a mission to compose the differences among these savages
which, he said, could "be easily affected by . . . some man
who understands the character of Indians. . . . I beg leave

to present the name of Colonel Augustus Chouteau. . . . I
would with great pleasure accompany him . . . but will not
accept any compensation for my services as the duty would
recreate my mind."[14]

But the restless exile found recreation for his mind sooner
than he anticipated and nearer to hand than the Santa Fé
Trail. The Cherokee war party was getting on with its scheme
to make an alliance with neighboring tribes and fall upon the
Pawnees and Comanches. A party of belligerent Creeks had
been approached. The whole project was to be threshed out
at a war-dance to take place on the Bayou Ménard in the
Cherokee country. So swiftly and secretly had the conspiring
Cherokees worked that the news did not reach Cantonment
Gibson until the braves were on their way to the rendezvous.
Anything could happen. From Canada to the Gulf the frontier
Indians were suspicious and discontented. On the plains war
existed, and troops had been ordered thither. A spark ignited
by a small combination of tribes on the Arkansas might envelop
the whole frontier. Colonel Arbuckle ordered his horse, and
calling Sam Houston, the two set out for the Bayou Ménard.

Surviving records of the next few moves are not clear, but
it appears that Arbuckle decided to stake everything on Houston's ability to stay the hand of the plotters. In any event,
Houston alone rode into the circle of astonished warriors,
while Arbuckle turned back. The following day Houston sent
the Colonel a lengthy report.

"After you left me last evening I attended the Dance &
Talk of the Cherokee [and the] Creeks and had the mortification to witness . . . the raising of the Tomahawk of War by
several Cherokees. The Creeks did not join . . . tho' I am
sensible that Smith [a Creek chief] will use every persuasive
in his power with them to [join this] . . . impolitic war
against the Pawnees & the Kimanchies. It is the project of a
few restless and turbulent young men who will not yield nor
listen to the Talk of their Chiefs. The great body of Chiefs
of the Cherokees are most *positively opposed* to the war: and
I have pointed out to them the ruinous consequences which must
result to them. . . .

"The Creeks assured me that they would not begin a war without Genl Jacksons consent, but . . . I have some fears. . . . I have been informed (but vaguely) that some Osage, Choctaw, Shawnee & Delewares are to join the Party, and in all make it some 250 or 300 warriors. I will not yet give up the project of stopping the Cherokees until all hope is lost, and there are yet fifteen days . . . before they will actually start for home. . . .

"It is not difficult to perceive that the most turbulent among the Cherokees are very solicitous that Cantonment Gibson should be broken up and all troops removed without the I. T. . . . I will predict that in the event of a removal of the U. S. Troops . . . that in less than twelve months . . . there will be waged a war the most sanguinary and savage that has raged within my recollection."[15]

Sam Houston knew that his report would go to Washington without delay, thus enabling him to address the authorities without assuming to do so. The letter to Arbuckle would tend to allay the apprehensions of Jackson who had been disturbed by the word he had received of Sam Houston's secret intentions in the West. The Arbuckle letter would show Houston's conduct to be quite correct—exercising his powers not to involve the Indians in war, but to avert such a thing. It would show him sympathetic with the Administration's desire to concentrate the remaining eastern Indians in the West.

This on one hand. On the other, Sam Houston's reasons for favoring the migration differed from the reasons of the Administration which wished the East to be a white man's country. Houston cared nothing for that, but the more Indians in the West the more power in the hands of Houston, in return for which he was willing to labor to better the lot of a reduced people with all the energy of a boiling mind that craved forgetfulness and nursed vague and bitter notions of revenge. Sam Houston's ultimate aim at this juncture is something no one can say. It is doubtful if Houston himself knew whither he was heading or wished to head. But the ideas of Oo-loo-te-ka, the ablest Indian in the region and the exile's closest counselor, were clear and definite.

The Raven had taken no step that did not comport with his foster-father's dream of empire. In six weeks he had established his influence with three of the four principal "agency" tribes in the Southwest. He enjoyed the confidence of the Commandant of all the United States troops in the country. He had stirred to temporary activity Auguste Chouteau through whom he proposed to extend his sway over the wild tribes of the plains, whose benevolent neutrality would be the least that Oo-loo-te-ka's project would require. Now he was engaged, with Oo-loo-te-ka, in trying to forestall a purposeless war that would imperil any possibility of such neutrality.

Houston addressed the war-dance on July 7, 1829. Mobilization of war parties was to be delayed for fifteen days. That much time remained in which to prevent the war. Houston, Arbuckle and every Indian leader who was for peace did their utmost. They succeeded, and the tomahawk was not raised.

With war forestalled, Sam Houston took the road without a day's delay for Fort Smith, Arkansas, fourteen miles from the Choctaw Agency. The Choctaws were the remaining immigrant tribe of importance to which Houston had not bound himself by ties of obligation. In this business The Raven had been adroit. In no case, excepting the crisis on the Bayou Ménard, had he approached an Indian uninvited. In every instance the Indians had solicited his counsel—first the Cherokees, then the Osages, then the Creeks. The Choctaws came to Houston, finding him, conveniently, at Fort Smith.

The gullible Choctaws were in a plight worse than the other western émigrés. Their agent, Captain William McClellan, was an honest man, but Washington had ignored his letters. Houston hurried to the agency and wrote the Secretary of War a stiff account of the robbery of the Choctaws by white interlopers. He told Major Eaton that he had assured the chiefs that their treaties with General Jackson would be kept. Houston might have done more had not illness cut his visit short, but he had won the lifelong friendship of the Choctaws.

An important work was now complete.

# CHAPTER X

## PAGAN SANCTUARIES

### 1

THE winged symbol of a "great destiny" had flown furiously and far. Sam Houston stood at the threshold of things of which destinies are made. His flagging forces whipped up by whisky, The Raven had thrust himself into a position of leadership over seven thousand Indians who controlled the country from Missouri to Texas and westward to the great plains. He had accomplished this in the space of eight weeks. Activity, activity—anything to "recreate my mind" and turn it from the perils of introspection.

Yet there was a limit to which a physique so remarkable as that of Sam Houston could be driven. At the end of the long ride from the Choctaw country The Raven reeled from his horse at Oo-loo-te-ka's wigwam with the stamp of a desperate illness upon him.

It was August, a month of which white men stood in dread. Even transplanted Indians, particularly those accustomed to the salubrious air of the southern mountains, were stricken by the pestilential heat that fell like a dead damp weight upon the swampy lowlands of the Arkansas Valley. The garrison at Cantonment Gibson had buried men until there were more soldiers in the graveyard outside the stockade than on the muster-rolls within.

At Oo-loo-te-ka's they helped The Raven inside a log hut and laid him on a mat of corn-shucks. His limbs trembled, his skin was yellow and hot to touch. He was burning with a malarial fever, which had reached a stage that was usually fatal.

Chief Oo-loo-te-ka's was not a Christian household. Although friendly to missionaries, he kept to the gods of his fathers and the punctilio of the ancient religion, with its medicine-men who regarded white physicians as their professional adversaries. To this habitation the stricken man had come in preference to Cantonment Gibson where there was a hospital (of a sort), or to a missionary station with its staff surgeon.

The scene at the wigwam must have been a weird one. The Cherokee word for disease means "the intruder." The intruder comes through the influence of ghosts and witches which only the intervention of certain gods can dispel. The treatment of the sick, therefore, was an office of the clergy—the shamans or medicine-men who were also poets wonderfully learned in the forms of a worship as colorful and as complete as any of the ceremonial religions of the East. In the belief of the old Cherokee practitioners, fevers were the work of insects and worms in revenge for being trodden on. To confound their destructive efforts the gods of the Great and the Little Whirlwind must be summoned from their pantheons in the air, the mountains, the trees and the water.

Every step was associated with the fantastic realm of mythology that encompassed the whole being of the Cherokee and touched and tinctured everything he knew, through the five senses, of the world about him. First the medicine-man beat up some bark of the wild cherry tree or tobacco leaves and heated the mixture in water over seven coals, representing the seven clans of the Cherokee people. Filling his mouth with this brew, he faced his patient toward the sunrise and intoned first to the gods in the air:

"Listen! On high you dwell. On high you dwell—you dwell, you dwell, for ever you dwell, for ever you dwell. Relief has come—has come. *Hayi!*"

With the interjection, "*Hayi!*" the medicine-man ceremoniously blew the medicine from his mouth on symbolic parts of the patient's body, making four blowings in all—four, like seven, being a sacred number.

The shaman then addressed the gods on the mountain. Four more blowings and the gods in the trees were summoned. Drenching the patient again, the priest called upon the gods in the water and then recited in a whisper a long petition to the Little Whirlwind to scatter the disease "as in play," that is, as the wind scatters the leaves. After this he blew his breath on the subject, chanted more ritual and enacted a pantomime. Lastly, he addressed the Great Whirlwind:

"Listen! O now again you have drawn near to hearken, O Whirlwind, surpassingly great. In the leafy shelter of the great mountain there you repose. O Great Whirlwind arise quickly. A very small part [of the disease] remains. You have come to sweep the intruder into the great swamp on the upland. You have laid down your paths to the great swamp. You shall scatter it as in play so that it shall utterly disappear.

"And now relief has come. All is done. *Yu!*"[1]

This rite was repeated at dawn and at dusk for four days. There was much more to the treatment, however, and the thirty-eight days that The Raven lay in his foster-father's wigwam afforded to the devout of Oo-loo-te-ka's family opportunity to reveal their familiarity with the rich repertoire of formulas and charms. Through the burning nimbus of his delirium, sounds of the conjurer's rattle reached the ears of the sufferer. . . . Poetic imagery. . . . Pagan nummery. . . . A vision of a  yellow-haired girl bending among the flowers of an old-fashioned garden.

John Thornton, the chief's youthful letter-writer, had learned something of the white man's medicine from Doctor Weed, the mission physician at Dwight. It may be that John got Doctor Weed to visit the sick man, although no mention of it appears in the mission records. It may be that John himself did some blood-letting or administered Peruvian bark and nitre to reinforce the simples of the shamans. The missionaries prayed for Sam Houston or other occasions; possibly on this occasion they mingled their supplications with the entreaties of the heathen Cherokees. In any event when September brought a measure of relief from the heat, the glassy-eyed man on the pallet of corn-shucks began to improve, and he was able to read a letter that had been carried down from Cantonment Gibson. As soon as he could hold a pen he answered it.

"Cherokee Nation
"19th Sept 1829

"My dear Sir,

"I am very feeble from a long spell of fever which . . . well nigh closed the scene of all my mortal cares, but I thank my God that I am again cheered by the hope of renewed health. I would not write this time but I cannot deny myself the pleasure of tendering you my heartfelt acknowledgement of your kind favor which reached me when I was barely able to peruse its contents. It was a cordial to my spirits and cheered me in my sickness. . . .

"The solicitude which you have so kindly manifested for my future welfare cannot fail to inspire me with a most proper sense of obligation. . . ." However, "to become a missionary among the Indians is rendered impossible for want of that Evangelical change of heart so absolutely necessary to a man who assumes the all important character of proclaiming to a lost world the mediation of a blessed Savior. To meliorate the condition of the Indians—to prevent fraud and peculation on the part of the Governments agents among them and to direct the feelings of the Indians in kindness to the Government and inspire them with confidence in its justice and magnanimity towards the Red People have been the objects of my constant solicitude and attention since I have been among them. . . .

"I pray you to salute your family for me and be assured of my sincere devotion. . . .

"Truly your friend
"SAM HOUSTON

"Genl Jackson
"President U. S."

A postscript added:

"I hope to take and send you between this and Xmas some

fine buffaloe meat for your Xmas dinner or at farthest the 8th of Jany!"[2]

## 2

The President of the United States was not the first to whom Sam Houston had revealed a want of that evangelical state of the heart necessary to commend the God of Israel to the heathen. The missionaries had learned as much. The lines to Jackson were written while Houston was under the influence of a deep emotional experience, as it is impossible to believe that one so sensitive to such impressions could have remained untouched by the aura of religious devotion which during his illness had enveloped the household of his foster-father. These unenlightened barbarians had unhesitatingly commended an unbeliever to the mercies of their gods. Five months before two clergymen of Nashville had found "good grounds" for sending a penitent fellow-follower of Christ into exile unblessed.

On his arrival in the Indian country, Sam Houston had been sought by the principal missionaries who desired the friendship of a personage so important. During all the years he lived with the Indians the missionaries, though they never liked him, continued to approach Houston for favors of many kinds. He helped them more often than not, and never was hostile. He treated them with the respect that had been a part of his childhood training in religion, and saw that others did the same—which was something of an undertaking in that part of the world.

The story is told of Sam Houston's meeting in Fort Smith with a white man of evil reputation when drunk. He was roaring about town declaring his intention of "licking" a missionary named Williams.

"I understand you are looking for Mr. Williams," Houston remarked.

The man said he was.

"I am Mr. Williams," said Sam Houston.

"That can't be," said the man. "I know Williams when I see him."

"That is the same as calling me a liar," said Houston, drawing two bowie knives from his belt. "Take your choice."

The white man accepted an alternative of apologizing to Mr. Williams.[3]

Even Dr. Marcus Palmer, of the Fairfield Mission, for whom Houston formed a warm regard, failed to "convert" The Raven or to change his habits, which the local clergy found a fertile subject for criticism.

Sam Houston's attitude toward the missionary idea more nearly resembled that of an intelligent Indian than a Christian concerned even nominally with the spread of his creed. Houston admired the missionaries for the dangers they braved, and the hardships they met unflinchingly in the name of their faith. He appreciated the uprightness of their personal characters and their honesty with the Indians. They were living proofs that white men were not necessarily blackguards. Oo-loo-te-ka, though he deplored the slight inroads they made on the tribal faith, felt that the good they did outweighed the harm, and permitted services in his wigwam. These friendly relations were the rule, but not the invariable rule. The Osages had trouble with Reverend Benton Pixley, and White Hair, the friend of Agent Hamtramck, wrote to Jackson:

"Father, we moved our people towards the setting sun and left the Missionaries two days march toward the rising sun,

"Father—one of them followed us and has been living on our land though we gave them land enough. . . .

"Father, He has quarrelled with our men and women and we hear he has also quarrelled with all the white men who our Great Father has sent here to do us good. . . .

"Father—we have enough of white people among us without him, even if he was good. . . . He forgets his black coat . . . disturbs our peace and many other things. . . .

"Father, we hope you may live long and be happy."[4]

The missionaries also encountered difficulties in acquainting the untutored with the merits of civilization's economic system. Washington Irving scribbled an example on a fly-leaf of the journal he kept at the time he made Sam Houston's acquaintance in the West. "Old Father Vail addressed the Indians on the necessity of industry as a means to happiness. An Indian replied—Father I dont understand this kind of happiness you talk of. You tell me to cut down tree—to lop it—to make fences—to plough—this you call being happy—I no like such happiness. When I go to St. Louis I go to see Chouteau—or Clarke.—He says hello—and negro comes in with great plate with cake, wine &—he say eat, drink. If you want anything else he say hello—three—four, five, six negro come and do what we 'want. that I call happy. he no plough. he no work. he no cut wood."

But in his chosen field of religion the missionary found the hardest rows to hoe. This was particularly true of those laboring among the Cherokees with an old-established and well-organized "church" of their own. Cephas Washburn, head of the Dwight Mission, the most scholarly Protestant missionary in the region, learned that his interpreter had enlightened a congregation as follows: "Mr. Washburn tells me to say to you that in the sight of God there are but two people, the good people and the bad people. But I do not believe him. I believe there are three kinds; the good people, the bad people, and the middle kind, like myself." The interpreter who knew the Cherokee mind better than Mr. Washburn doubtless sought only to lead his countrymen from error by easy steps. He was dismissed for his pains.

Cherokees who were troubled by witches were told that if they should accept Christianity the witches would be powerless to molest them. Some made the experiment only to discover hell-fire and brimstone, after which they were glad to return to the comparatively minor discomforts the witches might inflict. The case of Tah-neh was more involved, however. Tah-neh was the wife of The Girth, son of Oo-loo-te-ka. She was a sister-in-law, therefore, of The Raven. Her struggles with the doctrinal subtleties of the Christian gospel were witnessed by him.

In the Dwight Mission records the account runs:

"Tah-neh is deeply distressed. Her mind is greatly perplexed with some of the doctrines. . . . It is obvious that her heart is hostile. . . . When we told her that a condemned heathen in the world of retribution would be punished with less severity than a rejector of gospel grace she . . . expressed a wish that she had never heard of the gospel. She continued for several weeks . . . opposing her only Deliverer till she felt herself wholly lost . . . & that she must have a Savior or perish. Now she [has] returned to the L. J. C. . . . we trust with tears of real repentance."[5]

But in the estimation of Mr. Washburn Tah-neh's return to the Lord Jesus Christ was belated. "Hope" was all that could be held out to her. She must, Mr. Washburn said, undergo a period of instruction and apprenticeship. This term of uncertainty lasted for two years, after which Tah-neh was conducted to the mission and given "a very particular" quizzing as to her "humility, meekness, deep penitence & humble trust in GOD." This time her proofs were acceptable; she was baptized and her heathen name exchanged for that of Naomi. A few weeks later Naomi became hopelessly insane.[6]

As far as can be learned no other member of Oo-loo-te-ka's household was ever converted. Sam Houston was not converted. The covert hostility of the missionaries persisted as long as The Raven remained in the Indian country. In this matter, as in others, he gave no one his confidence. He explained nothing. Twenty-five years later, a spiritually broken man, grappling with a deep interior question of conscience, knelt with a woman to pray. Not until then can one understand the desolation sown by two Tennessee ministers whose view of their responsibilities had bereft Sam Houston of his faith.

## 3

Houston's illness was followed by a long period of convalescence, with much to do and little strength. His whirlwind entry into the Indian melodrama had left a trail of loose ends. The Indian agents and traders were almost a unit against him, and while Houston lay helpless grass had not grown under their feet. Susceptible Indians were being stirred up. Unless Houston could consolidate his position much of the ground gained would be lost. In this situation The Raven decided to specialize on the two most important Indian groups—the Cherokees and the Creeks—which were also the nearest to hand.

The first event of importance was the payment of the Cherokees' annuity. This took place at their agency in October, about a month after Houston was up and about. An annuity disbursement was always a great occasion and this particular disbursement to the Cherokees promised to be an occasion without precedent. A fortune in gold was due to be paid over—the fifty thousand dollars lump indemnity due under the treaty of 1828, the two thousand dollars annuity due under that treaty and various sums due under earlier treaties. The tribesmen and their officials and the white and mixed-breed complement usual to such occasions, began to pitch camp on the prairie about the agency. Whisky runners, traders, speculators, soldiers and attachés of the Indian Bureau—from Cantonment Gibson, the Three Forks, Fort Smith and even distant Little Rock they came—the rag-tag and bobtail of the frontier. Thus Major E. W. du Val, the Cherokee agent, made his second visit to his charges in their new home. Thus a bevy of light though thrifty ladies from the Arkansas capital made their first visit to await the shower of gold. Thither repaired also a tall man whose fashionable buckskins hung loosely upon his gigantic frame.

Major du Val made an announcement to the Cherokee chiefs. There would be, it seemed, no shower of gold. A murmur of dismay must have swept the tents of the camp-followers, until they learned that the agent's words should not be taken in too narrow a sense. Literally there would be no shower of gold, but actually there would be something much better. In default of currency, certificates of indebtedness would be distributed among the Indians. To get "hard" money from an

Indian was never a difficult task. To paper money he attached no importance whatever.

The result was a free-for-all. "Merchants," wrote Houston, "who had connections with the agents, purchased up these certificates in a fraudulent manner for a mere song. . . . A Mackinaw blanket, a flask of powder and even a bottle of whisky was often all these defrauded exiles ever got for the plighted faith of our Government."[7] Agent du Val himself opened a store to facilitate trade in certificates. The agent's brother opened a whisky running station, and in six weeks he had sold two hundred and fifty barrels of liquor.[8]

"In this manner," continued Houston in subsequent review, "whole tribes were preyed upon. . . . We cannot measure the desolating effects of intoxicating liquors among the Indians by an analogy drawn from civilized life. With the Red man the consequences are a thousand times more frightful. . . . The President . . . only hears one side of the story, and that, too, told by his own creatures. . . . During the entire period he resided in that region [Houston speaks of himself, Indian fashion, in the third person], he was unceasing in his efforts to prevent the introduction of ardent spirits among the Indians; and . . . this, too, was a period when he was far from being a practically temperate man himself."[9]

The swindlers' harvest was not what it might have been, however. Watt Webber, who was a Cherokee official, got his hands on a considerable amount of certificates. Ben Hawkins, a half-breed Creek of influence, got some. Houston seemed concerned with these transactions, which outraged the feelings of Agent du Val, but when Mr. du Val heard that Houston himself had carried away certificates to the value of sixty-six thousand dollars, official indignation knew no bounds.

The Cherokees who had entrusted Houston with their paper felt differently about it, however, and the Nation invested him with a privilege not previously granted to a white man, by this means checkmating a scheme of Du Val to circumscribe The Raven's activities:

"Whereas, an order has been published by the agent of the Cherokee Nation, requesting all white men who reside in the Nation . . . to comply with certain rules. . . . Now, Be it known. . . . That Samuel Houston, late of the State of Tennessee, has been residing in the Nation for sometime past and . . . In consideration of his former acquaintance with; and services rendered the Indians, and . . . our confidence in his integrity, and talents . . . We do . . . irrevocably grant him forever, all the rights, privileges and immunities, of a citizen of the Cherokee Nation . . . as though he was a native born Cherokee. . . .

"In witness whereof we have this day set out hands this 21st day of October, 1829.

his

"Walter + Webber Prest Commt

"Cherokee Nation     mark

   "Illinois       his

"Aron + Price vice President

mark

his

"Approved John + Jolly Principal Chief"[10]

mark

The one-time congressman, governor, protégé of Jackson and aspirant to the presidency no longer considered himself a citizen of the United States.

4

In the wigwam of Oo-loo-te-ka a pen scratched at the dictation of the first Chief.

"Great Father,

"My son (Gen^l Houston or) the Raven came to me last spring . . . and my heart embraced him. . . . At my wigwam he rested with me as my son. He has walked straight. . . . His path is not crooked. . . . He is now leaving me to meet his *white* Father, Gen^l Jackson, and look upon him and I hope he will take him by the hand and keep him as near to his heart as I have done. He is beloved by all my people. . . . When you look upon this letter I wish you to feel, as though we *smoked* the pipe of peace together, and held each other by the

hand, and felt, as one man.   We are far a part but I send my
heart to *my* friend Jackson, and the Father of my people!"[11]

John Jolly affixed his X mark and the letter was directed
to "Gen^l Andrew Jackson President U. States."   The letter-
writer on this occasion was not young John Thornton, but The
Raven himself.   The new citizen of the Cherokee Nation was
too useful a man to remain a private tribesman.   He had been
raised to the rank of ambassador and was in readiness to depart for the seat of the Great Father in Washington.

The appointment had not been made according to regular
form in open council.   Secrecy surrounded The Raven's departure.   But Jackson was advised through a mutual friend.
"I am on my way to Washington and perhaps New York. . . .
Many will be the conjectures as to the object of my trip, and
it will be . . . neither to solicit office or favors of . . .
the President. . . . My only study shall be to deport myself . . . as can no wise embarrass his feelings, nor his circumstances. . . . Write to Judge White's care [in Wash-
ington].   If this were not done the curious would open my
letters as they have done this summer."[12]

The Raven slipped away early in December, but weeks
elapsed before it was learned whither he had gone or why.
Some of the missionaries were much put out.   They had
counted on Houston to undertake to raise money for them in
the East.   Houston's boyhood friend, Captain John Rogers, Jr., was disturbed.   Watt Webber had gone east with
Houston, and Rogers did not like Webber.   He wrote to
Jackson, expressing his distrust of Webber, and by inference
included Houston in his insinuations.

Near Fort Smith, Houston and Webber encamped by the
side of the river near the residence of Major du Val, the
Cherokee agent, who transacted his affairs from the civilized
side of the Arkansas line.   With them was John Brown, an
eastern Cherokee recently come West, with whom Oo-loo-te-ka
was dickering to bring about his cherished reunion of the
tribe.   Du Val rode down to invite General Houston and his

friends to supper. At the house Du Val took Houston aside. They had had a few drinks together, when a clerk of Du Val's appeared bearing a letter which the agent opened and read. Then he handed it to Houston. The communication was to warn Major du Val that Houston was on his way to Washington to prefer charges against the agent. Du Val asked if this were true.

"Substantially," said Houston.

Du Val demanded that Houston put his charges in writing. Houston asked for pen and paper and did so, in duplicate. One copy he kept, the other he gave to the agent and took his written receipt for it. Major du Val renewed his invitation to dine but Houston and his Indian friends excused themselves and withdrew to prepare their own meal over a fire.[13]

## 5

On the day before Christmas, the palpitating little steamer *Amazon* trudged up the Mississippi. To the left lay the pine-dressed lowlands of Arkansas. On the right a more conspicuous shore now and then attained the dignity of a bluff that gave an air of aspiration to the unpeopled scene. This was Tennessee.

Tennessee! A tall man in a blanket and turban surveyed the prospect from the deck, and in the course of the day recorded certain Christmas Eve reflections:

"Composed on Dec 24th 1829

"There is a proud undying thought in man,
That bids his soul still upward look,
To fames proud cliff! And longing
Look in hope to grace his name
For after ages to admire, and wonder
How he reached the dizzy, dangerous
Hight, or where he stood, or how—
Or if admiring his proud station fell
And left a name alone!!
This is ambitions range, and while it seeks
To reach . . .

Beyond all earthy names,
And stand where millions never
Dared to look, it leaves content
                                   . . . the
Companion of a virtuous heart! . . .

"There is a race of mortals wild . . .
Who range the desert free
And roam where floods
Their onward currents pour
In majesty, as free as Indian thoughts,
Who feel that happiness and
Content are theirs.
*They* owe no homage to written rules
  . . . no allegiance to idle forms
                              . . . which
Virtue dare not own!
But proud of freedom,
In their native words, they
  . . . pitch their hopes of endless joys
In fields where game of never
Dying sort . . .
Delights the hunter's soul."[14]

Sam Houston never claimed to be a poet and later in life
conceived a curious prejudice against that form of expression.
But he could not forget Tennessee.  Four days later he wrote
to Judge John H. Overton, of Nashville:

"Passing near to the borders of a land so dear to me as
Tennessee, and reflecting upon . . . my life . . . I should
be wanting in justice to my feelings . . . were I to suppress
the expression of my most grateful and friendly regard.  In
prosperity you regarded me well, and generously, but when
the *darkest*, direst hour of human misery was passing by you
called to *sustain* me by the lights of age, philosophy, and friendship. . . . The hour of anguish has passed by, and my soul
feels all that tranquility conscious gratitude can bestow.  And
it is in this state of feeling that my heart . . . recurs, in
gratitude, to the man, who dared . . . diminish the weight of
misery, which I had been doomed to feel!"[15]

# CHAPTER XI

## Notions of Honor

### 1

On St. Patrick's Day of 1830 General Duff Green marched into the President's house exuding an air of importance. But Duff Green invariably looked important. It became his position as proprietor of the great *United States Telegraph*, charter member of Jackson's "kitchen cabinet" and, allowing for a personal point of view, President-maker.

In the President's private study, Duff Green saw three men about a littered desk, their heads together "in earnest conversation." They were the President, the Secretary of War and the ambassador of the Cherokee Nation of Indians. When Editor Green entered a palpable silence fell—a thing really difficult to avoid when time-tried associates who have privately begun to distrust each other unexpectedly meet under circumstances not calculated to diminish suspicion. The old salutes have a hollow sound. What is one to say?

Duff Green said nothing.

### 2

The vindicators of Eliza Allen did not feel that they had bungled their work. Houston's reputation was gone—and he was gone. Although the achievement had the appearance of permanence, a word from Jackson would insure this. There would be naught to fear from the man who, in banishment, retained the capacity to strike otherwise confident hearts with vague alarms of a return from Elba.

131

Andrew Jackson was chivalry embodied. "I never war against women and it is only the base and cowardly that do." He sought the presidency to wipe the smirks from the shifty countenances of his wife's traducers. Alas, a broken-hearted widower had composed a brave epitaph for "Rachel Jackson . . . whom slander might wound but could not dishonor," and plunged himself into the quixotic championship of Peggy Eaton. Surely one so generous would not withhold the mantle of his gallantry from Eliza Allen.

General Jackson had given patient audience to Sam Houston's enemies. He had listened to their stories, but said nothing. From Houston's friends came a few pitifully vague letters, and the President was three months in making up his mind what to do. Then, Indian intrigues notwithstanding, he wrote Houston a letter, which the exile, in reply, called "a cordial to my spirits," continuing:

"From the course which I had pursued in the relation to the cause of my abandonment of society—my absolute refusal to gratify the enquiring world—my entire silence because it comported with my notion of honor . . ."

"Because it comported with my notion of honor." This was putting it in rather general terms. The man who had conducted a prospective Cabinet officer to a shotgun wedding usually received more explicit answers to his inquiries. But Sam Houston told him no more, even in the exhilaration of feeling at the assurance that he retained the friendship of the great and loyal Jackson.

"Had a sceptre," continued Houston, "been dashed at my feet it would not have afforded me the same pleasure which I derived from the proud consciousness not only that I deserved but that *I possessed your confidence!* The elevation of your station . . . contrasted with that of a man who had ceased to be all that he ever had been in the world's eye; was such as would have justified you in any inferences, the most damning to his character and prejudicial to his integrity. You disregarded the standard calculations of mankind and acted from an impulse peculiar to yourself."[1]

An inquiring world was not immediately informed of this understanding between Andrew Jackson and the broken exile. Houston's enemies continued to importune the President. This was the state of affairs when Sam Houston reached Washington on January 13, 1830.

His arrival was the sensation of the week. It was one thing for Washington to receive a barbarian dignitary, and another to receive one who looked the part. Indians in claw-hammer coats were getting too common. With his fine eye for the proprieties, The Raven made no attempt to imitate the externals of a prosperous congressman. He presented himself in the costume of the wigwam. For every occasion there was a new blanket, and the metal ornaments on the ambassador's buckskin coat tinkled pleasantly as he walked. While flustered Washington was trying to determine what to do, the President made the decision. He invited The Raven to an entertainment at the Executive Mansion. The Tennessee avengers had their answer. Sam Houston's "notion of honor" satisfied Andrew Jackson.

The Allens made no attempt to conceal their displeasure, but their political partners were more discreet. Nevertheless, reprisals were planned. From a congressman with a foot in the enemy camp, Houston learned that he was to be visited with "a fate most appalling to humanity" should he return to the West by way of Tennessee. Moreover, he knew Duff Green to be his secret enemy.

## 3

The urbane Secretary of War spoke first. The President and General Houston, Major Eaton said, were discussing an important contract for supplying rations to the Indians newly emigrated or about to emigrate across the Mississippi. The present ration, costing twenty-one cents, was unsatisfactory.

General Houston had volunteered to supply a superior ration for eighteen cents. A saving of twelve thousand dollars a day! Think of it.

Duff Green did not share the Secretary's enthusiasm. Surely, he replied, General Houston had miscalculated. There was no saving to the government at eighteen cents a ration, but a great loss. Beef bought on the hoof in Illinois and Missouri could be distributed for much less than eighteen cents.

Jackson and Houston changed the conversation, and presently Duff Green took his departure, reflecting that if Eaton were after a puff in the *Telegraph* for Sam Houston's ration scheme, he was barking up the wrong tree. What with protecting the precious Peggy, the *Telegraph* had done enough for the Eaton family.

The next day Green found the President alone. Jackson said Houston was practically certain to get the contract. Duff Green raised his eyebrows. Hadn't the President better look into the matter more closely? Duff Green said that he had been examining figures, and the ration could be provided for six cents. Jackson turned in his chair. "Will *you* take it at *ten?*" Green said he would not. "Will you take it at twelve cents?" Green said he was not a bidder, and the President began to fuss with papers on his disorderly desk.

Duff Green went home and wrote a letter to the Secretary of War. The eighteen-cent contract might "enrich a few who are concerned in it but will . . . impair the fair name of the President which it is your duty and mine to guard."

While these high-minded words of caution were on their way, another letter was written at the Green residence—by a house-guest of the publisher, John Shackford, of St. Louis, making a formal bid for the ration contract at seventeen cents.

Affairs moved briskly. Shackford reduced his proposal to fifteen cents to meet competition. Houston countered with a bid of thirteen cents, submitted in the name of John Van Fossen, of New York. Other bids ran as low as eight cents. Shackford needed money, but the editor of the *Telegraph* had other motives for opposing the interests of The Raven. Houston had obtained the dismissal of five Indian agents, including du Val and Hamtramck. Green was a friend of Hamtramck and had opposed his removal. Moreover, the Peggy Eaton petticoat war was in full swing with Vice-President Calhoun, a relative of Green by marriage, getting the worst of it. Green saw the disguised hand of Sam Houston at work against Calhoun, and the Tennessee vendetta received a powerful ally.

Against this coalition Sam Houston stood alone. He declined to exploit Jackson's friendship, but otherwise he intrigued with the nimblest. Yet, the only words of concern for the Indian discoverable in a voluminous record of this sordid episode were uttered—with no thought of public effect—by Sam Houston when he wrote to Van Fossen: "Justice to the Indians . . . a full ration, and of good quality . . . must be a 'sine qua non.' "

The tempest whirled to a tame pause. The request for bids was withdrawn, and no one got the contract.[2] There the matter rested for two years.

4

Sam Houston was not the only outcast sheltered by Andrew Jackson that winter in the white "Castle" on the Avenue. John Eaton had dutifully married Peggy. Washington has seen strange sights in its time and has acquiesced, but on this occasion the transformation from tavern belle to Cabinet lady stopped the wheels of the social machinery. Firstly and finally, Society would not accept the amiable Peg.

Jackson canvassed the field for supporters. He appealed particularly to Calhoun and Van Buren. Mr. Van Buren responded handsomely. He gave a party for Mrs. Eaton. He got two of his bachelor friends, the British and the Russian ministers, to be nice to her. Mr. Calhoun would have done as much—if he could. He understood what was going on, but unlike Van Buren, Mr. Calhoun had a wife whose cooperation was essential.  Mrs. Calhoun refused to cooperate, and nothing could move her.

Mr. Van Buren redoubled his attentions.  Jackson began inviting the Secretary of State on horseback rides and calling him "Van."  Mr. Calhoun bit his nails and made lame excuses; he was in a desperate fix.  In the fulness of time the President heard that not for the first time had a certain fastidious South Carolina gentleman declined to stand with forthright Andrew Jackson.  Shade by shade, color was applied to the dark picture that Sam Houston three years before had etched about the famous letter of 1818 on the Florida campaign.

In the midst of this came Houston's dramatic reappearance in Washington—a towering figure in a bright blanket, grand, gloomy and peculiar, that paced the worn carpet of the presidential smoking-room, brooding and drinking.  The Raven did not scruple to impart fresh significance to his old accusation.  The bright blanket he wore stirred no memories calculated to soften his resentment toward John C. Calhoun.

Lewis, Eaton, Sam Swartwout and others of the original anti-Calhoun combination were on hand.  The encirclement of Mr. Calhoun was complete.  Duff Green could do little more than postpone the crash which obliged Mr. Calhoun to resign the vice-presidency.  This came after Houston, taking his own good time, had departed for the Indian country.  By the light of a dying fire in the Wigwam Neosho Sam Houston spent more than one summer evening in contemplation of the sweets of a subaltern's revenge.

5

April in Tennessee.  Azaleas flamed in a landscape where spring's work already was complete.  The slender figure of a young woman in black moved along the paths of an old-fashioned garden beside a house that overlooked the Cumberland.  Her oval face wore an expression of infinite loneliness.  Inside the house men were talking.  The young woman in the garden had watched them arrive: Former Governor Hall, Squire Alexander, General Eastin Morris, Lawyer Guild, of Gallatin, Captain Douglass and so on. They were shut in a room with her father. . . . A year this month, April. And still the secretive meetings, the maddening talk, talk.

As the men conversed they passed from hand to hand a letter that had never been answered. The woman in the garden knew every word of this letter. The signature at the bottom was a bold one with a rubric under it: SAM HOUSTON—her husband.

But one thing, one overwhelming thing, known to the men in the room was as yet unknown to the girl in the garden. Sam Houston was in Nashville! He had defied them.

This was the reason for the conference. Circumstances had changed within the year. The chivalrous championship of Eliza Allen now rested on strange premises. The champions trembled in the fear of exposure. They knew that Houston knew of their predicament. But they did not fear exposure by him. It was Eliza, the object of all their tender solicitation, who destroyed their peace of mind. She wanted her husband back.[3]

This cast of affairs had come about in a peculiar way. The proud Allens had a valid grievance against the man with a brilliant future into whose eager arms they had persuaded an unwilling daughter of their house. Sam Houston had accused his bride of a terrible thing. Then on his knees he had begged her forgiveness and the pardon of her family; but by her code and theirs amnesty was not possible.[4] Houston seemed to understand. His humiliation was complete. Without criticism or comment he had set his feet upon the path of retribution suggested by his personal ideas of honor. He never expressed resentment toward the Allens, and in later years they softened toward him.[5] As to Carroll, Houston hated him with a grim and abiding passion which the Tennesseean reciprocated. Forty years after the event, when Sam Houston and Eliza Allen were in their graves, a member of the old Carroll clique who had attained distinction in life, published a vituperative account of the marriage.[6]

The emotions of Eliza Allen had been the first to grow clear. Did she perceive the exploitation of herself and her family by a resourceful politician who had bound them all to the wheels of his chariot?

Everything went back to the circumstances attending the marriage. The enchantment of the crowded autumn hour when Eliza made her promise had been of brief duration. While donning her bridal gown, she had wept. Her hands trembled during the exchange of wedding vows. She felt that she loved another, but of Sam Houston's love for her there was no doubt. That night was passed at Eliza's home. When they were alone Houston spoke of his bride's nervousness "which convinced him some secret had not been revealed. Before retiring he frankly told her of his suspicion, asked a frank confession and pledged her that he should work her no injury. His frankness and firmness led to the confession that her affections had been pledged to another . . . and that filial duty had prompted her acceptance of his offer."[7] They rested apart.

The second night was spent at Locust Grove. In the morning Mrs. Robert Martin stood thoughtfully tapping a window of her mansion on the Pike. The chatelaine of Locust Grove had seen something of the world. Eight presidents and the Marquis de Lafayette skim through the pages of her unpublished memoirs. She was pondering the sight she beheld from her window. A beautiful snow had fallen during the night, and on the blanketed lawn Governor Houston and the two lively brunette Martin girls were engaged in a hilarious snow battle.

Mrs. Martin's reflections were interrupted by a step on the stairs. Eliza was coming down. "I said to her, 'It seems as if General Houston is getting the worst of the snow-balling; you had better go out and help him.' Looking seriously at me Mrs. Houston said, 'I wish they would kill him.' I looked up astonished to hear such a remark from a bride of not yet forty-eight hours, when she repeated in the same voice, 'Yes, I wish from the bottom of my heart that they would kill him.' "[8]

Martha Martin was Sam Houston's friend. She kept well the secret of that morning, and the couple journeyed to Nashville to pass the days in comparative seclusion. As far as any one could learn they were happy. Houston was busy with preparations for the campaign against Carroll. He made a journey from home—to Chickasaw Bluffs, one account says; to Columbia, in Maury County, according to another; but Cockrell's Spring seems to have been the place. The return was unannounced and unexpected. What the scene was no one can know. It has been said that Eliza was weeping over old love-letters.[9] It has been said that she was in a man's arms—a supposition not favored by the evidence.[10] In any event, provocation was such that Sam Houston accused his wife of infidelity.

The fearful indictment had scarcely fallen from his lips when doubts assailed him. It was the old story of jealous rage and terrible suspicions: a moment of wild accusation and a lifetime of regret. Naturally, Eliza desired to clear her name. By mutual consent the matter was laid before a third party and then, by means unexplained, the news reached the Allens. There was no repairing anything after that.

Eliza went home. Houston wrote her father a letter saying he believed his wife "virtuous." He followed the letter to Gallatin, and begged an interview with Eliza. It was granted on condition that an aunt remain in the room. Many, many years after, when passions had cooled, this aunt's story was told. "He knelt before her and with tears streaming down his face implored forgiveness . . . and insisted with all his dramatic force that she return to Nashville with him. Had she yielded to these entreaties what the future may have brought to them none can tell. As it was there were many years of sadness to be endured."[11]

Ah, had she but yielded! It was Eliza's turn now to regret. But she was brave. She took counsel of the intuitions of her heart and did a womanly thing. Setting aside the sacred code, she said she wanted her husband.

At the same time Eliza was loyal to her men-foik. She had no wish to involve them in a painful repudiation of declarations they had made to preserve her fair name. And there was Carroll; the security of his throne lay in keeping Sam Houston out of Tennessee. Lastly and least explicable was the position of Sam Houston himself. The ardor with which he declined the sympathy of the world suggests a compensating consolation that he had been able to afford himself. A whisky-whirled, romantic brain, brooding in forest solitudes, had turned inward. Houston had shouldered the blame and taken his punishment. He thought this enough. Yet the lash of a hundred untruths, of high names and low motives, pursued him in exile. Eliza's feelings had veered a full cycle; her husband's did the same. Again they were at opposite poles, Eliza entreating, Houston holding aloof. What caused this? Had Tiana Rogers taken the vacant place in his heart? And again, in the very fierceness with which Sam Houston, to the last day of his life, repelled the breath of scandal from Eliza Allen lurks a disturbing thought. . . .

### 6

At whatever expense to their own pride, or peril to the political fortunes of Carroll, the Allens had the courage and the tenderness to attempt a reconciliation. From a letter of Houston's it appears that they approached Houston on the subject and only when rebuffed by him—"when they had lost all hopes of a reunion"[12]—had they sought to justify before the world the uncomfortable plight in which Houston's changed attitude had thrust them.

With Sam Houston in Nashville, a short thirty miles away, the family was alarmed lest she fly to him "and I would not receive her."[13] The decision of the conference, dominated, it appears, by the lieutenants of the equally anxious Carroll, was to take measures not only to avert this, but also to guard the dangerous secret that Eliza had forgiven her husband. To make matters properly secure "they sent Mrs. H. to Carthage,"[14] where her Uncle Robert, the ex-Congressman, lived.

These maneuvers were screened by an energetic thrust at Houston. On April twenty-sixth, five days after Houston's arrival in Nashville, a meeting of "citizens of Sumner County" assembled at the court-house in Gallatin. The gathering was very respectable. George S. Crockett presided, and Thomas Anderson, Esquire, was appointed secretary. Lawyer Guild explained the business before the body, which formally "Resolved, that the following gentlemen be appointed a committee to consider and draw up a report expressive of the opinion entertained of the private virtues of Mrs. Eliza H. Houston and whether her amiable character had received an injury among those acquainted with her, in consequence of the late unfortunate occurrence between her and her husband, General Samuel Houston, late Governor of Tennessee, towit: Gen. Wm Hall, Wm. L. Alexander, Esq., Gen. Eastin Morris, Col. J. C. Guild, Elijah Boddie, Esq., Col. Daniel Montgomery, Thomas Anderson, Esq., Capt. Alf. H. Douglass, Isaac Baker, Esq., Mr. Robt. M. Boyers, Maj. Charles Watkins and Joseph W. Baldridge, Esq., and that said committee meet at the Court House on Wednesday next and report."[15]

This gave the committee forty-eight hours in which to perform its delicate mission. But the work was finished on time, and at a second meeting the committee's report was read and approved. Following this a motion was adopted requesting "the editors of the State of Tennessee who feel any interest in the character of the injured female . . . to give the foregoing report and proceedings in their respective papers."[16] But not until Sam Houston had left Tennessee were editors provided with copies of the proper material.

A slight recurrence of his Indian fever detained Houston in Nashville until a fortnight after the meeting in Gallatin had adjourned sine die. He had some shadowy knowledge of what had taken place and was not impatient to know more, calling the affair an example of the political generalship of William Carroll.

On his tour of Tennessee Sam Houston had held his head high. He showed himself where it was not supposed to be safe to go. This boldness had its little victories. The threats purveyed in the nervous effort to keep Sam Houston out of Tennessee died to a murmur in the path of his progress. Despite the formal frowns of the best people, throngs surrounded him wherever he appeared.

The mother of a small boy in Knoxville said, "Now, John, do you not go near him. The people have little to do to honor such a man." The flesh is weak. Not only did John go near the notorious traveler, but he shook his hand and then ran home to confess his crime. But mother became so engrossed in the recital of her son's adventure that she forgot to punish him.[17] A little girl in Nashville "was half afraid of Cousin Sam in his strange Indian garb, and yet so strongly did he attract me that I kept very close by my mother's side that I might lose nothing he should say."[18]

Houston's friends made their usual fine display of fidelity, but the result emphasized rather than disguised the fact that the ex-Governor was an outcast where a year before he had been an idol. Still, they urged him to remain in Tennessee. He would have only to explain, to tell his side of the story in order to overthrow Carroll and win back what he had lost. The proposal met the insurmountable obstacle that had defeated Houston's friends the year before. Their man would explain nothing. Only God, he said could understand and "justify" his course.[19]

7

On the Mississippi below St. Louis Houston read in a newspaper the findings of the Sumner County citizens:

"The Committee appointed to express the sentiments of this meeting in relation to the character of Mrs. Eliza H. Houston, and the causes which led her to separate from her husband, beg leave to present that . . . very shortly after the marriage Governor Houston became jealous of his wife, and mentioned the subject to one or two persons, apparently in confidence; yet the Committee are not informed that he made any specific charges, only that he believed she was incontinent and devoid of affection . . . [for] her husband. . . . He rendered his wife unhappy by his unfounded jealousies and his repeated suspicion of her coldness and want of attachment, and she was constrained by a sense of duty to herself and her family to separate from her infatuated husband . . . since which time she has remained in a state of dejection and despondency.

"The Committee . . . are informed that Governor Houston had lately . . . returned to Nashville on his way to Arkansas where they understood he has located in the Cherokee Nation, and it has been suggested that public sympathy has been much excited in his favor, and that a belief has obtained in many places abroad that he was married to an unworthy woman, and that she has been the cause of . . . his downfall as a man and as a politician, whereas nothing is farther from the fact; and without charging him of . . . baseness of purpose, the committee have no hesitation in saying he is a deluded man; that his suspicions were groundless; that his unfortunate wife is now and ever has been in the possession of a character unimpeachable, and that she is an innocent and injured woman. . . .

"The Committee have had placed in their hands a letter from Governor Houston to his father-in-law written shortly after the separation. . . .

" 'Dear Sir— . . . Whatever had been my feelings or opinions in relation to Eliza at one period, I have been satisfied . . . and believe her virtuous, [as] I had assured her last night and this morning; this . . . should have prevented the facts from coming to your knowledge and that of your wife.

" 'I would not for millions that it had been known to you. But one human being knew anything of it from me, and that was by Eliza's consent and wish. I would have perished first; and if mortal man had dared to charge my wife or say aught against her virtue, I would have slain him.

" 'That I have and do love Eliza none can doubt and that I have ever treated her with affection she will admit; that she is the only earthly object dear to me God will bear witness. . . .

" 'Eliza stands acquitted by me. I have received her as a virtuous, chaste wife and as such I pray God I may ever regard her, and I trust I ever shall. She was cold to me, and I thought did not love me; she owns that such was one cause of my unhappiness. You can think how unhappy I was to think I was united to a woman who did not love me. That time is now past, and my future happiness can only exist in the assurance that Eliza and myself can be more happy, and that your wife and yourself will forget the past, forget all and find lost peace— and you may be assured that nothing on my part shall be wanting to restore it. Let me know what is to be done.

" 'Your most obedient
" 'SAM HOUSTON.' "[20]

Seven months later, when "my motives should have the character of reflection," Houston spread that newspaper before him and wrote a long letter. In all the years of bitterness and farce that this blighted romance engendered, this letter represents Sam Houston's solitary attempt to parry a blow:

"Cherokee Nation, Wigwam Neosho, 7th Dec. 1830
"To Genl Wm. Hall :-
"Sir—When I resigned into your hands, the office of chief magistrate of the State of Tennessee, I could not have supposed that any act of yours, or association of your name, would . . . render it necessary for me, in the vindication of my feelings and character to address you."

Ex-Governor Hall was not, however, to take this as an "unkind" reflection, and the same applied to other members of the committee, though Houston could not forbear remarking the "imposing array of Titles—as I presume to render the proceedings of the committee at a distance more weighty and Dignified." Without naming him the writer indicated William Carroll as the "*mover*" of the proceedings in which innocent men had been misled.

"The resolutions originating the committee declared in substance that the object in view, was adverse to the character of no one, but for the purpose of offering respect, and confidence where it was due. But how far . . . the proceedings . . . accord, with this declaration, I shall take leave to examine. . . .

"The committee say that 'they deem it unnecessary at this time to animadvert on *my* conduct and character, except so far as it may be inseparably connected with the investigation,' etc. Now sir, it is evident to me that this observation was not only intended as a reflection upon my general character, but was designed to acquire for the committee a reputation for . . . magnanimity; and thus decently dressed the Report and charges were to *insinuate* their way to the world. . . . It is then alleged by the committee 'that they are informed, that *I had* returned to Nashville on *my* way to Arkansas, where they *understood* I had located myself in the Cherokee Nation.' Now I readily admit the correctness of this understanding . . . why was this really made a part of the report? . . . The reason obviously was that I ought to be proscribed in society, that others (than the party concerned) might be enabled to exult . . . over the memory of an exiled man. . . .

"The report then proceeds to state 'And it has been suggested that public sympathy has been excited in his favor; and that a belief has obtained in many places abroad that he was married to an unworthy woman' etc. By whom were those suggestions made? . . . How were . . . these facts . . . ascertained? Or were they facts at all or rather were they *only suggestions* made for the purpose of furnishing a ground of accusation against me. . . . I courted the sympathy of no one. . . . I have acquiesced to my *destiny*, and have been silent."

Houston took up the letter to his father-in-law. "It seems to me to have been a favorite object with the *mover* who incited the call of the committee to give publicity" to that letter. "And however much I may regret its publication, and certainly can derive no pleasure from adverting to it," Houston begged to correct an "error."

"The committee states 'that the letter was written shortly after the separation.' This is not the truth! It was written *previous* to the separation; but as it failed in restoring harmony, the separation occurred immediately. . . . So far as the feelings of the heart are expressed in the letter I have nothing to regret. . . .

"Now, Sir, a few general reflections. . . . Was it thro' me, or by my agency, or seeking that this *private* and *domestic* circumstance was ever extended beyond the family circle? . . . No, clearly not, as my letter published by the committee shows!—Yet all the consequences resulting from the affair are perseveringly visited upon me, even in exile in the wilderness. Had a moment of public excitement produced a committee . . . there might be some excuse . . . but when a twelvemonth had passed, it seemed to be uncalled for. . . . Had the committee not attacked my reputation as I deem, improperly; but had pursued their object, the reparation of an injured Lady, and the feelings of her family, I do most solemnly assure you, sir, I would never have addressed you . . . for it is impossible for me to cherish other than . . . the sincerest wishes for their happiness."

The communication closed by giving General Hall permission "to publish this letter, that my protest may be judged as well as the report of the committee."[21]

## 8

In the Sumner County resolutions the enemies of Sam Houston for the first time offered something more palpable than whispers to define their accusations. The emphasis is not on the fact that Sam Houston had uttered an accusation, however serious, against his wife, but that he spread "abroad" his suspicions. A curious charge: uttered against a man whose attitude toward the whole question could be expressed by the one word "silence," it seemed to call for clarification.

Before the world Sam Houston at last had challenged his accusers to prove what they said. He did not stop there. He charged them with the gravest duplicity. *They* had talked.

Sam Houston's friends might have done much with the letter from the Wigwam Neosho. It supplied the long-sought fuel they required for a back-fire against the conflagration of calumny which they had never believed to arise from facts discreditable to their man. The letter was moderate. Had sensation been the writer's primary aim Houston could have achieved it in fuller measure by disclosing Eliza's actual attitude toward the chivalrous championship of her cause.

But Houston's friends could do nothing. They never saw the Wigwam Neosho letter. It had been entrusted to the wrong man. William Hall had tasted power from a ruined man's cup and had found it sweet. He was Carroll's man now, and he suppressed the letter, which if given to the world might have changed the course of a nation's history.

Houston accepted the behavior of Hall as he accepted everything concerned with the tragic romance—in silence. In the beginning he had said that if his character could not stand the shock let him lose it. He never publicly amplified that statement, except as there crept into his memoirs, published years later, an atmosphere of distrust of the white race. He had found the Caucasian's capacity for "coldness" and "treachery" superior to that of an Indian. Near the close of his stormy life, Sam Houston said he had yet to be wronged or deceived by an Indian, but that every wound he had known was the work of those of his own blood. Of the source of this disillusionment he never spoke, and the mystery of his perfect reticence cast a long shadow.

# CHAPTER XII

## THE WIGWAM NEOSHO

### 1

MAY is the radiant month on the Arkansas. Sam Houston returned more tranquil in mind, despite the incidents of his journey, than he had been since the debacle. In Washington he had gained more than he had lost. In Tennessee the very lengths to which his enemies had gone, seemed, in a sense, reassuring. At any rate The Raven appears to have recalled that in a previous existence he was a member of Andrew Jackson's literary bureau. He took up the quill again.

"The Indian of other days stood on the shore of the Atlantic. . . . He was monarch of the wilds. . . . That age has gone by—the aboriginal character is almost lost in the views of the white man. A succession of injuries has broken the proud spirit and taught him to kiss the hand which inflicts upon him stripes—to cringe and ask favors of the wretch, who violates his oath by defrauding him out of his annuities, or refusing him money promised by treaties."[1]

These lines introduced a series of articles on the Creek Indians published by the Arkansas *Gazette* of Little Rock. They were signed "Tah-lhon-tusky" and appeared currently in the same newspaper with a series on the Cherokees over the signature of "Standing Bear."

The writings of Tah-lhon-tusky and of Standing Bear are still useful to students of Indian annals. The style is more vigorous than is usual for a historian, but the substance is

148

reliable.   Not improbably was the author's form influenced by
the tenor of some examples of the art of literary criticism
as it was cultivated on that frontier.   The editor of the *Gazette*
adjudged one such item "of too personal a cast for admission
into the columns of our newspaper."   He printed it, therefore,
in a supplement which was also reserved for dueling challenges.
"The only objection . . . one can urge against this mode of
publication is the expense of printing as the circulation of the
Supplement is co-extensive with the circulation of our newspaper."

"To STANDING BEAR *alias* Gen. SAMUEL HOUSTON, Sir: I
have seen . . . a communication in the Arkansas *Gazette* . . .
[calculated] to injure the private and public character of the
late Agent of the Cherokees. . . . But, sir, you may rest
assured that the mere ridiculous, feeble and contemptible as-
severations of every *vagabond* and *fugitive* from the just indignation of an offended community . . . will neither be regarded by his friends nor credited by his enemies."   And so on
for a bristling column, after which, "without wishing, sir, to
triumph over *fallen greatness* . . . I will now bid your tur-
band honor adieu, leaving you in the enjoyment you may find
in your new matrimonial alliance, hoping your fair bride may
induce you to make a prudent husbandry of whatever resources
you may have left, awaken you to a sense of your own degrada-
tion and in the belief *'stat magni nominis umbra.'* [signed]
TEKOTKA."[2]

If such care-free use of language tried the patience of
Standing Bear he gave little sign of it in his reply, which was
rather temperate and convincing.[3]   After answering a long
train of counter-accusations, he observed that there had been
no refutation of the original charges.   The rejoinder is so
thorough as to draw attention to the single point upon which
Standing Bear had nothing to say, thus affording ground for
the inference that he intended to treat his "new matrimonial
alliance" as the private concern of himself and the fair bride
in question.

2

Tiana Rogers was a living link with Oo-loo-te-ka's island in Tennessee, where a runaway boy with a copy of the *Iliad* and a rifle had learned the meaning of love and much of the meaning of life. When life seemed without aim and without hope he had turned again to the people among whom he had experienced the greatest happiness he was ever to know. In a year he had managed to reconstruct some fragments of that earlier Elysium, which Tiana was to make the more complete.

He remembered her as a half-naked sprite not more than ten years old, a part of the vague background of the halcyon interlude on the enchanted island. She was a half-sister of The Raven's chums, John and James Rogers, her mother being Jennie Due, whereas John's and James's mother was Elizabeth Due, Jennie's stepmother. Old Headman Rogers had confined his selections of wives to one wigwam. So had John and James, barring James's earlier misadventure with Susy. Their wives were the Coody sisters, Lizzie and Nannie. Indeed, nearly every one The Raven had known in the old days—the girls to whom he had made love, the boys with whom he had roamed—had married by now, some of them rather often. But Tiana was free.

She had been married, it is true—to David Gentry, a blacksmith, and consequently a man of affairs. She was David's second wife, his first having been Mary Buffington, Tiana's aunt. David was no longer a factor, however. What had become of him I do not know: whether he had fallen in battle with the Osages, or whether he and Tiana had simply "divided the blanket." Tiana, however, was more than a mere marriageable widow of thirty about whom crept the wraith of old desires. She was tall and slender and, on testimony from impartial white sources, she was beautiful. The whites sometimes called her Diana.

Moreover, she was socially eligible to become the wife of an adopted son of the Supreme Chief. The Rogers were of distinguished tribal lineage, their name and their strain of Caucasian blood coming, by tradition, from a British officer of the Revolution. They were related to the Black Coats, the Bushy-heads, the Rattlingourds, the Little Terrapins and most of the principal families on the Arkansas, including that of Oo-loo-te-ka himself. Tiana's half-brother, Captain John, succeeded Oo-loo-te-ka as first chief, and his grandson, William Charles Rogers, was the last chief to rule the Cherokee Nation. The family is still important in eastern Oklahoma. Will Rogers, of Claremore, Oklahoma, and Beverly Hills, California, is Tiana's nephew, three generations removed.

In the summer of 1830 The Raven left his foster-father's lodge for one of his own with Tiana to cheer the hearth. Where the marriage ceremony took place, or whether there was any ceremony, is not known. Tiana was a widow and custom did not require a great to-do over a lady's second mating, which is one of the things that raises the study of Cherokee genealogy above the commonplace. But the Cherokees considered Sam Houston and Tiana Rogers to be man and wife, and this under no inability to discriminate between a marriage and a liaison.

This view, however, was not shared by the missionaries who were endeavoring to popularize "mission weddings." But the fact that Eliza Allen had declined to sanction a divorce would seem to have left the white clergy without alternative—or Houston either, for that matter. The missionaries saw many alliances' on the Arkansas in an unfavorable light, and from this view the Rogers family was not exempt. Tiana's younger sister, Susannah, attended Mr. Washburn's school at Dwight. Her classroom record terminates with this notation:

"In the summer of 1824 it seems that she had imbibed a strong attachment to a young native. . . . She tried by indirect means . . . to excite a reciprocal regard. . . . Failing in this she resorted to open and explicit means. She . . . proposed to abscond with him. . . . This proposition was rejected but in a way not to expose her folly and indelicacy. She however was so much disappointed . . . that she left the school" and "married a white man of considerable enterprise and intelligence."[4] Eighteen twenty-four was leap year.

A great many young Rogers attended the Dwight School. Cynthia, a niece of Tiana, was "active" and "amiable," but "for want of parental . . . example she was vain, giddy, fond of dress and impatient of wholesome restraints. . . . She absconded with a most worthless and abandoned white man who had another Cherokee wife." Eliza Rogers was "active in body and mind" and made "rapid improvement," which was neutralized, however, by being "exposed to the wicked example of her father's house." The Rogers had not relinquished the native religion. Betsy Rogers, another niece, was an inattentive "scholar" and "excited more mischief than all the other pupils." At the age of fifteen "she was married to a profligate and abandoned white man who came to the nation as a merchant. . . . Peace and tranquility have long ago been banished from their dwelling."[5]

But there was peace and tranquillity at the Wigwam Neosho where The Raven established his bride. This dwelling-place was near the Neosho River, a little above Cantonment Gibson, and thirty miles from the lodge of Oo-loo-te-ka. Houston bought or built a large log house and set out an apple orchard. There he lived in style, transacting his affairs and entertaining his friends. There was no concealment. Tiana was his wife, her barbaric beauty a part of the solace he had found, as he said, amid "the lights and shadows of forest life."

## 3

To the boom of the morning gun, the Stars and Stripes slid to the top of a tall sapling pole at Cantonment Gibson, and the stout gate at the terminus of the military road from Fort Smith swung open for the day. A weather-beaten sergeant took his stand by the gate, serenely conscious of his rôle as symbol of the authority of the United States. Any one failing to meet the approval of this non-commissioned officer's scrutiny entered the post under guard to explain himself at headquarters. The pathway to the squat log building that served as headquarters passed a pillory and a wooden horse, where minor culprits expiated their crimes under a blistering sun. At the doorway of headquarters a smart-looking orderly in a cavalry uniform inquired the business of callers. On the twenty-second day of July, 1830, the commandant was within. He was reading a letter.

"Colonel Arbuckle. Sir: I have the honor to inform you of the arrival of my Boat . . . with an assortment of goods which I will proceed to open and make sale of so soon as convenient. . . ." This was not news. Sam Houston had made no secret of his purpose to enter the trading business. All Three Forks had heard of that stock en route from Nashville, and of the owner's intention to sell it to the Indians at "honest" prices.

"You are the only public officer in this country to whom I will or could report, . . . Capt. Vashon [the new Cherokee agent] not having arrived. . . . My situation is peculiar and for that reason I will take pains to obviate any difficulty arising from supposed violation of the intercourse laws." Supposed violation! "I am a citizen of the Cherokee Nation and as such I do contend that the intercourse laws have no . . . bearing upon me or my circumstances." Ah!

"I ordered to this point for my own use and the convenience of my establishment, five barrels of whisky (four of Monongahela and one of corn), one barrel of cognac brandy, one of gin, one of rum and one of wine. . . . The whiskey excepting one barrel will be stored with the sutler Gen'l Jno. Nicks, subject to your orders . . . and not to be used . . . without your knowledge or consent—nor shall one drop of whiskey be sold to either soldier or Indian. . . . [because] I entertain too much respect for the wishes of the Government—second— too much friendship for the Indians and third too much respect for myself.

"So soon as my establishment is opened I will request of you that you will (if you please) direct an officer or officers to examine and see that there is a perfect agreement between my report and the stores on hand. . . . I have the honor to be . . . SAM HOUSTON."[6]

The bland presumption of his correspondent might have ruffled a man of less poise than Matthew Arbuckle. There were, as Colonel Arbuckle doubtless knew, old treaties that gave the Cherokee Indians a peculiar national status. But the Colonel's instructions had nothing to do with these treaties. After sleeping on the matter, Arbuckle forwarded Sam Houston's interesting communication to the War Department, with comment.

General Houston, he said, was jealous of his privileges as a Cherokee citizen, "and being rather impatient of restraint has on some occasions made remarks . . . which might be regarded exceptionable." Colonel Arbuckle was not an alarmist, however. He was disposed to regard Houston's indiscreet talk as "the result of momentary excitement," arising from the controversies over his Indian writings. Nevertheless the Colonel had the honor to suggest "a decision . . . with respect to the Right of Genl Houston to absolve himself from his allegiance to the United States."[7]

The War Department viewed the case in a serious light. "The right contended for by General Houston, as a citizen of the Cherokee Nation, to carry on trade with the Indians without being licensed . . . as required by the laws of the United States, would, if admitted, tend to overthrow the whole system of Indian trade as established by Congress, under the power conferr'd by the General Government by the Constitution 'to regulate trade and intercourse with the Indian Tribes.' . . . General Houston will therefore be required to give bond and obtain (as other traders have to do) a license from the Indian Agent." The government would make an important concession, however. "Indian traders are not allowed to take Spirits into the Indian Country, but . . . Genl Houston . . . may be permitted . . . to take [the nine barrels of liquor] . . . to his own residence" and keep them for his private use.⁸

Washington had spoken with firmness and courtesy. The Wigwam Neosho replied in like tone, as equal to equal. Washington's demands, Sam Houston said, had not "materially changed" his situation. He had no intention of selling liquor to Indians. But this arose from moral compunctions of his own and not from a spirit of obedience to the intercourse laws or the Constitution of the United States, as "I consider them having no kind of bearing on my case." How could they? Houston was not a citizen of the United States and had "removed without the jurisdictional limits . . . beyond the bounds of all legal process" thereof. The power of Congress to regulate trade and intercourse with Indians was designed to exclude "the influence of foreign [European] nations from among the Indians" and not to curb the legitimate rights of any tribesman.

The government's invitation to apply for a trader's license was respectfully declined. Any other course would compromise the sovereignty of the Cherokee Nation. "It would be an acknowledgement that their act of naturalization was . . . void, and that as a nation they had no rights in community, and by their boasted advantages acquired by treaty . . . had only contrived themselves in the hopeless position of vassalage. . . . With great respect I have the honor to be Your Obt. Servant."⁹

Bold words. Suppose Washington should chance to compare them with the words that the chief, Oo-loo-te-ka, had sent a trusted envoy to speak to the Georgia Cherokees. "Make a wall to the east . . . preserve the sinking race of native Americans from extinction." Comparison was possible, for by means unknown, Oo-loo-te-ka's remarkable letter had found its way into the files of the War Department. If The Raven did not propose to make a wall to the east, what did he propose?

Washington pondered the case. Secretary Eaton asked Attorney-General Berrien for a ruling in the matter, indicating the embarrassing consequences that would ensue if Houston were upheld.[10] In a lengthy opinion Mr. Berrien did as much for his Cabinet colleague as circumstances permitted. He "thought" Sam Houston's position untenable. The Cherokees enjoyed "peculiar privileges." They held their land by a title "different from the ordinary Indian title of occupancy." Nevertheless, "the grant to them is a grant of soil and not of sovereignty." Therefore, Sam Houston could not "by establishing himself within the limits of this tribe, and incorporating himself with it . . . withdraw himself from the operation of the laws of the United States."[11]

Mr. Berrien's opinion was not final, however. As he wrote, the Supreme Court of the United States was considering the identical question that Sam Houston had raised. The eastern Cherokees, fighting to retain their lands, had brought suit, as a foreign nation, against the state of Georgia. Georgia contended that the Cherokee Nation was not a foreign nation and therefore was ineligible to sue a state of the Federal Union. The decision of the Supreme Court was awaited in suspense. It was made public in January of 1831, a month after the ruling of Mr. Berrien.

The court was divided. The opinion of Justices Thompson and Story recited that as treaties never suspended empowered the Cherokees to declare war and make peace, to regulate their internal affairs and to send to Washington a "delegate" whose rank was that of an ambassador, the Cherokee Nation of Indians was sovereign and independent, and within the meaning of the Constitution, a foreign state.

This supported the logic behind the whisky maneuvers of Sam Houston. It was not, however, the prevailing opinion of the court. Chief Justice Marshall and the four remaining justices held the Cherokees to be a "domestic" and "dependent" nation, which therefore had not the right to sue the state of Georgia. This overthrew the contentions of Houston and answered the most delicate question that has been raised in the course of our Indian relations.

4

"The fruit of this world turns to ashes and the charm of life is broken," wrote Sam Houston.[12] The days of tranquillity at the woodland wigwam were at an end. The year of 1831 saw the nadir of Houston's fortunes. The sustaining passion for activity that lifted him out of himself during his first months in the Indian country had failed. In his own words he "buried his sorrows in the flowing bowl . . . gave himself up to the fatal enchantress" alcohol.[13] The eagle's wings had drooped.

The Cherokees conferred a new name on their white counselor—Oo-tse-tee Ar-dee-tah-skee, which means Big Drunk.[14] When Big Drunk was in character a retinue of loyal Cherokees would follow him about to forestall complications, but not always with success. A young white clerk at Houston's trading-post displeased his employer and was challenged to a duel. Friends of Houston protested that the clerk's social station precluded him from participation in an affair of honor.

"I've always treated him as a gentleman," roared Houston, "and I'll treat him as a gentleman now."

This improved the morale of the clerk. He was ready to fight.

The meeting took place, and at the count both parties fired. Neither was hit, and seconds intervening persuaded challenger and challenged that honor had been vindicated. But Houston did not learn for some time afterward, if ever, that neither weapon was charged with ball ammunition.

On another occasion Houston quarreled with his foster-father and struck the old man. Others who were near attempted to seize The Raven and succeeded only after they had pummeled him unconscious. The old Chief was greatly distressed over the necessity of this extremity and bathed his errant son's bruises. Overwhelmed by remorse The Raven made a formal apology before the National Council.[15]

Whether Sam Houston complied with the War Department

order, the constitutionality of which the Supreme Court's decision upheld, to apply for a trader's license, is disclosed in no record discovered by this writer. The presumption is that he did—not that it matters. When Sam Houston alluded, as he often did, to the government's special use of the waters of destruction as an aid to negotiation with Indians, he spoke, in a measure, from close experience. Taking a base view of the matter, what better disposition could the Government have made of those nine barrels of liquor than to let Sam Houston take them home and drink them up?

His Indian writings lost coherency in a purple haze of controversy in which the author was displayed as "a *Greeneyed monster* . . . a slanderer of man and deceiver of woman" who "opposed the views of the United States" and fomented "discord" among the tribes "by speaking disrespectfully of their Agents."[16] Houston being on the unpopular side of the Indian question, eastern papers copied more of this sort of thing than of the embarrassing accusations they were designed to refute. His influence over the Indians wavered and some practical jokers among the Cherokees led to his place in the council house at Tah-lon-tee-skee a grotesquely painted negro tricked out in exaggerated imitation of The Raven's style of dress.

The year was a blurred gyration from place to place, from scheme to scheme. For some time Houston had been involved in a deal to purchase a salt works on the Neosho with the idea of making a million dollars. This blended into a reckless impulse to reclaim the reins of political power in Tennessee, entailing a foolhardy trip to Nashville, a ridiculous letter to the newspapers[17] and a painful time for Houston's friends. A permanent result of the visit was a portrait for which Houston posed as Marius amid the ruins of Carthage. This smashing Old Hickory of the Romans had always appealed to Houston, and I hope it is not too much to fancy the possible inspiration of the painting: Houston in the wilderness approached, like Marius by the lieutenant of Sextilius, and making answer, **"Go** tell that you have seen Caius Marius sitting in exile among the ruins of Carthage!"

Leaving Tennessee, "through with civilization forever," the unhappy man paused at Fort Smith to dicker with a whisky runner in broken English and then to plunge dangerously into Indian politics. The National Council of the Cherokees ratified the grant of citizenship previously bestowed by a special committee. There was a new gesture toward the West smacking of Oo-loo-te-ka's earlier visions of empire. Houston projected a trip to the plains with Chouteau to cultivate friendly relations with the wild tribes. This proposal faded in favor of a private expedition to the Rocky Mountains.

The Rocky Mountain project was something that recurred and recurred. Houston loved to talk about it. Two years before this talk had thrilled the Irish adventurer, Haralson. Half-breed Watt Webber was next to fall under the spell. He began accumulating capital for the trip. At present Houston had an appreciative listener in Captain Bonneville of the Cantonment Gibson garrison. Benjamin Louis Eulalie de Bonneville was born in France during the Terror and had been private secretary to the Marquis de Lafayette during his second visit to the United States. A shelf of Latin and Greek, the plays of Racine and poems of Maître François Villon lined a wall of his cabin in Officer's Row. Bonneville had long yearned to explore the Far West. Between the classics, the Rocky Mountain scheme and a bottle on the table, Houston and the vibrant baldheaded little Frenchman would talk all night.[18]

Schemes, dreams, fancies, phantoms. . . . There was another recurring vision about which Sam Houston dared not speak too much: Texas. The very necessity for discretion may explain the vitality of any fragment of rumor touching Texas. The thing was intangible, but it was there. It formed the most seductive part of the aura of romance and enigma that overhung the exile and kept people juggling with his name from the Back Bay of Boston to the camps by the Rio de los Brazos de Dios.

Sam Houston's passion for justice burned as fiercely as ever. Few men did more to subvert his plans than Colonel Arbuckle and Captain Vashon, yet no criticism of either ever passed Houston's lips, because he knew them to be honorable men and honest public servants. The same passion inspired his impulsive efforts in behalf of proud old Nathaniel Pryor, of the Three Forks, a first cousin of the Governor of Virginia. During the final stages of Houston's effort to force recognition of Cherokee sovereignty, he was urging at the same time the appointment of Captain Pryor to the Indian service when such an appointment would surely raise another obstacle to any attempt to diminish the government's authority among the Indians. But he knew Pryor to be a deserving man who would treat the Indians decently.

"It is impossible for me," Houston wrote Secretary Eaton, "ever to wish, or solicit, any patronage from the Government for myself, or anyone connected with me—but to see a *brave, honest, honorable* and *faithful servant* of that *country, which I once claimed as my own—in poverty with spirit half broken by neglect I must be permitted to ask something in his behalf!*"[19] He also wrote to Jackson setting forth Pryor's unique qualifications, and induced Arbuckle to write. Pryor received a five-hundred-dollar-a-year place, but died shortly afterward.

Sam Houston's enemies were never quite sure where they stood. The man was inconsistent: consider his refusal to drink with an Indian and his opposition to the Cherokee ball plays, which had become orgies of Roman proportions. Big Drunk went on his toots alone, or at Cantonment Gibson where he was always welcome at the bachelor officers' mess. Old accounts tell of casual strollers along the paths about the post stepping aside to avoid the buckskin-clad form of the squaw-man unconscious among tree-stumps.

With his visible fortunes at their lowest ebb, friends remained who were loyal and enemies who were afraid of Sam Houston. Officers' wives still lingered at their calico-curtained windows for a glimpse of the solitary figure whose tremendous downfall had been encompassed by a love-affair, of which, in all his rambling talk, he never spoke. They saw him lost in the contemplation of a little buckskin sack that was suspended by a thong about his neck. Mumbling to a Cherokee witch charm! A natural error, perhaps; but in reality the little sack contained Eliza Allen's engagement ring. The Raven avoided the society of the officers' ladies, but eyes no less wistful on that account strained to follow the dimmed star of an unfortunate gentleman.

## 5

In August of the dark year a letter from Tennessee was delivered at the Wigwam Neosho. In September Sam Houston climbed the slope of Baker's Creek Valley in Blount County to the porticoed house on the hillside. There he wept at the bedside of a "heroine," his mother. Elizabeth Houston pressed the hand that wore another ring, with a motto in it. And then she died.

In October Sam Houston was back at the Wigwam. In November he sat with the National Council of the Cherokees. In December he was on his way east again. A change had come over The Raven. There are times when a man must stand up.

# CHAPTER XIII

## A Hickory Cane

### 1

Black Coat, the second Chief, was in charge of the Cherokee delegation with which Sam Houston departed for Washington in December of 1831. Although Houston was not
officially a member of the mission, the delegates' instructions
and the petition they carried "To Andrew Jackson, Great
Father" were in his handwriting. The latter conveyed a recital of grievances, with a paragraph tucked in to regularize
a considerable purchase of land Houston had made from
"Chouteau's half-breed Indian bastard children," as Agent
Vashon phrased it, disliking ambiguities.[1]

For the journey the venerable Creek Chief, Opoth-ley-ahola,
gave Houston a handsome buckskin coat with a beaver collar
and a hunting knife to adorn the belt. The travelers stopped
off at Nashville and Houston showed them through the Hermitage. While inspecting the grounds he used the new knife
to cut a hickory sapling about as big around as a man's thumb
and fashion himself a walking cane. The party reached Washington in January of 1832 and accommodated themselves at
Brown's Indian Queen Hotel in Pennsylvania Avenue. A few
days later Houston gave the cane to a friend in Georgetown.

There had been changes in Washington since Houston's
last visit. Peggy Eaton was not in town and the place was
duller for it. She was in Florida where her husband, by grace
of Andrew Jackson, was governor. Echoes of the piquant

162

Peg's political disturbances still resounded in the marble halls, however, as on March 31, 1832, when William Stanbery, Member of Congress from Ohio, in the course of a broad criticism of the Administration, inquired, "Was not the late Secretary of War removed because of his attempt fraudulently to give Governor Houston the contract for Indian rations?"[2]

The words of Mr. Stanbery brought Houston to the foyer of the House chamber determined to "settle" the matter there, but James K. Polk hustled him out into the fresh air. Houston then sent Representative Cave Johnson, of Tennessee, to Stanbery with a note containing the formal inquiries that etiquette required to precede a challenge to a duel. Johnson was made to promise, however, that should Stanbery refuse to receive the note he would not assume the quarrel himself. Stanbery declined to reply to "a note signed Sam Houston." "I'll introduce myself to the damned rascal," said Houston. Mr. Stanbery armed himself with two pistols. Houston put away his evil-looking knife and asked his Georgetown friend if he could take back the cane for a few days.

**2**

On the evening of April thirteenth Houston, Senator Buck- ner, of Missouri, and Representative Blair, of Tennessee, were chatting with Senator Felix Grundy in the latter's room. Houston took his leave, and Buckner and Blair joined him in a walk along the Avenue. The three had covered about half the distance to Brown's Hotel when Blair recognized Congressman Stanbery crossing the street. Whereupon, Mr. Blair turned and walked "rapidly" away.

It was dark, except for the dim street-lamps. Houston approached the man in the street. "Are you Mr. Stanbery?" he asked politely.

"Yes, sir," replied the latter.

"Then you are a damned rascal," exclaimed Houston, slamming the Ohioan on the head with the hickory cane.

Stanbery was almost as large a man as Houston. He threw up his hands. "Oh, don't!" he cried, but Houston continued to rain blows and Stanbery turned, as Senator Buckner thought, to run. Houston leaped on his opponent's back and dragged him down. The two rolled on the pavement, Stanbery yelling for help. Houston could not hold and punch at the same time, his right arm having been useless in such emergencies since the battle of To-ho-pe-ka. Stanbery managed to draw one of his pistols. He pressed it against Houston's chest.

Buckner heard the gunlock snap, saw the flint strike fire. But the charge did not explode, and Houston tore the weapon from Stanbery's grasp. Houston then stood up, landed a few more licks with the cane and, as a finishing touch, lifted the Congressman's feet in the air and "*struck him elsewhere*," as Senator Buckner rendered it in his evidence at Houston's trial, ladies being present.

## MOST DARING OUTRAGE AND ASSAULT

was the head-line in General Duff Green's *United States Telegraph*, followed by brutal details. But the article wound up with observations which Houston himself could hardly have improved upon.

"What gives more importance to this transaction is the known relation that Houston bears to the President of the United States. . . . He was the individual who placed in the hands of General Jackson Mr. Monroe's letter to Mr. Calhoun that made so important a part of 'the correspondence' between the President and Vice President. Although he left Tennessee under circumstances that produced the greatest excitement, took up his residence among the Indians and adopted their costume and habits; and although the proof that he contemplated a fraud upon the government is conclusive, yet . . . he is still received at the Executive Mansion and treated with the kindness and hospitality of an old favorite. . . . We have long seen, that tactics of the Nashville school were to be transferred to Washington and that the voice of truth was to be silenced by the dread of the assassin But we have not yet taken fear as our counsellor."[3]

After this, further reference to a hickory cane cut at the Hermitage was labor of supererogation. General Green, with his powerful newspaper, had quit the Jackson entourage with Mr. Calhoun. Bursting to even the score, he raised the trouncing of Stanbery greatly above the altitude of a common brawl.

## 3

From his bed Mr. Stanbery dispatched a note to Andrew Stevenson, the Speaker of the House, describing how he had been "waylaid in the street . . . attacked, knocked down by a bludgeon and severely bruised and wounded by Samuel Houston, late of Tennessee, for words spoken in my place in the House of Representatives." This was read to the House, and a resolution was offered for the arrest of Houston.

This parliamentary move brought to his feet James K. Polk, the President's voice in the House of Representatives. Mr. Polk would not admit that the House had the power to arrest Sam Houston in the matter involved, but the vote was one hundred and forty-five to twenty-five for arrest.

On the following day the galleries were crowded and every member was in his seat when the prisoner, wearing his fur-collared buckskin coat and carrying his stick of Hermitage hickory, walked down the aisle of the House chamber beside the sergeant-of-arms. He halted before the Speaker's desk and bowed. Speaker Stevenson, a friend of the accused, read the formal arraignment. Houston asked for twenty-four hours in which to prepare his defense. He was granted forty-eight hours.

Houston reappeared with Francis Scott Key as his attorney, although the defendant virtually conducted his own case. Asked to plead to a charge of assaulting Representative Stanbery for words spoken in debate, Houston said he had not molested Mr. Stanbery for words spoken in the House, but for remarks imputed to Mr. Stanbery by a newspaper. After vainly trying to get Mr. Stanbery to disavow or affirm the published statements, Houston added that on an "accidental" meeting he had given way to his feelings and struck the Congressman with "a common walking cane." This was interpreted as a plea of not guilty and the trial of Sam Houston before the bar of the House of Representatives was set to begin on April nineteenth.

It continued for a month, growing in public interest until everything else in the current news was eclipsed. *Niles' Register*, of Baltimore, which prided itself on its reports of the proceedings of Congress, fell days behind on the regular doings of the Senate and the House, so great was the space required to report the Houston trial. The *Register* was moved to deprecate a public taste so thirsty for details of this raffish proceeding.

4

Mr. Stanbery was the first witness. The bumps on his countenance were Exhibit A. Houston conducted the cross-examination, opening with the statement that the witness had made an accusation of fraud.

"Had you then or have you now," he asked, "any and what evidence of the correctness of such imputation?"

Several of Stanbery's friends objected to the question. Mr. Polk demanded an answer. By a vote of one hundred and one to eighty-two the House ordered Mr. Stanbery to reply.

"It was no part of my intention," he said, "to impute fraud to General Houston."

Senator Buckner told of the encounter as he had witnessed it. Mr. Stanbery characterized the Senator's testimony as "destitute of truth and infamous," but withdrew the statement and apologized. The now celebrated cane was exhibited, hefted and passed from hand to hand. The defense showed that Mr. Stanbery had carried a pistol and had tried to shoot Houston, but the weapon was not introduced in evidence. The cane held the stage, unchallenged by any rival attraction.

On April twenty-sixth Mr. Key made the opening address for the defense. There was little in it to suggest the author of *The Star Spangled Banner*. He undertook to establish that Houston had not struck Stanbery for words spoken in debate but for words printed in a newspaper. The weak spot in this contention was that the words printed in the paper were a verbatim report of the debate. When he concluded, his client's chances of escaping conviction appeared to be rather slim.

This state of affairs distressed Andrew Jackson, and he sent for Houston. Speaking of it afterward, Sam Houston declared that he had never seen Jackson in such a temper. Houston was wearing the buckskin coat. The President asked if he had any other clothes. Houston said he had not, and Jackson tossed a clinking silk purse to his caller with the advice to dress like a gentleman and buck up his defense.[4] Houston went to a tailor and was measured for "a coat of the finest material, reaching to my knees, trousers in harmony of color and the latest style in cut, with a white satin vest to match."[5]

On the afternoon of May sixth Houston was notified that the defense would be required to close its case on the following day. That night a number of friends dropped into his room at Brown's Hotel. "Gentlemen," Houston is quoted as saying in a reminiscence of the occasion, "we sat late and you may judge how we drank when I tell you that Stevenson [the Speaker of the House, and presiding officer of the trial] at midnight was sleeping on the lounge. Bailey Peyton was out of commission and had gone to his room and Felix Grundy had ceased to be interesting. Polk rarely indulged and left us early."[6]

Houston awoke with a headache. "I took a cup of coffee but it refused to stick." A second cup behaved no better. "After something like an hour had passed I took another cup and it stuck, and I said, 'I am all right' and proceeded to array myself in my splendid apparel."[7]

5

Above the stately entrance to the chamber of the House stood a representation of History, a comely, though alert, young woman, by the hand of an Italian sculptor. Light draperies floated about her. On one knee she balanced a ledger, and gracefully exhibited a pen in perfect readiness to record whatever of interest that should take place within her view. A wheel of the chariot in which she rode served as the face of the clock of the House.

The draped dais of the Speaker faced the clock. At the hour of noon Mr. Stevenson called the House to order. The scene before him was notable. The hall was a noble adaptation of the Greek theater pattern. Shafts of sunlight descended from a glassed dome sixty feet, at its highest point, from the floor. Beneath a sweeping arch at the Speaker's back was a figure of Liberty at whose feet a marble eagle spread its wings for flight. On either side were flag-draped panels, one hung with a portrait of Washington, one with a likeness of Lafayette.

Every seat on the floor was filled and chairs had been placed in the aisles to accommodate the privileged overflow. A solid bank of men pressed against the colonnaded semicircle of wall. For two hours there had been no room in the galleries, where the diplomatic corps, gay with ribbons, the Army, the Navy and Society were authentically represented.

In front of the Speaker's dais the prisoner bowed to his guest of the evening before.

"Mr. Speaker," he said. The tone was one of ordinary conversation, but Houston's rich warm voice reached every part of the chamber. "Mr. Speaker, arraigned for the first time of my life on a charge of violating the laws of my country I feel all that embarrassment which my peculiar situation is calculated to inspire." Houston's perfect composure made this a gracious beginning.

"I disclaim, utterly, every motive unworthy of an honorable man." The tone was suddenly infused with passionate earnestness. If, when "deeply wronged," he had on "impulse" violated the laws of his country or trespassed the prerogatives of the House, he was "willing to be held to my responsibility. All I demand is that my actions may be pursued to the motives which gave them birth."

He stood before the House, he said, branded as "a man of broken fortune and blasted reputation." "I can never forget that reputation, however limited, is the high boon of heaven. . . . Though the plowshare of ruin has been driven over me and laid waste to my brightest hopes . . . I have only to say . . .

> " 'I seek no sympathies, nor need;
> The thorns which I have reaped are of the tree
> I planted; they have torn me and I bleed.' "

It was very effective. The galleries applauded, and as Houston awaited an opportunity to resume, a bouquet of flowers dropped at his feet. A woman's voice was heard above the hum:

"I had rather be Sam Houston in a dungeon than Stanbery on a throne!"[8]

Amid perfect silence Houston picked up the flowers. He bowed over them but did not raise his eyes.

Houston spoke for half an hour on the perils of legislative tyranny. He mentioned Greece and Rome. The errors of Cæsar, of Cromwell, of Bonaparte and of "the Autocrat of all the Russias" were displayed. Blackstone and the Apostle Paul were shown to be on the speaker's side. A well-turned period was closed with a quotation nine lines in length, beginning:

> "There is a proud, undying thought in man
> That bids his soul still upward look. . . ."

From this premise the speaker moved dexterously to the corollary that he had committed no offense for which the Congress could punish him without invading the private rights of a citizen.

Houston paused. His glance met the glance of History, then shifted to the flag that draped the portrait of Lafayette.

"So long as that proud emblem . . . shall wave in the Hall of American legislators, so long shall it cast its sacred protection over the personal rights of every American citizen. Sir, when you shall have destroyed the pride of American character, you will have destroyed the brightest jewel that heaven ever made. You will have drained the purest and holiest drop which visits the hearts of your sages in council and heroes in the field and . . . these massy columns, with yonder lofty dome will sink into one crumbling ruin. . . . But, Sir, so long as that flag shall bear aloft its glittering stars . . . so long I trust, shall the rights of American citizens be preserved safe and unimpaired—till discord shall wreck the spheres—the grand march of time shall cease—and not one fragment of all creation be left to chafe the bosom of eternity's waves."

That was all. Whether Francis Scott Key, who sat in the front row, felt like disowning certain feeble lines of his own, inspired by the bombardment of Fort McHenry, is a detail upon which history is remiss. But Junius Brutus Booth plowed through the crowd and embraced his old friend.

"Houston, take my laurels!"⁹

### 6

As soon as Speaker Stevenson could restore order, Mr. Harper, of New Hampshire, was recognized. He made a motion.

"*Resolved*, that Samuel Houston now in custody of the Sergeant-of-Arms, should forthwith be discharged."

Mr. Huntington, of Connecticut, was recognized. He desired to amend the motion of Mr. Harper by striking out all but the word "Resolved" and substituting the following:

"That Samuel Houston has been guilty of a contempt in violation of the privileges of this House."

The amendment was debated for four days. Mr. Polk contested every inch of the ground, but the House at length tired of the entertainment and voted one hundred and six to eighty-nine that Houston was guilty. He was sentenced to be reprimanded by the Speaker. The Stanbery wing sought to deprive Houston of the privilege of the floor of the House which he enjoyed as a former member of that body, but Polk struck back and defeated this, one hundred and one to ninety.

The reprimand took place on May fourteenth. Again the galleries were thronged and the aisles packed. Again Houston, the picture of composure, bowed before the Speaker, who bowed back, and began his unwelcome duty. He opened by alluding to the "character and the intelligence" of the accused "who has himself been honored with a seat in this House." "I forbear to say more," concluded Mr. Stevenson, "than to pronounce the judgement of the House, which is that you . . . be reprimanded at this bar by the Speaker, and . . . I do reprimand you accordingly."

But Mr. Stanbery was now showing more fight than he had that evening on Pennsylvania Avenue. He had Houston arrested on a criminal warrant charging assault. Further, he obtained a House investigation of the rations contract maneuvers of 1830. A jury convicted Houston of assault and he was fined five hundred dollars, but for some reason the trial attracted next to no attention. Duff Green seems to have been saving his thunder for the ration investigation which became another national spectacle. Green was so certain that Houston would be convicted of fraud that he announced his guilt in advance.

That was an era of latitude for the press. When Duff Green broke with Jackson, the President needing an organ in Washington, had induced Francis P. Blair to start the *Globe*. Blair was a westerner of the Jackson-Houston stamp in the matter of personal loyalties. His big house near the Executive Mansion was a haven of refuge for an old soldier in ill health, very weary, and at times as near dejection as one of Jackson's unconquerable spirit could be. The President would escape to "Blaar's," as he said it, in the broad North-of-Ireland way, slump into a big chair and smoke his pipe in peace. The *Globe* leaped to Houston's defense in the ration issue, and Andrew Jackson, busy as he was, found time to inspire Frank Blair's blunt pen.

The investigation was conducted by a committee of seven, of which Mr. Stanbery was the chairman. Houston conducted his own defense. The hearings were long drawn out. Stanbery was not impartial. There were many witnesses, some like Auguste Chouteau, from great distances. Duff Green was a tame witness. Houston practically ruined his testimony by a cross-examination conducted with Chesterfieldian courtesy. The evidence showed that Houston was the favored bidder of Eaton and Jackson, and only a failure of plans had prevented his obtaining the ration contract by secretive means and at enormous profit—perhaps aggregating a million dollars. Even so, the government would have saved money, and motives of envy, not patriotism, had kept the contract from Houston. After six weeks the committee reported by a divided vote that "John H. Eaton and Samuel Houston do stand entirely acquitted from all imputation of fraud."[10]

## 7

These triumphs were far-reaching. They stripped The Raven of his beads and blanket. They buried Big Drunk. They resurrected Sam Houston who passionately embraced as "my country" the land he had so bitterly repudiated only a few months before. Once more he was in the train of the eagle.

Houston understood what had happen'd. Reviewing the Stanbery episode in after-life he said: "I was dying out and had they taken me before a justice of peace and fined me ten dollars it would have killed me; but they gave me a national tribunal for a theatre, and that set me up again."[11]

No one was more pleased to see Sam Houston set up again

than Andrew Jackson. Houston was his friend. He was another good man to use, and what President ever had enough good men? The old intimacy was restored, it was like bygone times. We have the spiteful testimony of Duff Green that Houston practically lived at the Executive Mansion.

Sam Houston was always giving presents. Poor Aunt Rachel must have had a drawerful of such remembrances. The mistress of the President's House at this period was Sarah York Jackson, wife of Andrew Jackson, Jr., the Executive's adopted son. Sam gave her Eliza Allen's engagement ring.[12] From his discarded Indian wardrobe, he presented the President with an elaborate Cherokee ceremonial costume. Jackson had it among his trophies at the Hermitage when he died.

Like old times, indeed: Sam Houston one of the family—a renaissance of the days when this obedient servant traded horses, held offices and fought a duel for Andrew Jackson. His first thought, his constant thought, was to atone for the period of his delinquency. He would do something grand. He would capture an empire and lay it at his old Chieftain's feet—Texas, or the New Estremadura, as Houston used to say when his poetic fancy was on the wing.

# CHAPTER XIV

## THE MUDDIER RUBICON

### 1

THE thought of delivering the New Estremadura was not new with General Houston. For more than four years the refugee had been a factor in the complex Texas question, which one way or another had rippled the waters of our foreign policy since the Louisiana Purchase. One of the principal factors in keeping the question alive was Andrew Jackson, who felt a personal responsibility in the matter.

Our claim to Texas assumed this vast and vague region to be a part of Louisiana, but the authority of the assertion had been impaired by Mr. Monroe who had disavowed it to placate Spain during the rumpus following Jackson's seizure of Florida. Jackson had concurred in the repudiation, only to regret it and regard Texas as much the rightful prize of the United States as Florida. Before a year had elapsed after the renunciation, James Long, an ex-Army surgeon under Jackson, lost his life in an attempt to restore the province by means of a handful of armed adventurers.

Mexico then won its independence of Spain and inaugurated a new policy in Texas. Spain had prohibited immigration except by Spaniards. This kept Texas virtually depopulated, which Spain believed to be a protection to the northern frontier of Mexico. But that extraordinary rover, Moses Austin, by nerve and luck obtained permission to move into Texas with three hundred American families. Then Austin died and Spain was overthrown in Mexico. Stephen F. Austin took over his father's work. The Mexican Republic validated the grant and invited other settlers on attractive terms. A tide of immigration followed and by 1832 the white population of Texas had grown to twenty thousand, frontier Americans predominating. Austin had become a loyal citizen of his adopted country. This was not true of many others, however, who carried to Texas the definite idea of bringing it under United States sovereignty.

The significance of this trend was not lost on Washington. Mr. Adams asked Andrew Jackson to be the first minister of the United States to the Mexican Republic. He declined, and Joel R. Poinsett went to Mexico City, shortly to receive instructions to ask Mexico to accept the Rio Grande as the frontier. The startled Mexicans refused. Poinsett was asked to restate the offer with a cash inducement of a million dollars, but, feeling that this would only further antagonize Mexico, he declined to do so. On the other hand, he concluded a treaty in which the Sabine River was declared to be the boundary. Jackson saw Texas slipping from our grasp, and his irritation increased.

Becoming president, Jackson shelved the Poinsett agreement, which the Senate had not ratified, and reopened negotiations for the Rio Grande boundary. He was willing to pay five million dollars. Poinsett was replaced by a personal friend of Jackson, Anthony Butler. Butler tried to bribe the Mexican officials whose sanction was necessary to the relinquishment of Texas. His methods, lacking finesse, only served to throw Mexico into a state of alarm. The colonization laws were amended and eventually revoked to choke off emigration to Texas. Outcry against the acquisition of Texas also went up from free-soil New England which feared an increase of power to the slaveholding South, and Europe took notice: all very annoying to Andrew Jackson.

Into this darkening picture had plunged Sam Houston, trained in the Jackson school: Texas was ours—we were destiny-bound to bring it under the flag. When the spectacular ruin of his fortunes sent the ex-Governor storming southwestward, Texas, and not the Indian country or the Rocky Mountains, was the goal Sam Houston had in his mind. It was Jackson who changed these plans.

**2**

Houston had scarcely arrived in the Cherokee country when the President received word of his intentions. This came from Duff Green, moved by a sincere wish to discredit Houston. Green showed Jackson a letter from Congressman Marable, quoting Houston as saying that he intended to "conquer Mexico or Texas, and be worth two millions in two years." This came at a moment when Jackson was anxious to preserve an appearance of respect for Mexican sovereignty. The President believed the story that Houston had told Marable to be "efusions of a distempered brain," but he took no chances. "As a precautionary measure I directed the Secretary of War to write and enclose Mr. Pope, Govr of Arkansas, the extract [of Marable's letter to Green] and instruct him if such illegal project should be discovered to exist to adopt prompt measures to put it down and give the government the earliest intelligence of such illegal enterprise with the names of all concerned therein."[1]

Sam Houston entered the Indian country under surveillance, and his mail was intercepted and read. But Jackson was frank enough to write him a long letter. "When I parted with you on the 18th of January last . . . I then viewed you as on the brink of happiness and rejoiced. About to be united in marriage to a beautiful young lady, of accomplished manners, and respectable connections, & of your own selection—you the Governor of the State and holding the affections of the people—these were your prospects when I shook you by the hand and bade you farewell. You may well judge my astonishment and grief in receiving a letter from you dated Little Rock, A. T.

conveying the sad intellegence that you were then . . . an exile from, your country."

These lines were well calculated to soothe the torn heart of the fugitive, who surmised the sort of stories his enemies had carried to Jackson. Houston read on. "It has been communicated to me that you had the illegal enterprise in view of conquering Texas; that you had declared that you would, in less than two years, be emperor of that country by conquest. I must really have thought you deranged to have believed you had so wild a scheme in contemplation, and particularly when it was communicated that the physical force to be employed was the Cherokee Indians. Indeed, my dear Sir, I cannot believe you have any such chimerical visionary scheme in view. Your pledge of honor to the contrary is a sufficient guarantee that you will never engage in any enterprise injurious to your country that would tarnish your fame."[2]

The pledge was given, and honor was not a word that Sam Houston used lightly.[3] Consequently, letters like this, from John Wharton, of Nashville, could receive no satisfactory answer: "I have heard you intended an expedition against Texas. I suppose, if it is true, you will let your Nashville friends know of it."[4] Houston's silence seems to have puzzled Wharton, who went to Texas on his own account, writing again in October: "I . . . request you once more to visit Texas. It is a fine field for enterprise. You can get a grant of land, be surrounded by your friends, and what may not the coming of time bring about?"[5]

Sam Houston was as anxious as any one to know what time might bring about, but for the present he could only plan vaguely in the hope that time would induce Jackson to release him from his vow. Jackson appreciated Houston's disappointment and tried to divert his friend with the suggestion that he enter public life in Arkansas under the Jacksonian ægis. This Houston declined, but he considered, for a time, settling in Natchez, Mississippi, another good jumping-off place. Meantime, however, the web of Indian affairs caught him up and began to lead him along strange paths.  But Texas was never long out of his thoughts.

### 3

When Houston's first visit to Washington from the Indian country precipitated the rations controversy, the Cherokee envoy unburdened himself concerning another matter to Dr. Robert Mayo, a Jackson admirer and fellow-lodger at Brown's Hotel.  Some months later, while the Administration was wrestling with the whisky issue by which Sam Houston had raised the question of Cherokee sovereignty, Doctor Mayo unburdened himself to Jackson.  The President requested Mayo to put his story in writing, which he did in a letter dated December 2, 1830.

"Sometime in the month of February last . . . very shortly after General Samuel Houston arrived in this city, I was introduced to him at Brown's Hotel.  Our rooms were on the same floor and convenient for social intercourse; which, from the General's courteous manners, and my own desire to . . . do him justice in my own estimation relative to his abandoning his family and abdicating the government of Tennessee, readily became intimate. . . . He discanted on the immense fields for enterprise in the Indian settlement, in Texas; and recommended me to direct my destinies that way. . . . I had a curiosity now on tiptoe, to hear his romantic projections, for his manner and his enthusiasm were at least entertaining. . . . I learnt these facts and speculations, viz:

"That he was organizing an expedition against Texas; to afford a cloak to which he had assumed the Indian costume, habits and associations, by settling among them in the neighborhood of Texas.  That nothing was more easy to accomplish than the conquest and possession of that extensive and fertile country, [and] by the cooperation of the Indians in the Arkansas Territory and recruits among the citizens of the United States . . . [form] a separate and independent government. . . . That the event of success opened the most unbounded prospects of wealth and that . . . I should have a surgeoncy in the expedition, and he recommended me in the meantime, to remove along with him and practice physic among the Indians. . . .

"I declined . . . and . . . after this our interviews fell into neglect. . . . In the month of March [1830] Gen'l Houston visited Baltimore, Philadelphia and New York, and did intend to have gone as far as Boston. . . .

"Sometime in the month of June . . . I met a young gentleman . . . by the name of Murray, from Tennessee . . . [who] readily confirmed . . . as a thing of common rumor . . . that the general was organizing an expedition to take possession of Texas. . . .

"A few weeks ago a Mr. Hunter, lately dismissed from West Point, came to take lodgings in the house where I boarded. . . . Being in pecuniary embarrassments and unable to redeem his baggage . . . he fell to boasting of the funds he was daily expecting by the mail. . . . But, says he, all that is nothing to the unbounded prospects I have of wealth in the future. Indeed! I said, how is it that you can engender wealth? . . . Ah, says he, that is a secret. I will lay my life, said I, that it is a scheme upon Texas. He, hesitatingly, said, yes, something like it. And said I, General Houston is the projector and conductor of the enterprise? At this he was . . . impressed with the conviction that I knew all . . . and . . . set in to . . . writing my name on the table in cipher . . . and wrote the scheme [of the cipher] here enclosed."

Mr. Hunter further claimed to be "a bona fide agent of the recruiting service for this district; and that there were agencies established in all the principal towns, and various parts of the United States; and that occult code exhibited was the means of correspondence. That several thousand had already enlisted along the seaboard from New England to Georgia, inclusive. That each man had paid thirty dollars to the common fund, and took an oath of secrecy. . . . That they were to repair . . . as travellers to different points on the banks of the Mississippi, where they had already chartered steamboats."[6]

The credibility of Doctor Mayo has been assailed on the ground that he was a tale-bearing busybody, hostile to Jackson.

These criticisms are somewhat true, but the hostility came later, and has no bearing on his letter. Mayo may have been gullible and he may have stretched things a bit, but circumstances impel the conclusion that he reported with fair accuracy what he had heard. He expected a sweeping official investigation of his story, and was chagrined because Jackson did not order one. Barring the cipher, the essential details of the plotting as pictured by Doctor Mayo are supported by other evidence, as well as by the facts of the Texas drama, as they presently were to unfold themselves. Jackson himself, knowing all that he did of the Texas question, was sufficiently impressed to pass the Mayo story on to the authorities in Arkansas with instructions to maintain with "utmost secrecy" a fresh lookout over Houston's movements.

4

The discreet Houston did nothing to bring about an intervention of the spying officials. Rumors of his Texas conspiracy did not die, however. They were much alive in the Indian country, in the United States and in Texas as well, where it was understood that the exile was in communication with a young lawyer named William Barret Travis, who had brought with him from Georgia some forward ideas touching the future of northeastern Mexico.

Jackson pressed his purchase negotiations as hard as he dared, and Houston kept his word not to disturb the deep waters of diplomacy. So far so good, except that Butler's efforts at purchase exhibited slight prospects of success and presently Sam Houston was off on another tangent. His seemingly sudden notions of the sanctity of Cherokee sovereignty gave the Administration an amount of concern. In this instance also, Sam Houston took his medicine like a good Jackson subaltern, and there followed a period of comparative quiet on the Potomac, while on the Arkansas Houston was too greatly disconcerted by "the flowing bowl" for the critical application necessary to the execution of any settled plan. Shocked out of this hiatus by the death of his mother, Sam Houston burst upon Washington and lost no time proving that his genius for the spotlight retained its fine edge. The pummeling of Stanbery reestablished Sam Houston as a national figure and a trusted friend of the President. It was the springboard for his long-postponed leap to Texas.

The purchase negotiations still dragged, and many people, including Jackson, were becoming impatient. Texas was filling up with Americans who made little secret of their revolutionary intentions. This situation, coupled with the effronteries of Butler, increased the suspicions of Mexico, which fumblingly began to take measures.

But the laws forbidding American emigration could not be enforced. A law abolishing slavery met a similar fate. The Americans in Texas became bolder, and when Stephen F. Austin, their leader, showed himself too conservative, a headstrong minority began to take matters in its own hands. While the Stanbery affair was at its height the radicals discussed the possibility of inviting either Sam Houston or Billy Carroll, of Tennessee, to lead them.[7]

Jackson was getting in a corner, and he, too, took measures. Butler was prodded. Steps also were taken against the possible collapse of the policy of purchase. Houston spent his days and nights with Jackson men who thought it time for a Florida coup in Texas. He pressed his advantage. The President yielded, and with either the expressed or implied consent of his patron, Sam Houston made an excursion to New York to raise funds for a trip to Texas. The New Yorkers were sympathetic, but not so quick to part with their money. Eastern financiers had recently made heavy investments in Texas lands and a revolution was something that required reflection. Samuel Swartwout, now President Jackson's collector of the Port of New York, would cheerfully acknowledge that. So would old Aaron Burr.

Houston returned to Washington with the question of his

personal budget unsolved.  Whereupon, according to Buell, a
biographer jealous of Jackson's reputation, the President
loaned Houston five hundred dollars to start on his adventure[8]—a modest sum but Jackson's cash reserve was low.  The
President also clothed Houston with official powers and con-
cocted a confidential mission to Texas under a United States
passport.  Houston quietly left Washington, giving out that
he was bound for his wigwam on the Arkansas.  As usual he
stopped over in Tennessee.

5

The talk in Tennessee still revolved about Eliza Allen.
Neither the Stanbery affair nor Texas had diminished interest
in the parting of the lovers.  But in three years sentiment had
undergone a change.  Houston's policy of silence had begun to
tell.  Whether blameless or blameworthy, who could criticize
his conduct since the event?  He had said nothing; he had
done nothing except to withdraw.  By the outward sign no
detachment could be more complete, no oblivion more sincerely
sought.  Fragmentary glimpses of a fugitive figure, to-day in
the vortex of great events in the nation's capital, to-morrow
on a dim frontier ruling the camps of reckless men:  such was
the likeness that Tennessee had contrived of Sam Houston.
It appealed.  The exile had endowed his cause with a certain
dignity and his person with a modish flavor of romance.

The Stanbery affair was "good theater," and although Carroll was still in the saddle, Houston's return caused something
resembling an ovation in Tennessee.  "Wherever he went he
was received with every demonstration of regard. . . . Reason had resumed its sway over the public mind, and a strong
desire was manifested that he should again take up his abode
in Tennessee."  But in his own words, Houston "could not be
dissuaded from his purpose of returning once more to the
forest.  A sight of the spot where he had seen the bright hopes
that had greeted his early manhood, crushed in a single hour,

only awakened associations he wished to forget." Accordingly "he once more turned his face towards the distant wigwam of the old Indian chief" to seek "repose by the hearth-stone of a savage King—a biting satire on civilized life."[9]

Although these protestations served to disguise the traveler's descent upon Texas, there can be no doubt of the sincerity of the allusion to Eliza. Yet, as Houston wrote Lewis, had she eluded surveillance and come to him on the occasion of the memorable visit to Nashville two years before "I would not [have] received her."[10]  The tragedy that kept those two apart formed the very soul of Sam Houston's secret.  "Tho' the world can never know my situation and may condemn me God will justify me!"[11]

But God's justification had been slow in easing the torments of Houston's mind.  During the three and one-half years of his Indian life, Houston visited Tennessee four times.  On two occasions he saw his wife—if there is truth in stories that have been told and believed in Sumner County for nearly one hundred years.  They rest upon ground a reviewer must tread with caution, but the body of legend that surrounds Sam Houston is a part of the saga of his life.  The versions presented here seem the most agreeable with history.

This is the story of a girlhood friend of Eliza who was a bridesmaid at her wedding. "One day while Eliza was in the garden of the manor house . . . the housemaid announced that a stranger, a tall man, was in the reception room asking to see her. On entering the room she saw at a glance that the stranger was the late Governor artfully disguised. He arose and made his old time courtly salutation. . . . He did not suspect that his disguise was detected. . . . He conversed about the weather and the condition of the river. Neither did she in any way hint that she knew him but all the time the visitor was gazing at her as if to fasten her features more surely in his memory. Then he arose, made another profound bow and passed out going down to the river. There he entered a canoe, paddled to the opposite bank and disappeared."[12]

The other account I select is accredited to one Dilsey, a servant of the Allen family. The incident is supposed to have taken place on Houston's last visit to Tennessee before his departure for Texas. Dilsey was busy about her cabin near the "big house" when Marse Sam suddenly appeared, frightening the negress almost out of her wits. Winning her confidence with a present of silver, Houston persuaded Dilsey to call her mistress to the cabin. He concealed himself and thus harbored by a slave, is said to have gazed upon the face and heard the voice of his wife for the last time.[13]

## 6

The wisdom of Houston's impulse not to linger in the environs of Tennessee soon became apparent. Leaving Nashville, he stopped at Cincinnati. He had friends there who were interested in his Texas plans, and in any event the presence of one so notable was something to speak of on the wharf where the well-to-do promenaded and took their nip at the Orleans Coffee House that stood in a garden facing the steamboat landing. The theater bills announced that General Houston would attend the play on the evening of July twentieth.

The guest of honor with a party of friends arrived and entered a box. Their appearance was saluted with hisses.

"Turn him out!" "The damned scoundrel!" "Female purity!"

The play was forgotten. The curtain descended and the theater manager came out to see what was the matter. They howled him down. One or two of Houston's friends rose and attempted to speak. They howled them down. Sam Houston rose. His towering form, his confident self-command and unforgettable voice restored quiet to the theater.

"He appealed as a stranger," said a newspaper account,[14] "to the hospitality and patriotism of the audience." He recalled "having fought and bled in defense of his country, when his companions in arms were soldiers from Ohio."

"Don't hear him!" "Out with him!" "Female purity!"

The actors tried to sing the people into a good humor, but it was useless. The performance closed. "Houston and his friends succeeding in leaving the theatre without injury!"

About six weeks later, that is, in early September, 1832, Sam Houston received at Cantonment Gibson his passport requesting "all the Tribes of Indians, whether in amity with the United States, or as yet not allied to them by Treaties, to permit safely and freely to pass through their respective territories, General Samuel Houston, a Citizen of the United States, Thirty-eight years of age, Six feet, two inches in stature, brown hair and light complexion; and in case of need to give him all lawful aid and protection."[15]

The name of Texas does not appear in the document. But by the same post, or very nearly the same, came a letter from Houston's old friend, John Van Fossen, who could speak with less reserve. Van Fossen was a Jackson political appointee and had been close to Houston during the Stanbery episode. He regretted to hear "that your friends in New York may fail to furnish the means of prosecuting your Texas enterprise." "I hope," he continued, "it will not prove true, for I had indulged the expectation of . . . the most splendid results. I do not believe that that country will long continue its allegiance to the Mexican Government, and I would much rather see it detached through your agency . . . than . . . [by] purchase. . . . It has been your fortune to engross more public attention than any other private individual in this nation, and I am daily asked a hundred questions about this extraordinary man, Gen. Houston. I most ardently hope that I may ere long be able to say that you have triumphed over every obstacle that interposed against . . . *your wishes*."[16]

Houston passed the next three months settling his affairs. He was at Cantonment Gibson often. Things were quiet, and old Colonel Arbuckle was courting the lately widowed Sallie Nicks, who still served out grog although she was worth twenty-five thousand dollars. In November Washington Irving arrived at the post on his tour of the wild West, and Houston joined the distinguished visitor's escort on its way to the hunting-grounds. "Gov. Houston," scribbled Mr. Irving in his pocket note-book, "tall, large, well formed, fascinating man—low crowned large brimmed white beaver—boots with brass [?] eagle [?] spurs—given to grandiloquence. A large & military mode of expressing himself; I encamped last night at——, for, I slept last night. Old Genl Nix [Sallie's late lamented] used to say God made him two drinks scant."[17]

Not long thereafter The Raven said farewell to Tiana and left her possessed of the Wigwam Neosho, its fields and two slaves. Andrew Jackson's emissary took with him only Jack, the pony he rode; and Jack had no tail. Heading toward the Red River, Houston met Elias Rector, whom General Albert Pike has immortalized as the Fine Arkansas Gentleman who got drunk once a week on whisky and sobered himself on wine. The two rode together for a day and halted for a convivial hour before parting. Houston said it was humiliating to think of appearing so poorly mounted among a race of strangers who were connoisseurs of horse-flesh. It would be trying on the horse as well, for Jack, having no tail, would find the flies a pest in Texas. Saddles and bridles were changed, and Houston took leave of Jack with words that touched Rector.

"Houston," he said, "I wish to give you something before we separate and I have nothing that will do as a gift except my razor."

"Rector," said Houston, "I except your gift, and mark my words, if I have luck this razor will some day shave the chin of a president of a republic."[18]

On the first day of December, 1832, Houston was at Fort Towson on the American bank of the Red River, a sprawling, unfinished stream, normally more river-bed than river. On the other side billowed a vacant plain dressed in dirty red grass spotted with patches of jack-oak. This was Texas. On December second, while an eagle circled overhead, Sam Houston mounted the horse of the Fine Arkansas Gentleman and splashed into the muddier Rubicon.

# BOOK THREE

## DESTINY

"Your name & fame will be enrolled amongst the greatest
chieftains."
—ANDREW JACKSON.

# CHAPTER XV

## Don Samuel

### 1

Through the rain and the red mud of el Camino Real sloshed a dripping horse and a dripping rider. The weight of silver trappings jingling on his martingale and the radiant poncho to shield his fringed buckskins from the slanting downpour marked the unknown señor who fared the King's High Way as a personage of degree. Traveling eastward with Nacogdoches at his back, he had ridden more than a thousand miles in Texas, fording wild rivers, threading forests and crossing the featureless plain from San Antonio de Béxar. The gleaming stone and adobe town, drowsing through its second century of sunlight, had blessed the stranger with good weather and good company. The white contours of the outlying Álamo Mission, the plazas with their soft rugs of gray dust, shaded patios where guitars measured rich cadences and señoritas in flashing garments played with their fans: this seemed like a page from one of those idle novels the wayfarer had professed to deplore.

But it was reality, and the stranger had felt his weariness steal away under the influence of the poetry of Spanish names and the beautiful indolence of Spanish manners. A chance acquaintance met on the route had proved capable of marvelous introductions. The newcomer was entertained at the residence of Don Juan Veramendi, the vice-governor, who presented his guest as Don Samuel Houston.

With many expressions of regret, a few Spanish touches added to his costume and a few Spanish phrases to his vocabulary, Don Samuel had departed from Béxar. The breadth of Texas behind him, he crossed the turbulent Sabine and stood again on United States soil. At an inn in Natchitoches, Louisiana, he indited a letter under date of February 13, 1833:

"Gen. Jackson:

"Dear Sir:—Having been so far as Bexar, in the province of Texas . . . I am in possession of some information that . . . may be calculated to forward your views, if you should entertain any, touching the acquisition of Texas by the United States.

"That such a measure is desired by nineteen-twentieths of the population of the province, I can not doubt. . . . Mexico is involved in civil war. . . . The people of Texas are determined to form a State Government, and to separate from Coahuila, and unless Mexico is soon restored to order . . . Texas will remain separate from the Confederacy of Mexico. She has already beaten and repelled all the troops of Mexico from her soil. . . . She can defend herself against the whole power of Mexico, for really Mexico is powerless and penniless. . . . Her want of money taken in connection with the course which Texas *must and will adopt*, will render a transfer of Texas to some power inevitable. . . .

"Now is a very important crisis for Texas. . . . England is pressing her suit for it, but its citizens will resist if any transfer should be made of them to any power but the United States. . . . My opinion is that Texas, by her members in Convention, will, by 1st of April, declare all that country [north of the Rio Grande] as Texas proper, and form a State Constitution. I expect to be present at that Convention, and will apprise you of the course adopted. . . . I may make Texas my abiding place . . . [but] *I will never forget* the country of my birth. I will notify from this point the Commissioners of the Indians at Fort Gibson of my success, which will reach you through the War Department. . . .

"Your friend and obedient servant,

"SAM HOUSTON."[1]

Calculated as this casual-looking letter was to influence the course of the President of the United States, the accuracy of General Houston's survey forms a subject of interest. To whom had he applied for his information? What had been his observations?

2

From Fort Towson on the Red River General Jackson's envoy had ridden south to Nacogdoches, a distance of one hundred and eighty miles, with only two cabins on the way. As mission settlement, military post and border town, Nacogdoches had behind it an intermittent history of one hundred and fifteen years. Here the traveler took a short rest and pushed south-westward one hundred and eighty miles farther to San Felipe de Austin, on the Brazos River, a settlement of about thirty thrifty families, with two little taverns where guests, if numerous, slept on the floor. San Felipe de Austin was not designed as a resort for tourists. It was the capital of the famous colony where by virtue of attention to work, inattention to politics and the genius of Stephen F. Austin, several thousand emigrant Americans were attaining a sound prosperity. Already Austin and his work were widely known in the United States. Sam Houston went to San Felipe to consult this interesting man.

The empresario was absent in the interior of his vast domain. But in San Felipe Houston renewed the acquaintance of a Texan of scarcely less salient renown. Jim Bowie[2] was a sandy-haired giant from Georgia with an engaging smile and an adaptable way that made him equally eligible to the society of the old grandee families and the overnight camps of the frontier. He had stormed into Texas with the filibuster, Long, and ranged in and out of the place ever since, involving his name with legends of duels, Indian fights, slave smuggling, land speculations, and exploits with the celebrated knife that bears his name. He had married Ursula Veramendi, a daughter of the vice-governor, joined church and accumulated enough wealth to instal his family in a fine house in Saltillo.

In Jim Bowie Houston found a personality flavored to his liking. The two ate Christmas dinner together at San Felipe and rode to San Antonio de Béxar where Don Samuel unfolded his official papers and gave everything an appearance of regularity by conducting pow-wows with the Indians.

Houston never explained the nature of these interviews, except to say that their object was "confidential" between Jackson and himself, and that the ends "contemplated" were "accomplished."[3] The Secretary of War, however, to whom Houston submitted the results of his Indian conferences, found the report worthless and declined to pay an expense account of thirty-five hundred dollars which Houston enclosed.[4] I think this may support Houston's assertion that the objects of the Indian mission, which wears the aspect of a subterfuge, were confidential between the President and himself. Had the Secretary of War been a party to the secret he would have passed the expense account.

Before writing Jackson from Natchitoches Houston had found Austin and talked with him at length. Yet the story Jackson received was not derived from anything Stephen F. Austin had said. Nor is it likely to have come from Bowie who, despite his personal acquaintance with many of the advanced thinkers politically, was a Mexican citizen, connected by the strongest ties to the existing régime.

It is not difficult, however, to surmise the source of the partizan story that Houston passed on to Jackson. It might have come, lock and stock, from the astute and energetic Wharton brothers, William and John, who long had had their eyes on Houston as a handy man for the Texas radicals. It might have come from Henry Smith of Brazoria, who hated everything Spanish and believed in the divine right of Nordics, or from Sterling C. Robertson, a colony promoter from Tennessee, now engaged in a quarrel with Austin.

Houston had seen these men and others of their stamp. Their views had impressed him; Austin's had not. This was natural. Houston had known the Whartons in the old days in Tennessee. He had known Robertson there, and eleven years before had invested money in the bankrupt enterprise about which Robertson was disputing with Austin. From the councils of these gentlemen Houston had emerged to agitate Jackson with the sensational news of Texas twenty to one for annexation, and in virtual rebellion, having driven all Mexican troops from her soil.

## 3

An imposing dress, this, for the actual events.

In 1830 Mexican concern over American zeal to buy Texas, coupled with the imprudent declamations of Americans on both sides of the Sabine, had found expression in a law calculated to halt American colonization and encourage settlement by native Mexicans and Europeans. Henceforth Americans could enter Texas only under passports issued by Mexican authorities. This played havoc with the colonial empresarios, including Austin. But Austin had given such unfailing proof of his fidelity that he was able to obtain an exception in favor of his colony. The new statute also required the regarrisoning of the Texas military posts, long vacant, but the real grievances centered upon immigration and the collection of customs.

It remained for a swashbuckling Kentucky soldier of fortune named Bradburn, a colonel in the Mexican service, to make trouble between the troops and the inhabitants. He arrested William B. Travis and others on trivial charges, and one hundred and sixty armed colonists marched to their rescue. The prisoners were released, but this did not avert a brisk battle at Velasco where a small Mexican force surrendered and marched out of Texas on parole.

The prevailing sentiment was that Travis's friends had gone too far and the apprehensive colonists hit upon Antonio López de Santa Anna as the instrument to rescue them from a warm predicament.

General Santa Anna was leading a Liberal revolt against

the president, Bustamante.  The colonists adopted resolutions
representing their disturbances as an extension of the Liberal
battle-line against the hirelings of this convenient tyrant.  The
diplomacy succeeded and Texas began to speak well of General
Santa Anna, who was a man born to lead soldiers.  He needed`
troops now, and one by one the garrisons in Texas packed their
knapsacks and marched across the Rio Grande.  Within a few
weeks all were gone except the garrison at remote Nacogdoches,
whose commander, opposed to Santa Anna, elected to remain.
Nacogdoches made an armed demonstration, however, and
after some casualties sent commander and command on their
dusty way to the Rio Grande.

Mexico was now thoroughly immersed in civil war.  In October of 1832 Texas held a convention in San Felipe which
precipitated the first important show of strength between the
party favoring American acquisition and those opposed.
William H. Wharton led the acquisition party, but Austin, in
his quiet way, decisively defeated Wharton for presiding officer.
The Convention asked for a dissolution of the union with Coahuila and a separate state government for Texas, with free immigration and minor reforms.  It denied any desire for independence.

A few weeks later Sam Houston arrived in Texas.  The
next news from Mexico City was that Bustamante had been
driven from the presidency.  Then Texas heard of the "election" of Santa Anna, who would take office April first.  Texas
decided to restate its case to the victorious Liberal leader and
a call went out for the second Convention to which Houston
had alluded in his letter to Jackson.  Impulsive Nacogdoches
pressed Houston to be a delegate and he became a candidate of
the Wharton wing.  This was the situation when Houston
wrote to Jackson.

4

Don Samuel returned to Nacogdoches to find that he had
been unanimously elected a delegate to the Convention.  Where-

upon, Houston says he "took up his residence among his new constituents, who had extended him so generous a greeting."[5]

He did not remain with them long, however, because the Convention was called to order at San Felipe on April 1, 1833—the day that Santa Anna was sworn in at Mexico City. This time William H. Wharton defeated Austin for presiding officer, but Austin's moderating hand showed itself upon the work of the assembly which was practically a copy of that of 1832. Among the innovations, however, was a resolution of Houston's against encroachments on Indian lands and a constitution for the proposed State of Texas upon its separation from Coahuila, which the Convention again solicited in respectful terms. Houston pronounced the new constitution "one of the best extant." He is entitled to an opinion because he wrote most of it.

Austin was chosen to lay the Convention's requests before Santa Anna, and a week after the meeting dissolved he began the long journey to Mexico City. He expected to return in a few months, but Texas did not see Stephen F. Austin again for more than two years. Meanwhile, there was opportunity for Don Samuel to cultivate the acquaintance of his cordial constituents.

# CHAPTER XVI

## HALLS OF THE MONTEZUMAS

### 1

THE alcalde of La Villa de Nuestra Señora del Pilar de Nacogdoches was Don Adolfo Sterne, accomplished, among other things, as a linguist, speaking perfect German, good English, passable French and Spanish well enough for the time he had been at it. On his arrival in the Village of Our Lady of the Pillar of Nacogdoches, Sam Houston must have been delighted to find so influential a magistracy graced by Adolfo Sterne—otherwise Adolphus Sterne, a rosy little Rhineland Jew of many wanderings whom Houston had known as a transient member of the Monongahela toddy set at the Nashville Inn.

Señor Sterne's constituency, now Señor Houston's as well, lay on the King's High Way. This wretched path spanned the face of Texas from west to east. Forty-seven miles before drowning its sorrows in the Sabine, it dipped from the red plain to cross a pair of creeks. On the pretty little knoll between the streams was a Spanish mission about which had crept the inevitable Spanish town to pass three generations in somewhat troubled sleep, to die in its sleep, and in the fulness of time to be resuscitated by Yankee enterprise.

To and fro across the Sabine restless Yanks had swept with schemes in their heads and guns in their hands—fleeing justice, fleecing Indians, gambling in land and promoting shooting scrapes called revolutions. By these means Nacogdoches

196

and a good share of the Redlands, as East Texas was called, repopulated themselves with the driftwood of various adventures. There was at least one resident who had come southwest with Aaron Burr. Others had arrived before that with Nolan and with Magee, and afterward with Long and with Hayden Edwards, whom Austin had headed off by riding up from San Felipe with his personal militia. There were men who had consorted with the pirate Lafitte, the founder of Galveston and Spain's sleepless enemy. But Captain Lafitte, being a mariner careful of his personal dignity, had declined to concern himself with any of these amateur theatricals.

The law of 1830 closing the door on immigration, gave Nacogdoches a new importance as a smuggling center. This law slightly reduced the number of American immigrants, but materially changed their character. People who had anything to lose stayed at home. The Redlands and the unauthorized settlements about Galveston Bay entitled Texas to the picturesque fame acquired in those early days. "Hell and Texas!" took its place in the vocabulary of the 'thirties as a mild cuss word; a loose expression or Texas would have been mentioned first. When a citizen disappeared from his home community under cloudy circumstances he was said to have G. T. T.—Gone To Texas. Old Texas lawyers still tell of the newcomer who was so disturbed in mind over the circumstances of his coming that he went to an attorney for advice. "My friend," the lawyer said, "this is very serious. My counsel is that you leave this place before sundown." "Leave! Where'll I go? Ain't I in Texas now?"

The great principality of Stephen F. Austin was an exception to this rule. His colonists were selected for their industry and integrity, and his own labors seem incredible. He dealt with a central government at Mexico City and a state government at Saltillo, alike capricious, inexpert, often corrupt and always kaleidoscopic. He dealt with colonists whom hardships had disheartened and rendered distrustful. He was their military and civilian chief, their banker, broker, merchant and messenger. He led them against the Indians. He surveyed their lands, established jurisdictions, organized and administered a state. In this work Austin submerged the best years of his life—a starved anchorite who had pawned his watch, reduced his wardrobe to homespun and worn himself down in body and in mind.

He was not a man suited by temperament to a frontier life. His gentle instincts and quiet tastes, his love of order and of the amenities of cultured society, should have found a more congenial atmosphere. He appreciated music and poetry. He liked to dress well, to dance and to dine in the company of cultivated men and women. His rare and business-burdened visits to the cities were little white islands of bliss. All these things had Stephen Austin foregone from a sense of duty. Duty, always duty. Duty had drawn him to Texas by the side of that tempestuous visionary, his father. The old man died while still he dreamed, but he exacted from his dutiful son a promise to follow the rainbow—a pursuit that the elder Austin, if one may judge by his past, would have thrown up long ago.

But at length Texas began to prosper and Austin felt that a time might come when he should not be too harassed to marry. He picked a site on a hill, far up the Colorado, where one day he might retire and occupy himself with the creation of a great university to embellish the civilization that he had wrought in a wilderness. Stephen was dreaming as his father had dreamed when a merciful death intervened before the awakening. A new cloud flecked the sky of Texas.

At first this annexation talk did not disturb Stephen Austin. He was a Mexican citizen and an officer of the Republic. He had held up his hand and sworn fidelity to Mexico. Austin opposed annexation—tactfully, noiselessly, and kept his colonists with him. The Whartons put themselves at the head of the disturbing movement. They were competent. Texas began to fill up with men of a type inclined to listen to them. Austin looked upon Nacogdoches as an abode of insurgents and upon

Sam Houston as a dubious adventurer. This hurt Houston's pride.

At the close of the Convention of 1833 Austin had set out for Mexico City resolved to return as quickly as possible. The two-year delay was no fault of his.

## 2

Sam Houston took up his residence in Nacogdoches in time to be counted in the census of 1833, to which Alcalde Sterne was able to sign his name in certification of the luminous fact that the town had 1,272 inhabitants, as follows: bachelors, 319, spinsters, 291, married couples, 122, widowers, 9, widows, 34, minors under sixteen years of age, 375, of whom 183 were boys and 192 were girls. In which category Houston placed himself is not known, although a little later one encounters him officially herded with the bachelors and exceedingly attentive to Miss Anna Raguet.

Miss Anna was seventeen years old, a daughter of Colonel Henry Raguet, a Pennsylvanian of Swiss descent—merchant, landowner and substantial citizen—the sort of man Austin would have welcomed to San Felipe. He lived in the best house in town. He entertained generously, but as Anna was the apple of her father's eye, it was not every one he brought home to hear her play the French harp in the parlor. Miss Anna was a graceful translator of Spanish, and when this got out the provincial correspondence of some of the bachelors increased enormously.

Sam Houston became a permanent guest of Adolfo Sterne and won the affection of every member of the family. This assured his position socially as well as politically. In every way the hospitable Sterne home with its French-speaking Louisiana negro servants was more desirable than Brown's Tavern on the Plaza, where many another less fortunate bachelor made the best of it. The other hotel was the Cantina del Monte, Miguel Cortenoz, proprietor. Guests of the Monte were better off when they could arrange their affairs so as to sleep in the daytime, since Señor Cortenoz conducted a dance-hall and gambling room in conjunction with his hotel. Dances were also occasionally held at Brown's by one or another of the various Anglo-Saxon social sets, but there was entertainment at the Monte every night and a fandango once a week. These fandangos were supposed to be pretty tough affairs, despite the attendance of Americans attracted, as a fellow countryman assures us, by "the novelty of the scene."

Music at the Monte was furnished by an ancient Castillian in soiled linen who divided his attention between a violin and a long cigar. The principal entertainers were a Mexican dancing team. The girl was vivacious, with a mouth "pretty enough to kiss" from which drooped a cigarette in a fashion described as "very becoming." Her partner, a pasty-faced professional dancing man, seemed unworthy of association with such fresh beauty. Adjoining the ballroom was an airless chamber with smoke-blackened walls where a beak-nosed crone sat behind a tall table with a pot of black coffee at her side. She sipped the coffee and sold stiffer drinks to the perspiring dancers, sliding the glasses across a table-top that was slick from constant use.

Señor Cortenoz also had a daughter. Her name has not come down in history, but she, also, was the apple of her father's eye. In January of 1836 this child died of measles. Death has a great prestige with the Spanish. Life may be arbitrary, forcing an inconspicuous rôle upon one deserving of better things, but death makes one the central figure of a ceremonial as elaborate as the estate of the deceased can provide. Miguel Cortenoz closed his gambling room and gave his dance-hall people a night off. The body of his little girl was borne to the Monte and laid out on a table in the center of the ballroom floor with candles at her head and at her feet. Unfortunately the padre was absent from the parish, but the entire Spanish-speaking population of Nacogdoches left their mud and adobe domiciles, and were joined by a sprinkling of

Americans. All night they mourned with Miguel Cortenoz and glasses slid on the smooth table in the dark back room. In the morning the procession threaded the narrow streets to the enclosed square of consecrated earth and saw *la chiquita* laid to rest.

**3**

Sam Houston was not present at these solemn rites, being in another part of Texas at the time. Nor is there direct evidence that he was ever a steady patron of the house of Cortenoz. The English-speaking and Spanish-speaking sets, who called themselves respectfully Americans and Mexicans, did not mix. The latter contained a small number of polished people. The American set was subdivided into classes, ranging from the select Sterne-Raguet milieu to the more numerous following of an ex-Missourian known as the Ring Tailed Panther, reputed to have eaten raw the heart of an Indian. Houston was of the Sterne-Raguets, but he was also popular among the Mexicans. Probably no other American in the town could have adopted the radiant Mexican blanket as a part of his costume without giving offense to the Spanish element or losing cast with the Nordic gentility.

The Mexicans were outnumbered by five to one, but stood as a man opposed to the separation of Texas from the mother country. Houston had reported to Jackson that the Americans were twenty to one in favor of separation. This may have been true of the Americans in Nacogdoches, but in Texas as a whole the annexationists formed the minority party. Generally speaking, the less an American had to lose the more pronounced were his views in favor of separation. Henry Raguet was for independence, but a step at a time. He was more conservative than the leader of his party, W. H. Wharton.

But Houston was aggressive. Less than a year after his arrival in Texas, a party of newcomers was riding along the road between Nacogdoches and the new town of San Augustine. Twice in one day they passed a splendidly mounted horseman whose polite bows attracted favorable comment, especially from the ladies. That evening the party inquired at a wayside inn who the civil stranger might be. "That," they were told, "is Governor Houston, and he says there is going to be war in Texas before long and he means to figure in it."[1]

Governor Houston was often in San Augustine. On these occasions he stayed at the residence of Phil Sublett one of the founders of the town, and a large speculator in land. Houston had read up on the Mexican land laws, and his legal training was useful to men like Sublett. One night in the autumn of 1833, he arrived at his friend's house very late, and in such an eccentric state that he was unable to mount the stairs. Moreover, he appeared inclined to talk. Sublett thought this might be a good opportunity to get some first-hand information. He asked Houston why he had left Eliza Allen. The question restored Sam Houston instantly. He stormed from the house and called for his horse.[2]

But the long shadow had crossed another frontier.

4

Houston entered upon the practise of law in Nacogdoches and was admitted to appear before the Court of the First Instance presided over by Judge Juan Mora. This brought Don Samuel into professional association with such barristers as Vicente Córdova, Miguel Saco and Francisco Garrero, whose Castillian names had no shadowy counterparts on the alien side of the Sabine. Houston had some good clients: Phil Sublett, Frost Thorn, José Durst and others of the local land clique. The new lawyer's best client, however, was the Galveston Bay and Texas Land Company.

Organized on a mammoth scale in New York City, the Galveston Bay and Texas Land Company marked the entry of big business and politics into the unsettling affairs of Texas. Headed by Anthony Dey, a New York banker, and others whose relations with the Jackson Administration conveyed a reassuring implication, the company had no trouble finding money to pay for helpful services. This money was raised by the sale of stock to the favored few and land script to the small fry. The land script was a fraud.

These occupations linked Houston once more with his old friends, the Indians on the Arkansas. There is a tradition among the Cherokees that Houston sent word to Tiana to join him in Texas. This I do not believe, but half-breed Ben Hawkins and the Creek Chief, Opoth-ley-ahola, who had given Houston the fur-collared coat, did come to Nacogdoches on another matter. They agreed to settle their people on lands held by Houston's New York clients, and a part of the purchase price was advanced. In connection with this transaction it will be recalled that the earliest mention of Houston's designs upon Texas contemplated the use of Arkansas Indians as troops to help wrest the province from Mexico.

It appears that Houston carried on these activities without becoming a Mexican citizen. But if the Mexican Government was slipshod about the way foreigners exercised political privileges without becoming citizens, it diligently enforced the statutes withholding ownership of land from those not of the Catholic faith. Austin and his colonists, and other regularized settlers, had gone through the form of affiliation with the Roman Church.

Sam Houston joined the Catholic Church in the last half of 1833 or the first half of 1834, perhaps the latter. It would be interesting to know to what extent he was swayed by expediency and to what extent by Eva Rosine Sterne, the young Louisiana wife of the alcalde.

Investigation of Houston's Catholicism discloses little that one can interpret without aid of conjecture. It is understood that he was a "Muldoon Catholic," implying that he had been inducted into the faith by the learned Padre Miguel Muldoon, a friend of Americans and a practical man whose converts were numerous, and contributions to the ecclesiastical treasury correspondingly so. A Muldoon Catholic Sam Houston may

have been, although in his case the baptismal waters were
dispensed by Eva Rosine's confessor, a certain Père Cham-
bondeau, of Louisiana.  The church records in which Houston's
baptism should appear have been destroyed by fire, but a
daughter of Señora Sterne has left an account, based on her
mother's recollections.  The ceremony took place at the church
in Nacogdoches, Mrs. Sterne acting as the convert's "god-
mother, after which  . . .  he always addressed her as 'Madre
Mío.' "[3]  One hears from another source that after the church
ritual the alcalde gave a party on the porch of his home and
opened considerable wine.

It is not unreasonable to suppose that the pageantry of
the Catholic service appealed to Houston's color-loving soul,
and that certain articles of the creed were a comfort to his
buffeted spirit.  At the same time, Houston did not remain a
practising Catholic very long, if he was ever one.  Later he
joined his fellow Texas revolutionaries in protests against
religious tyranny that looked well in manifestos but had slender
basis in reality.

5

Estevan Austin, as he subscribed himself when among his
Spanish-speaking countrymen, arrived in Mexico City in mid-
July of 1833, half sick after an eleven weeks' journey.  He
supported Texas's application for a separate state government
with a plea vigorous to the point of bluntness.  Austin asked
that the matter be settled without delay.  How could any one,
least of all Austin with his reputation for tact and Job's
patience, have made such a request of a Mexican official?  A
part of the answer may be found in a private letter.  "I am so
weary that life is hardly worth having."

Delay followed delay.  The behavior of Santa Anna had
begun to disturb his Liberal supporters.  The air was filled with
uncertainty.  Having obtained somewhat less than half of what
he came for Austin finally turned his steps northward—to be
seized, snatched back to Mexico City and harshly imprisoned.

"I do not blame the government for arresting me," he wrote to the people of Texas, "and I particularly request that there be no excitement about it. . . . Keep quiet, discountenance all revolutionary measures or men . . . have no more conventions."

In Texas Sam Houston joined Austin in the counsel of calmness, inveighing against "unrestrained ebullitions of feeling," on the ground, as he afterward explained, that "they would be likely to plunge Texas into a bloody struggle with Mexico, *before she was prepared for it*."[4]

The barrister of Nacogdoches had changed his political views. He was now a moderate—favoring independence, but by one prudent step at a time. "All new States," he later wrote, "are infested, more or less, by a class of noisy, second-rate men, who are always in favor of rash and extreme measures. But Texas was absolutely overrun by such men." What Texas needed was a leader "brave enough for any trial, wise enough for any emergency, and cool enough for any crisis."[5] Houston had determined to be that man.

Within a few months resentment over Austin's imprisonment had died away so completely that the luckless man mistakenly believed political opponents in Texas to be conspiring to keep him in jail. This state of affairs suited the projects of Don Samuel, who quietly packed his bag for a journey.

### 6

Cincinnati and Tennessee obtained their customary glimpses of him. In the fall of 1834 he was in Washington. Jackson was still trying to purchase Texas and was still embarrassed by his envoy, Anthony Butler, who, failing to advance negotiations by bribery, was trying to stir Texas to rebellion over Austin's arrest.

One evening Houston met Junius Brutus Booth on the Avenue. Adjourning to Brown's Indian Queen Hotel they exchanged mutual accounts of themselves and

"industriously circulated the bottle.   Many a loud shout echoed
through the hall, and startled watchmen in the street.   As night
wore on excitement increased until . . . [Booth's] companion exclaimed—

" 'Now, Booth, let's have a speech to liberty—one of those
apostrophes to Old Roman freedom.' . . .

"The tragedian rehearsed . . . many of those electric
passages in defense of liberty with which the English drama
abounds.   His friend . . . caught up the words, and with
equal force, went through each speech in regular succession. . . . [At length Houston] sprang . . . to his feet,
and in the tone of one amid battle's din . . . exclaimed,

" 'Now, Booth, once more for liberty !'

"The tragedian ran through . . . a tale of Spanish conquest. . . .

"Before him stood at that lone hour, listening with an
intensity of thought and feeling which shown in his eyes . . .
one who had . . . the ambition of a Pizarro.   Quick as
thought he . . . repeated the words uttered by Booth. . . .
His spirit seemed to take fire ; and with an air so strange, so
determined, so frightful, that it seemed the voice of one inspired
he exclaimed at the close of a masterly rhapsody.

" 'Yes ! yes ! I am made to revel in the Halls of the
Montezumas !' "[6]

On another evening in a crowded drawing-room, Narcissa
Hamilton, a schoolgirl from Virginia, was presented to General
Houston.   She curtsied and asked her Cousin Sam if he remembered her.   What a question—did Sam Houston ever forget a
pretty girl?   Then, would he compose a little sentiment to that
effect in Narcissa's album?   Houston wrote rapidly while the
girl's wonder grew that one should be able to concentrate amid
such distractions.

> "Remember thee?
> Yes, lovely girl ;
> While faithful memory holds its seat,
> Till this warm heart in dust is laid,
> And this wild pulse shall cease to beat,
> No matter where my bark be tost
> On Life's tumultuous, stormy sea ;

My anchor gone, my rudder lost,
Still, cousin, I will think of thee."[7]

Narcissa treasured those lines as long as she lived.

Houston visited Baltimore, Philadelphia and New York. In New York he met stockholders in the Galveston Bay and Texas Land Company, and enjoyed himself socially. With one of these stockholders, Jackson's close friend Samuel Swartwout, Houston had some interesting conversations before he departed for the West.

Little Rock viewed the traveler homeward bound.

"Gen. Houston was one of the most magnificent specimens of physical manhood I have ever seen. . . . I first saw him on the public road a few miles out of town. He was riding a splendid bay horse, and his saddle and bridle were of the most exquisite Mexican workmanship and were elaborately ornamented with solid silver plates and buckles in profusion. He was enveloped in a Mexican 'poncho' which was richly ornamented with Mexican embroidery work. When again I saw him on the streets of Little Rock . . . it was hard to realize that this elegantly appearing gentleman had voluntarily given up home and kindred and official preferment to join himself to a band of half-civilized Indians, and had adopted their dress . . . and habits of life."[8]

In December of 1834 an Englishman arrived at Washington, Arkansas, an out-of-the-way log hamlet thirty miles from the Texas boundary. He wrote:

"I was not desirous of remaining long at this place. General Houston was here, leading a mysterious sort of life, shut up in a small tavern, seeing nobody by day and sitting up all night. The world gave him credit for passing these waking hours in the study of *trente et quarante* and *sept 'a lever;* but I had seen too much passing before my eyes, to be ignorant that this little place was the rendezvous where a much deeper game . . . was playing. There were many persons at this time in the village from the States lying adjacent to the Mississippi, under the pretence of purchasing government lands, but whose real object was to encourage the settlers in Texas to throw off their allegiance to the Mexican government. Many of these individuals were personally acquainted with me; they knew I was not with them, and would naturally conclude I was against them. Having nothing whatever in common with their plan, and no inclination to forward or oppose them, I perceived that the longer I staid the more they would find reason to suppose I were a spy."[9]

The stage was being set for the advance upon the halls of the Montezumas. The spear-carriers were jostling to their places in the wings.

# CHAPTER XVII

## REVOLT

### 1

IN THE autumn of 1835 Houston offered for sale four thousand acres of Red River land for twenty-five hundred dollars, one thousand in cash. The money was needed to defray some extraordinary personal expenses, including the purchase, in New Orleans, of a uniform with a general's stars and a sword sash to adorn it. Houston possessed a sword—the gift of an American Army officer at Fort Jessup, Louisiana. These preparations followed an action of the Committee of Vigilance and Safety which had commissioned Sam Houston "Commander-in-Chief of the forces" of the Department of Nacogdoches "to sustain the principles of the Constitution of 1824."

The new Commander scattered through the Redlands an appeal for recruits. "All that is sacred menaced by an arbitrary power!" "War is our only alternative! . . . Volunteers are invited to join our ranks with a good rifle and 100 rounds of ammunition." "The morning of glory is dawning. . . . Patriotic millions will sympathise in our struggles."

General Houston's first call upon the patriotic millions was published in New Orleans. "Volunteers from the United States will . . . receive liberal bounties of land. . . . Come with a good rifle, and come soon. . . . 'Liberty or Death! . . . Down with the usurper!' "[1]

A skirmish took place at Gonzales.

The curtain had risen on the Texas Revolution. In Houston's opinion it had risen prematurely.

209

**2**

Eight months previous General Houston had returned from his American tour to find Texas still quiet. Although no longer the toast of Liberals, Santa Anna had confined his suspicious gestures to the country south of the Rio Grande. Austin was out of prison, enjoying the gaiety of Mexico City.

Houston resumed his law practise, the difficult courtship of Anna Raguet and his leisurely plotting. With Austin free factional disputes came to life. This was hastened by the blunder of a relative of Austin who published a private letter from the prisoner, intimating that W. H. Wharton was keeping him in jail. Houston shared Wharton's indignation at the unjust charge, for nominally Houston was still of the Wharton party. But actually he was his own man, and took no one into his confidence. A letter of his to John Wharton:

"Last night, I had the pleasure of passing with your brother, and his company. . . . I . . . remained with them, until this morning; when we parted, for various routs and pursuits—I to my *law business* and *they* to the more animating pursuits of speculation.

"From your brother I learned the news of the colony, and of its politicks, for really, I was ignorant of them. . . . I heard with singular pleasure, that you were recovering the use of your arm! I had heard of the occurrence of the meeting, but never the particulars. . . . They gratified me much because they were in perfect accordance, with my estimate of you. . . .

"William shewed me his *card* in answer to Austins ridiculous letter of last August from Mexico. I think he has left the little Gentleman very few crumbs of comfort—I was provoked at his first letter of August, I must confess, that it awakened no other emotion in my breast, than *pity* mingled with *contempt*. He shewed the disposition of a viper without its fangs. . . . He aimed at me a few thrusts, but I will wait an interview with him before I make any public expose of . . . his political inconsistencies. . . .

"I am doing pretty well, and certainly, am one of the most steady men in Texas!"[2]

Houston permitted Nacogdoches to see him as he described himself to Wharton: a busy lawyer, a steady man pursuing the uneventful tenor of his way. What a contrast with Wharton—duelist, speculator and politician!

Radford Berry had succeeded Adolfo Sterne as alcalde. Houston filed with him the certificate of character required of aliens. "This is to certify that the foreigner Samuel Pablo [sic!] Houston is a man of good moral character and industrious, loving the constitution and the laws of the country, a bachelor without family and generally known as a good man. Nacogdoches 21 of April 1835. [signed] JUAN M. DOR."[3]

In a jury trial before Judge Mora that lasted a month, Houston defended José Lorenzo Boden and Justo Lienda, accused of inciting an Indian attack on white people, and obtained their acquittal.[4] While this case was in progress a young Georgian came to town with a plaintive story. He had put his fortune in a gold mine and the manager of the mine had vanished—G. T. T.—with his employer's investment. The fugitive was overtaken on the outskirts of Nacogdoches, but he had lost the money in a card game. One way or another, those Georgia gold mines were invariably losing propositions.

Lawyer Houston took the luckless proprietor before Alcalde Berry and witnessed the fact that "came and appeared the foreigner Thomas J. Rusk who deposed upon oath, stated and declared that he is a native of the United States of North America . . . his age twenty-nine years . . . that he desires to dwell under the wise and just government which offers the protection of its beneficent laws to honest and industrious men."[5]

The simple life. What, therefore, is one to apprehend from a paper like this?

"Sunday evening New York 10th May 1835
"My dear Houston
"Your very interesting letter . . . reminded me of old times and old scenes. . . . It was like yourself and therefore thrice welcome."

But to business.  There followed a long narration of how the writer had invested "$2750 Dollars" in Texas land and had nothing to show for it.  He feared that one Cabrajal had gone south with the money and asked Houston to investigate.  "Your description of Texas and the piece of land on Red River had made me too *appy* as poor old Gen[l]. La fayette used to say.  Why man, my 50,000 acres, if I should ever get them, will be a fortune.  Try hard therefore to get them for me."  Threaten Cabrajal with "exposure."  Say that "a good reputation will be worth more to him than a few thousands obtained by fraud."  An engaging observation, since it came from the Collector of the Port of New York, whose sticky fingers were to contrive the great scandal of the Jackson Administration, enriching contemporary language with the verb "to swartwout," meaning to pilfer.

"Your letter has set everyone crazy. . . .  Price is ready to abandon the District Attorneyship for . . . the 'newly discovered Paradise.'  Ogden Grosveneur & Doct Cooper, yr old friends are all mad to go there, and d——m me . . . if I would not like to pay you a visit in ducking season.  By the bye, the 11 Leagues on Red River is *due to me*, for my sufferings and trouble in that old Burr scrape of mine.—You need not say anything to the Mexicans about it, but I'm d——d . . . if I dont think they owe me a plantation for what I suffered in that expedition."

Sam Houston to assume the obligations of the defunct Aaron Burr—spicy suggestion, to say the least.  But not an impertinent one from Mr. Swartwout's point of view, especially since "If I mistake not Texas will be U States in 5 years, or an independent Empire, when you'l be King. . . .  My wife & Daughter are well and desire to be remembered to you.  Price will write you in a day or so.  Ever Yours Sam[l]. Swartwout."  And a postscript: "I am glad to hear that you think [manuscript torn] -ing sober for a while—till you get my land, I hope. I long to have a bottle of old Madeira with you."[6]

The five-year program was ruthlessly clipped to five months. Santa Anna lashed out and fell upon the State of Zacatecas, which had refused to accept his dictatorship. He sent his brother-in-law, Martin Perfecto Cos, to attend to Texas. While one lawyer was poring over his briefs in Nacogdoches, another barrister named W. B. Travis with twenty-five men drove a Mexican garrison from Anahuac and proposed a march upon Béxar, the remaining garrison town, before Cos could reinforce it. There was no march to Béxar, however, and Travis was widely denounced in Texas. Only when Cos issued a stupidly phrased order for the military arrest of the offender did popular opinion rally to his side.

On September first Stephen F. Austin arrived in Texas, and all eyes turned toward him. War or peace? Austin had been studying Santa Anna at close range for two years. "War," he said, "is our only recourse." Texas stood united—and unprepared.

## 3

In response to Houston's call to arms, Thomas J. Rusk organized a company at Nacogdoches. New Orleans also responded. "Americans to the Rescue!" shouted the *Bee*. There followed mass meetings, speeches, public subscriptions. Adolphus Sterne thrilled an audience with an offer to buy rifles for the first fifty recruits. The New Orleans "Grays" formed themselves and claimed the rifles. Houston's appeal spread like fire in powder. Men formed up in Georgia, in Mississippi, in Tennessee, Kentucky, Cincinnati and New York, where Sam Swartwout unloosened the strings of some heavy purses.

Houston could not tarry in East Texas to contemplate this gratifying response amid which even Miss Anna had thawed. She tied his sword sash, snipped a lock of his hair and sent her soldier to fight for Texas. He was not, however, to fight on a battle-field as yet. His first stop was at Washington on the Brazos, where he fell in with a party of delegates bound for San Felipe to attend the meeting of a Consultation that had been summoned to coordinate the manifold activities. Houston also had been chosen a member of this body. He found his fellow delegates in a state of excitement and of many minds. A letter came from Austin, commanding the army, requesting the East Texas forces. Houston has stated that he gave the last five dollars he had "in the world" to a rider to carry the order that sent Rusk and the other Redlanders to the scene of war. Then the General and the other delegates took up the march to San Felipe.

The main body of members to the prospective Consultation seem to have been on the ground when Houston arrived, but were unorganized and had accomplished nothing. The most striking figure present was Lorenzo de Zavala, Governor, Senator, Cabinet officer and Minister to France under various Mexican Governments, and hero of the revolution that had won freedom from Spain. This passionate friend of liberty had repudiated Santa Anna and fled to Texas, but he could do little with a band of distracted Americans. Neither could Houston. At length, however, he placed himself at the head of thirty of the members and set out for Austin's camp, a ride of one hundred and sixty miles.

The army was then five miles from San Antonio de Béxar, whither Cos had arrived with reinforcements. Invited to surrender, General Cos had crisply declined, and Austin's camp was a spectacle of divided counsels. In desperation Austin is said to have offered the command of the army to Houston who refused it in the interest of harmony. A dispute arose as to whether the Consultation members should stay and fight or depart and legislate. The army thought they should fight, but Houston and Austin addressed the troops on the necessity of forming a government. They carried their point by a vote taken on the field.

On November 3, 1835, the Consultation again sat down in San Felipe. Sam Houston appeared before it clothed not in his new uniform, but in his old buckskins—the garb of a citizen performing a citizen's duty of building an Anglo-Saxon state.

"My impressions of the consultation unfavorable," noted a passer-by. "Some good men but I feel sick at the prospect. Introduced to Bowie—he was dead drunk; to Houston—his appearance anything but respectable."

The man in buckskins dominated a delicate situation. As sincerely as any one, Sam Houston desired Texan independence, or annexation to the United States. He felt, however, that this result could be achieved only by a military victory over Santa Anna. To air such advanced views now would only alienate the support of Liberal Mexicans like Zavala. Houston challenged the Whartons on the question of independence. A hot fight followed, but Houston won, and the Consultation adopted a provisional decree of independence under the Constitution of 1824.

A constitution was written and a civil administration organized with Henry Smith, of Brazoria, Governor, and James W. Robinson, of Nacogdoches, Lieutenant-Governor. A legislative body called the General Council was created. Stephen F. Austin, W. H. Wharton and Dr. Branch T. Archer were authorized to borrow a million dollars in the United States. With one dissenting vote Sam Houston was elected commander-in-chief of the Armies.

4

Confused reports came from the Army. Houston heard that Austin had been displaced by Jim Bowie. This was an error, but Austin was having his troubles, most of which came from his own side rather than from Cos who hesitated to show himself outside of the fortifications. A plague had swept Bowie's beautiful wife and two children into the grave, leaving the lion-hearted Jim almost insane with grief. Abandoning his property he had plunged into the Texas struggle, drinking to excess and quarrelsome, but still a leader and a fighter. Marching ninety men from Austin's camp, he whipped four hundred of Cos's cavalry at Mission Concepcion, and crowned the victory by throwing up his commission in a tiff.

Houston established contact with the army by means of a confidential letter to James W. Fannin. Fannin was one of those personal mysteries not uncommon to early Texas. A Georgian about thirty-one years of age, educated at the United States Military Academy under the name of Walker, he had appeared in Texas as a slave-runner, in funds and a free spender. When the clouds began to gather in the summer of 1835, Fannin impetuously espoused the cause of the extremists and scattered his money liberally. At Concepcion he shared the command with Bowie. Perhaps it was his military training that attracted Houston, who offered Fannin appointment as inspector-general of the army with rank of colonel.

Houston did not think that Cos could be beaten without artillery. Therefore "wou'd it not be best to raise the *nominal* seige,—fall back on Labehai [La Bahai, better known as Goliad] and Gonzales . . . furlough" most of "the army to Comfortable homes, and when the Artillery, is in readiness, march to the Combat with sufficient force, and at once reduce San Antonio! . . . Recommend the Safest course! . . . Remember our Maxim, it is better to do well, *late:* than *never!*"[7]

In reply Fannin dispatched two letters within a few hours of each other. "With regard to falling back . . . I must admit it to be a safest course." On the other hand "I am fully convinced that with 250 men, well chosen & properly drilled . . . that the place can be taken by storm."[8]

Upon his own future Fannin dwelt at greater length, crestfallen at the offer of a mere colonelcy. "I . . . write . . . in haste and thank you for the tender . . . of Quarter [master] Genl." In great haste, it would seem, since the tender was of inspector-general. "I have not had time to consult my friends or the wishes of the Army. . . . I would prefer a command in the line if I could be *actively engaged.*" Were not two brigadier-generals to be selected? "If so . . . I respectfully request your influence for one . . . well satisfied that I can fill either of the posts, *better than any officer*, who has yet been in command.—Entertaining this opinion I will at least tender my services. . . . Others may succeed over me by intrigues . . . [but I shall] not quit camp to seek office; . . . prefer the post of danger; where I may seek the enemy & beat him."[9] "Liberty & Texas—our wives & sweet hearts."[10]

With these communications before him Houston pressed the appointment of inspector-general upon Fannin, and sent him to take charge of the principal rendezvous for volunteers that were streaming in from the United States.

## 5

The Commander-in-Chief paid little attention to the army before Béxar and pursued his better-late-than-never policy by sitting down at San Felipe to evolve a military establishment designed to withstand the wear and tear of protracted campaigning.

Like any frontier community Texas had always been able to improvise a fighting force equal to brief emergencies. Our history teems with the exploits of such "armies"—thrown together in a week, to campaign for a month and go home. The turbulent troops before Béxar were all for having a battle at once or for going home. Houston, the old Regular, did not feel that such a force could win for Texas. With too strong a preference for formally drilled troops and too little confidence in raw volunteers, he continued his arrangements for a regular army and volunteer regiments, to be carefully equipped and trained before they took the field. He clung to the idea of Indian allies, ordering these stores from New Orleans: "1000 Butcher knives 1000 Tomahawks well tempered with handles . . . 3000 lb chewing tobacco (Kentucky)."[11]

Events outmarched the organizer. The day this requisition went forward the siege of Béxar was at an end. The army was in the town, fighting from street to street.

On leaving for the United States, Austin had transferred the command to Edward Burleson, an old Indian fighter who, like Houston, feared to attack. But the army was tired of waiting. "Who'll go into Béxar with old Ben Milam?" was the droll proposal of that veteran plainsman. Three hundred and one men volunteered and the town was stormed in the face of artillery fire. Milam was killed, and the command passed to Francis W. Johnson. On the fifth day of battle Cos with fourteen hundred men surrendered. They were permitted to march back to Mexico under parole not to bear arms against Texas, and once more there was not a Mexican soldier north of the Rio Grande.

Texas went wild over the victory, and said that the war was over. Burleson, who had said that Béxar could not be taken without artillery, resigned and went home. Johnson was elected commander. Houston, who had said that Béxar could not be taken without artillery, published a call for troops in which he said that the war had just begun. "The 1st of March next, we must meet the enemy with an army worthy of our cause. . . . Our habitations must be defended. . . . Our countrymen in the field have presented an example worthy of imitation. . . . Let the brave rally to the standard."[12]

This proclamation failed of the effect intended. The recruits flocked to the leaders who had covered themselves with glory at San Antonio de Béxar. That victory had been a blow to Houston's prestige, and a movement to displace him as commander-in-chief took form.

This had its beginning with James Grant, a Scotch surgeon whose mines below the Rio Grande had been seized. He had taken advantage of Austin's caution to spread discontent among the troops, promising them wealth and glory in an invasion of Mexico. This talk so appealed to the troops that only the assault upon Béxar had forestalled a march on Matamoras. Doctor Grant was wounded in that action, which tightened his hold upon the soldiers. He won over the new Commander, Johnson, and the two concerted their efforts with members of the General Council of the civil government. The project was painted in glittering tints—Liberal Mexicans rising to greet the invaders—the rich spoils of the old cities of Tamaulipas and Neuvo Leon—the fruitful country—the salubrious climate: a veritable souvenir hunt to the Halls of the Montezumas. The Council succumbed to the seductive spell.

Houston opposed the Matamoras campaign. He pointed out that irrespective of party, the Mexicans invariably united to repel foreign invasions. He deprecated the idea of using the army to recover the confiscated estates of Doctor Grant. The real seat of his opposition was deeper than either of these objections, however. Houston knew that Mexican pride would attempt vengeance for Béxar. He wished to direct all efforts to creating an army capable of meeting Santa Anna and smashing Mexico's power north of the Rio Grande. Governor Smith sided with Houston, but Smith and the Council had never pulled together and the gap between them was growing daily.

While the battle at Béxar was in progress, José Antonio Mexía had appeared in Texas and offered his sword in defense of liberty. General Mexía was an enemy of Santa Anna and had fled to New Orleans. There he had won the confidence of a company of American filibusters awaiting a ship to join Houston in Texas. When six days at sea Mexía announced to these volunteers that their destination was Tampico, where General Mexía had decided to gather some laurels on his own account. Instead of welcoming Mexía, Tampico shouted "Death to Foreigners!" The General escaped to a small boat, but most of his followers were captured and shot.

Sam Houston saw excellent reasons for declining to avail himself of the services of this soldier. Mexía appealed to the General Council which voted him ten thousand dollars and other assistance for an invasion of Mexico. Governor Smith vetoed the appropriation, denouncing Mexía as an unprincipled adventurer. The Council repassed the ordinance over Smith's veto, but with a modification that wounded the sensibilities of the General who declined to imperil his "military reputation" in the interest of Texas, and left the country.

But Grant and Johnson remained at Béxar, the idols of the Army, while enthusiasm for their Matamoras project swept the country. Members of the Council conspired with the Béxar leaders, and on December fifteenth made the first move looking to the elimination of Houston. His headquarters were transferred from San Felipe to the out-of-the-way hamlet of Washington. Houston, however, delayed his going, and with Governor Smith formed a counter-project to prevent the Army from eluding their influence. Houston directed Bowie to organize an expedition and "proceed on the route to Matamoras." Bowie was also to keep open the near-by port of Copano. Word went to New Orleans for American volunteers to land at Copano and concentrate under James W. Fannin at Refugio Mission and at Goliad.

By these means Houston expected to place an effective body of troops under Bowie and Fannin, whom he trusted, and to steal a march on Grant by starting Bowie to Matamoras first. Should the feint appear promising of results, it was in Houston's mind to appear in person at the head of the army and avail himself of the glory. These dispositions also took account of the expected invasion by Santa Anna in the spring.

### 6

So far, so good. On Christmas Day Houston removed his headquarters to Washington. Inspector-General Fannin was instructed to extend the Commander-in-Chief's "best salutations to all volunteers," and to keep them quietly in camp. "The volunteers may rely on my presence at Copano at the earliest moment, that a campaign should be undertaken for the success of the army and the good of the country." This done, Fannin was to join Houston at Washington.[13]

In place of Colonel Fannin, Sam Houston's next caller of consequence was a courier from Béxar with news that Grant was on the way to Matamoras at the head of two hundred men, including the crack New Orleans Grays with Adolphus Sterne's new rifles. This upsetting intelligence was from Lieutenant-Colonel Joseph C. Neill, a Houston man left behind with eighty sick and wounded whom Grant had stripped of medicines.

The Commander-in-Chief wrote Governor Smith an excited letter. "No language can express the anguish of my soul. Oh, save our poor country! . . . What will the world think of the authorities of Texas?" Nothing remained but for Houston to buckle on his sword and pursue the miscreant who had stolen the army. "Within thirty hours I shall set out . . . I pray that a confidential dispatch may meet me at Goliad. . . . I do not fear,—I will do my duty!"[14]

On the night of January 14, 1836, Houston overtook Grant at Goliad. Styling himself "Acting Commander-in-Chief" Grant had gleaned Goliad of horses and provisions and his men were in high feather. Houston did not press the point of his authority, believing he would be in a better position to do so at Refugio Mission on the seacoast, whither Grant was bound. There Houston expected to meet a large concentration of loyal troops under Fannin and to find a supply depot.

The situation at Goliad would have been fraught with less anxiety had not Houston received from Neill the grave tidings that Texas was invaded. The Mexicans were on the march to attack Béxar. Houston had not reckoned on an invasion before another two months. Neither he nor any one else had credited Santa Anna with ability to move an army in the dead of winter over the storm-swept desert that lay between Saltillo and Béxar. Texan leaders one and all had been too busily spying on one another to inform themselves of the enemy's movements.

Houston acted resolutely. Bowie was at Goliad. He had missed Houston's order to anticipate Grant with a gesture toward Matamoras, so that detail of the Houston-Smith counter-strategy had miscarried also. Houston started a handful of men to Béxar under Bowie with instructions to "demolish . . . the fortifications . . . remove all the canon . . . blow up the Alamo and abandon the place. I would myself have marched to Bexar . . . but the Matamoras rage is so high, that I must see Col Ward's men."[15]

Ward commanded a well-equipped battalion that had just arrived from Georgia. Houston had entrusted its reception to Fannin. But what was Fannin doing? Houston found posted in Goliad a proclamation signed with Fannin's name, calling for volunteers to march on Matamoras and promising that the "troops should be paid out of the first spoils taken from the enemy."[16] At best this represented an act of grievous indiscretion. A looting raid would not win over the Mexican Liberals.

Hence the importance of pressing on to Refugio and getting hold of Ward's men and the supplies. The invasion had changed everything. Grant must be forestalled at any cost.

The "Acting Commander-in-Chief" took up his march for Refugio, and the regular Commander-in-Chief rode along with him, badgering the men in a good-natured way over the obstacles that lay in the path to Matamoras. In real emergencies Houston usually was the master, and he could always make himself agreeable to soldiers. His persuasions had begun to weigh with Grant's men when they rode into Refugio on the night of January twentieth.

At Refugio Sam Houston found a disquieting situation. Ward was not there. Fannin was not there. Not a pound of supplies was on the ground.

The following morning Grant's partner in intrigue, Johnson, galloped in with an explanation of these mysteries. The General Council had deposed Governor Smith. It had superseded Sam Houston as Commander-in-Chief, making James W. Fannin the actual head of the army. Fannin was in possession of Ward's battalion and of the supplies. Matamoras would be taken, Mexico smitten with fire and the sword.

## 7

"I had but one course left to pursue," Houston wrote to Governor Smith. "By remaining with the army, the council would have had the pleasure of ascribing to me the evils which their own acts, will, in all probability, produce. . . . I regard the expedition, as now ordered, as . . . [divested] of any character save that of piratical . . . war."[17]

Houston washed his hands of the business and took his leave, but not until he had done two small things that are important to history. He harangued Grant's and Johnson's men on the perils of a march to Matamoras and left them murmuring. He announced his candidacy as delegate from Refugio to a new convention that was to meet in Washington on the first of March to reorganize the government.

Houston left Refugio at night, accompanied by his personal aide, Major George W. Hockley. He rode in silence "troubled by the most painful suspense—whether to withdraw once more from the treacheries and persecutions of the world, and bury himself deep in the solitude of nature, and pass a life in communion with the Great Spirit, and his beautiful creations"— or whether "to boldly mark out a track for himself" and "trample down all opposition."[18] For all the mauling that he had received at the hands of the world, Sam Houston retained the sensitive nature of his boyhood. He was not a happy warrior, but a brooding man in the stormy quest of repose.

The evening of the following day, Houston resolved upon a course. He told Hockley he would mark the new track. He would set Texas free.

At San Felipe Houston talked over things with Governor Smith who still made some pretentions to authority. Smith went through the form of granting his military commander a furlough until March first, and Houston disappeared among the Indians. In his calculations for the subjugation of Texas, General Santa Anna had omitted little. On the west and the south he advanced with armies. On the north and east were Indians who had their own grudges against Texas. Santa Anna's agents were stirring the blood of the clans who numbered two thousand men at arms when Sam Houston took his place at the council fire of The Bowl, War Lord of the Texas Cherokees.

# CHAPTER XVIII

## The Retreat from Gonzales

### 1

On the twenty-seventh day of February, 1836, the urbane Colonel William F. Gray, of Virginia, rode into Washington on the Brazos. "Disgusting place," he wrote in his diary. "About a dozen cabins or shanties constitute the city; not one decent house in it, and only one well defined street, which consists of an opening cut out of the woods. The stumps still standing."

In New Orleans Colonel Gray had met Austin and the other commissioners. The city was enthusiastic and the commissioners had borrowed two hundred thousand dollars. After this, Texas itself was disappointing. The visitor was in San Felipe during a brawl between Smith and the Council, which had left Texas without army or government. But San Felipe professed indifference; if Santa Anna crossed the Rio Grande he should never return alive. A week later Santa Anna was well across the Rio Grande, and San Felipe was packing to go eastward. Colonel Gray made an early start.

In Washington he had expected to find Houston. He bore a letter for him from Stephen F. Austin. Colonel Gray found many other people in Washington who were looking for Houston, who, as far as any one knew, was still among the Indians.

Washington was a whirlpool of confusion. The vanguard of the flight before the invasion was arriving. Delegates to

224

the Convention that was to meet in three days had begun to appear. There were not roofs enough and many slept under the trees. Residents were joining the eastward march. Texas was beginning to perceive that Houston's elimination from the army had failed to produce the results anticipated. In any event where was he now? His name somehow inspired confidence. Colonel Gray thought the Convention must make quick shift of its business or starve, since Washington was down to a corn-bread and fat-pork ration.

On February twenty-eighth a courier on a hard-ridden horse galloped into town with what has been called the most heroic message in American history.

> "Commandancy of the Alamo
> "Bejar, F'by 24th 1836
> "To the People of Texas & all Americans in the world: . . . am beseiged by a thousand or more of the Mexicans under Santa Anna. I have sustained a continual Bombardment & cannonade for 24 hours & have not lost a man. The enemy has demanded a surrender at discretion, otherwise, the garrison are to be put to the sword . . . if the fort is taken—I have answered the demand with a cannon shot & our flag still waves proudly from the wall. *I shall never surrender or retreat. Then,* I call on you in the name of Liberty, of patriotism & & everything dear to the American character, to come to our aid with all dispatch. The enemy is receiving reinforcements daily & will no doubt increase to three or four thousand in four or five days. If this is neglected, I am determined to sustain myself as long as possible. . . . VICTORY OR DEATH.
> "W. BARRET TRAVIS
> "Lt. Col. Comdt."[1]

The crowd took up a collection for the courier and sped him on.

"The Acting Governor, Robinson, with a fragment of the Council is here," noted Colonel Gray. "He is treated coldly and really seems of little consequence." Houston was the man of consequence now. Refugio had chosen him as a delegate to the Convention.

On February twenty-ninth it rained. The Convention would form on the morrow. To what purpose? Cheerless weather; leaderless confusion; a sense of helplessness in the face of impending danger. . . . A sudden shout in the stump-studded street snatched the throng from its brooding. A rush of men converged about a figure on horseback. Houston had come.

"Gen'l Houston's arrival has created more sensation than that of any other man. He is much broken in appearance, but has still a fine person and courtly manners; he will be forty-three years old on the 3rd [2nd] March—looks older."[2]

Thus Colonel Gray who lost no time introducing himself.

2

Next day a norther swept in and the temperature fell to thirty-three degrees. In a fireless shed the Convention worked through the night and, among other things, wrote a Declaration of Independence which was adopted without a dissenting vote and immediately signed on March 2, 1836. Sam Houston was the John Hancock of the occasion, his flowing autograph as bold as ever. Eleven of the signers were natives of Virginia, nine of Tennessee, nine of North Carolina, five of Kentucky, four of South Carolina, four of Georgia, three of Mexico (two of Texas and one of Yucatan), two of Pennsylvania, two of New York and one each of Massachusetts, New Jersey, Ireland, Scotland, England and Canada. The birthplaces of three are not obtainable.

The approval of the declaration took place on Sam Houston's forty-third birthday. Only eleven of those who signed it were his seniors, the average age being just under thirty-eight. Delegate Houston sent his felicitations to Madre Mío—Citizeness Rosine Sterne of Nacogdoches—enclosing a pair of beautiful earrings. She wore them each succeeding March second to the year of her death.

On March fourth the Convention elected Sam Houston

Commander-in-Chief of the Armies of the Republic, and on Sunday, March sixth, while Washington was eating breakfast an express dashed in with tidings from the Álamo. The town hastened to the Convention Hall to hear the news, which proved to be the last lines Barret Travis was to give to the world.

"The spirits of my men are still high, although they have had much to depress them. We have contended for ten days against an enemy whose number are variously estimated at from fifteen hundred to six thousand men. . . . Col. Fannin is said to be on the march to this place . . . but I fear it is not true, as I have repeatedly sent to him for aid without receiving any. . . . I hope your honorable body will hasten on reinforcements. . . . Our supply of ammunition is limited."

Robert Potter of the honorable body moved that "the Convention do immediately adjourn, arm, and march to the relief of the Álamo." Sam Houston characterized Mr. Potter's motion as "madness." The Convention must remain in session and create a government. Houston would leave for the front. He would find troops and interpose them between the enemy and the Convention. And "if mortal power could avail" he would "relieve the brave men in the Álamo." Houston did not mention that the brave men in the Álamo were there because his order to blow up that death-trap had been disregarded.

When he finished speaking, the Commander-in-Chief strode from the hall and mounted his horse—a superb animal, richly caparisoned in the Mexican fashion. The fine uniform had succumbed to the recent tribulations, however. The General wore a Cherokee coat and vest of buckskin, but from his broad hat streamed a martial feather. The gift sword was at his side and in his belt a pistol. His high-heeled boots were adorned with silver spurs of Mexican workmanship, with three-inch rowels in the pattern of daisies. Followed by the faithful Hockley and three volunteers, one in a borrowed suit of clothes, the protector of the Republic rode to meet General Santa Anna and his well-appointed army of seven thousand men.

3

Houston started for Gonzales—a hundred odd miles westward and seventy-six miles from the Álamo—sending a courier ahead to order Fannin to join him. The Commander-in-Chief did not doubt that this officer would be glad to abandon his pretensions to the supreme command. Poor Fannin! His eyes were open to the incredible folly in which the pursuit of ambition and the conspirators of the Council had enmeshed him. He sat at Goliad, miserable and repentant, writing pathetic letters, asking to be extricated from his predicament that he might redeem himself as an obedient "company officer."

The departing gestures of Houston at Refugio had broken up the Matamoras expedition. Fannin had marched his command to Goliad and thrown up what he characteristically christened Fort Defiance. Grant and Johnson, stouter of heart though less troubled by the pricks of conscience, had started to Matamoras regardless, but when their followers dwindled to a hundred men they, too, were obliged to call a halt.

A short distance from Washington, Houston separated himself from his companions, dismounted and held his ear to the prairie. He returned with the announcement that he feared the worst for the Álamo. The firing there had ceased, he said. Otherwise he could have detected it from the earth, an accomplishment learned from the Indians.

At four o'clock on the afternoon of March eleventh, the Commander-in-Chief reached Gonzales. In a camp in the bend of the river on the edge of town were three hundred and seventy-four men under Moseley Baker, with whom Houston lately had quarreled. They possessed two days' rations and two cannon that would shoot. A third piece of artillery was in John Sowell's blacksmith shop. There was no news from the Álamo.

Houston started to form the men into companies, but was interrupted by the sudden shrieks of women in the town. Two Mexicans had arrived with the story that the Álamo had fallen and that the defenders had been horribly slain. Houston denounced the report and arrested the Mexicans as spies. Actually, he believed their story and dispatched fresh orders to Fannin, still rooted at Goliad, to blow up his fort and retreat.

In two days the army grew to five hundred men. Houston organized them into a regiment under Burleson, the Indian fighter, and instituted a program of drill calculated to get the men in hand for a reception of the unnerving news Houston knew he could suppress little longer. Already he had written Henry Raguet a fairly correct account of the battle with particulars, as he had them, of the deaths of Travis and Bowie. "Col Fannin should have relieved our Brave men. . . . He had taken up the line of march . . . [but] owing to the breaking down of a wagon . . . returned to Goliad, and left our *Spartans* to their fate!

"We are now compelled to take post on the east side of the Guadeloupe, and . . . watch . . . the enemy. . . . I [will] if possible prevent all future murders [of] our men in forts." The campaign was taking shape in the mind of Sam Houston. "We cannot fight the enemy ten to one, in their own country." Therefore retreat to East Texas and induce the enemy to divide his forces in pursuit. "I have no doubt as to the issue of the contest. I am in *good* spirits!—tho not *Ardent!!!*"[3] Miss Anna please note.

This letter was barely on its way when Deaf Smith, a famous plainsman and hunter, rode into camp with three actual survivors of the Álamo: Mrs. A. M. Dickinson, her fifteen-months-old baby, Angelina, and Travis's negro body-servant, Joe.

Mrs. Dickinson, who was young and attractive, had been taken to General Santa Anna's apartments after the battle. She held her head high. Her husband had perished on the walls. Her clothing was soiled with the blood of a wounded boy from Nacogdoches whom she had tried to save from the bayonet. General Santa Anna received her with perfect courtesy, and petted little Angelina. Placing a horse and his personal servant, Ben, at her disposal, he asked Mrs. Dickinson to convey the compliments of General Santa Anna to Señor Houston, and to assure him that the story of the Álamo would be the story of all who were found in arms against Mexican authority. Santa Anna said the rebels would be spared only if they laid down their arms forthwith.

Panic took the town and the army. The Mexican advance guard was declared to be in sight. Houston dashed among the soldiery, shouting to the assembly in his booming voice, and telling them to bring in the deserters who had fled. But twenty got away and their wild tales brought pandemonium to Texas.

### 4

Houston quieted the little town where thirty women had learned that they were widows. The army's baggage wagons were reserved for their use. Sinking his artillery in the river, Houston burned what equipage the men could not carry on their backs. At eleven o'clock the army, followed by one ammunition wagon drawn by four oxen, began its retreat.

"In the name of God, gentlemen," cried an old man, "you are not going to leave the families behind!"

"Oh, yes," drawled a voice from the ranks, "we're looking out for number one."

But Houston had left a mounted rear-guard under Deaf Smith to send the refugees in the wake of the army.

The night was warm and pitch dark. A mile east of the town the trail entered a forest of post-oak. The men sank ankle-deep in the sandy soil and expressed themselves freely on the General's order making them infantry. It was a serious compromise with dignity for a Texan to fight on foot. An hour before daybreak there was a halt. The troops dropped in their tracks and slept. At dawn the refugee train came up, and the women helped the soldiers get breakfast.

The meal was interrupted by a series of explosions. Santa Anna's artillery! Houston calmed them. The rear-guard was blowing up the poisoned liquor citizens of Gonzales had left for Santa Anna.

Fifty recruits came during the halt, but seeing the refugees, twenty-five departed to look after their families. The army emerged from the wood on the prairie, "as green as emerald," wrote a boy in the ranks, "and the sun, which had been obscured by clouds, shone out . . . greatly exhilarating our spirits." Houston rode alongside the column, pointing his finger and counting. "We are the rise of eight hundred strong," he said, "and with a good position can whip ten to one of the enemy."[4] This exaggeration of their numbers served to cheer the men.

Houston felt them in need of cheering. A courier had brought a message from Fannin who refused to retreat.[5] Houston surveyed the little column "which seemed but a speck on the vast prairie." "Hockley," he said, "there is the last hope of Texas. We shall never see Fannin nor his men."[6]

At sundown the army bivouaced on La Baca River. Houston found a man asleep on guard, ordered him shot and rejoined Hockley before the embers in the fireplace of a deserted cabin. The Commander-in-Chief whittled a stick and meditated. The only military force, properly speaking, in Texas was with Fannin. Grant and Johnson had been wiped out by Urrea whose dragoons would fall upon Fannin next. Houston tossed a handful of shavings on the fire. "Hockley," he said, "take an order," and dictated instructions to Major William T. Austin to hasten to the coast, find some artillery and rejoin the army on the Colorado in twelve days' time. Houston meant to fight.

On the next day the Commander-in-Chief heard that a blind woman with six children had been passed by. He sent a detachment back thirty miles to bring them in. From Houston the poor woman learned that her husband had perished at the Álamo. The widow and her brood tramped with the army to the Colorado, which was reached at Burnham's Crossing on March seventeenth. Terror-stricken settlers were strung for miles up and down the river, frantic to get across. They had abandoned their home at the words of alarm spread by the Gon-

zales deserters. Some had stopped to throw a few belongings
in a wagon, others had left dinners in the pots. Wives called
out their husbands' names, mothers searched for their children.
Houston rode among them saying that every civilian would be
safely over the river before a single soldier crossed.

The last of the troops were crossing when the Commander
espied two women seated on a log. One was an Álamo widow,
and both were utterly destitute. Houston gave them fifty
dollars and found them places in a wagon. These scenes affected the army and many volunteers left. There was nothing
to restrain any one except the personality of Sam Houston.

But losses were more than made good, and with six hundred
men, he went into camp on the east bank of the Colorado to
await definite word as to Fannin, reinforcements and artillery.
Discipline was maintained. The guard found asleep on La
Baca had not been shot, but the army understood that
his escape was a narrow one. This made pickets so vigilant
that one detained the Commander-in-Chief for identification.
Houston scattered couriers to the eastward to quell the panic
that paralyzed his efforts to form an army capable of giving
battle. He wrote the government that "if only three hundred
men remain on this side of the Brazos, I will die with them or
conquer."[7]

### 5

In assuming that Texas had a government Houston was, in
a broad sense, correct.

While he had been delaying his urgent march to rescue the
blind widow, the Convention at Washington received its first
intimation of the fall of the Álamo in a guarded letter from the
Commander himself. Next day Houston confirmed the disaster,
and deserters from Gonzales embroidered the horror. Part of
the Convention fled without ceremony. Other members got
drunk. Chairman Ellis attempted to adjourn the sittings to
Nacogdoches, but a well-knit delegate with a stubby beard
stood on a bench and told the members to return to their work.

The Constitution was slapped together at ten o'clock that night. At midnight the Convention elected the well-knit delegate provisional president of the Republic.

His name was David G. Burnet. Thirty years before he had deserted a high stool in a New York counting house to see the world. He was with Miranda's romantic but rash descents upon Venezuela. He had roamed with the wild Indians in the little-explored West. One bulge in his close-fitting coat was made by a Bible, another by a pistol; and he did not drink or swear.

Lorenzo de Zavala was chosen vice-president.

Burnet's Cabinet was elected on the spot. At four in the morning of March seventeenth the new Administration was sworn in, and the Convention took a recess for breakfast.

After the meal a remnant of the members came together again. "An invaded, unarmed, unprovided country," wrote Colonel Gray, the useful diarist, "without an army to oppose invaders, and without money to raise one, now presents itself to their hitherto besotted and blinded minds and the awful cry has been heard from the midst of their Assembly, 'What shall we do to be saved?'" When a fugitive dashed into town shouting the groundless rumor that Santa Anna's cavalry had crossed the Colorado, the question of salvation became a matter too intimate for parliamentary procedure. "The members are now dispersing in all directions. A general panic seems to have seized them. Their families are exposed and defenseless, and thousands are moving off to the east. A constant stream of women and children and some men, with wagons, carts and pack mules are rushing across the Brazos night and day."

Mr. Burnet called a Cabinet meeting, at which it was decided to transfer the capital of the Republic "to Harrisburg on the Buffalo Bayou, as a place of more safety than this." The removal began in the rain on the following day. Vice-President Zavala rode a small mule. At his side Johnathan Ikin, an English capitalist, slopped through the mud on foot, revolving in his mind some doubts concerning a proposed five-million-dollar loan. Mrs. Robinson, the wife of the late Lieutenant-Governor, also walked. Some one had stolen her horse.

Mrs. Harris, widow of the founder of the new capital, entertained the dignitaries of the government. Secretary of War Thomas J. Rusk and Colonel Gray dried themselves before her fire and rolled up in a blanket on the floor. The Secretary of Navy and the Attorney-General did the same. But the President, the Vice-President and the Secretary of State had a bed. Lorenzo de Zavala, Jr., embraced his father and, attended by a French valet, breasted the rainswept stream of fleeing humanity to join Sam Houston's Army.

## 6

The flight of the government did not diminish the difficulties of the Commander-in-Chief. "It was a poor compliment to me," he wrote to Rusk, "to suppose that I would not advise the convention of any necessity that might arise for their removal. . . . You know I am not easily depressed but, before my God, since we parted I have found the darkest hours of my life! . . . For forty-eight hours I have not eaten an ounce, nor have I slept." During the retreat "I was in constant apprehension of a rout . . . yet I managed as well, or such was my good luck," that the army was kept together. At Gonzales "if I could have had a moment to start an express in advance of the deserters . . . all would have been well, and all at peace" east of the Colorado. But the deserters "went first, and, being panic-struck . . . all who saw them breathed the poison and fled."[8]

Next day the outlook brightened. "My force will [soon] be highly respectable. . . . You will hear from us. . . . I am writing in the open air. I have no tent. . . . Do devise some plan to send back the rascals who have gone from the army. . . . Oh, why did the cabinet leave Washington? . . . Oh, curse the consternation that has seized the people."[9]

Matters continued to improve. Houston's determination to

fight brought a tide of recruits, until ultimately he had perhaps fourteen hundred men—poorly equipped, without artillery, but eager for battle. Houston maneuvered down the river, and the alert Deaf Smith captured a Mexican scout who revealed that General Sesma was approaching with seven hundred and twenty-five infantry and two field pieces. Sesma camped on the west side of the river two miles above the right wing of Houston's army, and sent for reinforcements. Lieutenant-Colonel Sidney Sherman, a dashing Kentucky volunteer with the best-looking uniform in camp, begged to cross and attack, but Houston refused.

For five days the armies faced each other in expectation of battle. There were a few brushes between patrols. On the evening of March twenty-fifth a Gonzales refugee named Peter Kerr galloped into camp shouting that Fannin had surrendered after a bloody defeat. The cry went up to fall upon Sesma at once. Houston seized Kerr and denounced his story. Sesma would be taken care of in good time. The soldiery went to bed and during the night General Sesma was heavily reinforced.

The only music in the Texan camp was tattoo and reveille beaten on a drum by the Commander-in-Chief himself, who had learned the art under Captain Cusack of the Mounted Gunmen in Tennessee. Each night between these calls, General Houston inspected the lines of sentinels, conferred with his staff, wrote dispatches and turned the pages of the *Commentaries* of Cæsar and *Gulliver's Travels*, which he had brought in his saddle-bags from Washington to read in his spare time.

There was an occasional hour for a talk with George Hockley. A fast comradeship grew between the General and his aide. They were old acquaintances and had come near fighting a duel in Nashville ten years before. But these mellow midnight conversations while his army slept carried Sam Houston back to days more remote. He spoke of his mother, of the consolation her teachings had been to his troubled life and of his will to reestablish himself as a mark of respect for her memory.

Reveille was beaten an hour before dawn, when the camp

stood to arms until full day outlined the west bank of the river where Mexican patrols lurked in the brush.   After breakfast the Commander-in-Chief would kick off his boots and sleep for three hours.   By mid-forenoon he was on his round of inspection, which carried him to every precinct of the camp.   Since joining the troops at Gonzales the Commander had used liquor sparingly, if at all, but carried a small vial of salts of hartshorn which he periodically dabbed to his nostrils.

The morning after the Fannin alarm Houston did not sleep. The soldiers saw their General sunning himself on a pile of saddles while he cut chews of tobacco with a clasp knife and studied a map.   The rumor spread that the General was planning a battle, and there was a great cleaning of rifles and clattering of accouterments.   Noon came and Houston had not begun his inspections.   Something was in the wind.   By mid-afternoon the atmosphere was tense when an order came to break camp, load the wagons and be ready to retreat at sunset.

The army was dumfounded.   What did it mean?   Detachment commanders went flying to headquarters to ascertain. They were told to return to their companies and carry out orders.   The army would march at sunset as directed.

Bewildered and complaining, the army left fires alight and picked its way eastward through the tall grass.   Seventy-five families were encamped on the river, hoping for a battle.   They fled.   "Among these was my own," one soldier wrote.   "I now left the army and with the families set out on the retreat."[10] Many of Houston's soldiers did likewise.

Six miles from the river the army bivouaced without fires and grumbled itself to sleep.   The first light of morning saw the column pressing on.   Staff officers rode up and down. "Close up, men.   Close up."   Major Ben Fort Smith of the staff asked Captain Moseley Baker what he thought of the movement.   Captain Baker replied in a loud voice.   He thought little enough of the movement, and unless reasons for the retreat acceptable to the Army were forthcoming, Sam Houston would be deposed from command before the day was over.

The march was so relentlessly pressed that Captain Baker did not find an opportunity to carry out his plan. That night, with thirty weary miles behind them, the men were too tired to care. They had covered the whole distance between the Colorado and the Rio de los Brazos de Dios and were bivouaced a mile from San Felipe de Austin. But sentiment against the retreat had grown, and after a few hurried interviews Captain Baker turned in, confident that the Army would throw off Houston's leadership in the morning.[11]

# CHAPTER XIX

## The Plain of St. Hyacinth

### 1

Reveille rolled in the darkness, and stiff men, casting grotesque shadows, fumbled about the breakfast fires. A bleak wind blew ashes in the coffee kettles. The Commander-in-Chief did not show himself, but after breakfast the punctual staff officers bounced through camp with brisk orders to form companies for the march.

Soldiers grumble as a matter of form, but those ably led acquire a habit of obedience that overbears many weaknesses of the flesh. The companies fell in, and only Captains Moseley Baker and Wily Martin sustained the bold resolutions of the night before. Lieutenant-Colonel Sherman sent Houston an announcement of their refusal to march. This brought Hockley at a gallop, shouting to Sherman to put the column in motion. "If subordinates refuse to obey orders the sooner the fact is ascertained the better!" The column moved, but the companies of Baker and Martin stood fast.

A furious rain caught the column toiling through a swamp up the west bank of the River of the Arms of God. Wagons stalled and men floundered in the mud. The sheer force of the downpour broke the ranks. The exertions of all the staff officers and of Houston himself were unable to preserve an appearance of military order. Stragglers began to grope back toward Baker and Martin. Houston paused under a tree, penciling an order to Baker to take post in defense of the river

238

crossing at San Felipe, and Martin at Fort Bend.  They complied.

For three terrible days Houston drove the stumbling column through the unrelenting rain, advancing only eighteen miles. On March 31, 1836, he halted in a "bottom" by the Brazos with nine hundred demoralized and mutinous men remaining of the thirteen hundred he had led from the Colorado five days before. Near by glowed the lights of Jared Groce's house, where in 1829 took place the first discussion on Texas soil to solicit Sam Houston to assist the fortunes of the restless province.

The country was in worse temper than the Army.  Houston's abandonment of the Colorado gave fresh wings to the terror that had been calmed somewhat by his halt and the expectation of a battle.  A fierce outcry broke from government and populace, which took little account of the strategic handicap Fannin's capitulation had imposed upon their General.  Although students of the military science, viewing the campaign in retrospect, entertain divided opinions on the matter, Houston believed that a victory on the Colorado would have been indecisive and a reverse irreparable.  General Santa Anna believed that the elimination of Fannin had made all Texas untenable for Houston, and arranged for an early return to Mexico City.

During the retreat came the paralyzing intelligence that Fannin and three hundred and ninety men had been executed in cold blood after surrendering, and of the massacre of a smaller band under Captain King.  General Santa Anna was keeping his word.  Texas shuddered and fled.  Mr. Burnet's government lost its grip and the flight of the population became a hysterical plunge toward the Sabine.

Sam Houston's rain-soaked and rebellious mob was the Republic's solitary hope—menaced by four Mexican columns sweeping forward to enclose its front, flanks and rear.  The profound wisdom of hindsight suggests that had the Commander given some explanation of his retreat, Army and country might have fared better.  But the inscrutable Indian brain of The Raven had divulged nothing and explained nothing. "I consulted none;" he wrote in the saddle, "held no councils of war. *If I err, the blame is mine.*"[1] And he had taken no notice of criticism.

The story grew that Houston meant to abandon Texas in a mad effort to induce United States troops on the Sabine to take up the war. That first wet night in the Brazos Bottoms, Houston wrote Secretary of War Rusk for news of the government's program, if any. "I must let the camp know something . . . [so that] I can keep them together."[2]

## 2

Sam Houston promised his mob a glorious victory and drove a parcel of beeves into camp for a barbecue. Then he began to remold the rabble into an army to receive the enemy, providentially delayed by the rains.

The Bottoms quaked with activity, and no trick in the repertory of the professionally trained soldier was neglected. Drills, inspections, maneuvers; maneuvers, inspections, drills. Units were revamped, two new regiments created, a corps d'élite of Regulars formed. Anson Jones was so dizzily yanked from infantry private to regimental surgeon that he complained of "having to do duty in both capacities" for several days. Discipline and esprit de corps began to return. Recruits came in. Scouts watched the encroaching enemy. Patrols watched the camp. Jackals caught plundering refugees were assisted out of their troubles at the nearest tree.

Encouraging reports from the United States were published to the Army. Wharton wrote to Houston from Nashville: "*Your name* . . . [will] raise 5000 volunteers in Tennessee alone. . . . Especially the Ladies are enthusiastic. . . . The Ladies have pledged themselves to arm equip & entirely outfit 200 volunteers now forming."[3] The lovely Nashville ladies! Miss Anna Hanna stitched a flag for her old beau. A woman in black on a river plantation flaunted, like a banner, her proud glance in the face of hostile family frowns.

Houston's difficulties were staggering. Burnet was an enemy. He had a spy on Houston's staff. The Commander-in-Chief intercepted one of this creature's letters, declaring that after abandoning the use of liquor Houston had taken up opium. A newly promoted major returned from Moseley Baker's outpost and began to sound out officers on a scheme to "beat for volunteers" to proclaim a successor to General Houston. Sidney Sherman—a full colonel now, his uniform the brightest sight in camp—was to be the man.

An Indian uprising threatened the refugees. Mexican agents were undoing the peace-work Houston had accomplished after leaving Refugio. "My friend Col Bowl," Houston wrote the war lord of the Cherokees, "I am very busy, and will only say how da do, to you!" The salutation took the form of a reminder that Houston had been the red man's friend and that the red man would find it to his profit to reciprocate. "My best compliments to my sister, and tell her that I have not wore out the mockasins which she made me."[4]

On April seventh Santa Anna reached San Felipe. Houston reinforced Baker, and for four days the Mexican artillery tried to force a crossing without success, although an American named Johnson, serving with the Mexicans, caused some discomfort by firing across the flooded river with a rifle. With this cannonade rumbling in his ears, Houston received a brief message from President Burnet. "Sir: The enemy are laughing you to scorn. You must fight."[5] The camp was in a frenzy of excitement. Leaders of the contemplated mutiny believed their hour had struck, but changed their minds when Sam Houston had two graves dug and affixed to trees about camp a memorandum saying that the first man to beat for volunteers would be shot.[6]

### 3

Word that Santa Anna had abruptly abandoned his attempt to cross at San Felipe found Houston in a buoyant mood. He had just received his long awaited guns—two iron six-pounders, the gift of friends in Cincinnati. Clad in a worn leather jacket, he was watching the camp blacksmith cut up old horseshoes for artillery ammunition, when a young soldier said that the lock on his rifle would not work. "All right, son," said General Houston, "set her down and call around in an hour." The boy came back, stammering an apology. He was a recruit, he said, and did not know that the man pointed out to him as a blacksmith was the Commander-in-Chief. "My friend, he told you right. I am a very good blacksmith," replied Houston taking up the gun and snapping the lock. "She is in order now."[7]

The next two days Houston devoted to moving his army across the Brazos, while Santa Anna crossed near Fort Bend. The Texans encamped on the premises of a well-to-do settler named Donahoe, who demanded that Houston stop the men from cutting his timber for fire-wood. General Houston reprimanded the wood-gatherers. Under no circumstances, he said, should they lay ax to another of Citizen Donahoe's trees. Could they not see that Citizen Donahoe's rail fence would afford the fuel required? That night the army gallants scraped up an acquaintance with some girls in a refugee camp, turned Mr. Donahoe out of house and held a dance.[8]

When the army left Donahoe's at dawn Moseley Baker demanded to know whether Houston intended to intercept Santa Anna at Harrisburg or to retreat to the Sabine. The General declined to answer. Seventeen miles from Donahoe's the road forked, the left branch leading to Nacogdoches and the Sabine, the right branch to Harrisburg. If Houston should attempt to take the left road, Captain Baker proclaimed that he would "then and there be deposed from command."[9] Rain slowed the march, however, and only by borrowing draft oxen from Mrs. Mann of a refugee band that followed the army, did the troops by nightfall reach Sam McCurley's, a mile short of the cross-roads.

Next morning a torrential rain failed to extinguish the excitement in the ranks. Which road would Houston take?

The menacing Baker thundered warnings, but the Sabine route had its partizans among the troops. All of the refugees favored it. The Commander-in-Chief treated the commotion as if it did not exist and without comment sent the advance-guard over the Harrisburg Road.

A wail arose from the refugees. There was a halt and a wrangle which Houston terminated by ordering Wily Martin to escort the refugees and watch for Indian hostilities to the eastward. The Commander-in-Chief thought this cleared the path for his pursuit of Santa Anna, but he had reckoned without Mrs. Mann. She demanded the return of her oxen. Wagon Master Rohrer, a giant in buckskin with a voice like a bull, brushed the protest aside as too trivial for the attention of a man of affairs, and cracking his long whip, addressed the oxen in the sparkling idiom of the trail. Whereupon, Mrs. Mann produced from beneath her apron a pistol, and, if rightly overheard, addressed Mr. Rohrer in terms equally exhilarating. General Houston arrived in time to compose the difficulty with his usual courtly deference to the wishes of a lady.

Three or four hundred men followed Martin, or departed independently, leaving Houston with less than a thousand to follow Santa Anna who rode with a magnificent suite at the head of a picked force of veterans. But Santa Anna was now the pursued and Houston the pursuer. General Santa Anna commanded the center of three armies. The rains, however, had fought on Houston's side, and there was a chance that by fast marching he might catch the Mexican Commander-in-Chief out of reach of his cooperating columns. Another factor in Houston's favor was the Sabine retreat story. Houston had never intended to fall back to the Sabine, but the report was so persistently circulated and never denied that the Mexicans included it in their strategic calculations.

Over the boggy prairie path, by courtesy the Harrisburg Road, Houston drove the little column fearfully. Nothing delayed the advance. Wagons were carried over quagmires on the backs of the men. The greatest trial was the guns. In camp the enthusiastic soldiers had christened them the "Twin Sisters," but now they thought of other names.

On the morning of April eighteenth the army reached the Buffalo Bayou, opposite Harrisburg, having covered fifty-five miles in two and a half days. Mounts and men were dead beat. Houston had never been in this part of the country before. He spent his nights in constant touch with the scouts and in the study of a crude map, covered with cabalistic pencilings of his own.

The army rested. Harrisburg was in ashes; Santa Anna had come and gone. Deaf[10] Smith swam the bayou and toward evening returned with two prisoners, a Mexican scout and a courier. The courier's saddle-bag bore the name of W. B. Travis—souvenir of the Álamo. It contained useful information. Santa Anna had dashed upon Harrisburg with eight hundred troops in an effort to capture President Burnet leaving Cos to follow. But the raid netted only three printers who had stuck to their cases in the office of Gail Borden's *Texas Telegraph*. Editor Borden and the government had fled to Galveston Island in the nick of time, with Santa Anna racing in futile pursuit to take them before they left the mainland. On his soiled map Houston traced the situation of his quarry, not ten miles away, groping among the unfamiliar marshes that indented Galveston Bay and the estuary of a certain nebulous Rio San Jacinto.[11] Sending his army to bed the Commander-in-Chief continued to pore over the chart. Two hours before dawn he slept a little.

After the daybreak stand-to General Houston delivered a speech. The "ascending eloquence and earnestness" put one impressionable young soldier in mind of "the halo encircling the brow of our Savior." "Victory is certain!" Sam Houston said. "Trust in God and fear not! And remember the Álamo! Remember the Álamo!"

"Remember the Álamo!" the ranks roared back. They had a battle-cry.

There was just time for a short letter to Anna Raguet's

father: "This morning we are in preparation to meet Santa Anna. . . . It is wisdom growing out of necessity."[12]

The pick of the army advanced, leaving the sick and the wagons with a rear-guard. After a swift march Houston made a perilous crossing of Buffalo Bayou, using the floor torn from a cabin as a raft. The column hid in a woods until dark, and then advanced warily, encircled by the scouts under Deaf Smith and Henry Karnes. At a narrow bridge over a stream—Vince's bridge over Vince's Bayou, men who knew the country said—the column trampled the cold ashes of Santa Anna's camp-fires. The night was black and the advance painfully slow. Equipment had been muffled so as to make no sound. A low-spoken order passed from rank to rank to be ready on the instant to attack. Rifles were clutched a little closer. One mile, two miles beyond the bridge, down a steep ravine and stealthily up the other side crept the column.

At two o'clock in the morning the word came to break ranks. In the damp grass the men dropped beside their arms. With the salt of the sea in their nostrils they slept for an hour; then formed up and stumbled on until daybreak, when their General concealed them in a patch of timber.

Some of the Vince brothers' cows were grazing in this wood. The army had a commissary! Throats were noiselessly cut and General Houston had given permission to build fires when a party of scouts dashed up. They had driven off a Mexican patrol and learned that Santa Anna was on the road to Lynch's Ferry. The butchers were called from their delectable task and the fires pulled apart. The men fell in to the banging of muskets and the clank of ramrods as old charges were fired and fresh ones sent home. The breakfastless army headed for Lynch's Ferry, three miles eastward. Santa Anna approached the ferry from the south, with five miles to go.

From the crest of a grass-grown slope Houston's army got its first view of Lynch's Ferry, lying at the tip of a point of lowland where Buffalo Bayou flowed into the San Jacinto River. On the farther side of the river was a scattering of unpainted houses—the town of Lynchburg. Behind the town bulged a round hill, the side of which was covered with people who gazed for a moment at the column filing down the slope, and then melted away. They were Texas Tories waiting to pilot Santa Anna toward the Sabine.

Having the choice of positions, Houston established himself in a wood of great oak trees, curtained with Spanish moss, that skirted the bayou just above its junction with the San Jacinto. He posted the infantry and cavalry in order of battle within the thick shelter, and placed the Twin Sisters on the edge of the trees so as to command the swelling savannah that lay in front of the woods. This semi-tropical prairie extended to the front for nearly a mile, thick with waving green grass, half as high as wheat. A woods bounded the prairie on the left, screening a treacherous swamp that bordered the San Jacinto. Swamp and river swung to the right, half enclosing the prairie and giving it a background of green a tone darker than the active young grass. Over this prairie Santa Anna must pass to gain the ferry.

The Texans were prepared to fight, but the presence of cows in the grass revealed the force of Napoleon's famous maxim. Again the fires crackled, and this time steaks were sizzling on the spits when the scouts came galloping across the plain. They said that Santa Anna was advancing just beyond a rise. The Twin Sisters were wheeled out a little piece on the prairie. The infantry line crept to the edge of the woods.

Santa Anna's bugles blared beyond the swell. A dotted line of skirmishers bobbed into view, and behind it marched parallel columns of infantry and of cavalry with slender lances gleaming. Between the columns Santa Anna advanced a gun. The skirmishers parted to let the clattering artillerymen through.

The Twin Sisters were primed and loaded with broken horseshoes. General Houston, on a great white stallion, rode up and down the front of his infantry. Under partial cover of a clump of trees, three hundred yards from the Texan lines, the Mexican gun wheeled into position.

Joe Neill, commanding the Twin Sisters, gave the word for one gun to fire. *Crash* went the first shot by Sam Houston's artillery in the war. There had been no powder for practise rounds. Through the ragged smoke the Texans could see Mexican horses down and men working frantically at their piece. Their Captain had been wounded and the gun carriage disabled.

*Crash!* The second Twin cut loose, and the Mexican gun replied. Its shot tore through the branches of the trees above the Texans' heads, causing a shower of twigs.

*Rat-tat!* The Mexican skirmishers opened fire and plumes of black dirt jumped in front of the Texas infantry. A ball glanced from a metal trimming on General Houston's bridle. Colonel Neill dropped with a broken hip.

The Texan infantrymen had held their beads on the dotted line for so long that their faces ached. Every dot was covered by ten rifles, for no Texan had to be told that when he shot to shoot *at* something. A row of flaming orange jets rushed from the woods and expired in air; the dotted gray line sagged into the grass and did not reappear.

The Twin Sisters whanged away and the Mexican gun barked back, but the state of its carriage made accurate aim impossible. Santa Anna decided not to bring on a general engagement, and sent a detachment of dragoons to haul off the crippled gun. Dashing Sidney Sherman begged to take the cavalry and capture the Mexican field piece, and finally Houston consented. Sherman lost two men and several horses, but failed to get the gun. General Houston gave him a dressing down that should have withered the leaves on the trees. A private by the conquering name of Mirabeau Buonaparte Lamar who had borne himself courageously was promoted to command the cavalry regiment, numbering fifty-three.

Sherman was considerable of a camp hero just the same; he and Deaf Smith who had captured the ferry-boat loaded with Mexican flour. Dough, rolled on sticks and baked by the fire, made the postponed meal notable, after which the men spread blankets by the fires and talked themselves to sleep over the big fight that was to take place in the morning. Less than a mile away, under the watchful eyes of Houston's scouts, flickered the camp-fires of the enemy.

On the twenty-first of April, 1836, reveille rolled at the usual hour of four, but a strange hand tapped the drum. The Commander-in-Chief was asleep, with a coil of rope under his head. He had left instructions not to be disturbed. It was evident that the anticipated dawn attack would not take place. The ranks silently stood to until daylight, precisely as they had done every other morning, except that the Commander-in-Chief slept through it all. Nor did the soldier hum of break-fast-time arouse him. It was full day when Sam Houston opened his eyes—after his first sleep of more than three hours in six weeks. He lay on his back, studying the sky. An eagle wheeled before the flawless blue. The Commander-in-Chief sprang to his feet. "The sun of Austerlitz," he said, "has risen again."[13]

An eagle over the Cumberland on that awful April night— an eagle over the muddier Rubicon—an eagle above the plain of St. Hyacinth. Did these symbolic birds exist, or were they simply reflections of a mind drenched with Indian lore? The eagle was Sam Houston's medicine animal. When profoundly moved it was from the Indian part of his being and not the white-man part that unbidden prayers ascended.

4

The camp was in a fidget to attack. It could not fathom a commander who sauntered aimlessly under the trees in the sheer enjoyment, he said, of a good night's sleep. Deaf Smith rode up and dismounted. The lines of the old plainsman's leathery face were deep. His short square frame moved with a heavy tread. The scout was very weary. Night and day he and Henry Karnes had been the eyes of the army, and considering the tax of the other faculties that deafness imposed upon a scout, the achievements of Smith elude rational explanation.

"Santa Anna is getting reinforcements," he said in his high-pitched voice. And surely enough, a line of pack-mules was just visible beyond the swell in the prairie. "They've just come over our track. I'm going to tell the general he ought to burn Vince's bridge before any more come up."

After a talk with Smith, Houston told his commissary general, John Forbes, to find two sharp axes, and then strolled past a gathering of soldiers remarking that it wasn't often Deaf Smith could be fooled by a trick like that—Santa Anna marching men around and around to make it look like a re-inforcement. Smith returned from another gallop on to the prairie. "The general was right," he announced loudly. "It's all a humbug." But privately he informed Houston that the reinforcement numbered five hundred and forty men under Cos, which raised Santa Anna's force to the neighborhood of thirteen hundred and fifty. Houston's strength was slightly above eight hundred.[14]

Houston later told Santa Anna that his reason for waiting for Cos was to avoid making "two bites of one cherry." But he did not care to see Filísola, who might turn up at any time with two or three thousand Mexicans. Handing the axes to Smith, Houston told him to destroy Vince's bridge. "And come back like eagles, or you will be too late for the day."

Unaware of these preparations, the camp was working itself into a state. To all appearance the General was wasting good time, and jealous officers were only too eager to place this construction on the situation. At noon John A. Wharton, the Adjutant-General, with whom the Commander-in-Chief was not on the most cordial terms, went from mess to mess, stirring up the men. "Boys, there is no other word to-day, but fight, fight!" Moseley Baker harangued his company. They must neither give nor ask quarter, he said. Resting on his saddle horn, Houston narrowly observed the Baker proceedings. He rode on to a mess that Wharton had just addressed. Every one was boiling for a fight. "All right," observed the General. "Fight and be damned."[15]

Houston called a council of war—the first and last, but one, of his career. The question he proposed was, "Shall we attack the enemy or await his attack upon us?" There was a sharp division of ideas. Houston expressed no opinion, and when the others had wrangled themselves into a thorough disagreement he dismissed the council.

At three-thirty o'clock, the Commander-in-Chief abruptly formed his army for attack. At four o'clock he lifted his sword. A drum and fife raised the air of a love-song, *Come to the Bower,* and the last army of the Republic moved from the woods and slowly up the sloping plain of San Jacinto. The left of the line was covered by the swamp, the right by the Twin Sisters, Millard's forty-eight Regulars and Lamar's fifty cavalry. A company from Newport, Kentucky, displayed a white silk flag, embroidered with an amateurish figure of Liberty. (The Lone Star emblem was a later creation.) A glove of the First Lieutenant's sweetheart bobbed from the staff. On the big white stallion Sam Houston rode up and down the front.

"Hold your fire, men. Hold your fire. Hold your fire."

The mastery of a continent was in contention between the champions of two civilizations—racial rivals and hereditary enemies, so divergent in idea and method that suggeston of compromise was an affront. On an obscure meadow of bright grass, nursed by a watercourse named on hardly any map, wet steel would decide which civilization should prevail on these shores and which submit in the clash of men and symbols impending— the conquistador and the frontiersman, the Inquisition and the Magna Charta, the rosary and the rifle.

5

For ten of the longest minutes that a man ever lives, the single line poked through the grass. In front lay a barricade of Mexican pack-saddles and camp impedimenta, inert in the oblique rays of the sun.

"Hold your fire, men. Hold your fire."

Behind the Mexican line a bugle rang. A sketchy string of orange dots glowed from the pack-saddles and a ragged rattle of musketry roused up a scolding swarm of birds from the trees on the Texans' left. A few Texans raised their rifles and let go at the dots.

"Hold your fire! God damn you, hold your fire!"[16] General Houston spurred the white stallion to a gallop.

The orange dots continued to wink and die. The white stallion fell. Throwing himself upon a cavalryman's pony, Houston resumed his patrol of the line.

"Fight for your lives! Vince's bridge has been cut down!" It was Deaf Smith on a lathered mustang. Rather inaccurately, the soldiers understood Vince's bridge to be their sole avenue of retreat.

Twenty yards from the works, Houston made a signal with his hat. A blast of horseshoes from the Twin Sisters laid a section of the fragile breastwork flat. The infantrymen roared a volley and lunged forward drawing their hunting knives. "Remember the Álamo! Remember the Álamo!"

They swept over the torn barricade as if it had not been there. Shouts and yells and the pounding of hoofs smote their ears. Through key-holes in a pungent wall of smoke they saw gray-clad little figures, with chin-straps awry, running back, kneeling and firing, and running back—toward some tents where greater masses of men were veering this way and that. The Texans pursued them. The pungent wall melted; the firing was not so heavy now as the Texans were using their knives and the bayonets of Mexican guns. The surprise lacked nothing. Santa Anna had thought Houston would not, could not, attack. In his carpeted marquee, he was enjoying a siesta when a drowsy sentinel on the barricade descried the Texan advance. Cos's men were sleeping off the fatigue of their night march. Cavalrymen were riding bareback to and from water. Others were cooking and cutting wood. Arms were stacked.

When the barrier was overrun a general of brigade rallied a handful of men about a field piece; all fell before the Texans' knives. An infantry colonel got together a following under cover of some trees; a Texas sharpshooter killed him, and the following scattered. Almonte, the Chief-of-Staff, rounded up four hundred men and succeeded in retreating out of the panic zone. Santa Anna rushed from his tent commanding every one to lie down. A moment later he vaulted on a black horse and disappeared.

General Houston rode among the wreckage of the Mexican camp. He was on his third horse, and his right boot was full of blood. "A hundred steady men," he said, "could wipe us out." Except for a handful of Regulars, the army had escaped control of its officers, and was pursuing, clubbing, knifing, shooting Mexicans wherever they were found. Fugitives plunged into the swamp and scattered over the prairie. "Me no Álamo! Me no Álamo!" Some cavalry bolted for bridgeless Vince's Bayou. The Texans rushed them down a vertical bank. A hundred men and a hundred horses, inextricably tangled, perished in the water.

Houston glanced over the prairie. A gray-clad column, marching with the swing of veterans, bore toward the scene of battle. After a long look the General lowered his field-glass with a thankful sigh. Almonte and his four hundred were surrendering in a body.

As the sun of Austerlitz set General Houston fainted in Hockley's arms. His right leg was shattered above the ankle. The other Texan casualties were six killed and twenty-four wounded. According to Texan figures the Mexicans lost 630 killed, 208 wounded and 730 prisoners, making a total of 1568 accounted for. This seems to be about 200 more men than Santa Anna had with him.

The battle proper had lasted perhaps twenty minutes. The rest was in remembrance of the Álamo. This pursuit and slaughter continued into the night. The prisoners were herded in the center of a circle of bright fires. "Santa Anna? Santa Anna?" the Texans demanded until officers began to pull off their shoulder-straps. But no Santa Anna was found.

The Texans roystered all night, to the terror of the prisoners who designated their captors by the only English words their bewildered senses were competent to grasp. A woman camp-follower threw herself before a Texan soldier. "Señor God Damn, do not kill me for the love of God and the life of your mother!" The soldier was of the small company of Mexicans that had fought under young Zavala. He told his countrywoman not to fear. "Sisters, see here," the woman cried. "This Señor God Damn speaks the Christian language like the rest of us!"

### 6

After a night of pain General Houston propped himself against a tree, and Surgeon Ewing redressed his wound which was more serious than had been supposed. While the Surgeon probed fragments of bone from the mangled flesh, the patient fashioned a garland of leaves and tastefully inscribed a card "To Miss Anna Raguet, Nacogdoches, Texas: These are laurels I send you from the battle field of San Jacinto. Thine. Houston."

The Commander-in-Chief also penciled a note which was borne as fast as horseflesh could take it to the hands of one who deserved his own share of the laurels—Andrew Jackson.

All day bands of scared prisoners were brought in. But no Santa Anna, no Cos. This was more than vexing. The Texans wished simply to kill Cos for violation of parole, but Santa Anna might escape to Filísola and return with thrice the army Houston had just defeated. With the President of Mexico in his hands, however, Houston could rest assured that he had won the war, not merely a battle.

Toward evening a patrol of five men rode into camp. Mounted behind Joel Robison was a bedraggled little figure in a blue cotton smock and red felt slippers. The patrol had found him near the ruined Vince's Bayou bridge seated on a stump, the living picture of dejection. He said he had found his ridiculous clothes in a deserted house. He looked hardly worth bothering to take five miles to camp and would have been dispatched on the spot but for Robison, who was a good-hearted boy, and spoke Spanish. Robison and his prisoner chatted on the ride. How many men did the Americans have? Robison said less than eight hundred, and the prisoner said that surely there were more than that. Robison asked the captive if he had left a family behind. "*Sí*, señor." "Do you expect to see them again?" The little Mexican shrugged his shoulders. "Why did you come and fight us?" Robison wished to know. "A private soldier, señor, has little choice in such matters."

Robison had taken a liking to the polite little fellow and was about to turn him loose without ceremony among the herd of prisoners, when the captives began to raise their hats.

"*El Presidente!  El Presidente!*"

An officer of the guard ran up and with an air that left the Texan flat, the prisoner asked to be conducted to General Houston.

Sam Houston was lying on a blanket under the oak tree, his eyes closed and his face drawn with pain. The little man was brought up by Hockley and Ben Fort Smith. He stepped forward and bowed gracefully.

"I am General Antonio López de Santa Anna, President of Mexico, Commander-in-Chief of the Army of Operations. I place myself at the disposal of the brave General Houston."

This much unexpected Spanish was almost too great a strain upon the pupil of Miss Anna Raguet. Raising himself on one elbow, Houston replied as words came to him.

"General Santa Anna!—Ah, indeed!—Take a seat, General. I am glad to see you, take a seat!"

The host waved his arm toward a black box, and asked for an interpreter. Zavala came up. Santa Anna recognized him.

"Oh! My friend, the son of my *early* friend!"

The young patrician bowed coldly. Santa Anna turned to General Houston.

"That man may consider himself born to no common destiny who has conquered the Napoleon of the West; and it now remains for him to be generous to the vanquished."

"You should have remembered that at the Álamo," Houston replied.[17]

General Santa Anna made a bland Latin answer that loses much in translation. Houston pressed the point. What excuse for the massacre of Fannin's men? Another Latin answer. Another blunt interrogation, and for the first time in his amazing life Santa Anna's power of self-command deserted him. He raised a nervous hand to his pale face and glanced behind him. A ring of savage Texans had pressed around, with ominous looks on their faces and ominous stains on their knives. Santa Anna murmured something about a passing indisposition and requested a piece of opium.

The drug restored the prisoner's poise, and formal negotiations were begun. Santa Anna was deft and shrewd, but Houston declined to discuss terms of peace, saying that was a governmental matter not within the province of a military commander. Santa Anna proposed an armistice, which Houston accepted, dictating the terms which provided for the immediate evacuation of Texas by the Mexican Armies. Santa Anna wrote marching orders for Filísola and the other generals. Houston beckoned to Deaf Smith, and the orders were on their way.

Houston had Santa Anna's marquee erected within a few yards of the tree under which the Texas General lay, and restored the captive's personal baggage to him. Santa Anna retired to change his clothes, and General Houston produced an ear of corn from beneath his blanket and began to nibble it. A soldier picked up a kernel and said he was going to take it home and plant it. A genius had opened his lips!

Houston's great voice summoned the men from their cordial

discussion of the mode of General Santa Anna's execution. "My brave fellows," he said scattering corn by the handful, "take this along with you to your own fields, where I hope you may long cultivate the arts of peace as you have shown yourselves masters of the art of war."

Irresistible.   "We'll call it Houston corn!" they shouted.

"Not Houston corn," their General said gravely, "but San Jacinto corn!"[18]

And thousands of tasseled Texas acres to-day boast pedigrees that trace back to the San Jacinto ear.   Three days after the corn incident, Houston had forgotten the name, however, and in his official report nearly wrote it the battle of Lynchburg.

7

When President Burnet arrived with as much of his travel-stained government as could be picked up on short notice, General Houston was receiving Mrs. McCormick who bore a verbal petition to remove "them stinking Mexicans" from her land.

"Why, lady," protested General Houston, "your land will be famed in history as the spot where the glorious battle was fought."

"To the devil with your glorious history," the lady replied. "Take off your stinking Mexicans."[19]

Mr. Burnet also found much to deplore, including General Houston's reported use of profanity.   He and his satellites swarmed over the camp, collecting souvenirs and giving orders without notice of the Commander-in-Chief.   Sidney Sherman and the new Colonel Lamar were much in the company of these statesmen.   Leaning on his crutches, Houston watched the government confiscate the fine stallion of Almonte, which, after the sale of some captured material at auction, had been presented to the General by his soldiers.   Had Sam Houston raised his hand those soldiers would have pushed Mr. Burnet into the San Jacinto.   Even greater tact was required to preserve the life of Santa Anna, whose guards would have slain him except for Houston.

The Commander's wound had become dangerous, and Doctor Ewing said he must go to New Orleans for an operation. When President Burnet and Cabinet boarded their vessel to return to Galveston Island, Houston was not asked to accompany them. When he applied for permission, it was refused. But the Captain of the boat declined to sail without the General, and Secretary of War Rusk and his brother carried him aboard. Mr. Rusk was still Houston's friend and had made the last part of the campaign with the Army.

Passage on a Texas naval vessel sailing for New Orleans was likewise refused, and Surgeon Ewing, who had accompanied his chief to Galveston Island against President Burnet's order, was dismissed from the service. Houston's condition was alarming. Doctor Ewing feared lockjaw would develop before he could reach New Orleans. While Houston was being lifted on board a dirty little trading schooner, Burnet regaled the vast refugee camp on the island with tales of the General's private life. When these reached the ears of a newly landed company of southern volunteers, a message written by a hand so stricken that it could hardly guide a pen was all that saved the official dignity of the Provisional President.

"On board Schooner Flora
"Galveston Island, 11th May 1836
"The Commander-in-Chief . . . has heard with regret that some dissatisfaction existed in the army. If it is connected with him, or his circumstances, he asks as a special favor, that it may no longer exist. . . . Obedience to the constituted authorities . . . is the first duty of a soldier. . . . The General in taking leave of his companions in arms, assures them of his affectionate gratitude.

"SAM HOUSTON."[20]

# CHAPTER XX

## "The Crisis Requires It"

### 1

For seven days the little *Flora* rolled in a storm before it beat into the churning Mississippi and at noon on Sunday, May 22, 1836, arrived at New Orleans. The levee was thronged with people.

Not since Jackson's victory at Chalmette had America been so stirred by a piece of military news. The story of San Jacinto was not believed at first. After the Álamo and Goliad, the extermination of the bands of Grant and Johnson, the flight of the government and of the people, and the dismal dispatches that Houston was falling back, still falling back, the overwhelming intelligence of the capture of the President of Mexico and the annihilation of his army was incredible. When the confirmation came cannon boomed, men paraded, and in the Senate Thomas Hart Benton called Sam Houston another Mark Antony.

General Houston lay in a stupor on the uncovered deck of the *Flora*. Captain Appleman believed his passenger to be a dying man. When the *Flora* touched the wharf a crowd surged on board, and the Captain thought that his boat would be swamped. They started to lift Houston from the deck. With a cry of pain and a convulsive movement of his powerful left arm he flung them off. A man bent over the sufferer. The years rolled back and Sam Houston recognized the voice of William Christy, with whom he had served in the United States Army. A band struck up a march; Houston told Christy to

258

hold off the crowd and he would get up by himself.  Leaning on
his crutches he lurched against the gunwale.

His wild appearance stunned the crowd.  General Houston's coat was tatters.  He had no hat.  His stained and stinking shirt was wound about the shattered ankle.  The music
stopped, the cheering stopped and a schoolgirl with big violet
eyes began to cry.  Her name was Margaret Lea.  As he was
lifted to a litter, General Houston fainted.

At the Christy mansion in Girod Street, three surgeons removed twenty pieces of bone from the wound.  Recovery seemed
by no means certain, and crowds lingered in front of the house.
On June second Houston received a few visitors, but fainted
during their call.  Ten days later bad news came from Texas.
Sam Houston gave his host a saddle that had belonged to
Santa Anna and, although his life was still in danger, set out
by land for the Sabine.

### 2

His strength failing on the journey, Houston was obliged
to lay over en route.  On July fifth he reached San Augustine
and found the town in a state that was a fair example of the
confusion prevailing in the Republic.  Burnet was impotent.
Few could keep track of the Cabinet, it changed so fast.
President Burnet had negotiated two treaties with Santa
Anna—one public, the other secret.  The former provided for
the cessation of hostilities and the return of Santa Anna to
Vera Cruz.  In the secret treaty Santa Anna promised to prepare the way for Mexican recognition of the independence of
Texas.  Two Cabinet members refused to sign the treaties,
holding that Santa Anna had forfeited his life.  One of these
was Secretary of War Mirabeau Buonaparte Lamar, the
afflorescent stranger who had led the cavalry at San Jacinto.

Nevertheless, Burnet hustled the prisoner aboard the Texas
man-of-war *Invincible* which was spreading canvas to depart
when the steamer *Ocean* entered Velasco harbor with two hun-

dred and fifty adventurers under Thomas Jefferson Green, of
North Carolina. Green boarded the *Invincible* and dragged
Santa Anna ashore in manacles while a mob on the beach howled
its approval. Burnet's humiliation was complete. The Army,
growing in numbers and in turbulence, scorned his authority.
The civil population, huddled in refugee camps or trekking
back to burned towns and desolated ranches, was a law unto
itself. The Executive blamed Houston for his troubles, and in
an effort to undermine the disabled leader's influence, shifted
Lamar from the Cabinet back to the Army which was commanded by Houston's friend Rusk.

The first letter Houston received in San Augustine was
from Rusk begging the Commander-in-Chief to hasten to the
army. "First they mounted you & tried to destroy you [but]
finding their efforts unavailing the[y] . . . have been ham-
mering at mee and really trying to break up the army. . . .
A vast deal depends on you. You have the entire confidence
of the army and the people."[1] Four days later he wrote again,
communicating a rumor that was to sweep Texas. Mexico, he
said, was contemplating a new invasion. Six thousand troops
were at Vera Cruz, four thousand at Matamoras. The Texans
were without supplies. "Confusion prevails in the Country.
The Cabinette I fear as a former Government has done, have
been engaged in trying to destroy the Army. . . . The Army
and People are Exasperated."[2] When, repeated Rusk, could
Houston place himself at the head of the troops? A sinister
idea had begun to lay hold of the grumbling soldiery.

To Houston the gravest feature of the situation was the
rumored invasion. Resting on his crutches, he appealed to a
mass meeting in San Augustine to support the government, and
one hundred and sixty men marched for the frontier. With
East Texas denuded of troops, the Indians grew restive and
once more terror took the hearts of the Administration.

General Gaines and his Regulars were on the American side
of the Sabine. Stephen F. Austin scrawled a note to Houston.
"It is very desirable that Gen Gains should establish his head

quarters at Nacagdoches. . . . Use your influence to get him to do so, and if he could visit this place [Columbia, the seat of government] & give the people here assurances of the good faith of Gen. Santa Anna in the offers and treaties he has made you & with this Govt" that also would be helpful.

At Phil Sublett's house in San Augustine, Houston took Austin's note from the hand of the courier. He penciled an asterisk after the word "treaty" and wrote on the margin, "I made no treaty." So much for keeping the record straight. At the foot of the sheet Houston added these lines: "General I refer this letter to you and can only add that such a step will . . . SAVE TEXAS. Your Friend SAM HOUSTON."[3]

Gaines declined to concern himself with treaties, but he sent some dragoons to Nacogdoches, Jackson describing the intervention as a measure to safeguard our frontier against the Indians.

## 3

No person in America had shown greater interest in the progress of the war in Texas than Andrew Jackson. The note that Sam Houston wrote on the battle-field was thrust into the hands of General Gaines at the international boundary, and Lieutenant Hitchcock risked his life in a dash through hostile Indian territory to save a few hours on the way to Washington. Jackson was recovering from a severe illness. He saw Hitchcock at once.

"I never saw a man more delighted," the young officer wrote in his journal. "He read the dispatch . . . exclaiming over and over as though talking to himself, 'Yes, that is his writing. I know it well. That is Sam Houston's writing.' . . . The old man ordered a map . . . and tried to locate San Jacinto. He passed his fingers excitedly over the map. . . . 'It must be here. . . . No, it is over there.'"[4]

In the flush of his ardor Jackson dashed off a note of congratulation to his old subaltern. Houston had won a victory greater than New Orleans. Houston had attacked; Jackson had stood on the defense. And after that, a second letter. Success to Texas! Money was being raised in the United States and Jackson's contribution, "was as much as I could spare."[5]

The occupation of Nacogdoches by Gaines stimulated recruiting in the United States.

"My brother Tom was just out of college and I was a freshman. Tom at once organized a Company of Volunteers in Washington, Pennsylvania. . . . We marched to Wheeling and took a little stern wheel boat named the '*Loyal Hannah*' for Louisville. . . . A boat arrived from below with word that . . . another steamer bearing President Jackson . . . would soon be along. I was color bearer . . . and had received the flag from the hands of my sister Catherine. . . . When we met his [Jackson's] boat the flag was lowered in salute and three cheers given. . . . Lemoyne, the great Abolitionist, was on that boat and demanded of the President why it was that armed bodies of men were allowed to recruit in the United States to make war on Mexico. To which General Jackson replied, 'That Americans had a lawful right to emigrate and to bear arms.' "[6]

Jackson considered that his official acts had been studiously correct. In response to protests from Mexico and murmurings in the chancellories of Europe, he had issued a solemn proclamation of the official disinterestedness of the United States. He had rebuked Commissioner Austin who during his tour of the States, had made so bold as to presume otherwise. He had directed his United States district attorneys to prevent violations of our neutrality. Indeed, upon receipt of this instrument, District Attorney Grundy, of Nashville, Jackson's home, had paused in his occupation of recruiting a company for Sam Houston to publish a stern warning. "I will prosecute any man in my command who takes up arms *in Tennessee* against Mexico and I will lead you to the border to see that our neutrality is not violated . . . *on our soil.*"[7]

Jackson's confidant, Samuel Swartwout, wrote to Houston:

"The old chief, encourages us to believe that you are not abandoned. . . . Genl Stewart left here the day before yesterday for Pensacola. His real object we suppose to be the command of the West India fleet preparatory to the reception of the answer from Mexico, to some queries or questions that the old man has sent to her. . . . We think your Independence will soon be acknowledged. . . . We shall press hard for annexation. . . . My noble Gen. you have erected a monument, with your single hand & in a day that will outlive the proudest . . . monarchies of the old world. . . . We have entertained your name in a proper manner . . . over the bottles by coupling your name and achievements with Washington and Jackson. . . . P. S. Mrs. Swartwout, one of your greatest admirers, sends her kindest regards to you, and my Daughter, now quite grown, begs me to say the same."[8]

From Congressman Ben Currey, of the intimate Jackson circle:

"You are by Genl Jackson Mr Van Buren Maj Lewis Colo Earle etc ranked among the great men of the earth. . . . I . . . raised a company of fifty men to join you. . . . Colo Earl has a splendid snuff box which he intends to send you by the first safe conveyance. I gave Mrs Addison formerly Miss Ellin Smallwood . . . a splendid entertainment on account of expressions of friendship for you evidences of which she wears on her finger. . . . I find in her album a poem in honor of you. . . . Hays is abusing you for not putting Santa Anna to death. . . . Genl Jackson says he is rejoiced at your prudence."[9]

Discredited old Aaron Burr sighed ruefully. "I was thirty years too soon."

4

When Houston heard of the kidnaping of Santa Anna, he stormed at the weakness of Burnet who managed, however, to retrieve the captive from Thomas Jefferson Green. Green rejoined the Army, which liked his style, and two colonels marched to overthrow the government and seize the Mexican President. Sam Houston halted them with a letter. "Texas, to be respected, must be considerate, politic . . . just. Santa Anna living . . . may be of incalculable advantage to Texas in her present crisis." Santa Anna dead would be just another dead Mexican.[10]

Burnet saw that his course was run. He called a general election to choose a new president and to ratify the constitution, but there was some embarrassment because the files of the Republic contained no copy of that document. In the exodus from Washington on the Brazos the Secretary of the Convention, Mr. Kimble, had disappeared with the manuscript. He ended his retreat at Nashville, Tennessee, however, giving the constitution to an editor who published it, but lost the original. A Cincinnati paper copied it from the Nashville sheet, and ten days after the call for an election Gail Borden's serviceable *Texas Telegraph* made a reprint from its Ohio contemporary. Burnet put a copy of the *Telegraph* in his desk, and the archives were in order.[11]

Austin and ex-Governor Henry Smith offered their candidacies for president and Texas began to stir—but not with enthusiasm for the election. The Mexican invasion scare had blown over, and the unoccupied army was out of hand again. General Thomas Jefferson Green was a big man now. He proposed an activity for the troops. "March immediately against the town of Matamoras . . . carry & burn the town destroy the main people if they resist & retreat . . . before they can have time to recover from their panic."[12] Rusk relayed word of the design to Houston but before anything happened useful George Hockley rode into camp with news that Sam Houston was on his way to the army!

The men were thrilled. The absent Commander-in-Chief had become a legend with the ranks. Rusk dashed off a long happy letter, Matamoras was eclipsed and the election came into its own as an object worthy of the Army's notice.

Sam Houston did not go to the army. He sat in tranquil San Augustine with his bandaged leg on a pillow, one of Phil Sublett's negroes in attendance and a Miss Barker reading from a novel.   Miss Barker had journeyed from Nacogdoches to cheer the wounded hero.   He said (but not to Miss Barker) that her blue eyes reminded him of Anna Raguet, who stayed at home.

5

Houston could have obliterated President Burnet and taken charge of Texas under any title that would have suited his whim, but he passed the warm July days in seclusion, bestirring himself only to save the life of Santa Anna and to keep Burnet on his uncomfortable seat.   The approaching election found General Houston still uninterested, except to remark that Rusk was a good man and might do for president.

Rusk was flattered.   He was popular with the army, and something like a boom began to agitate the ranks.   Thomas Jefferson Green pondered in his tent and informed Houston that Rusk would be "satisfactory."   But the paramount issue with General Green, was the execution of "Santo Ana."   "Great God when will this childish play cease."[13]

General Santa Anna himself was not indifferent to the paramount issue.   He smuggled a letter to the hermit of San Augustine, undertaking a delicate task of instruction.   *"Muy Estimado Señor. . . .* Your return has appeared to be very apropos . . . because it seems to me that your voice will be heard and properly respected."   The difficulties that confronted Texas "and . . . embarrass my departure for Mexico . . . you can easily remove with your influence in order that Texas may owe you its complete happiness."   The cause of Texas had been harmed by Houston's "absence, which is to be deplored.   Hurry yourself then to come among your friends.   Take advantage of the favorable time that presents itself and believe me, in all circumstances your affectionate and very grateful servant, ANT.o LÓPEZ DE SANTA ANNA."[14]

After a fortnight of meditation, the conscientious Rusk wrote Houston a fine letter of gratitude "that you should feel me worthy of the Presidential Chair but my age precludes me from running." General Rusk was thirty years old and had much to learn about politics. He was perplexed. Houston was his idol, and like Santa Anna, Rusk failed to understand why he should remain aloof. "This is an important office. I would rather vote for you than any other man."[15]

Rusk wrote on the ninth day of August. Texas would vote on September fifth. During the week ending August twentieth destiny showed its hand. Sam Houston's name was presented for the presidency by spontaneous meetings in various parts of the Republic. On August twenty-fifth, eleven days before the election, Houston consented to run. His announcement was the soul of brevity. "The crisis requires it." Houston received 5,119 votes to 743 for Smith and 587 for Austin. The constitution was adopted, and a proposal of annexation to the United States was carried almost unanimously. Mirabeau B. Lamar was elected vice-president.

Within certain limits Mr. Burnet could choose his own time for relinquishing office. He retired, however, with a degree of dispatch that moved his friend, General Lamar, to charge the President-Elect with unseemly precipitation in donning the toga. In any event on the morning of October 22, 1836, Burnet submitted his resignation and Congress ordained the inauguration to take place at four that afternoon. By chance or design Sam Houston was in Columbia, accessible to the committee of Congress which, in the execution of the time-saving program, conducted him to the big barn of a building that served as their meeting-place. Grumbling a little over the lack of preparation, General Houston advanced to a table covered with a blanket and took the oath.

The President made a speech, and in conclusion disengaged the sword of San Jacinto. The quotation that follows appears on page eighty-seven of the *House Journal*, First Session, First Congress of the Texas Republic, the words in brackets having been inserted by the official reporter.

"It now, sir, becomes my duty to make a presentation of

this sword—this emblem of my past office. [The President was unable to proceed further; but having firmly clenched it with both hands, as if with a farewell grasp, a tide of varied associations rushed upon him; . . . his countenance bespoke the . . . strongest emotions; his soul seemed to have swerved from the hypostatic union of the body. . . . After a pause . . . the president proceeded:] I have worn it with some humble pretensions in defense of my country; and, should . . . my country call . . . I expect to resume it."

Not every orator is a hero to his stenographer.

# CHAPTER XXI

## A Toast at Midnight

### 1

ALTHOUGH "the want of a Suitable pen" delayed the preparations of some preliminary papers, President Houston took hold of his responsibilities with little loss of time or waste of motion. The old barn at Columbia vibrated with his energy. Appointments, commissions, instructions, approvals, rejections, streamed day and night from a gaunt room wherein the Executive's labors kept three secretaries busy, Congress in a trance and the Cabinet in a state of prostration.

Everything had to be done, everything provided—instantly, it seemed. What was this? "In the name of the Republic of Texas, Free, Sovereign and Independent. . . . To All whom these Presents Shall come or in any wise concern: I, Sam Houston, President thereof send Greetings." Sam signed his name. He enjoyed doing that, for his swelling autograph was a work of art. But the paper called also for the great seal of the Republic. The President altered the document to read, "signed and affixed my private Seal, there being no great Seal of office yet provided." From his shirt he stripped an engraved cuff link, the design of which he impressed in wax upon the official paper.

The home-made heraldry on Sam Houston's cuff button served as the seal of the Texas Republic until Anna Raguet consented to assist in designing a permanent one. The button exhibited a dog's head, collared, encircled by an olive wreath,

below which was a script capital *H*.  Above the dog's head was
a cock and above the cock the motto: TRY ME.  This picto-
graph of the duel with White was a modification of the ancient
coat of arms of the Scottish barons of Houston which represented an incident in the life of an early soldier of the clan.

Sam Houston believed in the influences of heredity.  His
imagination was impressed by symbols and signs.  In his inaugural address he said that neither chance, design, nor desire,
but "my destiny," had guided his steps to the chief magistracy
of the new nation.  The rooster and the pups that figured in
the White duel bore sufficient kinship to the martlets and
hounds whose images had safeguarded generations of Houstons
to convince Sam that they might have something to do with
his future.

Houston chose a
notable Cabinet, induc-
ing his rivals for the
presidency to accept
portfolios.  Austin was
made Secretary of State
and Henry Smith Sec-
retary of Treasury.
Crushed by the stagger-
ing proportions of his defeat, Stephen F. Austin would have
gone to his grave an embittered man but for the magnanimity
of the victor.  Austin was ill and had prepared to isolate himself in a woodland cabin, but the impulse to duty remained,
and he accepted the most responsible and burdensome post in
the government.

Rusk again became Secretary of War.  Of the Army of
San Jacinto few remained in service.  Most of the early volunteers and professional adventurers having been killed off before-
hand, independence was won mainly by the old settlers with
family responsibilities.  They were now at home gathering the
first crop of San Jacinto corn.  Nevertheless, Texas had the
largest military force of its history, fed by daily arrivals from

the States. Their commander was Felix Huston, a forceful swashbuckler from Mississippi. The men wanted action, and on the lips of Felix was a dangerous word—Matamoras.

An obstreperous Army had upset one Texas Government and made another ridiculous. Secretary Rusk's attitude toward the Matamoras idea did not satisfy the President, and Mr. Rusk resigned after holding office a month. He was succeeded by William S. Fisher, a military adventurer but a staunch man who had proved his fealty at Brazos Bottoms.

The unrest of the Army increased. Felix Huston, wrote one of his men, "was as ambitious as Cortez. . . . It was his thoughts by day and his dream at night to march a conquering army into the 'Hall of the Montezumas.' During intervals at drill . . . he would pour floods of burning eloquence and arouse . . . passions by illusions to . . . the tropical beauties of the land far beyond the Rio Grande. . . . Had he chosen to do so he could have marched that army to Columbia with the avowed purpose of driving Sam Houston and the Congress into the Brazos River. . . . Felix Huston was a man of might but there was a mightier and far greater man in the executive cottage at Columbia. That man was Sam Houston. . . . Without a Herald and without parade he suddenly appeared [in camp]. His manner was calm and solemn. . . . The few men who had fought by his side at San Jacinto gathered around him as soldiers always cluster about a loved chief. . . . Houston's first act was to visit the hospital and inquire into the condition of the sick. . . . He reviewed the little army and addressed the men as a kind father would his wayward children. He told them the eyes of the civilized world were on them and appealed to them to disprove the calumnies sown broadcast against Texas. . . . His sonorous voice like the tones of a mighty organ rolled over the column. For a time at least the army felt his influence and it seemed as though all danger had passed."[1]

The duties of the Secretary of Navy were nominal since the Navy was detained in Baltimore for non-payment of a repair bill. James Pinckney Henderson, the good-looking and gay young Attorney-General, and Robert Barr, the Postmaster General, organized their departments on credit. Although the Republic was unable to pay cash for feed for the post-riders' horses, mail service was established and within four months a supreme court, district courts and tribunals in each of the twenty-three counties were in operation.

The administration of justice presented especial complications. The white population, distributed over an area the size of France, numbered thirty thousand. Hitherto, the process of atonement for crime in Texas had used up a good deal of rope, but with few objections on the whole.

The district judge selected for the upper Brazos was Robert M. Williamson, who had killed his opponent in duel in Georgia. When the lady in the case married a disinterested third party, the disappointed marksman came to Texas to devote himself to ranching and the elixirs of forgetfulness. One of Judge Williamson's legs being useless below the knee, he strapped it up behind him and substituted a wooden leg to walk on. This gave him the nickname of Three-Legged Willie.

On the first tour of his jurisdiction Three-Legged Willie was welcomed with the information that the inhabitants desired none of Sam Houston's courts there. Judge Williamson unpacked his saddle-bags, and establishing himself behind a table, placed a rifle at one elbow and a pistol at the other. His Honor had a way of snorting when he spoke. "Hear ye, hear ye, court for the Third District is either now in session or by God somebody's going to get killed."[2]

## 2

Shortly before his inauguration Sam Houston complied with a request of General Santa Anna to visit him at his place of confinement on a plantation near Columbia. The Napoleon of the West embraced his Wellington. His head did not reach the Texan's shoulders. He wept and called Houston a mag-

nanimous conqueror. He asked General Houston's influence
to obtain his release in return for which Santa Anna guaranteed
the acquiescence of Mexico to the annexation of Texas by the
United States.

The idea of using Santa Anna to assist in a solution of the
entangling diplomatic problems of the young Republic had
previously occurred to Houston. He had written Jackson
about it, but Jackson did not see how Santa Anna could
help. The Mexican Minister at Washington had warned that
no agreement made by Santa Anna while a prisoner would be
considered binding.

What to do with the distinguished captive was a puzzle.
There was still a healthy sentiment for his execution, and
General Santa Anna was eager to cooperate in relieving Texas
of the embarrassment of his presence. After the inauguration he addressed another letter to "Don Sam Houston: *Muy
Señor mío y de mi aprecio*," setting forth the pleasing intelligence that the diplomatic issues confronting Texas were "very
simple" of solution. Texas desired to be admitted to the
American union. The American union desired it. Only Mexico
remained to be consulted and Santa Anna would be pleased to
go to Washington and "adjust that negotiation."[3]

Houston was skeptical of any pourparlers that Santa Anna
might undertake, but he did wish to get him out of Texas.
"Restored to his own country," Houston said, Santa Anna
"would keep Mexico in commotion for years, and Texas will
be safe." Houston asked Congress for authority to release
the prisoner. Congress declined, and passed an inflammatory
resolution. Houston vetoed the resolution, gave Santa Anna
a fine horse and sent him on his way under escort of Colonel
Barnard E. Bee. Santa Anna borrowed two thousand dollars
of Bee and improved his wardrobe.

William H. Wharton had already started to Washington
as minister plenipotentiary with instructions to obtain the
recognition of Texan independence and annexation. But these
were not the only strings to the bow of Houston's foreign

policy. Should the attitude "of the United States toward Texas be indifferent or adverse," Mr. Wharton was to cultivate "a *close* and *intimate* intercourse with the foreign ministers in Washington," particularly the British and French.[4]

When Wharton had journeyed as far as Kentucky, he reported opposition to annexation by "both friends and foes" of Texas. "The leading prints of the North and East and the abolitionists . . . oppose it on the old grounds of . . . extension of slavery and of fear of southern preponderance in the councils of the Nation," while "our friends" proclaimed that "a brighter destiny awaits Texas." This bright destiny did not contemplate an independent Texas with strong friends in Europe, which was Sam Houston's alternative to annexation. It contemplated dismemberment of the Federal Union by the establishment of a slaveholding confederacy of which Texas should be a part. "Already has the war commenced. . . . The Southern papers . . . are acting most imprudently. . . . Language such as the following is uttered by the most respectable journals. . . . [']The North must choose between the Union with Texas added—or no Union. Texas will be added and then forever farewell to northern influence.['] Threats and denunciations like these will goad the North into a determined opposition and if Texas is annexed at all it will not be until it has convulsed this nation for several sessions of Congress."[5]

Wharton anticipated no difficulty in obtaining the recognition of Texan independence, however, which was necessary to repair the desperate condition of the Republic's finances. Wharton reached Washington in December of 1836, but was unable to see the President who was ill and working on his message to Congress. The message was expected to recommend recognition, and Congress was expected to grant it.

Every straw bearing on the course of events at Washington was watched with feverish interest in the barn by the Brazos. The enormous detail work of the Texan foreign policy was handled by Austin who proved Houston's ablest lieutenant.

Thus two of the greatest figures an American frontier has produced forgot their mutual distrust in the close association of unremitting labor. Despite frail health no task was too obscure for the conscientious Austin. "The prosperity of Texas," he wrote to a friend, "has assumed the character of a *religion* for the guidance of my thoughts."

On the night before Christmas Austin left his fireless room in the Capitol and retired with a chill. On the twenty-seventh he was delirious. "Texas is recognized. Did you see it in the papers?" With these words he ceased to speak, and Houston dictated this announcement: "The father of Texas is no more. The first pioneer of the wilderness 'has departed. General Stephen F. Austin, Secretary of State, expired this day."

### 3

The dying words of the first pioneer were not prophetic. The minute guns announcing his passing had not ceased to boom when newspapers from the United States arrived with Jackson's message to Congress, which contained these bewildering lines:

"Recognition at this time . . . would scarcely be regarded as consistent with that prudent reserve with which we have heretofore held ourselves bound to treat all similar questions."

Wharton was dumfounded. Could the man who spoke of "prudent reserve" be the same Jackson who had striven for fifteen years to annex Texas—countenancing the seamy diplomacy of Anthony Butler to that end, speeding Americans with his blessing to Sam Houston's Army, contributing to Houston's war chest, and advising the victor of San Jacinto on the conduct of Texan affairs?

Wharton went to work upon Jackson and in a skilful interview was both blunt and subtle. He appealed to the President's prejudices, his loyalties, his pride. Mexico, Wharton said, would print the message to Congress on satin.

Meantime, General Santa Anna arrived in Washington,

having charmed nearly every one he met during his leisurely journey. The North, especially, was able to appreciate the pleasing personality of the victor of the Álamo. "SANTA-ANNA" announced the Woonsocket, Rhode Island, *Patriot*. "How can we style him a tyrant . . . who opposed the efforts of rebels and used them with deserved severity" and "fought and bled to contravene the efforts of those who wished to substantiate . . . the horrible system of slavery?"

Jackson broached the subject of purchasing Mexico's assent to annexation. Santa Anna leaped at the idea. Wharton told Jackson that Texas would submit to no such indignity. The outcome of a long conversation, however, was that if Mexico could be quieted with a little "hush money," as Jackson expressed it, and the matter conducted with proper regard for the sensibilities of Texas, everything would be all right.[6] But the subject was dropped and Santa Anna departed for Vera Cruz after a round of ceremonial farewells in which the only amenity omitted was the repayment of Colonel Bee's two thousand dollars.

Continuing to pull strings, Wharton obtained the insertion in the diplomatic appropriation bill of a line providing for the expenses of a minister to the "Independent Republic" of Texas. The line was promptly stricken out, but Wharton did not give up. On February twenty-eighth, with Jackson packing to leave the Executive Mansion, a provision was inserted providing funds for such a minister "whenever the President may receive satisfactory evidence that Texas is an independent power." This seemed harmless and was allowed to remain.

Wharton flew to Jackson. He repeated all of his old arguments and invented new ones. In the afternoon of the last day of his term Jackson yielded. With one stroke of the pen he sent to the Senate the nomination of Alcée La Branche, of Louisiana, "to be Chargé d'Affairs to the Republic of Texas." With another stroke he remitted the fine of five hundred dollars a federal court had assessed against Sam Houston for thrashing William Stanbery. Close to midnight the Senate confirmed the appointment of La Branche, and Jackson and Wharton raised their glasses to Sam Houston's Republic.

Jackson would have preferred a toast to annexation, but for the first time in his life the old grenadier had been swerved from a course upon which he had set his heart. Jackson's love for the Union surpassed everything. The man who had defied the world in the dragooning of Florida retreated before the gathering tempest over slavery. It was a strategic withdrawal, however. Jackson had not abandoned his hopes for Texas. In one of his last conversations with Wharton, he said: "Texas must claim the Californias in order to paralyze the opposition of the North and East to Annexation. The fishing interests of the North and East wish a harbour on the Pacific."[7]

Balboa carried the standard of Spain to the Pacific. Sam Houston would carry the Stars and Stripes. The Florida imagination was not dead.

4

It was clear to Houston that his hopes, and Jackson's, must arise from the youthful soil of Texas rather than that of the District of Columbia. Texas must prepare to stand alone. At the outset, Houston had "determined to lay the foundations of the Texas Republic deep and strong . . . to be the ruler of the Nation and not of a party."[8]

The words have a regal ring, and it was this transfusion of Sam Houston's personality into the frail frame of the Republic that staved off chaos. Yet the regal tone was a disguise, the masquerade of a depressed and overworked man who lived in a shack, fighting the habit of drink to appear worthy in the indifferent eyes of a girl, who, thus far, had deferred her acknowledgment of the card from the field of San Jacinto.

The President participated little in the social life of his capital, and when he did flashes of the old warm-hearted conviviality meant tales for the ears of Miss Anna Raguet. To Dr. Robert Irion, a knightly young gentleman and the President's personal secretary, Sam Houston confided his troubles with a want of reserve uncommon for a man who had learned to obscure much. When Irion went home to Nacogdoches on a brief leave of absence, the President was very lonely. "Salute all my friends and dont forget the Fairest of the Fair!!!" "Write . . . and tell me how matters move on and how the Peerless Miss Anna is and does! I have written her so often that I fear she has found me troublesome, and . . . I pray you to make my apology and . . . salute her with my . . . very sincere respects."[9]

Since the peerless Anna was loath to correspond, the President contrived to get word of her by other means. Nearly every report thus received had Anna at the steps of the altar, although no two agreed as to the identity of the fortunate suitor.

## 5

In a vague region of the past, by a window that overlooked a river and an old-fashioned garden, sat another who awaited a letter. After San Jacinto, Eliza Allen's spirit had soared for a little on the wings of hope. Summer passed and flaming autumn approached to paint the woods by the curving Cumberland with the colors they had worn eight autumns ago when an overpowering young Man of Destiny swept her into his arms. Eliza's heart sank, but hope that declines to die drove her also to undertake the makeshift of despair.

"Washington City 6th October 1836
"Dear Gen<sup>l</sup>.

"I have now an opportunity of sending you a letter by a private conveyance . . . and . . . know that the subjects I will touch on will be more than interesting to your feallings.

"I passed through Tennessee on my way to this place; and spent two or three weeks there part of the time at my Brother Davids . . . in Lebennon. Mrs. Houston was there about the time the news that you had gained the victory over Santa Anna . . . reached that place. . . . She showed great pleasure at your success and fairly exulted. . . . No subject . . . was so interesting to her as when you were the subject of conversation; and she shew evident marks of displeasure and mortification if some person was to say anything unfavorable of you. . . . Some of her friends wanted her to git a divorce; and she positively refused; and said she was not displeased with her present name; therefore she would not change it on this earth; but would take it to the grave with her.—she has conducted herself with great surcumspiction and prudence and with great dignity of character so much that she has gained the universal respect of all that knows her She is certainly a most estimable woman; to have sustained herself as she has under all difficulties she has had to encounter.—I have dwelt on this subject as I believed it to be one that would not try your patience. . . .

> "I am dear sir, very respectfully
> "And Sincerely your friend
> "JNO. CAMPBELL

"His Excellency
    "Gen^l. Samuel Houston
        "President of the Republic
            "of Texas"[10]

And so Eliza—stretching her arms toward the man who one day had loved her so much as to surrender all that one can relinquish, save life. From the isolation of the trampled garden of her spirit she had followed the struggle for regeneration, perceiving in each singular achievement an extension of her regret.

But the great passion that had all but consumed the breast that held it was reduced to an ember, whose soft glow warmed a chamber of Sam Houston's heart merely for a memory. General Houston's answer to the letter of Eliza's distant cousin, Mr. Campbell, is not available. But when Sam's first cousin, Bob McEwen, to whose home in Nashville the Governor of Tennessee had brought Eliza as a bride, took up the theme of reconciliation, Houston told him it was impossible. Mr. McEwen conceded his cousin a right to the last word, but said that the door remained open. "Your wife desires such an event" and Houston's refusal notwithstanding, "many of your friends" persisted in the prediction that a restoration of the blighted romance would suitably crown Sam Houston's triumph in Texas. "You occupy the position of a second Washington," concluded Cousin Bob, and "I am gratified to learn that you have become a sober man."[11]

## 6

A fresh rumor that the Mexicans were massing for invasion sent the second Washington posting to Felix Huston's camp. "In a few days," he wrote Miss Anna, "I will set out for the army . . . and . . . if I win them you shall have more laurels."[12] The flurry blew over, and he wrote her a poem instead. "The greatest merit which it has is that it is intimately associated with you."[13]

The collapse of the Mexican threat was not an unalloyed blessing. Felix Huston became bolder in his plotting to alienate the Army. Sam Houston removed him from command and appointed Albert Sidney Johnston in his stead. Johnston was an honor graduate of West Point. Abandoning brilliant military prospects in the United States at the request of his young wife, upon her death, he had joined the Texan Army as a private soldier. When Johnston undertook to assume command Huston challenged him to a duel. Five fires were exchanged without effect, Johnston not aiming. On the sixth fire Johnston fell, seriously wounded. Huston rushed to his victim's side and acknowledged him the Commander of the Army.

Then came from Washington the great news of the third of March. Doctor Irion was again absent in Nacogdoches. "I have but a moment to say how do ye?" scribbled Houston. "You will have learned that we are Independent and recognized by the U. States . . . the last official act of Gen'l Jacksons life. This is a cause of joy. . . . My only wish is to see the country happy—at peace and retire to the Red

Lands, get a fair, sweet 'wee wifie' as Burns says, and pass the balance of my sinful life in ease and comfort (if I can). . . . My health, under you[r] Esculapian auspices, I thank God, is restored and my habits good."

Also his spirits. The writer proceeded to say that he would remove as soon as possible to the City of Houston, the prospective capital on Buffalo Bayou. The selection of this capital, named in the President's honor, had not pleased every one in Texas. Among those able to hold their enthusiasm in check was Anna Raguet. She had interrogated the President on the subject. Would not one of the established towns have done as well?

So the bitter went with the sweet. "I am informed," the President went on to tell his secretary, "that many ladies are coming to Houston and that society will be fine. We will not have the fair Miss Anna there—for she has a great aversion to 'Houston' and I dare not invite her . . . to a 'Levee' of the President. How sad the scene must be at my Levees,—no Mrs. H—— there, and many who will attend can claim fair Dames as theirs!!! You know the old adage, 'every dog,' etc., etc. My day may come!

"I pray you to salute all my friend[s], and . . . to Miss A., my *adoration*. . . . Ever yr friend, truly HOUSTON."

And a postscript:

"Irion. Miss Anna wont write me. Oh, what a sinner she must be."[14]

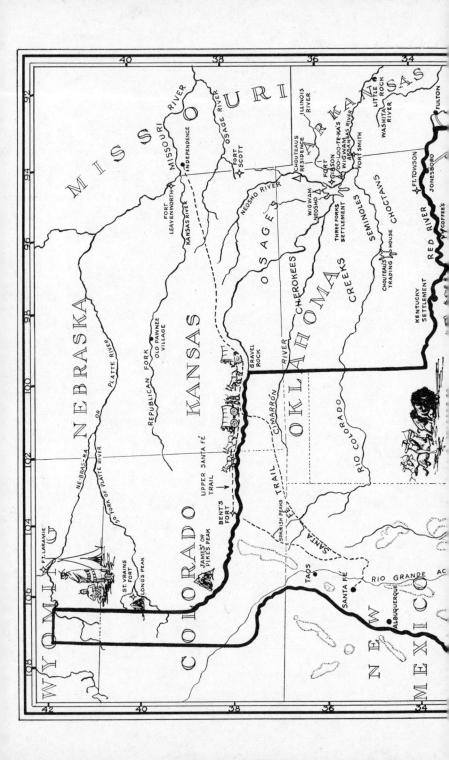

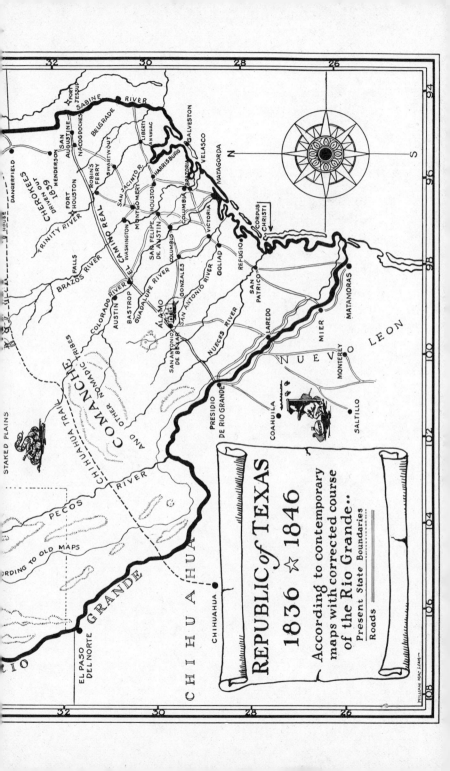

# CHAPTER XXII

## THE BACHELOR REPUBLIC

### 1

IN JANUARY of 1837 the steamer *Laura,* bound for the new capital, puffed up Buffalo Bayou in the wake of a yawl whose duty was "to hunt the city." The yawl stuck in the brush, giving the crew an opportunity to discover that they had passed the seat of government. An examination of the landscape disclosed "a few tents" and "a saloon."

When President Houston arrived in April, two taverns, "several" log cabins and "a few" saloons had been added. Timbers were being hauled for the new capital building and "all . . . was bustle and animation. Hammers and axes sounding . . . trees falling."[1] Sam Houston beamed with unblushing pride upon the busy scene. Forty-odd years before, identical emotions had stirred another tall Virginian striding the forlorn marshes of the Potomac.

The new place flourished. "Persons came pouring in until . . . a floating population had collected of some four or five hundred people." "Houses could not be built as fast as required," and town lots sold for five thousand dollars apiece. Of the resident population of "six or seven hundred persons . . . but one-half were engaged in any regular business . . . unless drinking and gambling may be considered such." Drinking "was reduced to a system, and . . . the Texians being entirely a military people, not only fought but drank in platoons." "Most of those who might be considered

281

citizens, were mere adventurers, who had pitched their tents for a time upon the prairy, to see what advantages might be seized upon in the combinations which were forming from the new elements that were about to create a new nation; with a view to depart should fortune prove unkind."[2]

From tent to tent moved Felix Huston who did not intend that fortune should prove unkind. He conveyed as much to a man with a scar on his cheek and a faded cloak worn with a certain grace; and Captain Alexandre Le Ray de Chaumont, whose sword had found employment in many lands, betook himself to the Army. On his rounds General Huston paid particular attention to the members of Congress, assembling for their second session. His object was a campaign against Matamoras which, once authorized by Congress, could hardly be ignored. Should Sam Houston attempt to do so it would be proper for the Legislature to commission a new leader to crown the republican standard with glory and enrich its treasury with the wealth of the Montezumas. So argued Felix Huston.

The President got wind of the plot, which was confirmed by reports from the Army, now twenty-five hundred strong. The soldiers were unpaid and in a mood for anything. Albert Sidney Johnston had nearly died of his duel wound, and was still unable to assume command. This left the restless rabble in the hands of Felix Huston who had disregarded his pledge of loyalty to the chivalrous Johnston.

There was no immediate cause for alarm, however. Felix Huston had been precipitous. The Congress would not convene until May first, and before that, on April twenty-first, would be the celebration of the anniversary of San Jacinto. The resources of the Republic had been taxed to make this occasion memorable. The prairie winked with the camp-fires of the gathering veterans, and the nights were lively with sounds of celebration. Their presence gave the President a feeling of security. These old-timers were, generally speaking, Sam Houston's friends. They had slight use for the battleless hosts whose conspiring chieftain continued to buttonhole congressmen.

On the evening of the twentieth all signs indicated a big time except for a shortage of girls for the ball. As Houston's population, floating and permanent, did not include more than eighty females, a committee had been named to find a sufficient number of dance partners. Invitations were scattered throughout the countryside, and the committeemen rode to neighboring settlements to make personal appeals. Many ladies had responded and nearly every roof in Houston was at their disposal while the men slept out-of-doors, but a count of heads still revealed an embarrassing deficit. The sun was sinking when a shout from the ragged street in front of the unfinished Capitol greeted an ox-drawn caravan creaking through the dust. The girls from Oyster Creek had come! Within an hour they were reinforced by the maidens from Brazos Bottoms. By midnight the Caney Creek girls were in and valor basked in the smiles of beauty.

Cannon proclaimed the dawn of the great day. The President accepted a silk flag sent to him by the ladies of New Orleans. He ordered it displayed from the liberty pole as the signal for the procession to march to the scene of the exercises.

When the parade formed Mr. Crawford of the British Consular Service stood at the head of the line beside President Houston. England rules one-fifth of the surface of the earth, and one reason for this is that her traveling representatives are usually on the ground ahead of competitors. It was time to march but the signal flag had not appeared. Fifteen minutes passed, and the column was getting impatient when finally the emblem of the Lone Star was broken out against the sky.

The delay had been due to the fouling of the halyards. A seaman from a vessel in the bayou had risked his neck to climb the peeled sapling and hoist the gift ensign to its place of honor. After the ceremonies, Houston called the sailor aside and gave him a deed to a town lot. A speculator had recently given the lot to Houston.

The ball was a tremendous success and lasted all night. "Dressed in a rich velvet suit," General Houston attended with Consul Crawford, "moving among the throng with a gallantry and grace which have always distinguished him; and during the dancing he remained perfectly sober."[3] The President chose as his partner for the grand march the wife of Congressman Moseley Baker, which an observer mentioned as an example of Houston's tact. Had Mrs. Baker been a homely woman, this might have been entirely true.

2

The date for the convening of Congress was May first. But as there was no roof on the Capitol it was impossible to assemble a quorum. A makeshift capable of keeping out the sun was patched up, and on May fifth Congress was opened with pomp. Consul Crawford occupied a seat of honor, and Sam Houston, wearing the velvet suit, made what was described as "a regal entrance."

He delivered an address, intended as much for the ears of His Majesty's representative and for Washington, as for the republican legislators. "We now occupy the proud attitude of a sovereign and independent Republic, which will impose upon us the obligation of evincing to the world that we are worthy to be free." The President's recommendations were detailed. He faced the uncertain future with an impressive dignity, urging legislation not alone for present emergencies, but for the foundation of a permanent system of government adapted to the future growth of a great country.

The favorable effect of the address was not of long duration. Obstacles seemed overwhelming and Congress turned to the alchemy of the facile Felix. Why sweat and labor to create a financial system when the end could be obtained so much more attractively by conquest? While Felix Huston worked upon Congress his second-in-command, Colonel Rodgers, stirred the camp which threatened to march on Houston, "chastise the President" and "kick Congress out of doors."

At two o'clock in the morning of May eighteenth, the President rolled Secretary of War Fisher out of bed and started him to the Army with sealed orders. On reaching camp Mr. Fisher read his instructions, which directed him to "furlough" the Army by companies, with the exception of six hundred men. The first company was ordered to Dimitt's Landing, the second to the mouth of the Brazos, the third to Galveston, and so on along two hundred miles of seacoast. The furloughs were unlimited, but liable to revocation at any time. Those not responding in thirty days would be tried for desertion.

The reading of the order threw the camp into an uproar, but the Army's leader was absent and Fisher could handle men. He segregated the units and had them on the march before Rodgers fairly realized what had taken place. By the time the tidings reached Felix Huston, the pawns in his game were hopelessly scattered in a mad scramble to get out of Texas before Houston should recall them to service which was, of course, the last thing the President intended to do. Relinquishing the stage to his remote kinsman, Felix sailed for New Orleans. Fortune had been unkind.

The President's difficulties were not at an end, however. The question of finance had reached a point of crisis. The troops left in service threatened to mutiny unless they got more to eat. The public officers had received no salary and a stream of resignations threatened to wreck the civil administration. The Minister to the United States was behind with his board bill, and Houston had stripped the coat from his back to clothe a ragged veteran of San Jacinto.

The Congress of the penniless Republic did what it could to reward valor. San Jacinto campaign men were given lands. Sleek speculators hovered like vultures. A jug of whisky or a sack of corn-meal and a few dollars in cash were all that many a poor soldier of the Revolution received for his bounty. "Erastus, usually called 'Deaf' Smith," was additionally recompensed, being allowed to take his pick of "any [public] house and lot in the city of Bexar" excepting only "forts, court houses, calibooses, churches and public squares," and the President ordered him to Houston to sit for a portrait to adorn some future Texas Hall of Fame.[4]

Congress had authorized the President to contract a five-million-dollar loan in the United States at ten per cent. But the panic of 1837 had tied up money in this country and the Republic scaled down its fiscal requirements. The President was empowered to borrow twenty thousand dollars at thirty per cent. interest, if he could not get it for less. A duty on imports was established ranging from one per cent. on bread to forty-five per cent. on liquor and fifty per cent. on silks, thus averting bankruptcy.

When Sam Houston entered his new capital city the audited claims against the Republic aggregated $606,945 with as many more waiting. Of this amount $1,569 had been paid, and an audited claim was worth fifteen cents on the dollar. Something had to be done. Congress passed a bill authorizing the issue of promissory notes to the amount of one million dollars. Houston vetoed it, saying that half of this sum would satisfy the need for a circulating medium and would be all that could be kept at par. The amount was limited to five hundred thousand dollars. Thus Sam Houston had in prospect a currency for his country, the value of which would depend upon ·the confidence he should establish for Texas in the eyes of the world.

3

In the sensitive field of foreign relations the first events were not favorable to the creation of a national prestige. The bright particular star of the Texan diplomatic corps, William H. Wharton, was in a Mexican jail. By dint of great effort the Texas Navy had been redeemed from pawn, and Mr. Wharton was coming home in triumph on a war-ship when the vessel was waylaid by two superior Mexican men-of-war and captured after a severe fight. John A. Wharton went to Matamoras under a flag of truce with thirty Mexican prisoners to obtain his brother's release. They locked up John also, and the two principal vessels remaining of the Texan sea forces began to sweep threateningly up and down the Gulf. The Whartons relieved the situation by effecting their escape, but the Texas war-ships were run aground by Mexican brigs, and once more the Texas Secretary of Navy was virtually a gentleman of leisure.

Martin Van Buren did not, as Mr. Cambreleng had expressed the wish, live a thousand years, and it is doubtful if he had a thousand sweethearts. But he followed Andrew Jackson into the presidency, which was more than Cambreleng had anticipated when ruminating upon the likely consequences of Peg O'Neale's betrothal. At the same time Memucan Hunt succeeded William Wharton in charge of the Texan Legation at Washington with the instructions to plug with Mr. Van Buren for annexation.

If old Jackson shrank from ugly visage of slavery what was one to expect of Martin Van Buren? No sooner had Hunt put out his feelers than the American Anti-Slavery Society set itself to defeat annexation. General Santa Anna was extolled as a friend of humanity and the pretensions of the Texas Republic were immortalized in Art:

> "Ho for the rescue! ye who part
> Parents from children—heart from heart—
> Up! patriarchs—and gather round,
> Ye who sell infants by the pound!"

The poet went on to chide the North, which

> "Pours her choicest scoundrels forth
> To fight for Texas lands—and slavery . . .
> Where proudly walk . . .
> The forger and the great unhung!
> Where Houston, chief of San Jacinto,
> Arrayed in Presidential dignity,
>             . . . plunges into
> Crimes which old Nick would scarce begin to."[5]

John Quincy Adams declared the annexation of Texas to be the first step in the conquest of the remainder of Mexico and of the West Indies for the establishment of a slave monarchy for our southern planters. When a resolution for annexation came before the House of Representatives, Mr. Adams held the floor for three weeks in speech against it. This closed the session, and the measure was not voted upon.

Minister Hunt's unpaid hotel bill had reached an uncomfortable total. He came home, and Sam Houston withdrew his offer of annexation. Diplomatic exchanges between the Republic of Texas and the United States on the boundary issue and other questions assumed a crisp tone. Pinckney Henderson, who was able to afford the luxury of foreign travel, sailed with credentials of introduction to the courts of St. James's and Versailles. Hunt was succeeded at Washington by Dr. Anson Jones, who established a line of credit at a different hotel. He also established himself in the confidence of a member of the American Diplomatic Service. Henderson had not as yet been received at court, but Jones's American friend stretched the proprieties sufficiently to place before the great Palmerston, British Secretary for Foreign Affairs, a letter calling attention to the growing importance of Texas. Did it not present a real opportunity for Great Britain to make a friend on the American continent? Lord Palmerston ruminated and wrote a memorandum. "The subject . . . is important."

4

Suddenly the sun came out. Brushing aside the cares of state, Sam Houston sat down at his disordered writing table to answer a letter from Anna Raguet.

"My Excellent Friend:
"Your delightful favor reached me on yesterday, and can assure you it was as grateful to me as the Oasis of the desert is to the weary pilgrim. . . . The Congress has gone on thus

far without much excitement—[and so on for a page concerning the state of the nation].

"Our friend Doct. Irion is well, and bids me present his much love to yourself. . . . Miss Ruth is married, and bids adieu to all her cares and coquetry. What a blessed exchange! Don't you say so? The beauty of New York has reached this place, and has commenced the destruction of hearts and happiness—but as my time admits of no leisure, thus far I am . . . untouched by her soft, blue eyes! . . .

"I am delighted to know that you are charmed with Whalebone—but I can't retake him, as I have now four very fine horses. . . .

"I regret that my friends should be visited by the Indians, or that any cause of alarm shou'd exist. Until our citizens learn prudence, we must be afflicted by such visitations. . . .

"This letter was commenced last night. . . . This morning I received an invitation to dine on tomorrow with the Fair New Yorker. . . . Should the gentlemen remain at wine, I withdraw to the parlor, and for the want of a competitor engross the smiles of the dear creatures.

"Again good-bye."

On the margin of page five General Houston wrote a few sentences, but since the paper is torn one can only discern:

"——and myself are reformed. Neither gets 'tight.' I have but ——ology 'I never drinks nothing.' "[6]

When John James Audubon visited Houston City, the Secretary of Navy acted as his escort. "We approached the President's mansion," the great naturalist wrote in his journal, "wading in water above our ankles. This abode . . . is a small log house, consisting of two rooms and a passage through, after the Southern fashion. . . . We found ourselves ushered into what in other countries would be called the ante-chamber; the ground-floor, however, was muddy and filthy, a large fire was burning, and a small table, covered with paper and writing materials, was in the centre; camp-beds, trunks, and different materials were strewed around the room. We were at once presented to several members of the Cabinet, some of whom bore the stamp of intellectual ability," and "to Mr. Crawford, an agent of the British minister to Mexico, who has come here on some secret mission."

The President being engaged in the opposite room, a stroll about the "city" was suggested. It was raining, and the party stepped into the Capitol, but the roof leaked, to the discomfiture of Congress as well as the tourists. Something to dispel the chill was in order, and Mr. Audubon was surprised that his host offered "his name instead of cash to the bar-keeper."

Returning to the Executive residence "we were presented to his Excellency," who wore the velvet suit and "a cravat somewhat in the style of seventy-six." He asked his visitors a few polite questions and led them into his private chamber, "which was not much cleaner" than the anteroom. There were introductions to members of his staff and friends seated on stools and a couple of camp-beds. The President asked the visitors to drink with him, "which we did, wishing success to the Republic. Our talk was short; but the impression made . . . by himself, his officers and his place of abode can never be forgotten."[7]

One of the beds in the private room was Sam Houston's. The other belonged to Ashbel Smith, Surgeon General of the Army. The cots in the reception-room were for guests. A third room, a lean-to back of the private chamber, served as kitchen and servants' hall for the President's two negro retainers, Esau and Tom Blue.

The hands of Esau were skilled at producing drinks. One afternoon the President was detained until late at the Capitol. Friends dropped in and apéritifs were served on the spot. One good story followed another until it was too late to go home. The company composed itself upon chairs, a table and the floor. The President was the first to awake.

"Esau! You, Esau!"

"Yes, Marse Gen'l."

"Water! Water!"

Where to get water at this time of night? Esau inquired.

At Aunt Lucy's, the President said.  Aunt Lucy was an aged negress who laundered the garments of statesmen at her shack on the bank of the bayou.  Esau returned without the water, but with a lengthy excuse.  The President stood at a window, looking first at the sky and then at his servant.

"Esau," he said, "can you believe that this is I, Sam Houston, protégé of Andrew Jackson, ex-Governor of Tennessee, the beloved of Coleto and his savage hosts, the hero of San Jacinto and the President of the Republic of Texas, standing at the dead hour of midnight in the heart of his own capital, with the myriad of twinkling stars shining down upon his unhappy forehead, begging for water at the door of an old nigger wench's shanty—and—can't—get—a—drop?"

Esau reflected upon the words of his master.  "Dat's jest right, Marse Gen'l.  We sho' ain't got no wattah."[8]

Dr. Ashbel Smith was a wiry man of medium stature whose indifference to his wardrobe was redeemed by the care he bestowed upon a close-clipped professional-looking beard. He was thirty-two years old, a Connecticut blue-stocking, educated at Yale and in France.  He was rich and had come to Texas to forget a girl.

The Surgeon General was a good conversationalist and the quiet charm of his personality contributed to the popularity of the ménage of the bachelor President of the Republic. The Executive residence was a scene of Rabelaisian entertainments.  Wonderful stories were told of these full-toned carousals.  Should the gentlemen weary of their own society it was only a short walk in the bracing air to the salons of Mrs. Mann and Madame Raimon—"ladies of some notoriety about the City of Houston," the virtuous Burnet recorded, representing General Houston in the act of acquainting his guests with "a number of fawn-necked damsels, whose naive deportment put upon one the idea practically of the Mussulman's paradise!"[9]

The temperate habits of Doctor Smith had their influence on his roommate.  At times the President presided at the revels, indulging in no more than an occasional sniff of the hartshorn vial, the custody of which was a special responsibility of the Surgeon General. On such occasions Houston usually drove his guests away early and, after a game of chess with Smith, would plant himself on the foot of the Doctor's bed and talk until daylight.

When General Houston received Indian callers no liquor was served. Treaties with all of the tribes were made during that summer, delegations constantly coming and going. "Brother, I wish to see you. . . . Send word to Big Mush . . . to the Kickapoos . . . the Caddoes. . . . I have a Talk that you will like to hear. Bring in the Treaty that I last made with you. It has ribbons and a seal on it. . . . Tell my sisters and brothers they live in my heart. SAM HOUSTON."[10] This to The Bowl. An Indian remaining overnight in Houston City invariably bivouaced in the President's yard. Occasionally Sam Houston would honor their camp-fires and, seated on a bearskin, praise the flavor of the dog-meat.

On other nights while the Surgeon General snored in his corner, the President would carry his candle to the littered table and write letters, pausing long between the paragraphs.

"It is past midnight. The toils of the day have passed by, and . . . the kind remembrance of my excellent friend is the first which claims my attention to the recollections of other days Sacred to Memory.

"You have been to New Orleans, and bye the bye, I have heard much, and, as usual, admired everything. You were the Belle of the City, and this was so much Glory for Texas. You claimed half the glories of the Victory of San Jacinto. I conceded them to you! Will you in return share with me your triumphs in the City of New Orleans? . . .

"You kindly say to me you were waited upon by 'your beautiful Miss Barker,' and 'I was much pleased with her.' I thank you for this, for . . . I wrote to you while I supposed you in Philadelphia that if she shou'd arrive there I wou'd be glad that you wou'd see her. I did this because when I saw her she presented to me a beautiful image so much resembling Miss Raguet that really I . . . was compelled to admire and wish to see her.

"Since then I have sent to her a trifling evidence of respect, which I dare not offer to Miss Anna, because she has not received from me the slightest token, and Miss B. had received a trifle from the spoils of San Jacinto when she was kind enough to dispense with Prudery and visit a soldier, prostrate and suffering under the influences of destiny. If I admired Miss Barker, it was because I admired others to whom she bore a striking resemblance! . . .

"It is half past two in the morning and this is Sunday. Should I remain longer from repose, I cou'd not look well at church. . . . Be so kind as to write to me—no matter what you write. . . .

"SAM HOUSTON

"Miss A. Raguet."[11]

There was no church house in Houston, but services were held in the Hall of Congress. A visiting divine, thinking he perceived in Texas a field for such gospel, announced a temperance lecture. The proposal was coldly received until Sam Houston asked permission to preside at the meeting. This brought half the town. The President delivered a moving sermon on the evil of drink, concluding with the advice to "follow my words and not my example."

5

A veil of exaggerated official courtesy did not obscure from Sam Houston the fact that Vice-President Lamar was his enemy. The antipathy went back to the Burnet régime when the artful influence of Houston had prevented Lamar from obtaining control of the Army and succeeding, possibly, to something more to his taste than his present eminently restful office.

Early in the summer of 1837 General Lamar returned to Georgia for a visit, but his friends in Houston remained on lookout. "I have with more vigilence than you are aware, watched the general procession of political movements. I find the President extreanly courteous when he out for general inspection, this seldom oftener than once in sunshine, between eleven & two, he . . . dresses himself gaudily in self peculiar taste viz. black silk velvet gold lace crimson vest and silver spurs takes a graduating glass, stops a moment before the miror . . . and adjusts his shappo . . . and lastly the requisite inibriating sip that makes himself again *Hector* upon his feet and no longe[r] the wounded Achilise of San Jacinto . . . and with a tread of dominion in his aroganic step strides . . . across his own nominated metropolis . . . to the bar keeper."[12]

This sympathetic portrait was followed by a lengthy account of the President's perfidy. To Lamar's friends he "laments much indeed" the Vice-President's absence, but to others he spoke "in an entire different stile." But General Lamar could be of good cheer. He was the popular choice for the president at the next election, and he might not have to wait that long. "Since Col Teals murder their has been much dicention in the army Johnson is here [in Houston] and in all probability will not return" to his command.

The murder of Houston's friend, Teal, had stirred Texas. Major Western, commanding the cavalry at Béxar, became almost too broad in his innuendoes about upsetting the "one-horse" government at Houston. Senator Everitt could not wait to leave his seat in the chamber to hasten a note to the absent Lamar. "Your presence is needed. . . . Higher duties in all probability will require Your presence E're . . . this Scrawl can Reach You. Houston worn-down by . . . Debauchery, is fast sinking under its Effects."[13]

Houston's health was not good, and his habits did not improve it, but fear of an assassin's bullet gave his friends their greatest concern for his safety.[14] In this situation Sam Houston called one of Lamar's spies to his residence and asked him to request the Vice-President to return to Texas, if he could do so without inconvenience, and assist in guiding the ship of state. Houston's advisers thought this madness, at which the old fox of San Jacinto must have smiled. General Lamar answered politely, but found excuses for prolonging his visit.

But there remained Major Western. By chance the loquacious William H. Patton, one of Houston's aides at San Jacinto, was departing for Béxar on private business. In wishing him Godspeed, Houston remarked that his own thoughts had been much on Béxar of late. Major Western was there. An exceptional man, Major Western, whose polished manners and diplomatic ability reminded one of Martin Van Buren. Now, the President was about to send an ambassador to England. The thing was to find the best fitted man. In strict confidence, what did Patton think of the qualifications of Major Western? Of course, not a word to any one; nothing was determined as yet.

When the President heard of Patton's arrival at Béxar orders were sent for Major Western to report at the seat of government. Houston received the Major cordially, but England was not mentioned. Time passed. Major Western approached Ashbel Smith. Had the Surgeon General heard the President mention the matter of a mission to England? The Surgeon General could not say that he had.

Pinckney Henderson's appointment was announced, but Major Western declined to believe it. The President was a better judge of men. When the truth came out, the Major was "disgusted." He returned to Béxar with ominous haste, where he found another officer in command of the cavalry and orders transferring him to an outpost.[15]

"The news of this country is not very interesting," the President wrote to Anna Raguet, enclosing a poem for criticism. "The frontier all quiet. . . . Dr. Irion is very well. . . . Miss Eberly & Miss Harris are both married—and doubtless both happy. People *will* marry on the *Brasos!* I saw on yesterday your schoolmate, Mrs Harrell. . . . Her husband is very kind to her. . . . I have heard of a *grand conclave of*

*Ladies* in Nacogdoches to settle *your* destiny and mine! Farewell."[16]

The ladies of Nacogdoches were not alone in the endeavor to influence destinies in Texas. For the one hundredth time a rumor of Mexican invasion ran through the country. Houston fell ill, and the Senate adopted a secret resolution "requesting & enjoining" the return of General Lamar.

But the news leaked and passions flamed in Texas. From Georgia Lamar posted westward. At Mobile he tarried to hold mysterious conferences about which hovered an old sweetheart, torn between aspirations for her adored and the peril of his undertaking. Missing a vessel at New Orleans, Lamar pressed on by the overland route along which desperados employed by Houston were supposed to lurk. "Come back to us instantly come back. . . . Your death is talked of . . . [until] I have lost the powers to think and can only repeat *come back.* OLIVIA."[17]

The man on horseback did not heed her. Never lacking personal courage, Lamar plunged into the Redlands and his apprehensive followers recovered their composure sufficiently to give him a banquet at San Augustine. On November ninth the Vice-President reached Houston. The town was in a ferment. General Lamar addressed the Senate. Peace, my friends, was his counsel. Let none fear for the security of Texas.

**6**

The triumphal entry was the work of talented amateurs—splendid as to external details, but otherwise fatally misconceived. The Old Fox extinguished the last spark of hope by an attitude of humilating indifference.

The fact is that the time was inopportune. Imperceptibly Sam Houston had installed a nation at his back. The Constitution was in operation; customs were collected; salaries were paid; immigration had increased. Henderson was writing commercial treaties with England and France. The currency—

called "star money" from the design on the notes—was a success. Beating down the opposition of Congress and of his own Secretary of Treasury, Houston had made this money receivable for customs on par with gold. This created confidence and star money rose to par for all purposes. The Capitol was finished—a handsome structure with a graceful colonnade of tall square pillars.

The Republic was a going concern—commerce reviving, mails delivered, courts respected. A drunken lawyer was arguing a case before Three-Legged Willie.

"Where is the law to support your contention?" interrupted the judge.

The lawyer whipped out a dirk.

"There's the law," he said.

Judge Williamson dropped the muzzle of a pistol over the bench.

"Yes, and there's the Constitution."[18]

A national character had been established—an embodiment of the character of the Republic's Chief Magistrate, who taught men to discriminate between the democracy of his habits, and the aristocracy of his ideals. The Navy was being rebuilt; the Indians were quiet; Mexican threats had ceased to intimidate. The civil administration was no longer clover for broken-down politicians, or the military service the apple of every out-at-elbows ruffler trailing a sword—as Captain de Chaumont had learned to his sorrow.

Sam Houston had built this out of chaos in little more than a year.

Of course Texas was still frontier. Jacob Snively went to Nacogdoches on official business. "I cannot find a suitable companion with whom to spend my evenings," he wrote the President. "The young men of this place are so singular . . . and the ladies" respond to nothing except "flattery. You, Yourself are aware of that. Last Sunday morning Mr. Michael Cossby was killed by Mr. Speight. At San Augustine Saturday evening Mr. Pinkney Lout [no flatterer, apparently] was also killed . . . by Mrs. Wright. . . . Miss Ana is well. She has many admirers, Messrs Kaufman, Hart & Hotchkiss. . . . I wish you were here."[19]

Houston promised to come for Thanksgiving, promised again for Christmas, but stayed away. His letters to Miss Anna were briefer. "Business" was his apology. "Our foreign relations . . . Lord Palmerston . . . state of the army . . . internal problems," engrossed his attention. "A recent report that ere this your *hand* and *faith* were both plighted," however, was received with a "thorn in the heart and hope with resignation for the best!!!" "The Cabinet, all being batchelors or widowers but one, have been somewhat deranged by the arrival of a *rich* and *pretty* widow from Alabama—young, too." "Christmas passed without much fuss. One Ball, *quite decent*."

Another letter from Nacogdoches:

"We have been looking for you every day since Christmas and none with more apparent anxiety than Miss Anna.—The other day it was believed you were but a few miles from town and all was joy and gladness but we were again doomed to disappointment. . . . We will celebrate the second of March . . . and conclude . . . by a splendid Ball.—May you be with us on that day—*Sic fata sinant*."[20]

This from the dashing Congressman Kaufman, apparently foremost among the corps of rivals. But whatever fate signified, Sam Houston remained in his capital on Independence Day, which was also his forty-fifth birthday.

On Washington's birthday there was a splendid ball in Houston at which Miss Dilrue Rose, of Bray's Bayou, made her début. "Mrs Dr. Gazley was dancing with the president. She, not feeling well, asked me to take her place." Alas! As little Miss Rose advanced to claim the vacant place "a pretty young widow, Mrs. Archer Boyd," pushed in ahead of her. "But I had the honor of dancing in the same set . . . [and] as there was to be a wedding in June and I was to be the first bridesmaid and General Houston best man, I didn't care."[21]

San Jacinto Day came first and was observed with a grand celebration and ball. "As Miss Mary Jane Harris, the belle of Buffalo Bayou was married" Miss Rose recorded the simple truth that "I came in for considerable attention." Alas once more General Houston did not dance—only "promenaded." Presently, however, he "was talking with Mother and some other ladies when Father presented Sister and me to the president. He kissed both of us. 'Dr. Rose, you have two pretty little girls.' I felt rather crestfallen as I considered myself a young lady."[22]

But neither widows nor pretty little girls were much in the President's thoughts. It was Miss Anna. Houston was now free. Tiana was dead and Cherokee roses bloomed on her grave.[23] Eliza Allen had been divorced—on the President's petition, presented by his attorneys before District Judge Shelby Corzine, of San Augustine. Mrs. Houston was represented by counsel, but there was no contest of the charge of abandonment. Everything was done as quietly as possible, but the news got out and there was a deal of whispered concern. While accompanying the President to an Indian conference, John H. Reagan, afterward Postmaster General of the Confederacy, adroitly asked the familiar question. Why had Houston left his wife?

"That is an absolute secret," Sam Houston said, "and will remain so."[24]

Anna Raguet received a version of the divorce story that shocked her. It is a simple matter to surmise what this version was. Under the Republic divorces were granted by Act of Congress, but for purposes of secrecy President Houston had empowered Judge Corzine to hear the case in chambers. This procedure seemed a little too regal for such a good friend of Houston as Barnard E. Bee who expressed to Ashbel Smith the opinion that the decree was "a fraud."[25]

"Miss Anna," wrote Houston. "Having learned by some agency that you were induced to believe that I had presumed to address you at a time when I must have been satisfied in my own mind that legal impediments lay in the way of my union with any lady . . . but one thing would remain for me to reflect upon. . . . Had I sought to win your love when I was aware that the same must have taken place at the expense of your happiness and pride and peace and honor in life, I must have acknowledged myself a 'lily liver'd' wretch!!! . . .

"Of this, enough. The enclosed letters contain the opinions of Gentlemen eminent in the profession of the law—obtained on the abstract question as to the legality of my divorce! The question was solemnly argued in court for the adverse party, and the judge on calm reflection rendered his decision to be recorded—which was done. . . .

"This much I have felt bound to say to you on the score of old friendship and a desire to evince to you that I have merited (at least in part) the esteem with which you have honored me in by gone days."[26]

Houston followed this letter to Nacogdoches. But the girl who held half of San Jacinto's laurels was lost to him.

## 7

Sam Houston returned to his capital in the rain alone. Cannon boomed across the prairie at his approach and an escort of the Milam Guards, the flower of the Army (possessing uniforms), galloped to meet the President. An epoch-making evening would now be complete.

The occasion was the Republic's salutation to the beaux arts in the form of the first professional theatrical performance under the Lone Star. The President was a few minutes late, but still in time for the state dinner to the cast. He ate in his wet clothes and a little doll actress from Baltimore confessed a difficulty in keeping her eyes on her plate.

Meantime the hall where the performance was to be held was filling up. The young ladies of Mrs. Robertson's fashionable boarding school were to have front seats, but when they arrived these places were occupied. The girls were marshaled into other chairs and from this point of vantage Dilrue Rose witnessed the entrance of the President and staff to the strains of *Hail the Chief*. But all of the seats were taken.

"The stage manager, Mr. Curry, requested the men in front who were gamblers and their friends to give up the seats. This they refused to do. Then the manager called for the police to put them out." This "enraged" the gamblers who drew "weapons and threatened to shoot. The sheriff called the soldiers. . . . It looked as if there would be bloodshed, gamblers on one side, soldiers on the other, women and children between, everybody talking. . . . The president got on a seat, commanded peace, asked those in front to be seated, ordered the soldiers to stack arms and said that he and the ladies would take back seats. This appeared to shame the gamblers. . . . [Their] spokesman said that if their money was returned they would leave the house as they had no desire to discommode the ladies."[27]

So the curtain rose upon "Sheridan Knowles Comedy *The Hunchback*," the performance concluding "with a farce entitled a *Dumb Belle, or I'm Perfection*."

After the show a player named Mr. Barker took a dose of laudanum for his nerves. It killed him, thus terminating the engagement. Tears blurred the borrowed bloom on the cheeks of the little trouper from Baltimore, who declared herself a widow, with two fatherless babies at home. The consolation of Mrs. Barker became a national matter. Her husband was given a fine funeral. The gamblers raised a purse of gold for the orphans, and General Houston placed the Executive Mansion at the bereaved artist's disposal until a vessel sailed for New Orleans.

Three days later came the June wedding that Dilrue Rose was counting on. "It was grand. . . . General Houston and I were to be the first attendants, Dr. Ashbel Smith and Miss Voate second and, Dr. Ewing and Mrs. Holliday, a pretty widow, third. At the last moment . . . Mrs. Holliday suggested that I was too young and timid, and that she would take my place. General Houston offered her his arm and Dr,

Ewing escorted me. As soon as the congratulations were over, General Houston who was the personification of elegance and kindness, excused himself and retired. Mrs. Holliday then took possession of Dr. Ewing and left me without an escort till Mr. Hunt introduced Mr. Ira A. Harris."[28] No widow intervening, Dilrue married Ira Harris.

## 8

Six months of presidency remained to Sam Houston who, under the Constitution, was ineligible to succeed himself. Things went awry. The contractor for the new Navy found the President "nearly all the time drunk."[29] Congress passed some foolish financial legislation over a veto, and star money dropped to ninety cents. A Mexican-inspired Indian outbreak terrorized the Nacogdoches country, and Houston's neglect of defensive measures brought a tide of denunciation. Star money fell to eighty cents. During an exchange of amenities, ex-President Burnet called Houston a half-Indian, the President retorting that his predecessor was a hog thief. Mr. Burnet challenged Houston to a duel, and Dr. Branch T. Archer, himself handy with the pistols, delivered the note. Houston brushed it aside, telling Archer to inform Burnet that "the people are equally disgusted with both of us."[30] Houston had a violent quarrel with his friend, W. H. Wharton. Wharton's hand dropped to his bowie knife. Houston raised his arms above his head. "Draw—draw if you dare!" Wharton did not draw.[31]

Samuel Colt, whose own career may explain his admiration for Houston, sought to smooth the pathway of the burdened Executive with a gift of a pair of handsome dueling irons. After trying them out on marks pinned to trees General Houston pronounced the new weapons to be superior to the run of pistols then in use. A local vogue for Colt's pistols resulted which enabled the Yankee inventor to sell as many guns in Texas during the next four years as he sold in the rest of the world. With this testimonial of approval the future of the Colt product was assured, notwithstanding an untimely bankruptcy due to a temporary absence of appreciation among the less discriminating.

Yet the reign of "Judge Colt" fell short of the President's ideal. By his personal example and otherwise General Houston had striven to discourage dueling in his powder-stained Republic. These efforts, however, received little support except in the case of Willis Alston, whom tradition identifies (but not to the exclusion of two or three other candidates) as the rival for Eliza Allen's hand over whom Sam Houston prevailed in 1829. Alston was a member of the celebrated North Carolina family and had made Houston's acquaintance when the two were in the United States Congress. After his father and two brothers had fallen in duels Alston killed a Georgia politician and came to Texas, where he killed a Doctor Stewart, and was executed by a mob in Brazoria. The fault of Mr. Alston involved the purity of the Code; he had used a sawed-off shotgun on Doctor Stewart.

Amid these events General Lamar's candidacy for president and that of Burnet for vice-president gained impetus. The befuddled opposition divided the field between two tickets which seemed to insure Lamar's election until one of the presidential aspirants, Chief Justice Collingsworth of the Supreme Court, a brilliant man who had wrecked his mind with drink, leaped from a steamer and drowned himself in Galveston Bay. This cleared the way for Peter W. Grayson, a lawyer of considerable ability and exemplary personal life. The Houston opposition took heart. Grayson was in the United States. While hastening home to press his campaign he was seized by a fit of mental depression, a malady against which he had waged a solitary struggle since the days of his youth. At a wayside tavern in Tennessee the sufferer penned a polite note asking the pardon of his landlord and blew out his brains.

Sam Houston attended the inaugural of Lamar and Burnet wearing a powdered wig and a costume of Washington's time. He delivered an oration not unworthy of association with another Farewell Address. Tears were in his eyes, and in the eyes of some who had come to sneer, when Sam Houston extended his great arms in an attitude of benediction and relinquished his Republic to the keeping of Mirabeau B. Lamar. "The day will come," said the *Telegraph and Texas Register*, which was not a partizan of General Houston, "when his name shall appear in the pages of the Texian story, unsullied by a single stain—his faults . . . forgotten, his vices buried in the tomb; the hero of San Jacinto . . . the nursling of Fame."

# CHAPTER XXIII

## THE TALENTED AMATEUR

### 1

MIRABEAU BUONAPARTE LAMAR had stepped into Texas with a sword in his hand and inquired the way to Sam Houston's Army when most people were headed in other directions. After the first skirmish at San Jacinto, General Houston raised the private of cavalry with the conquering name and air to command the mounted troops. His report of the battle mentioned the personal gallantry of Colonel Lamar.

As vice-president, Lamar's opposition and abortive coup d'état of 1837 followed the promptings of a nature that had derived ideas of grandeur from a doting uncle in Georgia who had christened him. Mirabeau Lamar regarded Sam Houston as a preposterous vulgarian who had humiliated Texas by his familiarity with Indians and rowdy whites.

In a polished inaugural address President Lamar foreshadowed a departure from the policies of his predecessor. Negotiations for annexation to the United States would not be resumed. A loftier destiny awaited Texas as an independent power, adorned by the graces as well as the sturdier virtues of Anglo-Saxon democracy. As a personal patron of the arts, General Lamar felt himself eligible to sponsor this extension of culture. He deprecated the fact that his achievements in the fields of war and statecraft had eclipsed his mastery of the violin and the merit of his lyrical verses. The inaugural ceremonies closed with a ball in the Capitol. "The elite of the land its beauty and worth were collected there," wrote Ashbel Smith, ". . . a large and overflowing assembly of noble and accomplished dames, of soldiers scholars and chivalrous gentlemen."

Sam Houston accepted the altered order of the times. One of the final acts of his Administration had been a house-cleaning of the Executive Mansion. Curtains were hung at the windows and carpets laid on the floors—though not until new planks were found to replace those lately pulled up for fire-wood by General Houston who had been unwilling to bring a pleasant evening to an untimely end. Houston closed his régime with a levee in which a suspicious mind might discover a trace of irony. "The rooms of the White House," noted the sprightly Smith, White House being a very new and smart expression, "were full to overflowing . . . a far less promiscuous assemblage than is commonly seen on such occasions. . . . The crowds promenaded to the movement of soft music . . . and . . . it was worth while to behold the elegant form and manly proportions of General Houston, to listen to the promptness and variety of his colloquial powers his facility and great tact to appropriate compliments as . . . he received the greetings of beauty and of talent."[1]

Moving into the refurbished establishment, General Lamar declared war on Indians, sent the Navy to help the rebellious province of Yucatan, recruited an army to frown across the Rio Grande, projected a national system of education, and began to lay out a new capital city. The money to defray these expenditures was printed while the President sunned himself in the contemplation of larger triumphs.

The site of the new capital was on the upper Colorado, beyond the remotest settlements, but with the maturity of the President's projects destined to be the hub of the greater Republic. The location was an inspiring one amid a collection of hills crowned by a violet haze, which long years before Stephen Austin had picked for his dream university. Although they named the new town Austin, the founders did not know of

Stephen's dream, but they were aware of the enthusiasm of General Lamar who had camped on the site during a hunting trip.

Sam Houston devoted the early months of the Lamar Administration to his personal affairs, which were prosperous, and then took a trip to the United States.

## 2

That nations make history is another fact that Mirabeau Lamar did not overlook. He began segregating material for the express purpose of assisting a future chronicler of the Texan story. By his industry were preserved thousands of documents, including this letter from Memucan Hunt, former Minister to the United States, dated at Jackson, Mississippi, July 13, 1839:

"General Houston was received with considerable attention at Columbus in this State, and on my reaching there, I was surprised to find how favorable an impression he had made. I do not think, however, when I left that place that my acquaintances continued to entertain . . . favorable views of him. . . . Only think how contemptible he acted, when I assure you that he mentioned the circumstances of the quarrel between him and myself, giving an unjust version of it, to a young lady, who he knew I would shortly visit. . . . This is almost as ridiculous, as his having burned off his coat tail, while in a state of intoxication, immediately after making Temperance speeches."[2]

The maiden of Columbus had not been the first young lady to share the confidences of the distinguished traveler. Before coming to Mississippi, Houston was in Alabama buying blooded horses and seeking capital for his Texas enterprises. The quest for capital took him to Mobile to interview William Bledsoe, who invited the General to his stately country home, Spring Hill. It was a radiant afternoon in May, and Mrs. Bledsoe was giving a strawberry festival on her lawn.

Emily Antoinette Bledsoe was eighteen years old. Her Parisian ancestry spoke in lustrous dark eyes, a vivacious manner and love for pretty clothes. In the presence of such a hostess Sam Houston was at his best. They were strolling in the rose garden when a girl came by carrying a dish of strawberries.

"General Houston, my sister, Miss Margaret Lea," said Emily Antoinette.

General Houston bowed very low.

"I am charmed." And he really was.

Sam Houston thought he had never seen anything so beautiful as the girl who regarded him with placid violet eyes. She was taller than Antoinette, and two years older. She was dressed less extravagantly. Her features were fairer and more tranquil. Her hair was dark brown, except for a gay band of golden ringlets circling her temples like a halo.

A young woman of less poise might have betrayed herself. Margaret's thoughts swept back to the unforgettable Sunday when New Orleans had received the victor of San Jacinto. The wild image of him, swaying against the gunwale, was burned in her mind. She had been incapable of dispelling the premonition that some time she would meet this romantic man, and the meeting would shape her destiny.

Emily Antoinette saw little more of General Houston that afternoon. At night a candle burned late in a room at Spring Hill. Margaret was writing a poem.[3]

### 3

General Houston visited Andrew Jackson at the Hermitage, and moved on to East Tennessee where he sojourned with a cousin, Judge Wallace, of Maryville. One evening a roomful of relatives was discussing Eliza Allen, who to every one's surprise had married a wealthy widower. Houston was lying on a couch, apparently not listening, when some one made an unnecessary remark. "Houston got up with eyes flashing," said Judge Wallace. " 'Whoever dares say a word against Eliza shall pay for it !' "[4]

In midsummer General Houston was in Alabama again, where he saw the Bledsoes, Margaret, and Mrs. Lea, her mother. He interested Mr. Bledsoe and Mrs. Lea, who was a widow and a keen business woman, in the money-making possibilities of Texas. They agreed to make a visit of inspection.

When the General departed Margaret wept. She had promised to be Sam Houston's wife. Many years later Margaret's pastor asked her how a girl of her environment could have risked her life's happiness in face of the warnings she received of General Houston's history and habits. Margaret's answer covered everything.

"He had won my heart."[5]

### 4

Houston reached Texas in a rage against Lamar's Indian war. The bleeding remnants of the Cherokees had been driven across the Red River to nurse their wounds in Oo-loo-te-ka's wigwams. In his eighty-fourth year The Bowl had led his braves in their last stand on Texan soil. When he saw that the day was lost, the venerable leader gave the signal to retreat, saying, "I stay. I am an old man. I die here." He fell, and a sword Sam Houston had given was pried from the red warrior's cold hand.

Houston reviewed the campaign in a savage speech at Nacogdoches. The Bowl was "a better man" than his "murderers." Houston's life was threatened as he left the hall and the speech estranged some of his oldest supporters in Texas, including Rusk, Adolphus Sterne and Henry Raguet. Nevertheless, Houston stood for representative in Congress for the Nacogdoches district and was elected. He journeyed to Austin where Anna Raguet wrote him a few letters and received pleasant, though not always prompt, replies.

Congress Avenue, the principal thoroughfare of the new

capital, was so wide and imposing that in wet weather communication between the rows of cabins on the opposite side was a serious undertaking. Inasmuch as some of the government departments were located on one side of the avenue and some on the other, this had a tendency to decentralize the Administration. Vehicles carried fence rails to pry the wheels out of the mud.

The one-story Hall of Congress stood on a little knoll just off the avenue. More "pretentious" was the two-story residence of President Lamar whose entourage Sam Houston disrespectfully dubbed "The Court of King Witumpka." Houston lodged on Congress Avenue in a shanty with a dirt floor. Here he held court of his own and, according to tradition, clad in moccasins and an Indian blanket, received the Count Alphonse de Saligny, the French Chargé d'Affaires. Saligny was a strutting little fellow with a patch of orders on his coat. The ex-President threw back his blanket and, striking his naked breast, indicated the scars of his battle wounds.

"Monsieur le Comte, an humble republican soldier, who wears his decorations here, salutes you."

The outcome of General Lamar's soaring schemes had begun to trouble Texans not blinded by partizanship. Paper money had fallen rapidly and coin was disappearing from circulation. In mid-summer, 1839, ex-Minister Anson Jones wrote in his private note-book more than he would have admitted in public. "Gen. Lamar may mean well . . . but his mind is altogether of a dreamy, poetic order, a sort of political Troubadour and Crusader and wholly unfit for . . . the every day realities of his present station."[6]

In November Doctor Jones arrived in Austin, a member of the Senate. Although friendly with Lamar the sly little Senator did not overlook the pits in the President's path. Sam Houston, holding court in his shack, satirizing and ridiculing, made matters no easier. Senator Jones believed Lamar to be doomed and wished to see him doomed, but not at the hands of Sam Houston. "Gen. H.," the Senator confided to his diary, "is not so strong in what he does himself, as in what his enemies do: it is not *his* strength, but *their* weakness—not his *wisdom* but their *folly*. Cunning, Indian cunning. . . . Old Bowles . . . learned him all he knows."[7]

As the Senator wrote he was fixing to out-cunning Houston. He was organizing a banquet, at which Sam Houston would be guest of honor and Anson Jones the toastmaster. In addition to members of the Houston group, Lamar men were to be invited, which might benefit an impartial chairman with a foot in both camps.

Although roads and weather kept many away, two hundred were present at the dinner which was "handsomely served." Forty-three toasts were drunk, eight of them to Sam Houston, whose name was received with nine cheers. When glasses were raised to "The President of the Republic," there was silence. Doctor Jones was rewarded for his trouble with a mention for the vice-presidency on a ticket headed by Houston. The editor of the Austin City *Gazette* thought Houston made "one of the most eloquent speeches we ever remember to have heard; and impressed us with a more favorable impression of his powerful intellect."[8] Alone in his room Toastmaster Jones penned a concise story of disappointed hopes. "No man is more completely master of the art of appropriating to himself the merit of others' good acts . . . than General Houston."[9]

The good acts of Doctor Jones emphasized Houston's leadership of the opposition which, except for a little informal sniping, permitted Lamar to run his course unchallenged. "I fear," wrote Jones on Christmas Eve, "that Gen. Houston does not care how completely L——r ruins the country, so that he can . . . say, 'I told you so; there is nobody but old Sam after all.' "

On New Year's Day, 1840, the Senator saw the country "going to the —— as fast as General H. can possibly wish." On February fourth Saligny was presented to the Senate with ceremony. That night the town was raided by Indians, and the cries of two inhabitants under the scalping knife brought Cabi-

net members from their beds.  The incident affected the poise
of Monsieur de Saligny, and this at a critical juncture in the
negotiations for a million-dollar loan in Paris.  Lamar quieted
the French diplomat's fears, however, and all was well until one
of Innkeeper Bullock's pigs broke into the Count's stable and
ate his corn.  Saligny's servant killed the pig.  Bullock
thrashed the servant and put the Count out of his hotel.
Saligny appealed to the Secretary of State for redress and,
failing to get it, departed for New Orleans.  The loan fell
through, and Texas money continued to decline.

5

Sam Houston found diversion from these events by flooding
the mails with impassioned letters to Margaret Lea.  He
begged her to come to Texas and marry him when her mother
and William Bledsoe should make their proposed trip.  Margaret said she would come and named the vessel.  Sam Houston
repaired to Galveston, from whence Lamar was informed that
"*The Great Ex* . . . awaits the arrival of his bride to be."[10]
There had lately disembarked at Galveston another traveler from Mobile who had come to Texas on a sentimental
journey.  It was Olivia.  From Houston City she sent wistful
messages—"Dinna forget me"—but the flushed dreamer at
Austin was very tardy with his replies.  The cares of state had
begun to harry Mirabeau, but he plunged buoyantly on, screening each failure with the mask of a grander scheme.  A variety
of matters were afoot—some, perhaps, without the President's
assent, since he had lost control of the country.  A revolution
supported by Texas filibusters was under way in northern
Mexico, with the eventual object, in Texan minds, of annexing
that territory to the Republic.  At the same time General
Lamar was striving for a peaceable rapprochement with
Mexico.  A detail of the plan, as alleged by Houston and
others, contemplated a matrimonial alliance with an old
grandee family.

The vessel that was to bring Sam Houston's bride-to-be anchored in the roads to the boom of the cannon fired by the ex-President's friends in the garrison. Touched by this tribute, which he took as a happy augury, General Houston set out in a dory to greet his intended. Mr. Bledsoe and Mrs. Lea were on the deck. But Miss Margaret? Not indisposed by the voyage, General Houston hoped.

"General Houston," said Nancy Lea, "my daughter is in Alabama. She goes forth in the world to marry no man. The one who receives her hand will receive it in my home and not elsewhere."[11]

## 6

Strong-minded and plain-spoken Nancy Lea, a Baptist minister's widow, had opposed her daughter's romance with Sam Houston, but despite herself she liked the man. There were kindred chords in their natures. After making investments in East Texas lands, Mrs. Lea and her son-in-law returned to Alabama and, with the rest of the family, renewed their persuasions upon Margaret.

In Texas those who could speak of such matters, argued with Houston. Ashbel Smith and Barnard Bee in particular sought to convince the ex-President that his "temperament" was unsuited to the quiet of the cottage. In view of "his terrific habits," wrote Bee, "I implored him . . . to resort to any expedient rather than *marry*."[12]

A month after her departure Sam Houston followed Nancy Lea to Alabama. Margaret had held out loyally, and the wedding was set for May 9, 1840, at the Lea residence in Marion. The guests arrived, the minister arrived and the musicians were ready to play when one of the men of the Lea family took General Houston aside. He said that unless Houston gave a satisfactory explanation of his separation from Eliza Allen the ceremony could not take place.

Sam Houston's tone was courteous, but it did not disguise the feeling that the manner of this ultimatum seemed calculated to place him in a trap. He told his questioner that there was nothing to add to what he had already said. The cause of that estrangement was something he had never told. If the wedding depended upon his telling now, Margaret's kinsman might "call his fiddlers off."[13]

### 7

The violinists swung their bows—a victory over the long shadow. As quickly as possible General Houston and his bride sailed for Galveston where the guns proclaimed that the Texas melodrama had acquired its bright-eyed ingénue.

"I see with great pain the marriage of Genl Houston to Miss Lea!" wrote Colonel Bee to Doctor Smith. "In all my acquaintance with life I have never met with an Individual more totally disqualified for domestic happiness—he will not live with her 6 months."[14]

Margaret conceived herself to be the instrument of General Houston's regeneration, and the beginning was auspicious. When three of Colonel Bee's six months had elapsed, Smith replied that Houston was a "model of propriety" and intensely devoted to his wife. He took her on his travels, but eventually this proved too fatiguing for Margaret, and five and a half months after the marriage they were separated for the first time, Mrs. Houston abandoning a tour midway while her husband hastened on to East Texas to attend court. He wrote to her from San Augustine:

"It is not that I expect to interest you much, for I have little, or no news, but My Love, I am so unhappy. . . . The world to me would be a sorry world, were it not, that I am willing, and even happy to endure it on your account. Every hour that we are apart, only resolves me, more firmly, not again to be separated from you. . . .

"Today is drisling and damp, and I am depressed and melancholy. I can not be happy, but where you are! . . . This morning while the chill was upon me, I felt as tho' I would yield every thing, & fly to you. . . .

"My love! I do sincerely hope that you will hear no more slanders of me. It is the malice of the world to abuse me, & really were not that they reach My Beloved Margaret, I would not care one picayune—but that you should be distressed, is inexpressible wretchedness to me.

"My dear! do be satisfied, and now in your feeble health, be cheerful, for that is all important to you, and my dear if you hear the truth, you never shall hear of my being in a 'spree'. . . .

"My heart embraces you. . . .

"Thine ever truly—<br>"Houston.

"P. S. 'Tis late in the day, & I will ride to pass the night with an old Batchelor friend. He is very old, and one of my first friends in Texas. He is the only Revolutionary soldier that I know in the Republic.          Thine Houston."[15]

Nine weeks later he left her again and journeyed to the outpost capital to attend the Fifth Congress.

8

In a shabby French boarding house a tall man with a weather-beaten look was writing a letter. A sword hung on the wall, and over it a tattered hat. The communication was addressed to Felix Huston:

"New Orleans Jany 28, 1841.

"Dear General

"Since I last had the pleasure of seeing you I have been . . . consoling myself with the hope that a big war would soon break out with England and furnish a broad field for enterprise for the myriads of Ardent & discontented spirits who are in the same threadbare condition as myself, but this hope grows daily less and less: for in this age of refined diplomacy a National injury . . . is frittered away in negotiation. . . . As every other means of subsistence is closed against me in this *happy and prosperous* community . . . I have come to the conclusion that . . . [Mexico] presents the favorist field to a military asperant that has offered itself within a Century. . . . Mexico is rushing upon her fate; her rulers have pledged themselves to the priesthood for a Consideration of a Million and a half dollars to Commence a Crusade against the heretics of Texas. . . . They will invade Texas with a force of 20,000 men which are already rendevousing at San Louis Potosi—what is to be the result? why Texas—helpless and . . . possessing by the shadow of a shade of Government will accept with avidity (and upon his own terms) the services of any individual who can bring into the field any force of Armed men. The consequence will be [the conquest of] . . . Mexico. . . . Thousands of . . . adventurous spirits will at once flock to the standard of *him* who can unite the heterogeneous mass which will necessarily compose the army of invaders.—The part which I have laid out for myself is humble. I have determined to go immediately to Texas and among my old associates and the disbanded soldiery to raise a force of from 5 to 600 men with which force I will take up a position which will . . . Command the valley of the Rio Grande . . . and strike . . . whenever the opportunity presents. . . . I will receive no Commission or authority from the Government of Texas and will be governed alone by the fixed principle of . . . rewarding those who serve under me with the riches of the land and the fatness Thereof—and in conclusion will have a potential voice in the disposition of the Conquered Country—You are the person named by every one as the leader who . . . must necessarily conquer Mexico. . . . The force of Guerillas which it is my intention to raise will . . . be . . . at your disposition. I . . . [write] for the purpose of ascertaining your views. . . . My threadbare condition prevents my calling upon you.

"Respectfully
"Yr Friend and Obdt Svt
"WILLIAM S. FISHER"[16]

Thus the Texas Republic after two years of Lamar—scorned by a coatless adventurer. It had been different in other days when as Sam Houston's Secretary of War the fortunes of Mr. Fisher and those of the Republic prospered together. The writer's remarks on the intentions of Santa Anna are worthy of notice. Mr. Fisher was lately returned from below the Rio Grande where he had found unstable employment as a colonel in the Mexican service.

The Fifth Congress saw the Lamar régime with its back to the wall. Worn out by anxiety the President had virtually abdicated the functions of his office to Vice-President Burnet who thumbed his Bible and thundered against Sam Houston. All of Lamar's schemes had failed. Texas money was worth twenty cents on the dollar, millions had been added to the public debt and credit was gone. The end seemed near.

The Administration met this situation as it had met others—with new plans. The first of these found expression in the Franco-Texienne Land Bill which proposed a territorial grant of astronomical proportions to a French company. The scheme was susceptible of glittering exploitation and for months it convulsed the country. Houston opposed it despite pressure and alluring inducements from Sam Swartwout and other easterners who had helped the Revolution. The bill was eventually laid to rest by Congress.

Lamar then staked everything on the capture of the rich revenues of the Santa Fé Trail. With the energy of despair the Administration leaders in Congress launched the program in stirring speeches about planting the Lone Star on the gray towers of el Palacio Real. Santa Fé and most of New Mexico lay within the boundaries of Texas as drawn in 1836, but the Republic had not attempted to assert its dominion there. Sam Houston said that to attempt it now would be foolhardy. He whittled sticks during the speaking and crushed the orators with ridicule.

Lamar was in no position to sustain this defeat. When Congress declined to sanction the expedition the President ordered a half million dollars from a New Orleans printer and proceeded on his own responsibility. Horses were purchased for a thousand dollars apiece—Texas currency—and the troops newly uniformed to make a brave showing. The venture was widely advertised and favorably noticed in the United States. The conquest was to be one of good will. Force was to be used only to repel attack. In June of 1841 the cavalcade marched. Soldiers, merchants with rich stores, financiers, diplomats and an editor of the New Orleans *Picayune*—a gallant facade contrived with the attractive incompetence that was the signature of Mirabeau Lamar. But the fine show and the respectable caliber of the cast created an impression which no amount of ridicule was able entirely to dispel.

### 9

The Lamar people said it was unfortunate that a presidential election must intervene before the results of the Santa Fé expedition should be apparent.

Another who regretted the approaching campaign was Margaret. General Houston had hastened from Austin as soon as his work was done and carried Margaret away to a summer home he had built—alack, for Anna—on a lovely spot by the sea called Cedar Point. They were very happy, and Margaret had every reason to acquire faith in herself as an instrument of regeneration. Margaret was as beautiful as any woman in Texas. She was more intelligent and had been much more carefully educated than the average of women there or elsewhere. She was an excellent musician and sang sweetly. At Cedar Point Margaret had only her guitar, but the population of Houston City was divided into two classes: those who had and those who had not seen the Houston piano! While not shunning society, Margaret cared little for it, or for the stir that went with being the wife of a famous public man. She was a home-maker.

Sam Houston was enjoying a life that had filled his heart with longing for many years. Delighted with his friend's happiness, Ashbel Smith proclaimed that Houston invariably set the fashion in Texas. Irion, Henderson, Hockley and "all the bachelors" were getting married. One fair match-maker had even "promised to marry me off"; and the doctor intimated that stranger things had already come to pass. Doctor Irion married Anna Raguet. This devoted friend had carried Sam Houston's love messages to Nacogdoches as long as hope remained. Anna named her first boy Sam Houston Irion.

When the campaign took Sam Houston away from Cedar Point, Margaret was oppressed by fears which the papers supporting the candidacy of Judge Burnet did little to allay.

"A hero was travelling—his labors were o'er,
But sad was the smile his countenance wore,
For . . .
. . . he'd sworn before God 'gainst taking strong drink.
'Now what will I do when my spirits are low,
Shall I take to friend opium? Ah! it is a worse foe—
By th' Eternal, I have it. To think more would be idle,
The Book that I swore on—why, it was not the Bible! . . .
So give me some whisky—'tis the cheer of Gods! . . .' "[17]

The traveler went his way with an assurance that irritated his adversaries. "It seems the big Mingo has been showing himself to his humble servants in San Augustine, who . . . seem sufficiently beatified if they can only touch the hem of his garment or be permitted to converse with *Esau*. He, the Mingo . . . says Lamar is a Mussell man and Burnett a hog thief; then Esau convives and guests disturb the neighborhood with bursts of cachination. . . . Send us the Journals of the two last Sessions of Congress I want them to operate with, against the Big Mingo."[18]

The operations were futile. With its currency as low as three cents and Santa Anna making gestures that looked like business, Texas voted overwhelmingly to restore the presidency to Sam Houston.

# CHAPTER XXIV

## WASHINGTON-ON-THE-BRAZOS

### 1

ON THE wind-swept thirteenth day of December, 1841, Sam Houston marched to the drafty frame tabernacle in Austin called the Hall of Congress, and with a grim curtailment of formality assumed receivership of the affairs of the Republic.

He burrowed into the Treasury records but failed to ascertain the amount of the public debt. One set of figures indicated something like twelve million dollars, while another ledger showed little more than half that sum. Aside from this confusion the state of the Treasury was simplicity itself. There was not the wherewithal to provide fire-wood for the presidential residence. (Fortunately, Margaret had remained in Houston City.) The debt was owed in gold. Revenues were received in paper from ninety-seven to seventy per cent. under par. The face value of the receipts was $33,550 a month, normal expenditures three times that. Commerce in the Republic had ceased to exist. The commander of a visiting French man-of-war reported the only market to be for hard liquors.

"It seems that we have arrived at a crisis," the President said to Congress. And in a personal memorandum: "Our situation is worse than it was on the 22nd of April 1836."

Houston reduced his own salary from ten thousand dollars to five thousand dollars a year, and many others in proportion. He suppressed an entire category of offices that had bloomed under Lamar, consolidated the War and Navy and the State and Post-Office Departments, and cut the pay-roll from $174,000 a year to $32,800. The Navy was recalled from Yucatan, peace emissaries sent among the Indians, and the horizon of foreign policy scrutinized with exceeding care. The President reposed his hope for the restoration of Texas in annexation to the United States or a European alliance. Since these policies were diametrically opposed, their management required tact. Anson Jones, who had brought Texas to the notice of Lord Palmerston, was appointed Secretary of State. He began to cultivate England and France—the latter being still rather cool over the pig indignity. Houston himself felt out the situation in Washington, where Tyler favored annexation rightly enough, but Congress could not be depended upon.

A new form of paper money was introduced which Houston made heroic efforts to maintain at a respectable rate of exchange. So sparingly was it issued that after three months the amount in circulation did not exceed forty thousand dollars. As fast as Lamar notes fell into government hands they were burned. Under these circumstances the new money—called "exchequers"—passed at par for several weeks, when, involved in a fresh whirlwind of troubles, it declined.

## 2

When Houston took office the country was in suspense over the Santa Fé expedition, which had not been heard of for months. Four weeks later the President got word that the entire command had been made prisoners and was being marched, with excessive brutality, to Mexico City.

The tidings inflamed Texas as nothing had done since the Álamo. Forgetting bankruptcy, forgetting everything, Congress adopted a resolution annexing the two Californias and all or part of seven other Mexican provinces—an area larger than the United States. In vetoing the measure Houston pointed out that the moment for a "legislative jest" was ill-chosen. Congress repassed the resolution over the veto and adjourned, the President having no wish to detain it for consideration of the graver consequences now at hand.

Some Mexican women of San Antonio de Béxar had brought the news that Santa Anna was gathering his forces for the attempted reconquest foreshadowed by Colonel Fisher. Houston left Austin in haste and placed Margaret aboard a vessel at Galveston bound for Mobile. An express from his private secretary followed the President. "It is impossible to know what may be the results of the reported invasion, if it should be true. I have, therefore, forwarded you both your public and private papers, in order that you may provide for their security."[1]

Twenty-four hours later this message came: "The truth at last. . . . San Antonio and Goliad have fallen! The enemy . . . will doubtless advance upon this place."[2]

The President reached for a pen.

"Galveston, March 10th, 1842. To Col. Alden A. M. Jackson, Sir. . . . [Place] the fort at the east end of the Island . . . in an efficient state of defense, in case of a descent of the enemy by sea."[3]

"To Brigadier General Morehouse, Sir, You will hold the troops in readiness to march at a moment's warning."[4]

"To Brigadier General A. Somervell, Sir. . . . Repair to . . . the army—take command of the same, and . . . maintain the strictest discipline. . . . If a man is taken asleep at his post . . . let him be shot. . . . Prudence will be of more importance than enthusiasm."[5]

"To P. Edmunds, Esq., Consul at New Orleans, Sir, . . . [Each] volunteer . . . *will be required . . . to bring with him a good rifle or musket with cartouch box, or powder horn, with at least one hundred rounds of ammunition . . .* and six months' clothing. . . . *None other* . . . will be received."[6]

The army marched and the enemy retreated, harried by the Texans until he passed the Rio Grande. Without a day's delay Sam Houston ordered all farmers released from service to "return to the cultivation of their fields." Scouts patrolled the border to warn of enemy movements.

A flamboyant letter came from Santa Anna, in reply to an unauthorized proposal by James Hamilton and Barnard E. Bee who suggested that Mexico acknowledge the independence of Texas in exchange for the payment of five million dollars exclusive of handsome bribes. General Santa Anna called the proposal an affront to his honor and declared that Mexico would plant "her eagle standard on the banks of the Sabine."

"Most Excellent Sir," replied Sam Houston. "Ere the banner of Mexico shall . . . float on the banks of the Sabine, the Texan standard of the single star, borne by the Anglo-Saxon race, shall display its bright folds in liberty's triumph on the Isthmus of Darien.

"With the most appropriate consideration, I have the honor to present you my salutation."[7]

This gave General Santa Anna food for reflection and doubled recruiting in the United States.

"Your favor under date of Parkersburg, Virginia, [received]. . . . If you raise a company . . . it must consist of at least fifty-six men, rank and file, completely armed, clothed, and provisioned for six months. . . . The remuneration for your expenses and services must come from the enemy. They have provoked the war and must abide by the consequences. The rules of honorable warfare will, however, be invariably observed. The field for chivalrous and eminently useful enterprise is now open. . . . The harvest is rich and inviting. . . . Come."[8]

Such letters streamed from Houston's pen night and day. Correspondence was not the whole of the President's burden, however. "Two hundred and fifty (250) dollars worth of sugar and coffee . . . for the troops at Corpus Christi" could be obtained only when Sam Houston personally guaranteed payment of the bill.[9]  The President praised Colonel Franks for his work as peacemaker among the Indians, regretting that it was "utterly impossible to furnish you . . . any pecuniary assistance.  There is not one dollar in the Treasury."[10]  The Navy again was in the hands of creditors. Mail service had been suspended.

Ashbel Smith sailed as minister to England and France, paying his own way, which was a boon to Texas but a blow to George S. McIntosh, the Lamar appointee whom Doctor Smith was to replace.  "With unfeigned reluctance" this disturbed diplomat wrote to Houston to say "that I am at this moment in Paris entirely *destitute* . . . and nearly $4000 in debt. . . . I have been forced to pawn my watches," and having nothing more to pawn only his diplomatic status fended off the fate that had overtaken the Navy.  "Mr. Smith my successor is in London and will be here in a fortnight.—His arrival will remove the only bar between me and imprisonment." Mr. McIntosh asked for five thousand dollars,[11] but Houston did not have it.  Ashbel Smith came to the rescue of his predecessor, however.

The President reestablished himself at Houston, and Margaret joined him there.  Congress was called to an extra session to make financial provision for the war.

### 3

General Santa Anna drummed his fingers over Houston's letter and withheld marching orders for the Sabine.  In some respects this meant additional trouble for Houston, with an idle Army on his hands.  Tempestuous volunteers swarmed from the United States, utterly unprovided for.  Starvation, insubordination and looting ensued.  Albert Sidney Johnston sent the President a challenge to a duel.  Houston handed it to his secretary, Miller.  "File this.  Angry gentlemen must wait their turn."

Adjutant-General Davis reported that he could restrain the men no longer. Texas must attack. The President replied in a fatherly fashion.

"My dear Sir, you have no idea of the pain you inflict on me, when you suggest to me the anxiety of the men to advance upon the enemy. . . . They will find that they are very young in service, and I fear—greatly fear—that we have again to see reenacted the scenes of Grant, Johnson and others, before our people will reflect. My heart is truly sick when I hear that men think seriously of doing *so-and-so*. Travis thought *so-and-so*, and so did Fannin. . . . When I want a movement made, I will order it. . . . How can men with naked feet talk of Matamoras, Monterey, and other places? This is all done by 'thinking.' Colonel Washington, and agents on whom I relied for obedience to orders, 'thought' that if they could get men here, all was right; and Colonel Gillespie is commended for assuming the generous responsibility of taking upon himself to send them contrary to orders. . . . This is *generosity*—this is what comes of the assumption of 'responsibility' in the face of orders reiterated by every boat. . . . The consequence will be that Texas will 'whip herself' without the assistance of Mexico. . . . Do the best you can. Truly thy friend, SAM HOUSTON."[12]

Another outbreak, and four days later the President addressed his Adjutant-General in a different tone. "I positively require the name of every deserter. I require the execution of every order. . . . You know what constitutes the offense of desertion. You know the penalty. . . . I expect it to be executed."[13]

The Army behaved for a while, and on June twenty-seventh Congress assembled. It declared a war of invasion, and passed a bill placing the President at the head of the Army with dictatorial authority. He could conscript one-third of the population able to bear arms and sell ten million acres of land. Army and populace applauded the sweeping provisions and when the President received the bill in silence there was general surprise. When it was rumored that he might return it with a veto, threats were heard of consequences the more patriotic opponents of Houston hoped to forestall. Memucan Hunt made a personal appeal to the Executive.

"The Bill presented for your consideration and signature opens to yourself a field for glory which has had no parallel since Napoleon crossed the Alps. . . . Call upon the choicest spirits of the land to rally to your banner. Challenge to the field your leading personal and political adversaries . . . and . . . you will find yourself at the head of an army which no Mexican force can withstand . . . the idol of both camp and country. . . .

"The opposite course—the veto of the bill—whilst it brings despair and desperation to a large and gallant portion of the country will disarm . . . your friends and sharpen the weapons of your enemies. . . . You stand before the world committed to an offensive war 'to the knife.' . . . Indeed I conscientiously believe that if you veto this bill there will be another assemblage of congress in sufficient numbers to form a quorum and legislate under the present constitution."[14]

Sam Houston scribbled at the foot of the letter, "Genl Hunt is on the highway to Mexico!" and passed it to Miller to file.

The tempest grew. Sam Houston was up to his Indian tricks. He had urged war. He had advised with congressional leaders on details of the bill in his hands. And for what purpose? To veto it and receive credit for lofty statesmanship at the expense of Congress? They said he did not dare.

Hard-looking strangers from the Army camps gathered in knots on the streets. Talk of assassination was in the air. Cabinet officers spoke of resigning to avert civil war. A guard was suggested for the President's house. Sam Houston scorned it, and Margaret stepped bravely into her rôle. Long after the lights in the town were extinguished the Executive Mansion was aglow. The windows were open. Forms crouching in the shadows beheld the stately figure of the President passing to and fro and heard the notes of the celebrated piano.

The President returned the measure to Congress with a

closely reasoned veto message. Having blown itself out before-hand, the opposition received the rejection without disturbance.

Houston's action concealed more than it disclosed. Like most hasty legislation the bill was faulty, but the motive behind it had been high and fine: a levee en mass, a fight to the last man and the last dollar. In refusing the crown the Texan Cæsar obviously had other plans.

And he kept them to himself.

4

In September of 1842 Santa Anna again raided San Antonio with a strong force under Woll who carried off a number of citizens, including the personnel of the District Court which was in session. Houston had to do something. He paraded twelve hundred men, made a warlike speech and sent them to invade Mexico. The force was not equipped for a campaign, but its departure stilled the popular outcry, and Houston gained time to improvise an issue in the arena of diplomacy, where he had made up his mind to risk everything.

In Washington the outlook was adverse. Once more annexation had been howled down by the abolitionists, William Lloyd Garrison putting the case succinctly: "All who would sympathize with that pseudo-Republic hate liberty, and would dethrone God." But this din diverted attention from Dr. Ashbel Smith who was treading softly the carpets of Whitehall and the tall corridors of Versailles.

As the Republic possessed few diplomatic assets, General Houston capitalized its liabilities. To the governments of Great Britain, France and the United States, he addressed a remonstrance against the San Antonio raid. It was an appeal for help, but its tone made an impression on the not essentially sentimental chancellories of Europe.

Three days after his message was on its way, the President indited another paper of state:

"To the Red Bear and Chiefs in Council:

"My brothers:—The path between us . . . has become white . . . and . . . the sun gives light to our footsteps. . . . I send councillors with my talk. . . . Hear it, and remember . . . I have never opened my lips to tell a red brother a lie. . . . Let the war-whoop be no more heard in our prairie—let songs of joy be heard upon our hills. In our valleys let there be laughter and in our wigwams let the voices of our women and children be heard . . . and when our warriors meet together, let them smoke the pipe of peace and be happy. Your brother, SAM HOUSTON."[15]

The Red Bear believed his brother. There was peace. "The great rains, like our sorrows, I hope have passed away. . . . The tomahawk shall no more be raised in war. Nor shall the dog howl for his master who has been slain in battle."[16]

The twelve hundred Texans marched to the Rio Grande, quarreled with their officers and marched home again, with the exception of three hundred men under ex-Secretary of War William S. Fisher, now captain of infantry. Placing a conveniently literal construction upon the expressed wishes of his Commander-in-Chief, this soldier of fortune crossed the Rio Grande in pursuit of the private plans of conquest. General Houston was much dismayed. To the war party at home he deplored the miscarriage of invasion. To England and France he disavowed the conduct of Captain Fisher.

Domestic troubles multiplied. Houston had seized the first opportunity to discredit Austin as a suitable place for the capital. During the spring and summer of 1842, he maintained the seat of government at Houston, but made no attempt to remove the archives, although the safety of the diplomatic file in particular was cause for concern. In the fall the capital was transferred to Washington-on-the-Brazos as a compromise, and Buck Pettis went to Austin for the archives. The citizens sheared the mane and tail of Captain Pettis's horse and sent the rider back without the papers.

The President dispatched Captain Thomas Smith to remove the records secretly. At midnight on December thirtieth Mrs.

Angelina Ebberly, a boarding-house mistress whose table had been depleted by the turn of affairs, saw a wagon being loaded in an alley back of the land office. She repaired to Congress Avenue where a six-pound gun had been kept loaded with grape since the days of the Lamar Indian wars. Turning the muzzle toward the land office, she blazed away. The shot perforated the land office and aroused the town. Captain Smith departed with what records he had, but these were captured at daylight and brought back. All records were then sealed in tin boxes and stored at Mrs. Ebberly's under day-and-night guard. An attempt to take them by force would have precipitated a civil war. Citizens of Austin offered to swap the archives for the President. When the proposal was declined they buried the tin boxes.

Houston's policy infused new life in Washington-on-the-Brazos. The President's proposal to commandeer Hatfield's saloon for the meeting-place of the House of Representatives encountered objections, however, in which a majority of the House appeared to concur. The sacrifice, they said, was disproportionate to the emergency. General Houston compromised by persuading a gambling establishment which occupied rooms above the saloon to surrender its quarters. One entered the legislative chamber by means of a stairway from the barroom. The Speaker experienced such difficulty in maintaining a quorum, however, that General Houston removed the steps to the outside of the building. The planks over the opening in the floor were not nailed down, and during a ball one of them slipped from the joists and a stout lady would have fallen through into the bar except for the presence of mind of Congressman Holland with whom she was dancing.

The Senate, smaller in numbers but not in dignity, met in a loft over a grocery whose principle staple was spirits. The rental of this chamber was three dollars a week. This and other drains upon the Treasury caused embarrassing delays in the remittance of public salaries, mitigated, however, by a senatorial prerogative permitting members to carry their blankets to the hall and sleep on the floor. The Department of War and Marine occupied a log cabin with one window. The sword, however, had had its day in Texas. An era of enlightened diplomacy had dawned. To this end Secretary of State Anson Jones was installed in a well-ventilated clapboard edifice in which the circulation of air was regulated by a system of rags in the chinks in the walls.

One must understand, of course, that these arrangements were impermanent. Sam Houston joked about his bivouac capital and solicited travelers not to leave Texas without viewing the handsome Government House—now temporarily a hotel—in Houston City.

The Department of War and Marine confessing an inability to lay hands on a conveyance of sufficient caliber, Wagon Master Rohrer moved the celebrated piano from Houston City by borrowed transport. This feat of engineering provided Texan diplomacy with an asset. The instrument was installed in the most pretentious edifice available for residential uses, and made the focal point of a scheme of appointment surpassed in splendor only by the grandee manors of Béxar. There were rugs on the floors, silver candelabra, and soft chairs tastefully covered with figured calico, concerning the choice of which the General had charged his purchasing agent "to select none such as will exhibit Turkey Gobblers, Peacocks, Bears, Elaphants, wild Boars or Stud Horses!!! Vines, Flowers or any figure of taste you may select. . . . Present Mrs. Houston & myself to Colo. Madam Christy."[17]

Captain Elliot, the British Chargé d'Affaires, and his wife were charmed by the hospitality of Margaret who dispensed from a silver service the best tea the New Orleans market supplied. The agreeable English couple found a pleasant social companion in the Captain's diplomatic adversary, Judge Joseph M. Eve, the United States Minister. Later the corps was increased by the arrival of the French representative and suite, the Vicomte de Cramayel, whom Ashbel Smith had sent to Texas in an optimistic frame of mind. The President and his lady did Texas no disservice when they were able to divert this circle from the discomforts to the picturesqueness of life on a frontier. On rainy days the Houston barouche, with Tom Blue on the box, was worth its weight in exchequers—which after sinking to twenty-five, were now worth fifty cents.

The President was missed by the congenial company at Hatfield's, where he rarely tarried longer than for a glass of bitters, flavored with orange peel. "I don't drink hard, but what I do take, I wish to be palatable," he wrote, telling a friend to save his orange peels.[18] Nor was this any new thing. A year before a correspondent had recorded that "On last Friday the Old Chief met a large collection of Ladies and Gentlemen, made them a Big Speech amid the shouts & welcome plaudits of the whole assembly. . . . We partook of 13 barbecued hogs & 2 thundering big beeves were roasted, with lots of honey, taters, chickens & goodies in general.—But strange to say it was a cold water doins. The old Chief did not touch, taste or handle the smallest drop of the ardent."[19]

There was some muttering about Old Sam putting on airs, but a rite that Washington accepted as a part of its day largely redeemed the airs. Each morning before breakfast the General appeared on his back porch with a basin of water and proceeded to shave, like all old soldiers, without a mirror. (One hopes the news got back to Elias Rector.) An interview with the President was a simpler matter at this time of day than during office hours; therefore every morning a delegation would gather about the back porch, to the annoyance of the colored cook. The current pride of the General's toilet was a pair of burnsides whose chestnut radiance compensated for the declining splendors of the once glorious head of hair, now visibly gray and scant on top. Still, in the shadow of his fifty-first year, General Houston presented as stirring a picture of manhood as one would be likely to encounter in capitals more populous than Washington-on-the-Brazos.

But the pride that was in his heart went deeper than that, deeper than the anticipation of any triumph he foresaw in the diplomatic picture-puzzle by which he was presently to agitate a large part of the world.  A consignment of linens and flannels had arrived at the Executive Mansion.  Margaret had begun to sew in her room and to exchange mysterious confidences with Eliza, the young negress who had followed her mistress from Alabama.  This secrecy availed little.  All Texas knew, Versailles knew, Whitehall knew and Washington knew that Sam Houston was to have a son.  That it could be other than a son the President did not pause to consider.  The name—William Christy Houston, after the General's old friend in New Orleans—had been tentatively decided.

General Houston was recalled from these contemplations by one who had lost a son.  Old Flaco, a noted Lipan Indian warrior, sent the message accompanied by a mustang stallion as a present to his friend.  His son, Young Flaco, a scout in the Texas Army, had been killed on the unfortunate Rio Grande expedition.  "So I wish my name altered & call me Seinor Yawney I dislike to hear the name of Flaco."[20]  The General sent eleven shawls to the bereaved mother and an expression of condolence to Señor Yawney:

"My heart is sad!  A dark cloud rests upon your nation. Grief has sounded in your camp.  The voice of Flaco is silent. . . . His life has fled to the Great Spirit. . . . Your warriors weep. . . . The song of birds is silent. . . . Grass shall not grow in the path between us. . . . Thy brother SAM HOUSTON."[21]

5

Captain Fisher, who had fought in northern Mexico as a regimental commander in the Mexican service, knew the country and many of the officers of the forces opposed to him.  With his three hundred he struck resolutely and took the town of Mier by storm.  The Mexicans counter-attacked with twenty-seven hundred men, and after sustaining a battle, which included a cavalry charge, for eighteen hours, Fisher negotiated a surrender to an old companion-in-arms.  The terms of the capitulation were immediately violated, and bound two and two, Fisher and his men started on the long march to Mexico City. The main body of men rose on their guards and escaped, but were recaptured. Santa Anna ordered them shot, but on the intercession of his officers the sentence was commuted to a "diezmo"—one in ten. The prisoners drew beans from a jar and the drawers of black beans were forthwith executed. Having taken no part in the attempted escape, Captain Fisher was not required to participate in the death lottery.

The Mier news was a blow to the diplomatic structure Houston was contriving. To calm Texas some gestures were necessary. Houston marched troops from A to B and published an announcement that Her British Majesty had been asked to intercede for the release of Fisher's men.

It was perfectly true. The request was embodied in a long and apparently guileless communication to Captain Elliot. After presenting the case of the prisoners, the President allowed himself to drift into another topic. "There is a subject now mooting in Texas which, it seems to me, will appeal directly to Her Majesty's Government: I mean the subject of 'annexation to the United States.' . . . I find from the incertitude of our position, that nine-tenths of those who converse with me, are in favor of the measure upon the ground that *it will give us peace.* . . .

"At this time the measure has an advocacy in the United States which has at no former period existed." The Captain knew what his correspondent meant by that. President Tyler had become its advocate. "From the most authentic sources, I have received an appeal" soliciting "my cooperation" to bring about "annexation." Interesting. The source of this appeal was something Captain Elliot must discover. The discovery was not reassuring. The appeal had come from John Tyler. But the Captain did not suspect that this had been managed by Houston himself—the President by the Brazos manipulating the President by the Potomac. Captain Elliot read on:

"The probabilities of the measure succeeding in the United

States are greater than they have been at any former period. . . . The *South* is in favor of it for various reasons. The *West* and *North* because of a monopoly of the trade of Santa Fe and the Californias . . . [and] the bay of San Francisco." A menacing hint of the Stars and Stripes on the Pacific! The whispered words of old Jackson were serving his pupil well.

But how simple for England "to defeat this policy" and insure the "national existence" of the Texas Republic. "It is only necessary for Lord Aberdeen to say to Santa Anna: 'Sir, Mexico must recognize the independence of Texas.' Santa Anna would be glad of such a pretext. He could then say to the Mexicans: '*You* see how I am situated; and I cannot go to war with England.' . . . This state of things would . . . leave him free to establish his power and dynasty."[22]

Before it was seen whether this seed would sprout tares or flowers, another strain threatened the thin strands by which Texan diplomatic hopes were moored. The Navy of the Republic, consisting of three vessels, was at New Orleans where its commanding officer, Post Captain Moore, treated the President's communications with an imposing indifference. Money had been sent to release the vessels from the hands of creditors, but they were not released, and Captain Moore troubled himself with no explanations. Earmarks of an understanding between the Post Captain and the creditors were rather distinct. Houston made a secret arrangement to sell the Navy, and dispatched two commissioners to convey this surprise to Captain Moore.

But the Commander of the Texas sea forces was not the man to be thus despoiled. Post Captain Moore was no Paul Jones, but he had sailed more than one *Bonhomme Richard* under the Texas flag, and had maintained it independently of a national treasury, frequently innocent of the price of a coil of rope. If, as alleged, some of the Captain's financial methods savored of the offense of piracy, it would be well to remember that seamen must live. Captain Moore had had his tiffs with officialdom before. On one occasion a discussion over authority took place on his own deck.   The dangling of a few malcontents from the yards composed this difference of opinion.

The commissioners did not discharge their mission.   Captain Moore showed them brighter prospects.   Certain gentlemen of New Orleans—among them the President's friend, William Christy—were financing a freebooting cruise for the Navy. The estimated profit would be eight hundred thousand dollars of which Captain Moore offered to turn over four hundred thousand dollars to the Texas Treasury.   Sam Houston's answer was an order for the fleet to proceed to Galveston. Accompanying the order was a document rumbling with whereases that proclaimed Captain Moore a pirate and called upon all nations in amity with Texas to secure his person. Houston said the proclamation would be invoked unless Moore brought the vessels to Galveston.

Moore started on the raiding expedition, and Houston published the proclamation.   Moore's backers shook the earth with righteous rage, and the stout mariner was himself somewhat distrait.   But nothing could move Houston.   Moore turned up at Galveston and challenged Houston to a duel.   The President ignored it.   The mighty Post Captain was broken and executive authority spared a critical loss of prestige.

## 6

Lord Aberdeen, the successor of Palmerston in the Foreign Office, consented to intercede for the Texan prisoners, and scarcely had he done so when a curious thing happened.   James W. Robinson, former lieutenant-governor and a leader of the conspiracy that overthrew Houston as leader of the Armies in January, 1836, was one of the captives General Woll had carried off from San Antonio.   Robinson suddenly turned up in Texas with an offer from Santa Anna to end hostilities on condition that Texas acknowledge the sovereignty of Mexico, retaining autonomous powers.   Robinson would have been harshly dealt with but for Houston, who construed Santa

Anna's proposal as confirming the assurance to Elliot that what the Mexican ruler wished was a face-saving excuse to conclude peace.

Houston dispatched a reply in Robinson's name. The writer deplored the ill-success of his mission. The situation had been misjudged. The only discoverable notice Houston had taken of Santa Anna's letter was an idle inquiry concerning the accuracy of the translation. With that the President had gone quietly about his business of forming a huge army for the invasion of Mexico. Still, the writer believed "that Houston would prefer peace" on honorable terms. To this end Robinson suggested that Santa Anna release all Texan prisoners and declare an armistice.

Santa Anna was encircled by pressure for peace. The United States acted through jealousy of England. England raised her commanding voice lest the United States gain an advantage. France sided with England.

The ostensible victory was England's. Her Majesty's sloop, *Scylla*, raced into Galveston harbor with word that the British Chargé at Mexico City had induced General Santa Anna to request an armistice pending a meeting of peace commissioners. A truce was agreed to, and Lieutenant Galan, of the Mexican Army, arrived in Washington with proposals for a peace conference at Laredo. Houston appointed George Hockley and another as delegates.

There was rejoicing on the Brazos. In London and at Versailles men who moved the destinies of Christendom complacently traced lines on unfamiliar maps. Sam Houston's name was on the lips of kings. "I was at the Palace of St. Cloud a few days since where the Royal Family are spending the autumn," wrote Ashbel Smith. "Louis Philippe . . . is a careful observer of events in Texas. I also had a somewhat long conversation . . . with Leopold, King of the Belgians, now on a visit to France."[23] A biographical dictionary of world figures was to be published in Paris. "Allow me accordingly to suggest my dear General that Mr. Miller . . .

draw up a sketch of your life and forward the same to me. . . . Such a history would be read here with great avidity, and illustrate one of their maxims that 'truth is stranger than fiction.' . . . The triumph of your peace policy amid such and so great annoyances . . . at home is scarcely less signal . . . than is your victories over foreign armies in the field. . . . With many most respectful compliments to Mrs. Houston—I trust I may at this time congratulate."[24]

The congratulations were in order. Sam Houston, Jr., was ten weeks old, and William Christy, in addition to a presidential rebuke for his rôle in the Navy episode, was without a namesake in Texas.

The grain harvest of 1843 was the most bountiful in the Republic's history. Trade expanded and exchequers mounted to par—passed par and sold at a gold premium over United States currency. His enemies confounded, his friends never more ardent, Sam Houston trod the borders of the Brazos with a buoyant step, "looking better than I ever saw him in my life. He has a garment of fine Broadcloth, in the style of a Mexican blanket, lined with yellow Satin, with gold lace all around it."[25] Not since the heyday of Jackson had a public man commanded such devotion of his followers. He was their "Old Chief."

The Potomac looked upon a different scene. The spirits of Mr. Tyler were low. And in a strangely still house on the Lebanon Pike out of Nashville, shuffled the Old Chief of another decade, weak and ill and the prey of vague alarms.

# CHAPTER XXV

## The Lone Star Passes

### 1

General Mirabeau Lamar continued his labors to light the steps of a future historian of the Republic, which he yet hoped to reclaim from Sam Houston. There is a hearsay account to the effect that no suitable chronicler appearing, the ex-President himself eventually refined this material into a narrative and carried the manuscript to New York for publication. There, so the story goes, the manuscript was lost under circumstances more entertaining, though not less dismaying, than in the classical case of Carlyle.

In any event only the Notes have come down to us. The compiler called the era of negotiation which his adversary's second Administration conveyed into being a "climax of audacity . . . [which] shames the talents of Taleyrand." General Lamar's choice of a verb implies dissatisfaction, but no flagrant impropriety can be discerned in a comparison of Sam Houston's diplomacy with that of the luminous French exemplar of the art.

In this affair Sam Houston's principal instrument was his Secretary of State, Anson Jones, who had begun life as a country surgeon in western Massachusetts. The President instructed him carefully. The foreign policy of the Republic must "be as sharp-sighted as lynxes and as wary as foxes."[1] Doctor Jones could understand this language. While no Talleyrand, the Secretary's talents for a lynx-fox game were

338

not contemptible. He had proved this as minister to the United States when he brought the harassed Republic to the sympathetic notice of Lord Palmerston. He had proved it during the Lamar régime, when he ran with the hare and hunted with the hounds so successfully as to recommend himself to the choice of Houston for the important portfolio he now held.

And he was proving it at the present time. "December 31st—The close of the year 1843, the conclusion of Gen. H.'s second year of his second term of office and of the second year of my term of Secretary of State. Affairs in the main have been managed agreeably to my wishes and advice, and the country has recovered from its extreme depression." But "Gen. H. and myself are drifting away from each other hourly. . . . I may have to play the part of 'Curtius,' and if so, am prepared to make a sacrifice like his." He was "content," however, "to let Gen. H. be 'Cæsar,' for it is only by yielding to his vanity that we can get on together."[2]

These reflections were for the Secretary's diary and nothing appeared on the surface to mar the harmonious official relations between the Cabinet officer and his Chief. The Secretary felt himself drawn away from his Chief by a force that not uncommonly complicates the lives of public men, namely, the pursuit of ambition. Doctor Jones desired that Texas remain an independent nation, greatly extend its boundaries, and become the dominant power of the Western World. He saw for himself a place in history as the architect of this greater Republic. The thought was not new, and since Doctor Jones was not a constructive genius, one wonders from whom he imbibed the essentials of the grand program. It is impossible to evade the presumption that he imbibed them, leastwise in part, from Houston.

Aside from Anson Jones the man at this time most intimately associated with Sam Houston's lynx-fox game was Elliot, the British Chargé d'Affaires. Captain Charles Elliot, Royal Navy, was an honorable servant of his Queen—a self-contained, courteous gentleman whose blue eyes reflected the solitudes of remote lands and remote peoples. He wore a big, flopping white hat and smoked a pipe continuously. Moreover, the Captain was familiar with the forces of the Oriental mind, in many respects similar to those of the Cherokee Indian. He had come to Texas from the Opium Wars in China where he had served his Queen too conscientiously to suit the London merchants who obtained his transfer. China to Texas: all in the day's work for Captain Elliot, one of that indispensable brigade of homeless Englishmen, trooping hither and yon over the face of the world, in the end to leave some bundles of yellowing dispatches in Chancery Lane, a foot-note in history, a forgotten grave in an alien clime—and an Empire.

The Captain's arrival in the Republic had been unpromising. "A Blanket on a Plank" was the best bed he could find on Galveston Island, until his American colleague, Judge Eve, offered half of his own cot. On the way to Houston City his steamer stuck on a sand-bar, and the emissary stepped through a hatch in the dark, dislocating a rib. Although practised to "hard rubs of all kinds," the Captain in one of his early interviews with Houston confessed an inability to "digest the modification of saw-dust, which they call 'Corn bread.'" The President admitted that life at Washington-on-the-Brazos was "rather raw." "And He," observed Captain Elliot, in his punctual dispatch, "has been accustomed to the elaborate comforts of an Indian wigwam." But General Houston held out hope for better things. Margaret arrived, the piano was brought up and the Captain himself was joined by his wife.

At a moment when Captain Elliot's opinion of Texas was least favorable, he gave his government this picture of the Chief Executive. "The President is General Houston of your acquaintance." The note was addressed to H. U. Addington, Under Secretary for Foreign Affairs, who, as a young attaché at the Washington legation, had explored night life with Congressman Houston, of Tennessee. "His career during too large an interval between that time and this, has been strange and wild. . . . A domestic tempest of desperate violence, and calamitous consequences; habitual drunkenness; a residence of several years amongst the Cherokee Indians; residing amongst them as a Chieftain, and begetting sons and daughters; a sudden reappearance on this stage with better hopes and purposes, and commensurate success,—but still with unreclaimed habits. Finally, however, a new connexion with a young and gentle woman brought up in fear of God, conquered no doubt as women have been from the beginning and will be to the end by a glowing tongue, but in good revenge making conquest of his habits of tremendous cursing, and passionate love of drink."

Nevertheless, "whatever General Houston has been, it is plain that He is the fittest man in this Country for his present station.—His education has been imperfect, but He possesses great sagacity and penetration, surprising tact in the management of men trained as men are in these parts, is perfectly pure handed and moved in the main by the inspiring motive of desiring to connect his name with a nation's rise."[3] And a month later: "General Houston has two sides to his understanding, one very clear indeed, and the other impenetrably dark.—Let him speak of men, or public affairs, or the tone and temper of other Governments, and no one can see farther, or more clearly.—The moment he turns to financial arrangements you find that He has been groping on the dark side of his mind."[4] Since Sam Houston's brilliant administration of his country's finances suggests that in these matters he saw clearly enough, one suspects the existence of a dark side to the mind of the confident and experienced Captain. The British diplomat had underestimated his man.

## 2

England had long had an eye on Texas. In 1830 one of her statesmen declared that American domination of the Gulf coast must end at the Sabine. When the Republic was proclaimed, England's first query was: Will it be permanent? A month after San Jacinto, the British Minister at Mexico

City wrote his government that Mexico would never reconquer Texas, and for three years continued to insist that England secure the friendship of the young Republic.

Still, Pinckney Henderson had cooled his heels in London without obtaining recognition, although France acknowledged Texas in 1839, and Belgium and Holland in 1840. For the time being England resisted even the pressure of her own commercial interests for a trade treaty. England had not abated her resolution to keep Texas out of American hands, but the United States had simplified this by rebuffing Texan overtures for annexation until Houston, to avoid humiliation, withdrew the offer.

England had every reason to oppose the expansion of the United States, with its consistent anti-British policy. Slavery was an international question. England had emancipated the blacks of her West Indies, momentarily placing those colonies at a disadvantage in trade with the Southern States. Self-interest reinforced the moral motives prompting the Empire to crusade for the liberation of American negroes. Should Texas, as the gateway to further conquests of territory, become American it was believed by many, notably the slave extensionists of the South, that the "peculiar institution" of negro bondage would be guaranteed a future safe from embarrassment by the hostility of the North, of England, or of any one. Forward thinkers in the South already foresaw a union of the Slave States with Texas under separate government.

If England could perpetuate the independence of Texas, and at the same time induce it to free its slaves, she would achieve at one stroke the crowning triumph of isolating and eventually destroying slavery in the United States, and of sponsoring a rival North American nation that might outshine its older sister. Emancipation of slaves was the price England desired Texas to pay for recognition. As Texas began its astonishing recovery from the disasters of Lamar this became the "darling wish of England," as Ashbel Smith reported from London. England had been informed by observers on the spot that if any conquering were done, it would be the conquest of Mexico by Texas. With this in view England changed her mind about recognition, and in June of 1842 received the Republic into the family of nations, shuttling Captain Elliot with uncomfortable haste on the long arc from China.

Sam Houston at the moment was pounding the tocsin to rouse up American adventurers for an invasion of Mexico. He had proclaimed war to the hilt and the members of Congress were gathering in Houston City for their memorable special session. While the famous bill conferring dictatorial powers upon Houston was being written, word of English recognition came, almost unobserved in the general commotion. It was then Houston staggered his country by dropping the war.

France played England's tune on a scratchy second fiddle. To promote the welfare of royalty, Louis Phillipe wished to substitute for American expansion a new nation under obligation to heads that wore crowns. The affable and ornamental Cramayel was replaced at Washington-on-the-Brazos by the Comte de Saligny, of the pig incident at Austin. But Saligny, who had been told that he resembled Napoleon, seldom intruded nearer to the scenes of action than his wine cellar in New Orleans.

The designs of Europe had the effect of rekindling sentiment for annexation in the United States. The great personage of this sentiment was Jackson, who had lain low for several years, awaiting a propitious time to renew the campaign. He, too, had envisaged the acquisition of the Pacific Coast and northern Mexico by Texas, believing this dowry would remove the objections of the industrial North. But the concept had changed. This conquest now seemed possible under trans-Atlantic auspices. Although he had a personal pride in the matter, Andrew Jackson viewed the annexation of Texas from the high ground of national interest. Obviously, Mexico was not to hold this vast region much longer. Should it fall to a power obligated to Europe by any ties, the consequences to the United States would be very serious.

The partizans of annexation who made the biggest splash, however, were the slave expansionists. In 1833 Jackson had stamped down the disunion activities of their leader, Calhoun, but without exterminating the seed. The imprudence of this group had done much to defeat annexation in 1837 and to assist the rise of the American Anti-Slavery Society. The abolitionists also behaved arrogantly and beat up a racket out of proportion to their importance. They served notice that on no terms could Texas enter the Union. But given a chance, there existed in the North the germs of an influential sentiment for annexation arising from the national policy of Jackson and from prospect of commercial advantage.

To this pivotal point in the destiny of a hemisphere had Sam Houston guided the fortunes of his nation which two years before was without credit for fire-wood to warm the quarters of its Chief Executive.

What was Houston's aim? He was accused of everything under the sun, being in the pay of Santa Anna included. Diplomacy of the Talleyrand school is not a frank subject, and while spots of the record are susceptible of clarification, this much withstands scrutiny. Jackson wanted Texas, and Houston went there to get it for him. Left in the lurch in 1837, Houston varied his tactics and prepared the Republic to stand alone. This had some effect on American sentiment but the change came so slowly that Houston and others doubted that it would ever be of any use. He made a skilful play for it, however. During the negotiations resulting in the truce with Mexico, he magnified the British assistance to Texas. This spurred to fresh activity old Jackson, who was not long for this world, but was determined to see Texas free of the paws of the British lion before he died. It was the lynx-fox game, but Elliot did not perceive it, nor did Jackson or John Tyler. Had either party smelled a rat the result might have been different. Certainly, Houston, who must secure the future of Texas one way or another, could afford no chances on the side of candor.

## 3

Twice during the autumn of 1843 Mr. Tyler had intimated that the United States would be happy to reopen the question of annexation. It was now Houston's turn to be indifferent, and he was bruskly so. "Were Texas to agree to annexation the good offices of the [European] powers would, it is believed, be immediately withdrawn, and were the treaty to fail of ratification by the Senate of the United States, Texas would be placed in a worse position than she is at present . . . without a friend and her difficulties with Mexico unsettled." Better to trust in the proved good offices of England and France than the doubtful promises of the United States, which "might again return the apathy and indifference towards us which has always until now characterized that government." But Tyler did not retreat. His Secretary of State, Judge Upshur, replied with Jacksonian bluntness. After insisting that annexation would not fail in the Senate, he threw the sword upon the council table. The United States would not forbear to see a rival power built up ón her flank. Should it be attempted "war will follow."

Old Jackson himself wrote to Houston. "You know, my dear General, that I have been, & still am your friend." "I have put down every where I heard them" the "slanders" of British intrigue "circulated against you." "You never could have become the dupe to England, and all the gold of Santana . . . could not séduce you from a just sense of duty & of patriotism. . . . My strength is exhausted and I must close. Please write to . . . your friend sincerely ANDREW JACKSON."[5] But the slander did not stay down. Jackson's faithful shadow of other days, Major Lewis, was at Tyler's side in Washington. His reports to the Hermitage were so alarming that Jackson wrote again.

The long letter, scrawled amid such apparent bodily and mental anguish causes one to hesitate to turn a page for fear the pen had been shaken from the enfeebled fingers before the

task was done. "My dear Genl I tell you in sincerity & friendship, if you will achieve this annexation your name & fame will
be enrolled amongst the greatest chieftains of the age. . . .
Now is the time to act & that with promptness & secrecy &
have the treaty of annexation laid before the United States
Senate where I am assured it will be ratified. Let the threats of
Great Britain and Mexico then be hurled at us,—if war the[y]
wish our fleet and army will freely fight them. . . . I am
scarcely able to write. . . . The Theme only inspires me
with the strength. . . . Let me hear from you if only three
lines."[6]

So the Old Chief, defiant and dying, yet entreating the one-
time subaltern he had threatened with arrest for too great
precipitation in the matter of bringing Texas under the flag.
The well-informed Elliot trembled over the effect of this intervention. His fear passed off, however, and he prompted his
government that Jackson had availed nothing with Houston.

The difficulties that confronted Houston in composing a
reply to the Hermitage were of no simple order. "So far as I
am concerned, or my hearty co-operation required, I am determined upon immediate annexation to the U States." The
words did not stand alone, however. The General wrote a
hundred times three lines. "Our situation has been peculiar"; "internal difficulties," "external dangers"—a great
responsibility rested upon Houston. He was duty bound to
keep himself free "to take any action . . . the future welfare" of his country might require. Moreover, the situations
of Texas and of the United States were not identical.
"Texas . . . could exist without the U States, but the U
States can not, without great hazard . . . exist without
Texas." "Now, my venerated friend, you will perceive that
Texas is presented to the United States, as a bride adorned
for her espousal. But if, so confident of the union, she should
be rejected, her mortification would be indescribable. She has
been sought by the United States, and this is the third time she
has consented. Were she now to be spurned, it would forever

terminate" the possibility of annexation. "Mrs. H. and my-self . . . unite in our prayers for your happiness. . . . It is our ardent desire to see the day when you can lay your hand on our little boy's head, and bestow upon him your benediction."[7]

This was carried to Tennessee by Miller, trusted private secretary of Houston, with instructions to add verbal assurances to lighten the blow. The anxieties of the old fighter were little abated, however. Continuing his persuasions upon Houston, he dispatched—as better became his style—orders to Washington, where a treaty was being drafted in secret by the Texan representatives and the State Dapartment.

But Houston, who had examined the situation with some care, had no confidence that this treaty could muster the two-thirds majority required for its acceptance by the United States Senate. He parried the curt note of Upshur with audacious counter-proposals and continued his mystifying course. On April 12, 1844, the treaty was signed, and ten days later Mr. Tyler laid it before the Senate. Had he turned loose a wildcat amid that decorous company the result would have been much the same.

Before Texas was aware of the Senate's reception, however, a copy of the treaty was received at Washington-on-the-Brazos. Elderly and urbane General Murphy, who had succeeded Judge Eve as American chargé, laid it before President Houston with as much dignity as he could summon to adorn a private audience. Murphy then exposed Tyler's trump card in the form of a communication guaranteeing Texas the protection of the United States during the pendency of the treaty. The result, General Murphy reported to his government, was gratifying. Houston scanned the treaty, and expressed "his hearty approbation of every part" of it. Then, reading the guarantee, the President "rose to his feet and gave utterance to his feelings of gratitude . . . for this distinguished manifestation of the generous and noble policy, which ruled the Councils" of the United States.

Ill health had sent Captain Elliot to Hot Springs, Virginia, followed by comforting personal and official assurances from "Thine truly, Sam Houston." But to Anson Jones fell the courtesy of informing the British diplomat of the signing of the treaty. It was, he said, "a source of great mortification to General Houston" and himself.

4

It became apparent that the friends of the treaty could not command all of the votes that General Jackson had ineffectually tried to convince Houston would be cast for ratification. The old grenadier took a new tack. Working to shunt the issue into the presidential campaign, he manipulated affairs with a deftness that would have brightened the shield of a politician in the prime of his powers. The original plan had been to keep Texas out of the campaign, and to conduct an orderly contest between Whigs and Democrats on the time-honored issues. The Whigs nominated Mr. Clay with this in view, and although they formed the anti-Texas party, the platform scrupulously avoided the dreadful question. But Jackson still ruled his Democracy. Thrusting the astonished Van Buren aside he nominated his personal spokesman and lieutenant, James K. Polk, on a bald platform of "Oregon and Texas."

Sam Houston had moved from Washington-on-the-Brazos to Houston City in order that he might more promptly receive tidings from the theater of war. Texas was prospering. Its white population had grown from thirty to more than one hundred thousand. Travelers came from afar to view the much talked-of country. The popular Captain Marryatt[8] wrote a book about the adventures of the Comte de Norbonne, an engaging young scamp from France who borrowed his way through the Republic, victimizing, in a small way, the President himself.

Another visitor, Mrs. Matilda C. Houstoun, a Scotch

woman of some literary pretensions, was touring the world on her yacht. Her especial desire was to see the President. She found him "wan and worn-looking" from his long watches at the helm of the Republic. But the tired countenance wore a "shrewd and kindly expression," and also, Mrs. Houstoun thought, some traces of the life that she had heard he had lived, a detail in which the traveler displayed a lively historical interest. They had a pleasant visit together. Mrs. Houstoun had married into the baronial family in Lanarkshire from which the President also was descended. She was struck by his singular attire and by "his courtesy to all classes." Although "a Tory at heart . . . General Houston's greeting to the free citizens—carters, or blacksmiths, as the case may be—is always kind and polite. It is 'How-d'ye-do, Colonel? How's Madam? Bad weather for the ladies!' . . . Never have I seen a man, especially one who had done not only the State, but the cause of humanity, such good service in his day, who was so unobtrusive in manner, and who seemed to think so little of himself."[9]

There was much to engross the thoughts of General Houston to the exclusion of his personal self. In the Senate the treaty was slipping and Jackson had not as yet succeeded in precipitating the issue into the campaign. In this situation the President wrote a lengthy letter, marked "Private," to Minister Murphy. It began with some mention of Mrs. Houston and Master Sam, and of a trip they proposed to make to Alabama. Otherwise, all quiet in Houston City—"no news of interest here" to report.

The letter-writer seemed driven afield where, fortunately, circumstances came to his aid. Indeed, "the times are big with events of coming circumstances, to Texas, and the world." Much depended upon the settlement of the question of annexation. Failure would work no embarrassment to Texas, however, and the writer covered five glowing pages with an enumeration of the advantages that would flow to the Republic should the measure be rejected. "No time has ever been so propitious for the upbuilding of a nation . . . as that which Texas at this moment enjoys, in the event that the measure of annexation should fail. Its failure can only result, from the selfishness on the part of the Govt, or Congress of the U States." But should it fail "the Glory of the United States has already culminated. A rival power will be built up," the dimensions of which Sam Houston proceeded to sketch for the American diplomat.

"The Pacific as well as the Atlantic, will be component parts of Texas," *i. e.*, the South would secede. Westward, Texas would reach out and take the mountain region, the Californias, and effect a friendly division of Oregon with England on the line of the Columbia River. Swinging south, Chihuahua and Sonora would fall under the sway of the Lone Star.

This prophecy "you will see by reference to the map, is no bugbear," no "fanciful" dream. It was cold logic applied to the future of the Anglo-Saxon race upon this continent, guided by political factors all too apparent. "Nothing" would prevent English-speaking people from becoming the masters of this illimitable domain. It was "destiny." Thus a new nation, sweeping from the Potomac to California, from the cool summits of Oregon veritably to the Halls of the Montezumas: such, said Sam Houston, would be the Texas Republic "in thirty years from this date."

Would the United States reject Texas again, or accept her and her fabulous heritage? "If the Treaty is not ratified I will require, all future negotiations to be transferred to Texas. I have written *much* more than what I expected, and it seems to me, that I have run into a prosaic strain."[10]

The purpose of this prosaic letter? Was it calculated to bolster the crumbling ramparts of the treaty party in the Senate? Hardly consciously so, for this issue more than likely would be decided before Murphy could forward the letter to Washington. Was it calculated to further Jackson's strategy involving the presidential campaign? This is possible: "future negotiations"—Houston *did* hold out hope beyond a rejection

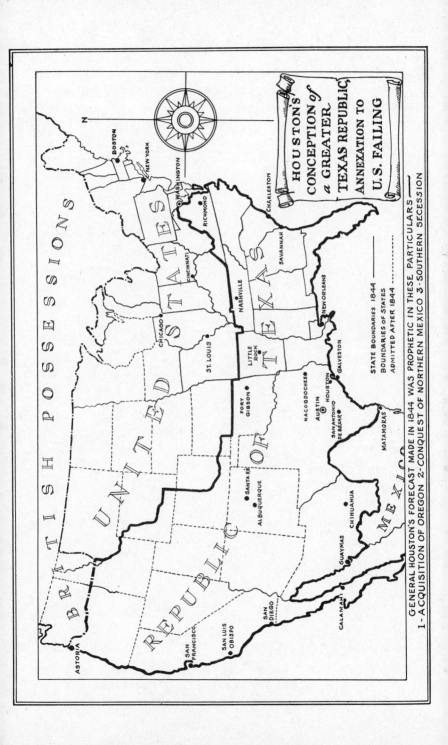

HOUSTON'S CONCEPTION of a GREATER TEXAS REPUBLIC, ANNEXATION TO U.S. FAILING

STATE BOUNDARIES 1844 ———
BOUNDARIES OF STATES ————
ADMITTED AFTER 1844 --------

GENERAL HOUSTON'S FORECAST MADE IN 1844 WAS PROPHETIC IN THESE PARTICULARS ——
1 - ACQUISITION OF OREGON 2 - CONQUEST OF NORTHERN MEXICO 3 - SOUTHERN SECESSION

of the Treaty, which hitherto he had declared should end every-thing between him and the United States. But the letter read two ways. There was nothing in it that could not be inter-preted to representatives of England and France as a tactful adieu to the United States. The old master of trente-et-quarante was still in a position to win—if not on the red, on the black.

Then came the nominations. How well Sam Houston knew James Knox Polk. When Houston became governor of Ten-nessee it was his friend Polk who moved up to fill the peculiar niche in the Jacksonian scheme thus vacated at Washington. Mrs. Polk was the most successful hostess in Nashville. Sam Houston had been a favorite at her board, and when the long shadow fell, her home and her friendship remained one of not many sanctuaries that civilized life afforded the exile.

Twelve days after Polk's nomination the Senate rejected the treaty. The same month Mexico ended the truce and re-newed the old threat of invasion. A revulsion of feeling against the United States swept Texas, stimulated by the Admin-istration press, which was under suspicion of British subsidy. Mr. Calhoun, now Secretary of State, sent Duff Green to do some countermining against the "pro-English" Houston, but General Green succeeded no better than he had succeeded in some previous undertakings against Sam Houston. Tyler sent Jackson's nephew, Andrew Jackson Donelson, to be chargé d'affaires. Donelson was the ablest of the United States envoys to Texas. He emerged from an interview with Houston, be-fuddled, disappointed, distrustful.

It was also campaign time in Texas. Under the Consti-tution Houston could never be president again. He quietly maneuvered the election of Anson Jones, and Captain Elliot professed his satisfaction.

The contest in the United States was spirited. "Polk—Slavery and Texas." "Clay—Union and Liberty." "James K. Polk and George M. Dallas—One for the devil and the other for the gallows." Polk won narrowly. His concealed influence having made two presidents within forty days, Sam Houston relinquished office with an air of resignation. Texas having been "spurned" again must now "work out her own political salvation." Flawless!

Yet the busy man could find time for lesser things. The past few months had been enlivened by an explosive exchange of compliments with Santa Anna. Before leaving Washington-on-the-Brazos, General Houston wrote to him again.

"The satisfaction with which on yesterday I laid down the cares and responsibilities of Government, was greatly heightened by the recollection that your Excellency had recently released from confinement all, save on[e], of the Texans who had been retained in prison. This act . . . did not disappoint me; and the only regret . . . arises from the knowledge that your Excellency has thought proper to withhold the same kindness from the unhappy Jose Antonio Navarro. . . . I approach your Excellency as a Private citizen . . . and ask as a personal favor . . . [the liberation of Navarro].

"I cannot close this note without tendering to your Excellency, my unaffected condolence in the bereavement which you have had the misfortune to sustain the loss of your late most excellent spouse."[11]

Navarro's escape relieved General Santa Anna of the obligation. Nevertheless, it was a curious ascendency that Sam Houston had over this attractive scoundrel. When he came to compose his grotesque autobiography, Santa Anna inserted a little tribute to Houston that blemishes the record of an otherwise almost irreproachable rascal.

## 5

Carrying his family to Huntsville, where the hills are reminiscent of Virginia, the General occupied himself with drawings for a plantation home on a large holding of land fourteen miles from town. He named the place "Raven Hill." . . . Raven Hill.

Margaret was as happy as a bride.

"To My Husband
*"December, 1844, on Retirement from the Presidency*

"Dearest, the cloud hath left thy brow,
  "The shade of thoughtfulness, of care
"And deep anxiety; and now
  "The sunshine of content is there."[12]

There were nine other verses. The home life for which she had prayed seemed assured to her and only one thing remained to make joy complete. Margaret had been wise and patient. A degree of success that others found incredible had prospered her forbearance. The time had come to shape the final goal. She asked her husband to join the Baptist Church.

## 6

Distractions of an earthly nature intervened. A stream of letters and visitors flooded Huntsville, and Andrew Jackson Donelson complained of the state of the road to General Houston's retreat.

The election of Polk had stirred the foreign offices of England and France. Ministers of the two nations hurriedly conferred. France balked at war, but England declared herself ready to go to any lengths to keep Texas out of American hands.

The United States was no longer indifferent to her peril. The Lone Star glowed ominously in the heavens—a concern more vital than slavery. National interests were prevailing over sectional interests. Northern opposition began to wane. Time was precious, and it was decided not to wait until the inauguration of Polk. A resolution for annexation was plumped before Congress, and Mr. Polk hastened to Washington to help Tyler force it through. Bedridden Jackson drummed out the last reserves of his strength. "The pressure of two Presidents and an ex-President is too much for us," an opposition Senator exclaimed. The resolution was adopted, and Tyler signed it on March 1, 1845, three days before leaving office.

On the twentieth of March a steamer arrived at Galveston with news of the action of the American Congress. Elliot and Saligny were there, but under the serious handicap of new instructions from their governments, for England who should now or never have taken a bold stand, had hedged. Nevertheless, the two set out for Washington-on-the-Brazos, in the hope of reaching there before Donelson should arrive, by another route, with the fateful tidings from the Potomac.

The European representatives outstripped Donelson and shut themselves up with Jones and Ashbel Smith who had been recalled from London to be Secretary of State. They went to the utmost limits allowed by their instructions, written four thousand miles from the scene of action. Feverish conferences lasted for several days and nights, with Elliot and Saligny beside themselves with anxiety lest Donelson arrive. Not without misgivings, Jones signed an agreement (1) authorizing England and France to negotiate at Mexico City for Mexican acknowledgment of the independence of Texas, (2) Texas consenting to annex itself to no country. Elliot was to fly to Mexico in disguise and bring this matter to pass, while Ashbel Smith sped back to Europe to take care of arrangements at that end. As a further safeguard Doctor Jones pledged himself not to call the pro-annexation Texas Congress for ninety days.

It looked like a good day's work for Queen Victoria, and for Louis of Orleans. As Captain Elliot and the Comte de Saligny rode out of town they met a horseman covered with dust. It was Donelson. Elliot and Saligny saluted. Donelson asked whether Congress had been convoked. Captain Elliot was sure he did not know; he supposed, however, that His Excellency the President awaited the advices of Major Donelson in the matter. Where, Donelson asked bluntly, was Sam Houston? Captain Elliot regretted that he could not say, "exactly." A vague menace about the earnestness of

Donelson prompted Saligny to send Jones a note to "be cheerful and firm . . . and, my word on it, everything will soon come out right."

There was a dash of the talented amateur in Dr. Anson Jones. Subtleties of the lynx-fox game that in more skilful hands shine as a commendable gift, by his manipulations wear the regrettable aspect of vice. Donelson got a rather formal reception at Washington-on-the-Brazos. The American proposal was taken under advisement and Jones declined to call Congress. The worried envoy hastened to Huntsville. Scant comfort from that source. Houston found fault with the American terms on the far-fetched ground that they were unjust in their disposition of public property and the matter of boundary arrangements.

But the competent Minister had not approached the Brazos Talleyrand with empty hands. He carried a letter from Jackson, who cordially chose to assume that opposition by Houston to the American terms was unthinkable. "I congratulate you, I congratulate Texas and the United States. . . . I now behold the great American eagle, with her stars and stripes hovering over the lone star of Texas . . . and proclaiming to Mexico and all foreign governments, 'You must not attempt to tread upon Texas!' . . . Glorious result! in which you, General, have acted a noble part."[13]

Nor was this all. Frank Blair had written in Jackson's old organ, the Washington *Globe*, that with the admission of Texas it would not be too much to expect a Chief Magistrate of the United States from beyond the Sabine. The Baltimore *American* mentioned Houston by name, with the remark that Jackson—and now lately!—had demonstrated that his ability to elect presidents remained unimpaired. The American Secretary of State, Jackson's friend Buchanan, gave an official cast to the seductive speculation. "Some of the high officers of Texas, supposing that their importance and their emoluments might be lessened by annexation, may prove hostile . . . but surely the hero of San Jacinto cannot fear that his brilliant star will become less bright by extending the sphere of its influence over all the twenty-nine States of our Federal Union."[14]

Ashbel Smith was on the ocean, fearful that the double game had been carried too far for comfort. But Smith was a man of stout fiber. Just before embarking he wrote to Houston. "My visit to Europe at this time will expose me to much censure, perhaps to obloquy; I am willing to risk it for the sake of my country. As to annexation the pinch of the matter will in my opinion be on the other side of the Sabine if any where, when the American Congress shall take a 'final action' on the same." For as the program stood the matter would go back to the American Congress, following any form of approval Texas should give to the resolution now before it. Yet, added Smith, regardless of personal hazard, Texas must play out its hand, for "nothing can bring" the United States "to a prompt decision, but the conviction that we can do without them." So fared Smith on his delicate errand, expecting annexation to be consummated and hoping, in that event, to be able to convince the "foreign Governments . . . that we have not been playing a deep game of hypocrisy."[15] But if, at the eleventh hour, annexation should slip Texas must have a port to steer for! "Sentiment," Sam Houston had written in his "prosaic" letter to Murphy, "tells well in love matters . . . but . . . the affairs of nations . . . have no soul, and recognize no *mentor* but interest."

Ere Ashbel Smith set foot on the soil of Albion the game was as good as up. Jones had surrendered, summoning Congress to consider the American resolution. Sam Houston was on his way to Tennessee.

The Master of the Hermitage was sinking. A godson of his, Edward George Washington Butler, who, one may faintly recall, once served Sam Houston in the important matter of buying a beaver hat in Washington, D. C., had gone to receive a final blessing. The hand of death was on the warrior's shoulder, but Texas filled his mind.

"Edward, what will Houston do?"

Edward referred the question to Huntsville. "Can it be possible that a native of Virginia and a citizen of Tennessee can so far have forgotten what is due to himself and his country as to lend himself for an instant to the representatives of England and France?"[16] What was that Sam Houston had said about sentiment? In any event, gathering up Margaret and Master Sam, he started for the Hermitage. Donelson dispatched in advance a letter to say that the fight was won. "Gen H. . . . has redeemed his pledge to restore Texas to the Union."[17]

This letter—it must have been this letter—was placed in the dying man's hand on June 6, 1845. On that day Jackson rallied from the brink of the grave, and spoke for hours of Texas and of Houston. "All is safe at last." His "old friend and companion-in-arms" had been true to his trust.[18]

On the following day the General sank again. Sunday, June eighth, dawned still and hot. The doctors said it would be a matter of hours. Major Lewis sat by his old Chief's side, and received from him three messages: one for Thomas Hart Benton, one for Frank Blair, one for Sam Houston. The family and the servants came in weeping. Propped against pillows, Jackson took his leave of each one. "I want to meet you all, white and black, in heaven." At six in the evening the head fell forward. The old soldier had laid down his arms.

At nine o'clock a coach driven at a gallop whirled through the gate. Mrs. John H. Eaton—Peggy—opened the door, and admitted General Houston and his family. For several minutes the towering, travel-stained figure stood perfectly motionless before the candle-lit couch of death. Then Sam Houston fell on his knees, and sobbing, buried his head upon the breast of his friend.

He drew little Sam to his side. "My son, try to remember that you have looked upon the face of Andrew Jackson."[19]

## 7

During General Houston's absence Captain Elliot stepped

ashore at Galveston from a French brig-of-war, with the Mexican agreement in his pocket. In a few hours he knew how the land lay, and raced toward Washington-on-the-Brazos, revolving desperate courses in his mind. They came to naught. England recoiled from the extremity of war.

Formal procedure incident to the absorption of Texas into the Union consumed nine months. Polk kept his eye on things in one theater and Houston in the other, too engrossed, alas, for much thought of theology. A state government was created. Sam Houston decided to take Thomas J. Rusk with him to the United States Senate. On the sixteenth day of February, 1846, the state officials-elect and citizens from far and near stood before the weather-stained tabernacle built in Austin by Lamar. At the close of an address that stirred tender emotions, Anson Jones, with his own hands, struck the tricolor of the Lone Star.

Sam Houston's arms reached to receive the folds lest they brush the ground. His Republic was the peculiar property of the ages.

# CHAPTER XXVI

## The Heritage

### 1

Though still young in years it had been the fate of Oliver
Dyer to see and hear enough of the great and near-great to
dispense with commonplace illusions.  Mr. Dyer was on the
shorthand staff of the United States Senate.  Yet his heart
leaped when he read in the papers that Sam Houston was to
be one of the new senators of Texas.  The name swept Oliver
back to his schoolboy days in Lockport, New York, when he
had joined a company to fight Santa Anna in 1836.  Like
many such companies it never reached Texas, but Oliver's admiration for the hero of San Jacinto remained intact, and
"not without apprehension" did he first lay eyes on the man
himself.

"I was not disappointed. . . . It was easy to believe in
his heroism.  He was fifty-five years old . . . a magnificent
barbarian, somewhat tempered by civilization.  He was of large
frame, of stately carriage and dignified demeanor and had a
lion-like countenance capable of expressing fiercest passions.
His dress was peculiar, but it was becoming to his style.  The
conspicuous features of it were a military cap, and a short military cloak of fine blue broadcloth, with a blood-red lining.
Afterward, I occasionally met him when he wore a vast and
picturesque sombrero and a Mexican blanket."[1]

More critical appraisers than Mr. Dyer felt the drama of
it when Sam Houston stood in the patrician Chamber and took

the oath, by that means resuming a place in American public life abandoned in heart-break and in mystery seventeen years before. The journey from the Brazos to the Potomac had been a sort of triumphal progress. At Nashville the Senator-Elect was entertained at the home of his old comrade, Dr. John Shelby. William Carroll was dead, and a blowout at the Nashville Inn assumed the quality of a hatchet-burying. Judge Jo C. Guild, of the reception committee, seemed a trifle nervous. Guild was the author of the famous Sumner County resolutions and probably had a hand in the suppression of the letter from the Wigwam Neosho. Houston led him aside and eased his mind. "Guild, you did a noble thing in vindicating the character of Eliza. I thank you and the citizens of Sumner County." At any rate so reads the Judge's memoirs.

## 2

General Houston had not emerged from his chromatic background empty-handed. He had brought with him Texas— a large parcel in itself, and larger still the heritage of territory that every one understood to be an eventual part of the Texas acquisition. A highly vocal minority in the United States was for immediate assertion of America's claim to this legacy. Mexico, also, was provocative. War seemed certain, and Senator Houston was made a member of the Committee on Military Affairs.

Houston was opposed to a Mexican war. White preparing for the ceremonial lowering of the Lone Star, he had counseled Polk on peace, believing that California and other territory could be obtained by the old Jacksonian plan of purchase. To this end Mr. Polk had instituted negotiations, but with slight success. Mexico severed diplomatic relations with the United States, notified the world at large that she was going to fight and prepared armies for the field. Polk's only answer in kind was to send Zachary Taylor, an officer of no great renown, to Corpus Christi, in Texas, with fifteen hundred poorly turned out Regulars. Houston again wrote to Polk, reiterating that there would be no war, but making a perfunctory "tender of my services if they can be useful to Texas or the U States."[2]

All winter Taylor sat on the sands of Corpus Christi acquiring a wide-spread reputation for military unfitness. His force was increased to thirty-nine hundred, but was managed so miserably that it degenerated into a carousing rabble. In January Taylor was ordered to the Rio Grande, two hundred miles away. He did not even know the road, and it was the eighth day of March, 1846, before he started. Three weeks later Houston took his place in the Senate.

A fortnight thereafter he made his first speech. Ignoring the Mexican question in which he was regarded as so important a factor, the Senator sought to turn the course of American foreign policy toward Oregon. The address was a long discursive improvisation, below the average of Houston's public utterances. The Senator was on unfamiliar ground. Nevertheless he took a strong stand and, shaking out the campaign banner of Fifty-Four Forty or Fight, supported the abrogation of the agreement with England for joint occupation of the disputed region. Some of the senators thought this would lead to war with Britain. What of it? countered Houston.

Much more was said on both sides, and the Mexican question moved into eclipse behind the Oregon dispute. England came down from her high horse and suggested that we renew our offer to compromise on the parallel of 49°. Polk stood firm.

Just when it seemed promising of lively possibilities, the Oregon issue was blotted out by the rattle of musketry on the Rio Grande. In two brisk little battles Taylor drove the Mexicans back to their own side of the river. The General's droll indifference to bullets won him a name with the troops. But the West-Pointers present could not understand how one could succeed by tactics that violated nearly every rule of the books.

Mr. Polk asked for fifty thousand volunteers, ten million dollars and, summoning Senator Houston to the White House, offered him a major-general's commission and the command of an army. Not without criticism, the President got his volunteers and his money, but he did not get Houston.

Although the embittered Lamar—among the first in Texas to fly to arms and to distinguish himself in battle—believed Houston to be "running" Polk, the intimate association of former days had not been renewed, and with the refusal of the commission their relations became rather formal. Houston supported the war in the Senate, however. His support was helpful and sometimes it was aggressive—as when he advocated a protectorate over Yucatan. At Raven Hill Margaret made a flag that Wood's Texas cavalry followed up the heights of Monterey.

But the war was foredoomed to unpopularity. The sequence of events on the Rio Grande was misunderstood. Taylor was assumed to be the aggressor, which he was not. Whatever his shortcomings, Mr. Polk did not provoke this war. He tried to avoid it, persevering even after these preliminary skirmishes and the call for troops. To this end his diplomacy was rather shady—a fact which, however, being little known is little urged against him.

3

General Houston's friends entertained high hopes for their man. Five months after he had taken his seat in the Senate, Ashbel Smith addressed his diary in a happy frame of mind. "Gen Rusk said Houston has behaved very well, and if he continues as he has done he will 'rent the White House.' "[3]

The suggestion long urged by Smith that Houston publish a Life of himself was carried out. A fluent hack named Charles Edwards Lester, a cousin of Aaron Burr, was installed in the General's apartments in the splendid National Hotel. There he toiled early and late, Houston himself editing, amending and dictating. Smith prepared reviews for the press. The completed product bore the title *Sam Houston and His Republic*, but even more arresting was a prefatory

## "WORD TO THE READER

"Before he begins this book or throws it down.

"I have lived to see unmeasured calumny poured on the head of an heroic man who struck the fetters from his bleeding country on the field and preserved her by his counsels in the cabinet. And I have lived to do justice to that man and that People by assisting the truth.

"This Book will lose me some friends. But if it lost me all and gained me none, in God's name, as I am a free man I would publish it. . . ."

After this, the book falls short of expectations. Although revealing something of what Monsieur de Talleyrand might have called that marvelous tact of omission, it is temperate and far more accurate than the run of campaign biographies of the period. It was widely read. In Texas old Burnet wrote to Lamar, a colonel in the field under Taylor, who replied: "Houston and *his* republic. *His* republic! That is true; for . . . I can regard Texas as little more than *Big Drunk's* big ranch."[4]

In this illustrious era of the Senate Texas was indeed proud to send a man who had taken his place alongside the mighty. Yet, Houston's reputation did not swell as his friends had hoped.

4

The Senator was lonely in Washington. Circumstances had changed since a buoyant youngster from the West, with the world before him, patrolled the Avenue intent upon the acquisition of a beaver hat in the proper mode. True, the return of Sam Houston made possible an interesting reunion, Daniel Webster being a member of the Senate and old Junius Brutus Booth a frequent caller from his farm in Maryland. But no foregathering of these mellow spirits is of record. The occupations Booth and Webster found to brighten their leisure had been foregone by General Houston.

Oh, there was a slip now and then, but the self-perpetuating aura of good-fellowship that for thirty years drew men to Sam Houston had paled. He moved in a circumspect world in which he had not found himself. After Texas, the heavy decorum of the Senate was irksome. After Texas, where Sam Houston had strode like some Gargantuan, the stage at Washington seemed close and crowded—a clamor of tongues, a press of figures, too many of which towered as high or higher than the Brazos titan trammeled by the support of a dubious war. Sam Houston was not used to such things. He was no longer young, and on every hand change, baffling change. The National Hotel with its private *bathtubs*, at which invading tourists came to gape, must have seemed positively indelicate. Everything altered and unfamiliar.

His temperament always a curious composition of opposites shifting with the mood between sociability and solitude, General Houston fell to taking long walks alone, often in the dead of night. Turning to the right from the pillared doorway of the National, near Sixth Street, one hundred paces along the Avenue would have brought the Senator abreast a ghost of bygone days—the swinging sign, displaying a gaudy Pocahontas, that saluted patrons of Brown's Indian Queen, last of Washington's old-time taverns. But white-aproned Jesse Brown no longer stood on the threshold to welcome the coming or Godspeed the departing guest. This good man, who maintained his office in the barroom, so as to see more of his patrons, had passed to his reward. The accolade of progress had touched his sons. They apologized for the old-fashioned place, and pulled it down to erect the magnificent Metropolitan which, with its five-story marble front, for years was the National's nearest rival. I find no record of General Houston's having stopped at the Metropolitan. He was at the grand opening at Willard's, however, and lived there during the closing scenes of his senatorship.

The decline of the drama in the capital was, in itself, almost enough to have driven old Booth to drink. The Washington, on Louisiana Avenue, of which Congressman Houston had been a favored patron, had been made into a hall for balls and assemblies. Another playhouse that had been on the popular Tennesseean's regular rounds about town was now the post-office. The remaining theater, the new National, was poorly supported. "The great diminution in numbers that were wont to attend the theatre," wrote George Watterson in his *New Guide to Washington,* for the year 1847, "has . . . risen . . . from causes which would seem to be antipodes, *religion* and *fashion.*" Balls, assemblies and church were the thing.

The Senator wrote long letters to Margaret, and received long replies, filled with testimony of his wife's affection, the affairs of the plantations, and the doings of the children—for now there were two, Sam and Nannie. But Margaret's recurring theme was theology. Her husband had only to acquire the consolations of faith to dispel the melancholy that was the badge of a soul unreclaimed.

On a Sabbath morning in the spring of 1846 General Houston threw his poncho across his shoulders and took up his gold-headed cane for a stroll in the sunshine. A few squares from the hotel he entered the E Street Baptist Church, the most fashionable of its demomination in the capital. From a pew near the pulpit he listened with rapt attention to the discourse of Reverend Doctor Samson. At the close of the service, the pastor shook hands with his flock. General Houston said he had come through respect for his wife, "One of the best Christians on earth."

On the next Sunday morning he returned to Doctor Samson's church, and on the next and the next. He whittled during the preaching, but his mind absorbed the sermons to an extent that astonished the pastor, who was also surprised by General Houston's knowledge of the Bible. The congregation cultivated the distinguished parishioner, who after every service would reward the piety of some little girl or boy with a toy that had taken shape under the magical strokes of the big ivory-handled clasp knife.

George W. Samson was a man of sound scholarship and a

master of the evangelical branch of his calling. In him Margaret discovered a wonderful ally. He prepared a sermon from the text in Proverbs, "Better is he that ruleth his spirit than he that taketh a city." This was followed by a series dealing with Israel's origin as a nation. The patriarch, Abraham, Moses, the law-giver, Joshua, the military founder of the Hebrew state, and the reign of the Judges were each made the theme of a discourse. It was the story of the settlement of a new land, of the conquest of heathen tribes, of fratricidal strife among jealous states not yet consolidated into nationality. The analogy struck home. Houston asked the pastor for a book to help him to beat down the doubts in his mind, and Doctor Samson placed in his hands a copy of Nelson's *Cause and Cure of Infidelity*.[5]

5

Two years went by. General Houston's Sunday routine was to attend church in the morning and in the afternoon write his wife a resumé of the sermon. Sometimes the Senator would miss a service, for the old instinct for motion remained and he traveled a great deal about the East. Newport and Saratoga beheld him in full sartorial glory. Once the General attended a church of the Unitarian faith and heard a learned advocate of its doctrines. There was an alarm over this, but nothing came of it. The arid intellectuality of that creed was not for the warm imagination of Sam Houston. The Baptists' chances were better.

In 1846 and in 1847 when General Houston was in Texas between sittings of Congress, Margaret and two local clergymen brought their persuasions and prayers to bear at point-blank range. But Houston would make no profession of faith, nor would he partake of the sacrament of the Lord's Supper, on the ground that he was spiritually unprepared.

It was a difficult time. As a young man whose follies were those of his day, Sam Houston had written to a friend about to depart among the Indians: "Solitude is the situation in which we can best ascertain our own hearts. There we derive no reflection from others, but are taught to make enquiry of our selves. . . . We can read the Scriptures, and pursue their preceps."[6] When the crisis came that swept Sam Houston clean of everything, including faith, he had sought the seclusion of the forests, and there examined his heart. Childhood beliefs, manhood convictions were gone. Deprived of the supports that ordinarily propitiate adversity, life seemed without hope. He caught at straws—an eagle on the wing—a "notion of honor." Upon them he had reestablished his life, with a protective coloring of skepticism to guard the sensitive soul underneath. This assailed, the vast arc of vacant sky loomed disquietingly.

The eventful spring of 1848 found Senator Houston back in Washington. It was a presidential year, and the General's absences from the E Street church were more frequent. This grieved Margaret who was approaching her third confinement.

"Huntsville April 12th 1848

"Dearest Love

"Another mail and no letter from you! I am distrest at it, but feel that in a few days, if I live, and nothing serious has befallen you, I shall get a great package from you. I can only write you a few lines, but I must write a——"

[The sentence is incomplete.]

"Saturday 22d—

"There is no doubt about it, my dearest Love, she is one of the loveliest little creatures you ever beheld. I mean our second daughter, for we are now the parents of three children. . . . You must look upon the unfinished paragraph of this letter as a great proof of my devotion to you, for I had endured much suffering, for a day and night, and in about 8 hours, the little one was added to our circle, but I thought I would make out a letter, as the mail was to go the next day. . . .

"What shall we call the little one? All I have to say is that it must be a family or fancy name, as we have too many friends to exercise partiality in that way. I enclose a lock of her hair [and] . . . a little white rose which she held in her hand, the first nap she ever took.

> "Thy fond and devoted wife
> "M. L. Houston"[7]

A fortnight later General Houston was assured that "our precious baby enjoys fine health and is beginning to look like her father. . . . She can stand on her feet, with as much strength, as most children three months old. She has the prettiest little hands and feet . . . and from the descriptions you have given me of your mother's I think they must be like hers." What shall they call her? Her father must suggest something. "She is becoming quite a young lady, to have no name. . . .

"Mrs Davis and Caroline have joined the church and Mr Creath expects to go down the first week in June to baptise them. . . . Your friend Mose Evans 'the wild man of Texas' has become a baptist and a very pious man. Sister Creath wrote to you about Albert's conversion. . . . My dear Love, I fear that you are suffering your mind to be drawn off from the subject of religion, by the political excitement of the day. . . . Oh when I think of the allurements that surround you, I tremble lest they should steal your heart from God. . . . There is something so bewitching in the voice of fame."

A postscript just before mailing told of a visit by Mr. Smith, a neighbor. "He told me two *good jokes* about you (to use his language), the affair of the *shirt button* and something about a fire not being kindled in your room, being the contents of a letter from his brother. My dear Love, you must quiet these things! I . . . pray with all my heart that you may be kept from the evil of this world and fitted for the joys of the next."[8]

## 6

General Houston received this letter at Barnum's Hotel in New York, whither he had gone on a political errand for his party. But beyond a contemplation of the evils of this world and the joys of the next, 1848 afforded small balm to any Democrat. The Mexican War was essentially the affair of the southern wing of the Democratic party. Having borne the burden of the criticism concerning it, the party managers felt entitled to any offsetting advantages. In the beginning a disconcerting situation had arisen, however. Houston, a southern Democrat, had refused a field command, and Zachary Taylor had gone on winning battles. Though a Louisianian and the owner of three hundred slaves, Taylor belonged, nominally, to the old southern Whig aristocracy. The Whigs needed a candidate who could poll southern votes. Party managers began toasting Old Rough and Ready. Mr. Polk took note and prepared to shelve General Taylor by handing over the principal theater of war to Scott at Vera Cruz.

Taylor was stripped of his best troops and in this situation Santa Anna confronted him with fifteen thousand men at Buena Vista. The Americans were barely five thousand, mostly volunteers. The presence of Santa Anna at Buena Vista represented a breach of trust that shook Polk's declining faith in human nature. When the war started the General was serving a term of banishment in Cuba. Desirous of avoiding further bloodshed, Mr. Polk dispatched Slidell McKenzie, of the Navy, to Havana with drawing privileges on a secret fund, to communicate the humane idea to Santa Anna. The Napoleon of the West departed for Mexico under protection of the United States gunboats but after seizing the government he announced a modification of the joint plan. Instead of surrendering the Army, he prepared to fight.

The battle of Buena Vista was terrific, but Taylor won and came home the unalterable hero of the hour. The Whigs passed up Webster and all of the other immortals for this unschooled soldier who had not cast a vote in forty years. The Democrats nominated Lewis Cass, a Cabinet officer under Jackson and a good man. Houston played a prominent part in the campaign, which from the outset looked like any one's victory.

The Whigs won as a result of a Democratic division in the state of New York. The fact that but for Sam Houston and Texas Zachary Taylor would have died an unknown frontier colonel was, however, a source of no satisfaction to either the Senator or his constituents.

The close of the war saw us in the possession of a new domain greater than the area of the original thirteen colonies. This realization of the expansionists' dream of heaven disturbed moderate thinkers. Many wondered whether so vast a realm could be held together under one central government. Taylor, who had a world of common sense, shrank before the sobering problem, and favored letting the Pacific coast go.

But this was the tremor of a moment. The territory was under the flag and there was little deep-seated disposition to relinquish any of it. The great problem was slavery. Would the new territory be slave or would it be free? The negro question had been pressing at the gates for ten years. With the great annexations under Polk the hinges parted and it burst tumultuously through.

The impact was first felt upon the discussions concerning the organization of the Oregon country. Senator Houston introduced an amendment to let the citizens of the territory decide the question of slavery. Mr. Calhoun inquired sarcastically the object of the amendment—"whether or not it was to give protection to Southern gentlemen." Houston replied that its object was to give protection to the citizens of Oregon. The discussion grew warmer, and a threat of disunion was made. The Senator of Texas arose in his place.

"I remember the cry of disunion," he said referring to Calhoun's abortive effort of 1832. "That cry reached me in the wilderness, an exile from kindred and friends . . . and wounded my heart. But I am now in the midst of such a cry . . . [and] have no fear. . . . It could not be to the interest of the North to destroy the South, notwithstanding the papers signed by old men and women and pretty girls, praying for abolition."[9]

Oregon Territory was organized as free soil. The slave extensionists, led by feeble but fiery Calhoun, uttered ominous warnings. They said the North was bent upon the ruin of the South, which must concede nothing. Houston refused to sign the bitter "Southern Address" of 1849. "It would excite the Southern people and drive them further on the road to separation from their Northern friends." Southern hotspurs were violent in their denunciation of the "traitor" to his section. It was not for the South to propitiate the North, they said, but to safeguard its political power.

Sam Houston answered this argument in a moving speech, "actuated," he said, "by as patriotic motives as any gentleman, North or South." He knew "neither North nor South" but "only the Union." He was a southern man, and he would contend for the rights of the South, but just as "ardently" would he "defend the North," when he believed its view to be right. He believed that "on this floor" he was a "representative of the whole American people." "On all occasions" he would maintain that position, believing the people of Texas would sustain him "for they are true to the Union."[10]

The gauntlet lay at the feet of the southern disunionists and northern agitators alike. On the fourteenth day of August, 1848, Senator Houston took his courageous stand, from which no form of entreaty, personal or political threat, or enticement of fame could bring him to recede. The national skies were black with clouds that presaged the storm-clutched chaos of the 'fifties. North and South, public men glided hither and thither, peering from this window and that, to know what to make of it and what to do. From conviction or convenience most of them prepared to sail with the winds of their particular section, whither they might blow. Sam Houston was a mariner of mature experience in troubled waters. He could tack with the best of them. But this time, in advance of all the rest and practically alone, he gave out his course, close-hauled his bark and whipped into the gathering gale.

# CHAPTER XXVII

## The Forlorn Hope

### 1

In 1793, when Sam Houston was born and carried about the comfortable house on Timber Ridge by the black nurse Peggy, slavery was a declining institution whose painless extinction was taken as a matter of course by persons of forethought. The country was in the hands of the men who had waged the Revolution, with its emphasis upon the Rights of Man. A slave owner, Mr. Jefferson, had written an unfriendly reference to the institution in his Declaration of Independence, but the passage was stricken out, representatives of the maritime interests of New England who had a good thing in the slave-carrying trade protesting as stoutly as any. Nevertheless, the lofty views of human rights expressed by the fight for national liberty were definitely impregnated with a coolness toward slavery. This gained ground the more readily because it inveighed against a custom that had become demonstrably unsound economically. George Washington found it cheaper to hire a hand than own a slave and foresaw in the end of bondage the elimination of a wasteful factor in plantation management.

But in this same year of 1793, Eli Whitney, of Massachusetts, marketed his cotton-gin that made the cultivation of this staple an occupation in which slaves could be employed with profit. One new state followed another in the rearing of the cotton kingdom that issued from the generous soil of the South.

industrial New England, which wove cotton into cloth, had less use for slave labor than before. By 1804 every Northern State excepting hybrid Delaware had either freed its slaves or arranged for gradual emancipation, usually providing that children born of slave parents should be free upon reaching the age of twenty-five. A similar proposal in Virginia attracted a large and influential following.

In this geographical reallocation of socially and economically distinct cultures, the moral issue was not stressed at first. Opposed interests were separated primarily by economic barriers. The South preferred to buy abroad, where most of its cotton went, because Europe sold more cheaply than New England. New England, naturally, wished to protect its industries with a tariff. The time came when slavery was denounced in the halls of Congress as a "crime," and the South began seriously to gird itself for defense of its "peculiar institution"— defense meaning expansion to maintain the political equilibrium.

In 1820 Clay's Missouri Compromise cooled passions on both sides and deferred the crisis, but by 1830 the struggle had been renewed.

The third decade saw the dawn of the gilded age of slavery times. Romantic, rich and reckless, a new South bloomed like an astonishing tropical flower. Fortunes were made and mansions built by men who had been poor a few years before. New plantations were known to pay for themselves with a second crop. Ice transported from Maine chilled the mint juleps that planter barons sipped in their magnolia-scented gardens. The conservative aristocracy of Virginia and the Old South elsewhere—except South Carolina where Calhoun led the radicals—was overborne by these sudden ascendants to wealth and power. The equivocal manners of the parvenu, insinuating themselves into the counsels of the South, matched the harsh behavior of the northern radicals, threat for threat, hard name for hard name.

In 1807 when Elizabeth Houston and her nine children moved to Tennessee, responsible southern thought regarded slavery as an evil, for which, however, a solution seemed no longer quite apparent. Northern meddling tended to solidify the South. This was furthered in 1831 when Nat Turner's ghastly slave rebellion in Virginia took sixty white lives. Turner was said to have read abolition literature. A resolution to abolish slavery failed in the Virginia Legislature because the people did not wish the free blacks on their hands. For better or worse the negroes were a fixed part of the population, and the South believed they could only be controlled as slaves. A slave's lot was not what abolitionists represented it to be, however, and with all its defects, the charm of southern life was preferred by most European visitors to the United States.

One southern white family in five owned slaves. The white population of the South in 1860 was 9,000,000. The number of slave-holders was 384,000, the number of slaves, 3,950,000. The great nobles of the cotton kingdom owning fifty slaves or more did not exceed 8,000 heads of families.

Many features of this oligarchy were molded, to a degree, by the necessity of opposition to northern extremists. To say that Garrison, the father of the American Anti-Slavery Society, which had such a hand in the molding, failed to appreciate the South's problems is hardly enough. His advocacy of "the immediate enfranchisement of our slave population" was savage and lawless. But his society grew slowly. In 1840 it was short of 200,000 members which, distributed among a free state population of 9,729,000, is not impressive.

The northern threat was very real, nevertheless. The North had grown less colorfully but more soundly than the South. By 1850 it had nearly twice the white population. Wealth and political influence were more broadly distributed. The trend was to hem the South about with an inflexible ring of free states and strip it piecemeal of its disproportionate political power. The South saw this as slow destruction, and resisted. But the North was firm and only the British menace wrung its consent to the admission of Texas.

Sam Houston had observed these portentous changes with

peculiar penetration. The annexation of Texas brought its problems to the United States, but it was our best way out. Texas came in as a Slave State, but the status of the great domain beyond the mountains which formed its dowry was to be determined. North and South buckled on their armor, and the session of Congress that was to convene in December of 1849 was anticipated with a sense of apprehension.

2

The preceding summer heard open threats of secession. General Houston declined to be drawn into controversies, except to say that while standing for southern rights, he stood also for national rights. He had a way of changing the subject to his new place in Huntsville, to which the family repaired on leaving Cedar Point, the summer residence on Galveston Bay. Margaret disliked the isolation of Raven Hill, and the General had provided her with a third home and a great yellow coach in which to travel from one to another.

The new Huntsville house bore some resemblance to Sam Houston's birthplace in Virginia. It stood on spacious grounds at the edge of the village, which prided itself on being a replica of an old-fashioned southern community. In the side yard General Houston erected of squared logs his particular sanctum, where he could whittle and scatter papers and pipe ashes to his heart's content. What tidying he permitted was entrusted to Joshua, the plantation blacksmith at Raven Hill and out-of-doors factotum about the Houston estates. The principal furniture consisted of a pine table and the great oak chair with a rawhide bottom that had served General Houston as President of the Republic. The walls were lined with books—a law library, the old favorites of classical and standard literature—and Nelson's *Cause and Cure of Infidelity*. Here the General spent many hours each day and took his visitors.

In mid-November he set out for Washington. His first letter en route was from East Texas.

"Douglass
"18th Nov 1850

"Dearest

"I am here, and as I have time to write I am happy to do so. . . .

"The day has passed quietly for me, for I had no company in the stage. . . . I can tell you no news of this section only that my friend Hogg has been acquitted for killing Chandler. . . .

"If God wills I shall press on my journey so as to have as much time as possible to spend with our relations in Alabama. I have no expectation that any thing important will transpire until after Holy Days.

"I do pray that you may be cheerful in my absence and not repine at what is unavoidable. . . .

"As it is Sunday night I will not write to you on any matters of business.

"My love to all
"Ever thine
"Houston.

"Margaret
"P S Tell Sam, Nannie, & Maggy, that I have preserved all the roses and chrysanthemums which they gave me."[1]

"Maggy" was the baby, named for her mother.

The early weeks of Congress saw a confusion of suggestions to which no great attention was paid. The nation awaited the voice of Henry Clay. The return of Clay to public life appealed to the imagination. For six years the Great Compromiser had lived in retirement with his blooded horses and his blue-grass. In 1820 and again in 1833 this moderate southern statesman had calmed the seas of national politics troubled by slavery.

In January of 1850 he laid before the Senate an expertly balanced program to which Sam Houston had contributed some important ideas. Mr. Clay made a two-day speech in support of his proposals. He spoke as an old man whose remaining ambition was to give his country peace. He portrayed the glories of the Union, which he and every other old man present had seen born and grow. He said these could be preserved if each side would pursue a reasonable course of give and take.

The speech was answered by Calhoun who championed disunion in a dramatic utterance. Mr. Calhoun also was an old man and his sands were almost run. Too weak to deliver his reply to Clay, he was conducted to his place in the Senate while his words were declaimed by a friend. Nothing would satisfy this uncompromising patriarch but a constitutional amendment, perpetuating the balance of power between the sections. Furthermore the North must cease its propaganda against slavery. Otherwise, "let the states . . . part in peace."

As the author of this defiance tottered from the Chamber he accidentally confronted Mr. Clay. Old Calhoun jerked his head erect and met the glance of his adversary in the partizan battles of more than thirty years. For a few seconds neither spoke. Then they fell into each other's arms. The Senate never saw the venerable firebrand again. He was dead in four weeks.

Daniel Webster eulogized the memory of his southern colleague in the Chamber, but by this time he, too, had brought his long public career to a remarkable close. In a powerful address he had supported the Clay compromises and killed his own chances for the presidency. Our greatest orator and one of our greatest statesmen, Webster embodied the qualities that distinguished the New England gentleman of a fading era. He was the last man to grace the Senate in a blue broadcloth coat with brass buttons. Few public men in our history have been more greatly revered. This popularity he sacrificed to safeguard the Union. The North rang with denunciation. "Webster is a fallen star! A Lucifer descending from the heavens!"

Sam Houston also braved the hostility of his homeland. He was the first senator of prominence to support Clay on the floor. He spoke with great solemnity. "I must say that I am sorry that I cannot offer the prayers of the righteous that my petition be heard. But I beseech those whose piety will permit them reverentially to offer such petitions, that they will pray for this Union, and . . . ask of Him who buildeth up and pulleth down nations . . . [to] unite us. I wish, if this Union *must* be dissolved, that its ruins may be the monument of my grave."

The South, and especially Texas, resented these words. The country beyond the Sabine had sustained itself outside of the Union and did not doubt its capacity to do so again.

This had no effect on Houston. When the Southern States held a convention in Nashville, he ridiculed the meeting and the Texas delegates in particular. He refused to acknowledge the leadership of Jefferson Davis, whom he dismissed as "cold as a lizard and ambitious as Lucifer." In the contest at hand Houston was on the winning side. The Clay proposals were eventually adopted, and the Kentucky Senator died in room number sixteen of the National Hotel, serene in the belief that he had rescued his country from danger. During the long struggle the personal breach between General Houston and Jackson's old enemy was healed and Houston traveled to Lexington to attend the funeral.

### 3

The time had come to cast an eye over the field in quest of candidates for 1852. Despite the industry of party leaders and of business interests who wished to keep the slavery question out of politics, party lines swayed before the pressure. The Democratic party, in general terms the party of the West, was shifting its center of gravity southward and had altered in other respects since its domination by the Union-loving Jackson. The conservative Whig party, uniting the old blue-stocking elements of New England and the southern seaboard, was drifting northward.

In neither case was a majority of the political change-abouts perfectly satisfied with its new environments. But there were no other places to go, since the old party mechanisms remained sufficiently staunch to resist attempts at building new parties. The changed internal conditions of each party complicated the work of selecting candidates, however.

Had the Democrats maintained the party of Jackson, General Houston's fight for the compromises of 1850 would have stood him in good stead. This contest had gained Houston the approval of the moderates everywhere. In the spring of 1851 Ashbel Smith, not an inferior observer, made a tour of the country and sailed for a holiday visit to Europe, writing to Houston from London. "Without a shadow of a doubt public opinion at the North as well as the South regards you as decidedly the strongest candidate of the Democratic party; and many Whigs have expressed to me their opinion that you could be elected."[2] Houston's strength was with the people, however, rather than with politicians, which rendered his resources in a large measure inarticulate. As a remedy, Smith suggested steps "to secure the attendance of the right sort of men from the several states in the next convention."

Houston did little about this, however. Seemingly he did little about anything calculated to enhance the fortunes of an aspirant to office. The country was at the feet of the visiting Hungarian patriot, Kossuth, who especially desired to cultivate General Houston. The General met him politely, but that was the extent of his welcome to the popular idol, whom he felt should be at home fighting. Then there were the Indians. Sam Houston embraced their emissaries in public and made speeches about their wrongs. Befriending an Indian or snubbing a hero has made no public man any votes, notwithstanding that America ultimately wearied of the splendid Kossuth.

Opposing politicians did not neglect the opportunities presented by this unconventional behavior. After all, was not this fabled hero of San Jacinto just a wilful and aging eccentric who dressed peculiarly, whittled for children, distributed copies of Nelson on infidelity and wrote touching sentiments in ladies' albums? It was charitably whispered that a too tardy relinquishment of more entertaining habits might be responsible for this decline. The opium story seems to have been usefully revived. This tale was first sponsored in 1836 by Major James H. Perry, Texas Army, and Burnet's spy who had broken bread with Sam Houston as a member of his staff. Major Perry had abandoned the military profession, however. He was now pastor of a well-attended church in New York City, and still blackening the character of General Houston.

The General did not go about a great deal socially, although he was still a favorite of the type that ladies vaguely called "interesting." In a hostess's memory book containing sentiments by the hands of Zachary Taylor, Hannibal Hamlin, John C. Calhoun and Jefferson Davis, he wrote:

> "Woman is lovely to the sight,
> As gentle as the dews of even
> As bright as morning's earliest light
> And spotless as the snows of Heaven."[3]

This attitude moved one wit to predict that if General Houston were elected president he would have a Cabinet of women who would boss him.

Although by no means indifferent to Ashbel Smith's political efforts, Houston's replies to his letters were filled with personal things. Smith was lonely, and Houston's repeated advice was to marry. There was also young Miller, the Senator's former secretary. "Write by return mail and in better spirits. I mean better Heart. . . . Get married Miller while young!!!" "Absence does not lessen my affection for you, tho it increases my anxiety! Will you not marry Miller? You must do so!"[4]

When Thomas Boyers, of Gallatin, Tennessee, called, the Senator showed him more than the perfunctory attentions. "Very adroitly and after more than one interview, he led me to speak of his wife [Eliza], and then succeeded question and question, many of them of the most trivial character in regard to her."[5] Mr. Boyers did not record the substance of his replies, but he may have spoken without reserve for, after all, there did not seem to be a great deal to relate. After the Texas divorce Eliza's sudden marriage to Dr. Elmore Douglass, of a wealthy county family, had been a surprise in view of her previous refusal to countenance admirers or suggestions of divorce. Eliza was twenty-nine when she remarried, and Doctor Douglass much older, a mild widower and father of a large brood of children. Eliza had borne him three or four more heirs. This considerable family lived very quietly in the shaded town house in Gallatin, spending the summers on a plantation.

Peaceful Gallatin was disposed to forget and, tacitly, to forgive, but in Nashville discussion of the General's political future not unnaturally recalled the past. If the memory of an aged surgeon has served him rightly, an aspect of the historic estrangement was discussed at the University of Nashville in a lecture by a learned member of the medical profession.[6]

General Houston continued his faithful attendance at church service, but as a penitent outside the fold, absenting himself from communion on the ground that to partake would constitute a sacrilege. The spiritually serene years of Sam Houston's life had been spent with the Indians whose world invisible had soothed his soul when the white man's world, including the vice-regents of its gods, was in arms against him. This made matters difficult.

A clergyman in Texas went over the Scriptures with General Houston in an attempt to convince him that he might taste the wine of communion without offense. Returning to Washington the General wrestled with the issue all winter, and on March 6, 1851, he filled Margaret's heart with joy. "Tomorrow is our communion day at E Street Baptist Church. If the Lord spares me, I expect to attend and partake of the sacrament of our Lord's supper. . . . I know I am a sinner and . . . I feel that I do not love God as I ought to. . . . Pray for me dearest. . . . Thy devoted SAM HOUSTON."[7]

Thus time went by. As the nominating conventions approached, General Houston's friends felt that the situation of their man was hopeless. Congressman Andrew Johnson, of

Tennessee, wrote to a relative: "Dan the God-like is considered out of the fight. . . . Scott will be the Whig nominee." As to the Democrats, "All agree that if Sam Houston could receive the nomination he would be elected by a greater majority than any other person."[8] Johnson was a real Jacksonian, and therefore biased in Houston's favor, but this was not true of Sumner, of Massachusetts, who, after a talk with Houston, confessed his astonishment "to find himself so much of his inclining. . . . With him the anti-slavery interests would stand better than with any other man."[9]

The Whigs, whose two lone presidential victories had been won by military idols of no political experience, put up Winfield Scott. On the forty-ninth ballot the Democrats nominated the obscure Franklin Pierce, of New Hampshire. Houston did not permit his own name to go before the Convention, but supported Pierce whose devastating victory over Scott was hailed as a guarantee of the permanence of the Compromise.

### 4

But northern radicals took another view. "There is no hope," wrote Wendell Phillips. "We shall have Cuba in a year or two, Mexico in five." A "vast slave empire united with Brazil" would darken the hemisphere. There was some cause for this warning. Pierce panned out an instrument of the southern ultras, and was repudiated by Sam Houston, thenceforward a senator without a party.

The effort to add Cuba to the slave domain was renewed, although less violently than in 1851 when a son of the Attorney-General of the United States died before a firing squad in Havana. Better luck now attended William Walker, a young Tennesseean of the type that twenty years before made good lieutenants for Houston in Texas. With a band of Americans he subdued Nicaragua, declared himself president and sent an ambassador to Washington.

The triumphant southerners advanced on a broad front.

Their first thrust was audacious. It contemplated the destruction not only of the Compromise of 1850, but of the Missouri Compromise, which had been the steadying force in our internal affairs for more than thirty years. Stephen A. Douglas, a Democrat of Illinois, burning with presidential ambition, introduced his Kansas-Nebraska Bill, the mischievous features of which were inspired by a southern radical, Atchison, of Missouri. This measure would open the whole West from Iowa to the Mountains to slavery by the principle of "squatter sovereignty," which permitted the residents to decide whether they should have slaves or exclude them. The tacit assumption was that the northern part of this territory would be free and the southern part would be slave.

This attempt at the literal leveling of the work of 1850 and of 1820, about which had grown a patriotic regard, was testimony of a new spirit. Yet such was the composition of the Senate, and the astuteness of the managers of the bill, that early chances of success crystallized into certainty. No state was more ardent for the bill than Texas, and General Houston was not expected to oppose his electorate. Still, "incredible as this may be," a correspondent of the Richmond *Enquirer* heard "that General Sam Houston, of Texas, will vote against the Nebraska bill. . . . Nothing can justify this treachery."[10]

It was quite true. Houston not only voted against the bill, being the only southern Democrat to do so, but he led the hopeless opposition with a clarity of vision not surpassed by any senator on the floor. He foresaw the consequences of reopening the agitation allayed in 1850.

At a night session General Houston stood beneath the concentric circles of gas-lights to make his closing address. The galleries were filled.

"I had fondly hoped, Mr. President, that having attained my present period of life, I should pass the residue of my days, be they many or few, in peace and tranquility. . . . My hopes are less sanguine now. My anxieties increase. Sir, if this repeal takes place, I will have seen the commencement of the agitation, but the youngest child now born, will not live to witness its termination." The speaker recalled the compromise of 1820. He reviewed the "drama" of 1850. What necessity had arisen for the destruction of these bulwarks? "None." "I ask again, what benefit is to result to the South from this measure? . . . Will it secure these territories to the South. No, sir, not at all." On the contrary "it furnished those in the North, who are enemies of the South, with efficient weapons."

Senator Houston cited a factor not mentioned elsewhere in the debates. What provision would be made for the forty thousand Indians inhabitating the domain in question? He made a plea for them, although with "little hope that any appeal I can make for the Indians will do any good." Nor was this the last time that The Raven detained an impatient Senate with his eloquence to ask justice for "a race of people whom I am not ashamed to say have called me brother."

His conclusion was brief. The symbolic eagle above the chair of the presiding officer was draped in black for Webster and Clay. Must this badge of woe also represent "a fearful omen of future calamities which await our nation in event this bill should become a law? . . . I adjure you, harmonize and preserve this nation. . . . Give us peace!"[11]

Four days later the bill was passed. Houston was pilloried at mass meetings in the South. The Texas Legislature and the Texas State Democratic Convention formally censured him, and notice was served that with the expiration of his senatorial term Sam Houston's public career would close in disgrace.

## 5

There was work for the big yellow coach that summer in Texas. Mrs. Houston had asthma, and thinking to benefit her by the higher altitude, the General built another residence at Independence, where her mother lived and ran the Baptist Church. This gave the Houstons four homes, each maintained in readiness for instant occupancy. The General himself preferred Huntsville, though Houston City held a place in his heart. The old Capitol building, once his pride, was still accessible as the Capitol Hotel.

The march of years had not diminished his passion for motion, and the Houston family, with its cluster of little ones, whose number methodically increased to seven, became as mobile as cavalry. A notion to trek would strike the General. In an hour the children would be rounded up by Margaret and the maids. With trunks lashed to the boot, a surplus negro or two perched on the top and a flourish of Tom Blue's long whip, the great yellow carry-all and four horses would be off in a cloud of rolling dust, General Houston leading the way in a single-seated top buggy beside the gigantic Joshua, his driver. . . . On, on—always in flight.

But the long quest for spiritual repose ended that autumn when, at the close of a service, Sam Houston knelt before the altar in Independence and asked to be received into the church. The bell in the tower, a gift of Nancy Lea and so inscribed, tolled the tidings, which in clerical circles assumed the scope of a national event. On the nineteenth of November, 1854, the convert waded the chilly waters of Rocky Creek and was baptized by Reverend Rufus C. Burleson.

"The announcement of General Houston's immersion," recounted a church periodical of wide repute, "has excited the wonder and surprise of many who have supposed that he was 'past praying for' but it is no marvel to us. . . . Three thousand and fifty clergymen have been praying for him ever since the Nebraska outrage in the Senate."[12]

Another Rubicon had been crossed.

"Well, General," remarked a Texas friend, "I hear your sins were washed away."

"I hope so," Sam Houston replied. "But if they were all washed away, the Lord help the fish down below."[13]

General Houston engaged to pay half of the minister's salary—"My pocketbook was baptised, too"—and shortly afterward was riding horseback when his mount stumbled.

"God damn a stumbling horse!"

John H. Reagan, with whom the General was traveling, professed to be shocked. Houston dismounted, knelt in the road and asked forgiveness.

## 6

The ensuing session of Congress revealed the harvest of the Kansas-Nebraska Bill to be as General Houston had prophesied. Missourians streamed across the line to hold Kansas for slavery. New England sent emigrants and adventurers to dispute the issue. The result was armed conflict. The first shots of the Civil War were fired, not at Sumter, but at Lawrence.

This sobered neither the South nor the North. Knives and a pistol were drawn in the House of Representatives, and Congressman Brooks, of South Carolina, answered a philippic of Senator Sumner by cudgeling the statesman from Massachusetts nearly to death at his desk. "Last night I was to a Party at Speaker Banks," Houston wrote to Margaret, "and saw 'Uncle Toms Cabin' alias Madam Beecher Stowe. She is certainly a hard object to look on. I . . . ate an ice cream & left."[14] From Houston the words sound ungallant, although even moderate southerners regarded the mild Mrs. Stowe as something of a demon. Her novel was the most widely read piece of literature in the world. Not since Cervantes laughed away Spain's chivalry had the pen launched such a blow at an institution.

There was some recrudescence of General Houston's prestige. The Democracy of New Hampshire endorsed him for the presidency and endeavored to stampede the country for his nomination in 1856. The General had no party behind him, but a new party had become inevitable. In this lay the hope of those who believed Sam Houston to be the man to o'ermaster chaos and lead the nation from ruin. Out of a curious secret society called Native Americans, or Know-

Nothings, from a formula in its ritual, was emerging a political organization that gave promise of becoming this national union party. In 1854 it carried several states and continued to gain. It elected Houston's friend, Banks, speaker of the House and began to look to the Texas Senator as national standard-bearer. But the Whig party collapsed, and the northern wing, going over to the Know-Nothings practically in a body, vitiated the prospects of that organization, already handicapped by the anti-Catholic, anti-immigrant doctrines of the secret order. A new grouping, calling itself Republican, marched from the West and claimed the day.

The overturn of party definitions was complete. The Democratic party, founded by Thomas Jefferson as the party of human rights, had become very deeply involved with property rights—negroes in bondage. The Republican party, descendant of the Federalists of Hamilton, became in this particular a champion of human rights. The name Republican was chosen because Jefferson had used it. Rather despite themselves at first, the Republicans were more sectional than national in their outlook. Many new party men were opposed to the radical type of opposition to slavery, however, and thought well of Sam Houston whose name they cheered in their New Jersey Convention.

So the realignment for 1856: a failure of nationalism and a triumph of sectionalism. But not without misgivings! The Republicans nominated Frémont, the California conquistadore, who, as Benton's son-in-law, was supposed to appeal to the Jacksonians; the Democrats nominated Buchanan, of Pennsylvania, a Jackson follower with a colorless record; the American party (Know-Nothings) nominated Millard Fillmore and Andrew Jackson Donelson! In a rather melancholy letter of advice to a young friend, Sam Houston gave lengthy reasons for supporting the Fillmore ticket. They could have been reduced to three words: Save the Union![15]

Mr. Buchanan was elected in a fairly close contest. Fillmore carried one state—Maryland.

The southern extremists remained in the saddle and rode heedlessly on, not without the spur of northern provocation pricking their flanks. The Dred Scott decision opened the entire West to slavery. The triumphant southerners cut the tariff again and began their successful assaults upon the New England ship subsidies. Sam Houston had fought his fight to harmonize the factions and had failed; so had every other man. His term had until 1859 to run, but his career in the Senate was over. He turned to preserve, if possible, his turmoiled Texas from the wreck.

In August of 1857 a governor was to be elected. Against the advice of friends and without resigning from the Senate Houston announced his candidacy. The Democratic party and the political machinery of the state were in the hands of the radicals. Waiving the need of party, press or general electioneering paraphernalia, he ran simply as Sam Houston. It seemed a forlorn hope, although it was by no means a foolhardy one. Houston's political capital could scarcely sink lower, and he might redeem it. Sam Houston had been in tight places before in Texas.

The campaign was violent. The regular Democratic nominee was Hardin R. Runnels, a square-jawed fighter. But Mr. Runnels was unfamiliar with political methods of the spacious days of the Republic and of Sam Houston's prime. His adversary simply changed the calendar on him.

Sam Houston had spent too much of his life in the camps of the frontier to swing free in the stultifying atmosphere of the futile Chamber on Capitol Hill, but in Texas he was himself again, carrying the action to his enemy in regular Brazos Bottoms style. Issues were nothing, personalities everything, and the surprised Runnels found himself on the defensive. Back and forth across the plains and up and down the strings of towns that dotted the watercourses, rolled Sam Houston in his old top buggy. The summer was hot, and he would peel off his shirt and harangue the folk clad in a rumpled linen duster that reached from his neck to his ankles. He stirred the people. He quickened them as they had not been quickened since 'thirty-six and 'forty-two. He said things on the stump for which another man would have been shot. This appealed. A legendary hero had come to life—the weather-beaten figure of "Old Sam Jacinto" himself, with a heart for any fortune and a hand for any fight.

While General Houston was speaking at Lockhart, Judge W. S. Oldham, a Runnels lieutenant, rode up and began taking books from his saddle-bags.

"Be still, my friends, be still," Sam Houston said. "I will report the cause of this commotion. It is only Oldham, only Oldham. He is opening some books, but they are not the bank books he stole and sunk in the White River, in Arkansas."

The Judge bit his cigar in two.

"He wants to have me assassinated!" roared Houston, adding that Oldham had signed a circular declaring Sam Houston should be "handled without gloves." Drawing from his pocket a pair a large buckskin gloves, the General put them on and gingerly produced a copy of the paper in question. "Here it is," he said. "This paper is too dirty to handle without gloves." Adjusting his spectacles the General began to read from the circular, which characterized him as a traitor.

"What!" he challenged, throwing the document to the ground. "I a traitor to Texas!" Old Sam took several steps, hobbling, as he occasionally did, on the San Jacinto leg. "Was it for this I bared my bosom to the hail of battle—to be branded a traitor in my old age?"

The crowd went wild, for in the preoccupation of his oratory the General's duster had become unbuttoned, revealing to the world that bosom, covered with hair "as thick as a buffalo mop," by one spectator's estimate.

Retrieving the round robin Houston asked permission to read the names signed to it.

"Williamson S. Oldham—though he stole and sunk those

bank books in the river and ran away to Texas, he is not yet in the penitentiary.  J. M. Steiner—a murderer.  John Marshall—a vegetarian—he won't eat meat and one drop of his blood would freeze a dog. . . ."[16]

At Brenham Houston's right to speak in the court-house was questioned.  It was quite all right, the General told the assembled citizens.  "I am not a taxpayer here.  I did not contribute to buy a single brick or beam in this building, and have no right to speak here.  But," and here his tone changed, "if there is a man within the sound of my voice who desires to hear Sam Houston speak and will follow me hence to yonder hillside under the shade of yon spreading live oak on the soil of Texas I have a right to speak there because I have watered it with my blood!"[17]

Runnels won the election by 32,552 votes to 23,628.  Houston wrote Ashbel Smith a humorous letter, telling the wary old bachelor not to be downcast, but to come to Huntsville and meet "one of the Grandest girls, said to be, in America.  Oh, I do want someone who has seen other days in Texas, to talk with!  Come and see me, I bind myself to make you laugh."

### 8

During the last eighteen months of his term, Senator Houston occupied most of his hours in the Chamber with a knife and a pine stick.  In March of 1859, his thirteen years of service were up.  The General made a round of farewell visits including one to the White House, recalling that forty-five years before, as a furloughed soldier with an arm in a sling, he had gazed upon its ruins.

Thanks to the steam cars which with many vicissitudes ran by relays the whole distance to New Orleans, the trip to Texas could be accomplished in eight days.  The countless times in his restless life that Sam Houston had journeyed to and from Washington!  The city he had seen grow from a spraddling village occupied a peculiar place in the many-chambered magazine of his destiny. It mattered not how rudely or how far away events might fling him. With the precision of a thing ordained, he'd pick a path unerringly back. It was incredible now, that by some pass of circumstances, he should not retrace the familiar course.

This was not to be. When Sam Houston crossed the Sabine and set foot on Texas soil, he was never to leave it again.

# CHAPTER XXVIII

## The Last of His Race

### 1

A YEAR before his return to Texas as a private citizen General Houston had forecast his entry into the "sheperdizing business," and promised to round out his days tending sheep on a hillside. The arrival of a collection of blooded rams from Louisiana lent verisimilitude to the proposal. Governor Runnels desired ampler assurances, however. He was thinking of reelection.

The Governor's misgivings were borne out. When Mr. Runnels was renominated, the sheep scheme faded into the empyreal blue and Sam Houston announced his candidacy as an independent "opposed alike to the Black Republicans and the little less dangerous fanatics and Higher law men at the South."

Two years before Houston had conducted the only sort of campaign by which he could hope to gain anything. He had not expected to win the election, but to make a showing and encourage the frightened opposition to the radicals. In this he professed to have succeeded beyond his expectations. Now the tables were turned. The radicals were alarmed and afraid to speak their minds. The Convention that nominated Runnels defeated a resolution in favor of the resumption of the slave trade, and on the stump the Governor repudiated a desire for "immediate" secession. How could such pretense hope to prevail against Sam Houston? He gave his adversaries no peace. In a campaign more dignified than that of 1857, he drove home his arguments against disunion. Two cargoes of savages were landed from Africa on the Texas coast. Houston made the most of it. The election was his by a vote of 36,257 to 27,500, or close to an exact reversal of the majority of two years before.

It was a second San Jacinto. Sam Houston regained the troubled stage of national affairs. What manner of man was this Texas trojan, who single-handed had thrown back the southern extremists for their first defeat in eleven years? The South smarted under the reverse, and the party leaders in Texas had recourse in childish fury. In the Legislature an appropriation for furnishings for the Executive Mansion was obstructed by a controversy whether Sam Houston, who had lived in a wigwam, should be surrounded by civilized luxuries at public expense. The House debated whether it should offer its quarters for the inaugural ball and, if so, whether the carpet should be removed. The formalities of administering the oath of office to the Governor-Elect became a subject for biting allusions.

Houston made his own inaugural arrangements. Instead of taking the oath in the House chamber before the Legislature and a select few, he delivered his inaugural address on the portico of the Capitol. A vast crowd stood on the sloping lawn. "When Texas united her destiny with that of the United States," Houston told them, "she entered into not the North nor South. Her connection was . . . national."

Thus nine months after leaving the Senate Sam Houston assumed for the seventh time the helm of affairs in Texas. On five of the occasions preceding he had triumphed: twice as president of the Republic, once as commander-in-chief of the Armies and twice as first citizen, when he had thwarted chaos during the regimes of Burnet and Lamar. Once, as commander-in-chief, he had failed, but to retrieve personally what he had lost. Houston had proved the only leader from Austin down consistently capable of handling Texas which, in its greatest crisis, turned to him again.

### 2

The Governor plunged into his duties with enormous energy. Within a month he had Legislature, state departments, and even county officials in a whirl of activity, reorganizing the governmental machinery of the state. Texas was thinking more of of its own concerns and less of the agitation dividing the nation. In the Governor's eagerly awaited message to the Legislature,[1] national issues were subordinated to local problems, but not without the calm assurance that "Texas will maintain the Constitution and stand by the Union."

An aid to the General's program was Juan Nepomucino Cortina, by profession a bandit. Señor Cortina had formed for himself a principality, embracing several Texas counties on the lower Rio Grande and a corresponding strétch of domain on the Mexican side of the river, enabling him to exercise the rights of citizenship in two republics. His greater success was on the Texas side, where he had his personal envoy in the Legislature, controlled the custom-house at Brownsville and maintained an understanding with several sheriffs, one of them being his brother. After the election of Houston, whom he had opposed, Cortina made a demonstration of his power. Riding into Brownsville, he held the city by force until obliged to retire before Mexican Regulars from Matamoras to whom American citizens had appealed for protection. While Mexican soldiers policed the streets of Brownsville, Cortina withdrew to his fortified hacienda, the Rancho del Carmen, nine miles away, and summoned reinforcements. When Houston took office the desperado had five hundred fighting men, and the border was in a state of alarm.

Sam Houston sent three companies of Texas Rangers to attend to Cortina. A body of United States Regulars preceded them, however, and in a pitched battle drove the bandit over the Rio Grande. Texas approved and was wholesomely diverted, while Houston's political enemies observed uneasily that during the excitement the Governor had assembled a rather heavy concentration of military power which he kept within easy reach.

The border diversion sustained an interruption when a communication arrived from the Governor of South Carolina. In view of "the assaults upon the institution of slavery, and upon the rights . . . of the Southern States" the time had come for these states to hold a convention to take measures "to protect . . . their property from the enemy." To this end the South Carolina Legislature had appropriated one hundred thousand dollars "for military emergencies."

"With the spirit of courtesy which should actuate the Executive of one State in his intercourse with that of another," General Houston laid the communication before the Legislature, accompanied by a lengthy message.[2] "The Union was intended to be a perpetuity." The Governor reasoned against the abstract right of a state to secede. But granting this right, the principle of secession was ruinous. Should the South form a new Confederacy, it would only split into smaller fragments eventually.

A fierce fight followed in the Legislature. This body believed overwhelmingly in the abstract right of secession and had a majority in favor of the overt act. Sam Houston controlled agile minorities in each house, whose leaders he inspired with courage and with craft. Majority and minority reports were brought to the floor. In a bewildering battle Houston confused issues and outwitted the majority. Texas did not accept the South Carolina invitation.

So another personal victory, but the question was: How long, with his handful of followers, could Houston keep it up? He managed, however, to juggle until the Legislature adjourned. But the calm was momentary. An issue fraught with greater dangers was at hand—the fatal presidential campaign of 1860.

## 3

The Democratic party was now the only one in Texas. Even Houston, maintaining himself from day to day by dint of desperate improvisation, called his driven little band Union Democrats. Texas sent to the National Convention at Charleston a delegation headed by ex-Governor Runnels, instructed to go whole hog with the radical wing of the party. In framing the platform the southern group lost a point to the northerners, and the Texans with forty-odd other delegates walked out of the hall. The remainder cast fifty-seven ballots to select a nominee. Douglas polled a majority on every ballot, but under the two-thirds rule there was no choice.

Earnest efforts were made to bring the factions together. A spokesman for the powerful New York delegation visited a caucus of the Texans. There was a simple way out, he said. Nominate Sam Houston and New York would give him a majority of one hundred thousand. The Texas chairman voiced the sentiment of the delegation. "Sir, by——! I am the individual Sam Houston recently thrashed for Governor and anything that is laudatory to him is d——d unpleasant to me!"[3] Peace measures failing, the Convention adjourned for two months, to reconvene in Baltimore on June eighteenth. The bolters agreed to meet in Richmond on June tenth. Irretrievably divided was the party of the white-haired warrior who had flung in John C. Calhoun's face: "Our Federal Union—it must be preserved!"

Two days before the curtain rose on the disaster at Charleston, the twenty-fourth anniversary of San Jacinto was observed. General Houston remained with his family, but there was the usual pilgrimage to the battle-field with firing of guns, display of flags, foregathering of old soldiers. The assemblage adopted a resolution.

"We have fallen upon evil times. Political jobbers have maneuvered and squabbled, when they should have labored for the public good; they have invented new questions to distract the public mind; they have arrayed one section against another. . . . The time has now arrived when . . . men of whatever section who love their country should unite upon candidates of national" rather than sectional character.

"Therefore, be it *resolved* . . . That we recommend our distinguished fellow-citizen, General Sam Houston, as the people's candidate for the presidency— . . . [and ask] all conservative men, of all parties, in all sections of our Union" to support him.[4]

The action at San Jacinto struck fire in every quarter of the country. People approved, but politicians bitterly disapproved. There were parties enough and candidates enough as it was. The "regular" Democrats went ahead and nominated Douglas. The southern bolters, deaf to pleading, chose John C. Breckinridge, of Kentucky. The Republicans were more careful and more astute. Taking notice of the Houston sentiment and of what it meant, they rejected their shining light, Seward, as too extreme in his opposition to slavery, and compromised on a newcomer in national politics, Abraham Lincoln, of Illinois. Sam Houston even received a few votes for vice-president in the Republican Convention. Houston's southern enemies promptly made the most of this, especially since the nomination went to Hannibal Hamlin, of Maine, whom the South had been taught to believe was a mulatto.

A formidable body of voters was content with none of these selections, however. Mr. Breckinridge was no southern hotspur, and some of the hotspurs responsible for the Richmond Convention, fancied his choice to be a concession. They might have nominated Jefferson Davis. But the North was in no mood to discern such fine distinctions and regarded the Breckinridge candidacy as a studied slap. Even more greatly inflamed was the South by the nomination of Lincoln. Again, it was not the man. Despite his "house divided" speech, Lincoln's views of slavery were too moderate for most abolitionists. The northern radicals, unable to get a man more to their liking, were bound to support the ticket, however. Douglas was tarred with the Kansas-Nebraska blunder.

Thus the anxious interest centering upon the remaining nomination to be made. Calling itself the National Union party, the new political group had engaged an unused Presbyterian church in Baltimore and prepared to hold a Convention, beginning May ninth. The choice of name was a happy one. National Union expressed precisely the sentiment of the vast, independent, voter-group whose ideas had not been met by any of the three nominations preceding. Partizans of the previous nominees booed the Baltimore affair and the San Jacinto "nomination" in the same breath, but they were really disturbed. A profound interest welled from the people who sought only a leader "to grasp this sorry scheme of things entire . . . and . . . remould it."

San Jacinto had spoken, and it seemed with the voice of genius. The demand for Sam Houston as the National Union candidate exceeded that of all others whose names adorned the inevitable roster of "eligibles." His Texas triumphs were fresh in the public mind. He had strength in every part of the country. Lincoln, Douglas and Breckinridge were, each one, the choice of a section. That Houston would obtain the National Union nomination was not doubted. Correspondents of the New York *Herald*, *Times* and *Tribune*, arriving in Baltimore the day before the sessions opened, were a unit in predicting the selection of the former Texas Senator. The Houston headquarters were at Barnum's Hotel, those of John Bell, his only rival deserving of notice, at the slightly less swagger Eutaw House.

But a sudden fear caught at the heart of the Houston managers. If the dead hand of the Whig party, which already had done so much to ruin the budding aspirations of one national union party, should dominate this Convention, Houston and everything were lost. Senator Bell was a Union man from Tennessee with a good, mediocre record, but in no sense a national leader or a figure of national caliber. He was an old-line Whig, however, and strong with the surviving remnants of that defunct party, which like a thousand industrious moles, had burrowed into the structure of the new hope that was to express its ideals at Baltimore.

How deeply had the moles bored in? During the organization of the Convention on the first day, it was apparent that they had bored rather far, but neutral observers still gave Houston the best chance. The impress of his personality and the prestige of his attainments were definitely upon the Convention, which sought to imitate the tactics by which the Texas victories had been won. Dispensing with much time-honored campaign baggage, including a platform which few ever read and fewer understood, Houston had substituted a watch-word, "The Constitution and the Union!" The National Union party decided to do without a platform in favor of a slightly expanded copy of Sam Houston's battle-cry, "The Constitution of the Country, the Union of the States, and the enforcement of the laws."

General Houston did not appear to benefit by this tribute, however. The night following the first sessions witnessed further switching to Bell, and the Houston phalanx of New York delegates was broken into. "The old regular-died-in-the-wool Whigs cannot swallow the independent soldier-statesman from Texas," wrote the *Herald* man in his dispatch.

The next day nominations were in order. "Let us know no party but our Country and no platform but the Union," said Washington Hunt, of New York, the presiding officer, repeating almost verbatim a recent phrase of General Houston. Gustavus A. Henry, the first orator of Tennessee, gave the name of John Bell. Texas was next on the roll of states. It offered Sam Houston. The nomination was seconded by Delegate Gerard, of New York, who made the best speech of the Convention. He went to the point at once. "We can't carry New York with Bell but we can carry it with Sam Houston." "Give us this man, whose blood once ran like water in defense of the union now imperilled; who fought the Indians when they were enemies and lived with them when they were friends; who has been governor of two states; who has drawn his sword in defense of two republics; who has been president of one and is now on his way to that high office in the other. Give us this man who puts his party behind him, . . . a man like old

Jackson, who knows no party when enemies attack his beloved Union. Give us this man and we will decorate the City of New York with banners, go to the Country and with emblems of devotion to the union, sprinkle the blood of its defenders on the lintels of every door."[5]

It was useless. Bell polled 68½ votes on the first ballot, Houston 57, and 128½ were scattered among eight other aspirants. On the second ballot Bell was nominated. The listless choice for vice-president was the superannuated scholar, Edward Everett, of Harvard University—a solid Whig ticket.

The result at Baltimore took the heart out of the nationalist effort, and one by one editors who had been too forehanded removed from their mastheads the announcements reading: "For President, General Sam Houston of Texas." It was a hard fight to lose.

4

Sam Houston had failed to gain the leadership of a new party, but the renewed evidences of his national stature encouraged his friends in Texas and awed his adversaries. The feverish spring and summer of 1860 brought many very real consolations to the fighting Governor. Sam Houston was surrounded by his family for the longest period since Sam, Jr., had been a baby. The Executive Mansion was a habitation deserving of its title, and the Governor's large and happy domestic circle enhanced its splendor. The long and exacting hours of labor would have been too great a tax upon the Executive's strength except for Margaret, who superintended her husband's diet and guarded his periods of rest like a sentinel.

The Mansion was the scene of social gatherings amid which the General moved with the grace of yore. The Nashville gallant of forty years gone by was a grand seignor, whose popularity with the fair had diminished little. General Houston was never merely "pleased" to meet one, but "honored" to make the acquaintance of gentlemen and "charmed" or "enchanted" in the case of women, who were invariably "my lady" or "madame." A favored visitor to the Mansion was Emily Antoinette, the sister of Margaret, although there had been a time when Emily Antoinette stood rather higher in the favor of her sister's husband than of her sister. The wealthy Mr. Bledsoe had died and Emily had not worn her weeds long enough to suit Margaret, when she married Charles Power who had made a fortune in the diamond mines of Brazil. The new brother-in-law settled in Texas, had a sharp eye for business, and Houston liked him. At forty-eight Emily imported her dresses from Paris and defied the oblivion of middle age—something of a social experiment in 1860.

This, General Houston would have been the last to deprecate. His own wardrobe was as noteworthy as ever, and his jewelry more so. A friendly political opponent, encountering the General in company, began to rally him on his passion for personal adornment. "Yes, yes," said Houston. "This watch fob you see has a story connected with it. General Lafayette gave it to Andrew Jackson" under such and such circumstances, and "General Jackson gave it to me." So on through a display of four or five finger rings, watch, gold-headed cane and gold-encased pencil. A tale went with each and the absorbed hearers lost the point that the General's critic wished to emphasize. One thing General Houston passed over in his inventory, however—a plain gold band, quite thin now, worn on the small finger of the left hand. It was his mother's mottoed ring. Through every vicissitude of life, Sam Houston had carried this talisman, the simple story of which no man knew.

General Houston could not see too much of his children. All seven were at home, except Sam. The girls went to the town school in Austin, and Mrs. Houston instructed them at home in Latin and in music. Maggie was the studious one. At the age of twelve she helped her father with his correspondence. Sam, who attended Colonel Allen's military academy at Bastrop, was a tall, well-mannered boy of sixteen, above average in his studies and his popularity with the girls. The General was proud of Cadet Houston and, during the busiest days of his life, found time to write long letters to his son.

"Don't smoke, nor chew . . . [or] carry concealed weapons. . . . I look upon you as the one on whom my mantle is to fall. . . . It is natural that I should desire you to wear it worthily, aye nobly, and to give [it] additional lustre."[7] "Remember your Creator in the days of your youth . . . & my Dear boy never associate with those who . . . sneer at the teachings of the Bible."[8]

But there was less of this than one might expect. For the most part Houston's letters to his son were filled with family and neighborhood news, not to mention Sam's girl friends— Tula Clay, "the fair haired Octavia," Miss Rosa, Maggie Willis, Maggie Ragsdale and Miss Oldham, who looked "as blooming as a Pink, & attractive as a swamp cabbage."

"I wish you to pay more attention to Languages, History, Geography and Grammar than to mathematics." Geometry had been one reason for the father's brief stay at Porter Academy. The reading of poetry also was listed as a waste of time! "Lamar wrote poetry." Penmanship, however, was important. "Be sure my dear Boy to catch your pen, far from the end. This I never learned. Had I it would have been a great thing for me." "I have procured for you Caius Marius sitting on the ruins of Carthage. . . . You will be instructed & delighted, as he was one of the Proudest Romans."[9]

Marius again—a patriarch of seventy maintaining his seventh consulship by the sword, while civil war wet the paving stones of Rome. Sam Houston sustained his seventh reign in Texas by force of personality and the ability to govern men. He had not been popular in Austin since the "archive war." The story is told that when he arrived as governor a citizen of hard reputation mentioned that it would not be wise for Sam Houston to show himself on the streets. The Governor heard that this man was entertaining the diners at a local hotel with his threats. He went to the hotel and without a word seated himself directly opposite the man. The tavern's clientele trod softly, but nothing occurred to disturb General Houston in the leisurely consumption of his meal.

These things were useful. They kept green the tradition of an accepted courage that excused Sam Houston from duels. They formed a part of the invisible force that kept Cortina immured within the Mexican half of his domain, and restored the law's majesty on the frontiers.

"Sam Huston. Govnr. . . . I have bin reElected to the office of Assessor and Collector of Sansaba County. . . . Send me a SixShooter of the largest size and Buoy knife. E. Estep."[10]

"Sir I have the Honor to report the success of Capt Clark and myself in over taking the horse theives that you will recollect seeing us on their trail in Austin on the 4th of July you'll also recolect Col John Burleson giving my little son Kossuth an introduction to you in your buggy who told you he had heard so much talk of you that he expected to see a man big as an Elephant whereupon after a few more words you presented him to 50 ct what do you think he did with it Governor permit me to tell you that he bought a rope that hung the thieves. . . . J. B. Barry 1st Sargant Bosque County minute men."[11]

5

Although personal and political animosities made it a bitter pill, Houston gave pro forma support to Bell, and tried to prepare the people for the election of Lincoln. He left a sick bed to address a union rally at Austin urging that the success of the Republicans would afford no reason for secession.

In Texas the Governor continued as much in the public eye as any candidate. The individuality of Sam Houston was a part of the common domain, like the Llano Estacado. Steamboats and babies basked in the reflected glory of the magic name. Now that a few miles of railway had been laid down in Texas one read this head-line in the *Republican:*

"LOOK OUT FOR
SAM HOUSTON!"

For such was the name of "the new and splendid Locomotive" of the Southern Pacific Railroad.

In the same newspaper:

"GREAT WAR!!!
"Messrs Cohen & Bredig
"Have Declared a Great War

"against . . . E. Schwartz. . . ."
whom one infers to have been an unethical competitor.

The trend of informed political opinion did not agree with Messrs. Cohen & Bredig. The North would not fight. Displaying a lady's handkerchief one speaker volunteered to wipe up every drop of blood that should be spilled over secession. Another orator offered to drink every drop.

## 6

The election passed off fairly quietly in Texas. Before the result was known General Houston wrote to his son. "Your Dear Ma sends you by stage a bundle with eatables in it. I hope they may be agreeable to your palate." Whatever the result of the election, "If an attempt should be made to destroy our Union . . . there will be blood shed. . . . I wish you to write Cousin Mart Lea . . . and beg of him never to drink a drop of liquor . . . [but] don't let him know that I have given you the hint."[12]

The count of the ballots revealed that, although receiving less than two-fifths of the votes cast, Lincoln had a small popular plurality and a good majority in the electoral college. Bell ran last, polling 590,000 votes to 847,000 for Breckinridge, 1,365,000 for Douglas and 1,857,000 for Lincoln. Texas cast 47,000 votes for Breckinridge, 15,000 for Bell and none that were counted for Douglas or Lincoln.

Bonfires burned and Lone Star flags appeared. Secession seemed a certainty. Houston's Huntsville neighbors addressed a petition for guidance to the Governor. Houston's answer was to be calm and reflect. "Mr. Lincoln has been elected upon a sectional issue. If he expects to maintain that sectional issue during his administration, it is well that we should know it. If he intends to administer the government with equality and fairness, we should know that. Let us wait and see."[13]

Houston was deluged with petitions to call the Legislature. On November twentieth Ashbel Smith arrived in the capital, bearing such a petition. Sam Houston received his friend affectionately, and two days later published a Thanksgiving Day proclamation, asking citizens humbly to beseech Divine direction "in this hour of peril." All petitions to summon the Legislature were rejected, but the tidal wave of secession sentiment rolled on. The narrow ground on which Sam Houston stood began to crumble beneath his feet when members of his own Administration whom he had carried into office on a Union ticket deserted their leader. While Houston penned his Thanksgiving proclamation, a little knot of officials gathered in the office of the Attorney-General. On December third they disclosed their plan for circumventing the Governor. A petition was placed in circulation calling for the election of delegates to a Convention to meet on January twenty-eighth to decide the future of Texas.

The call swept the state. Prominent men vied for precedence in affixing their names. Preparations for the election went ahead, and the result was never an instant in doubt.

Between two fires, Houston chose to deal with the Legislature. He summoned it to convene on January twentieth, eight days in advance of the meeting of the Secession Convention.

On December twentieth South Carolina seceded, and an electric thrill ran through the South.

Mississippi, Florida, Alabama, Georgia and Louisiana left the Union. The simulacrum of a government at Washington did worse than nothing. Poor, negligible old Buchanan, wringing his hands in impotent befuddlement! An agonized bystander stretched his arms to heaven. "Oh, for an hour of Old Hickory Jackson!" As for Sam Houston, Senator Iverson, of Georgia, invited "some Texan Brutus" to "rise and rid his country of the hoary-headed incubus."

### 7

The Texas Legislature convened amid tumult, but gave respectful attention to the reading of a message which stands as one of Sam Houston's greatest public papers. The larger part of it was devoted to a comprehensive review of the internal affairs of Texas, outlining sufficient work in this field to occupy the lawmakers for a year. But there was something more. "The peculiar attitude of our relations with the Federal Government will, I trust, command . . . earnest attention. . . . While the proud structure of government, built by our fathers, seems tottering in ruin . . . we may not alone contemplate the scene and await its total downfall. . . . Ere the work of centuries is undone, and freedom, shorn of her victorious garments, started out once again on her weary pilgrimage, hoping to find another dwelling place, is it not manly to pause and avert the calamity."

The Governor permitted himself a tactful use of the sectional vernacular of the period. "The election of the Black Republican candidate to the presidency" was regrettable, "but the Executive yet has seen in it no cause for the . . . immediate secession of Texas." Houston shifted his line of defense. He contended no longer against the right of secession, but against the wisdom of it. He counseled delay. "Let the record of no one rash act blur" Texas's page in history.

But the Secession Convention, decreed to convene in ten days, bore upon the Governor like an engine of destruction. Houston fell back upon a strategy he had plied before with success. He ignored the Convention. In the entire length of his message there was no allusion to its existence. Yet, it might be that "the people, as the source of all power," should desire to speak their wishes as to "the course that Texas shall pursue." In any event the Legislature should study the matter. "Should the Legislature in its wisdom deem it necessary to carry a convention of delegates fresh from the people, the Executive will not oppose the same. . . . May a kind Providence guide you aright."[14]

A time there had been in Texas when Houston ruled by the hypnotism of his words and of his presence. That day was waning. The Legislature ignored the message and occupied itself with provisions for the comfort of the Secession Convention which, it was decided, should meet in the hall of the House of Representatives. It met on January twenty-eighth, and the Legislature, overriding a veto, recognized its authority.

The presiding officer of the Convention, Oran M. Roberts, an associate justice of the Supreme Court, conducted matters with a marked regard for the sensibilities of the Governor. Whether one liked Sam Houston or not, all conceded the strength his adhesion would bring to the secession cause. When one delegate called Houston a traitor William P. Rogers choked an apology from him. Rogers was a cousin of the Governor. An ordinance of secession was drafted, with a proviso for submission to the voters, intended as a concession to the views of the Executive.

The Convention was to vote on the ordinance at noon on February first, and Rogers headed a committee to invite the Governor to honor the occasion with his presence. Long before the hour designated the galleries were crowded, with special places for the legislative, judiciary and executive officers of the state. The seat of honor at Judge Roberts's right was reserved for Sam Houston.

On the stroke of twelve the Governor made a majestic entrance. Amid "deafening" applause Judge Roberts welcomed him graciously. Every eye was on Sam Houston's countenance. It told them nothing.

Amid perfect silence the Secretary read the ordinance of secession. Not a muscle of Houston's face moved. The clerk began to call the roll.

The first seventy delegates on the alphabetical list answered, "Aye."

"Hughes," read the clerk. Thomas Hughes, of Williamson County, was first and always a supporter of Sam Houston.

"No!" he shouted.

The effect was one of stupefaction. Then a cry of disapproval swept the hall.

After another stretch of "ayes" three more negative votes were cast in the face of increasingly hostile demonstrations.

"Throckmorton." James W. Throckmorton was leader of the Houston minority in the State Senate—tall, slender, magnetic and the best parliamentarian in Texas. It was his thirty-sixth birthday. "Mr. President, in the presence of God and my country, and unawed by the wild spirit of revolution around me, I vote, No!"

Judge Roberts announced the adoption of the ordinance by a vote of one hundred and sixty-seven to seven. Attorney-General Flournoy led a company of ladies down the aisle. They unfurled a Lone Star flag, and the tableau was over.

## 8

Interest veered to the military situation that Sam Houston had contrived on the Rio Grande. This concentration of troops, the largest in the country, long had been a source of concern to secessionists throughout the South. They were uncertain of the officer in command, Colonel Robert E. Lee. They had an ally, however, in the Secretary of War, who replaced Lee with General D. E. Twiggs. Governor Houston diplomatically asked the new Commandant to transfer the military property in Texas to the state authorities. Twiggs said he would do so "after secession," and with the passage of the ordinance he yielded troops and stores to a Committee on Public Safety created by the Convention.

On February twenty-third Texas was to vote on the secession ordinance. After a few Union meetings had been broken up, and speakers stoned, Sam Houston took the stump—a Dantonesque gesture in the face of certain defeat. After his second speech, at Waco, his life was threatened. At Gilmer he was challenged to express his "honest" opinion of Thomas Jefferson Green who was stumping Texas for secession. "He has all the characteristics of a dog except fidelity," replied Sam Houston. The Governor intended to close his tour with a speech from the balcony of the Tremont House in Galveston, but the behavior of the crowd was so ugly that his friends begged him not to appear.

Houston faced the mob. "There he stood," wrote an admiring northerner who was present, "an old man of seventy years, on the balcony ten feet above the heads of the thousands assembled to hear him, where every eye could scan his magnificent form, six feet and three inches high, straight as an arrow, with deep-set and penetrating eyes, looking out from heavy and thundering brows, a high forehead, with something of the infinite intellectual shadowed there, crowned with white locks, partly erect, seeming to give capillary conduction to the electric fluid used by his massive brain, and a voice of the deep basso tone, which shook and commanded the soul of the hearer; adding to all this a powerful manner, made up of deliberation, self-possession, and restrained majesty of action, leaving the hearer impressed with the feeling that more of his power was hidden than revealed."[15]

There was silence. It was not as yet given to Texans to withstand the Presence.

"Some of you laugh to scorn the idea of bloodshed as the result of secession," said Sam Houston. "But let me tell you what is coming. . . . Your fathers and husbands, your sons and brothers, will be herded at the point of the bayonet. . . . You may, after the sacrifice of countless millions of treasure and hundreds of thousands of lives, as a bare possibility, win Southern independence . . . but I doubt it. I tell you that, while I believe with you in the doctrine of state rights, the North is determined to preserve this Union. They are not a fiery, impulsive people as you are, for they live in colder climates. But when they begin to move in a given direction . . . they move with the steady momentum and perseverance of a mighty avalanche; and what I fear is, they will overwhelm the South."[16]

At the moment the South was overborne by an avalanche of a different character. Jefferson Davis rode to his inauguration in a carriage drawn by white horses. A granddaughter of ex-President Tyler fired the ceremonial cannon. The oath was administered in front of the stately Capitol of Alabama. "The man and the hour" were proclaimed to have "met," and the day closed with an illumination and a ball.

Five days later Texas voted. Eighty-one counties reported majorities for the ordinance. Seventeen voted for the Union. Twenty-seven counties, including some of the most populous, submitted no official figures. The result was 39,415 for secession and 13,898 opposed.

Houston's stand attracted much attention in the North, but the Buchanan government did nothing. While the election returns were being tabulated the Governor started on a trip from Austin to Belton. En route he stopped overnight at the home of Elias Talbot in Georgetown where a stranger who introduced himself as George D. Giddings handed General Houston a letter from Abraham Lincoln. Once in office Mr. Lincoln promised to support Houston in his endeavor to keep Texas in the Union, offering to land a large force of Federal troops on the Texas coast.

Returning to Austin Sam Houston held the second, and last, council of war of his career. David B. Culbertson, J. W. Throckmorton, Benjamin H. Epperson and George W. Paschal were summoned to the Executive Mansion. All were Unionists. Houston showed them the letter from Lincoln and asked their advice, beginning, military fashion, with the youngest person present.

This was Epperson. He favored resistance. Culbertson was next. He opposed resistance. The majority of people in Texas were for secession, and to make their homes a battle-ground would not change their opinions. The third to speak was James Throckmorton, ablest and most effective of Houston's adherents in Austin. He supported Culbertson. Paschal did the same.

The Governor stepped to the fireplace and dropped the letter of Abraham Lincoln into the flames.

"Gentlemen, I have asked your advice and will take it, but if I were ten years younger I would not."[17]

### 9

On March fourth the Convention declared Texas an "inde pendent sovereignty" and adjourned for dinner. Leaving the Capitol grounds, members saw posted on the gate a "Proclamation by the Governor of the State of Texas," announcing that an election had been held, with a result "appearing . . . in favor of 'secession.'" That was all. No mention of the Convention.

Judge Roberts sent a committee to ascertain the meaning of the proclamation. The Governor said he would explain himself to the Legislature, which was to reconvene on March eighteenth.

The Convention was not to be thrust aside. By a vote of one hundred and nine to two it declared Texas a part of the Confederacy, and ordered all officials to take the oath of allegiance. The ceremony for state officers was set for noon on March sixteenth. A great crowd of them was on hand. When the hour struck R. T Brownrigg, Secretary of the Convention, called out:

"Sam Houston."

There was no answer.

"Sam Houston! Sam Houston!"

Silence.

"Edward Clark."

Lieutenant-Governor Clark took the oath to support the Confederate States of America and was declared successor to the "vacant" office of governor.

In the Executive Chamber General Houston was at his desk, writing. The words have an imperishable quality.

"Fellow citizens, in the name of your rights and liberties, which I believe have been trampled upon, I refuse to take this oath. In the name of my own conscience and my own manhood . . . I refuse to take this oath. . . . I love Texas too well to bring strife and bloodshed upon her . . . [and] shall make no endeavor to maintain my authority as chief executive of this State except by peaceful exercise of my functions. When I can no longer do this I shall calmly withdraw, leaving the government in the hands of those who have usurped my authority, but still claiming that I am its chief executive. . . .

"It is, perhaps, meet that my career should close thus. I have seen patriots and statesmen of my youth one by one gathered to their fathers, and the government which they have reared rent in twain. . . . I stand the last almost of my race . . . stricken down because I will not yield those principles which I have fought for. . . . The severest pang is that the blow comes in the name of the State of Texas."[18]

General Houston crossed the Capitol square to the Executive Mansion, and seated himself on the south porch to await the end. His view commanded the State-House. Perhaps faintly he caught the sound of the cheering.

Shortly before one o'clock the throng began to stream from the building. From one of a group passing the Executive residence—a little fellow with a squeaky voice—Sam Houston heard the tidings of his fate.

The veteran's face was gray.

"Margaret," he said, "Texas is lost."[19]

# CHAPTER XXIX

## Stars to Clay

### 1

THE "bonnie blue" banner of the Confederacy gleamed beside the ensign of the single star. The new flag had experienced its baptism of fire on the field of Manassas in Virginia. Houston City celebrated the victory, Main Street a pageant of fresh uniforms and crinoline.

What nonsense that old villain Houston had preached to frighten the tender-hearted! With Manassas had vanished every doubt of a speedy end to the war. Every promise of the secessionists had been borne out, every foreboding overthrown. Union men who had followed Sam Houston had little to say in July of 1861. A few had left Texas, some were lying low, but the majority had proclaimed their error. No cringing coat-turning, this, but a genuine part of the emotional outpouring for Texas. "My State right or wrong!" James Throckmorton had said, and joined the Army.

During the spring Houston had tarried at Huntsville and then sought the deeper seclusion of Cedar Point by the sea. "He has sunk out of sight, leaving but a ripple on the surface."

In the exhilaration that thrilled Houston City and peopled its promenades, none seemed to recognize the countenance obscured by a shaggy beard, or the tall stooped form of an elderly man in loose-fitting country clothes who clumped Main Street with a great cane. At the high-toned Capitol Saloon hardly a head was turned when the old man received from the hand of the bartender a glass of anemic ginger water and retired to a table to sip alone and, it is possible, to reflect that under this roof Sam Houston had made Texas a nation and ruled it.

At the bar a party of staff officers clinked their glasses and demolished Yankees faster than Beauregard had dreamed of. One of them ventured that it would afford him pleasure to run his sword through the heart of that coward and traitor, Sam Houston.

Leaving his ginger water the old man made his way to the bar. He corrected the stoop in his shoulders.

"Here is the heart of Sam Houston, and whoever says it is the heart of a coward or traitor lies in his teeth!"[1]

On another day General Houston was seated on the balcony of the City Hotel when a parcel of recruits for the Second Texas Infantry called out a respectful greeting. They were just boys. Leaning on his stick, the General started to tell them in a paternal way some of the things that young soldiers should know. A bystander made a sneering remark.

Sam Houston threw down his cane and spoke in a new tone. Having himself gone to war as a boy, he had a feeling toward these young men that only an old soldier could understand. All honor to them. But this was not to say that the war was right or reasonable. One swallow did not make a summer, and one victory would not win the war. Emblems of triumph floated in Texas now. Time would see badges of sorrow in their places. But these boys went to battle with his blessing. His prayers would follow them, "that they may be brave, trust in God and fear not."[2]

General Houston returned to Cedar Point to learn that he had blessed his own son. Sam, Jr., had joined Ashbel Smith's company of the Second Texas. Margaret was in tears. Her husband consoled her. What else was there for a boy of spirit to do?

**2**

Yet, General Houston had nourished other ambitions for his son. Such ambitions! For months his mind had dwelt on them: The sword of San Jacinto in a younger Sam Houston's hand; deeds of glory in Texas; a dream of dynasty; the restoration of His Republic—and His Son's.

Since the early foreshadowings of disaster the grand imagination had been at work. As remote as 1857 the General had speculated upon a possible resurrection of the Lone Star in event of the disintegration of the Union. Sam Houston believed that, given time, he could, in any situation, bring Texas to his bidding. North of the Red River lay the Indian country, where the career of The Raven formed a part of the tribal legends. To the south shimmered the castles of the Montezumas.

Toward the end of the short sharp struggle at Austin over secession, Sam Houston's methods had been more transparent than was usual for him. His idea was to accept a separation from the Union, then quickly disperse the Secession Convention and gather all authority into his own hands. "I can see your motive in this," wrote Houston's brother-in-law, Charles Power, "which is to endeavor to get this state to go it alone looking to a disruption of the new confederation. . . . I should like to see yr program carried out but General . . . the die is cast. . . . The only portion of the State that will be for the Lone Star is Galveston. . . . I advise you as a friend to yield quietly to the majority. . . . Pass quietly into quiet retirement and let them fight it out, and posterity will give you a page of History which is as much as the greatest can expect, the disorganizers may have their day but will go down without paeons being sung to their memories."[3]

The advice of Emily's husband seems to have weighed with the Executive, who could have gathered to himself a band of men who would have sold their lives dearly. But Houston had retired peaceably—so peaceably that his opponents were uneasy. "Ex-Governor Houston," said the Austin *Gazette*, "is at last willing to acknowledge that Texas is out of the Union. He now declares himself in favor of the Lone Star Republic, and opposed to the Southern Confederacy. He will use his influence to cause the rejection of the permanent constitution of the Confederate States."[4]

This opposition, too, failed to materialize; yet apprehension did not down. Before he had been in office a month, Governor Clark began to contribute to the worries of Jefferson Davis. "An effort will soon be made . . . to establish an independent republic, and one of the most effective arguments will be that the Confederate States have supplied the place of U. S. troops consisting of 2800 men with only one regiment. The people of Texas have been positively assured that their protection would be far more perfect under the Confederate States than it was under . . . the old U. S. and on that assurance we now rely."[5]

While these things were going on Sam, Jr., was at military school in an atmosphere that gave his father much concern. General Houston was glad when the term ended, and he could bury the boy at Cedar Point, sending him in advance of the family to "mind the corn and the cord-wood . . . destroy the cockleburs in the fields and yard." As for politics, the General hoped Sam would not believe what he saw in the papers. "They lye to suit the market. Do you my son not let anything disturb you, attend to business, and when it is proper you shall go to war if you wish. . . . It is every man's duty to defend his country and I wish my offspring to do so, at a proper time and in a proper way. We are not wanted or needed out of Texas, and we may soon be needed and wanted in Texas. Until then, my son, be content. . . . Tula Clay and all are well. . . . Thy father, affectionately."[6]

The family moved down to the seashore and General Houston continued his subtle occupation of sowing distrust, in which, as invariably happened, external events seemed to spring unbidden to his aid. A stream of complaints poured upon Mr. Davis. Texas resented the presence of recruiting officers from across the Sabine. A Texas regiment had been raised by an outsider and marched east without local authority. A demand for eighteen regiments had specified infantry, when all the world knew that Texas cavalry had no equal on the globe. But the dominant consideration was the supposed need for troops for local defense. On one frontier were the Indians. On another a rumor of invasion by way of Missouri stole surreptitiously from the sharp brain of a white-haired schemer shuffling the cards for his last cast for fortune. The result was a mounting tide of sovereignty, the legacy of the Lone Star. Houston could wish for nothing better.

He was anxious, however, about his boy. Sam had gone off to a near-by encampment where a group of young fellows were drilling with the vague intent of absorbing themselves into the new regiments requested by Richmond. "I had hoped, my dear son," his father wrote, "that in my retirement my mind would be engrossed . . . with . . . matters concerning my family alone, and to live in peace." But this was not to be. "In the train of events now transpiring I think I perceive disaster to Texas.

"I know not how much statesmanship Lincoln may have, or Generalship at his command . . . but looking at matters as they seem to me his wise course, I would say," would be to launch an offensive from Missouri against Texas. In this "Texas . . . can look for no aid from the Confederacy." She "must either succumb or defend herself. . . . My son . . . your first allegiance is due" to Texas, "and let nothing cause you in a moment of ardor . . . to assume any obligation to any other power whatever without my consent. If Texas demands your services or your life . . . stand by her.

"Houston is not, nor will be, a favorite name in the Confederacy! Thus you had best keep your duty and your hopes together, and when the Drill is over come home. . . . When will you come home? my son? Thy Devoted Father, SAM HOUSTON."[7]

Immediately after writing this letter General Houston made his visit to Houston City, returning to learn that his son was a Confederate soldier.

### 3

The boy asked his father's forgiveness and received it. When the Second Texas was mobilized on Galveston Island, General Houston became a frequent visitor to the encampment. He slept in the Colonel's tent but ate with the men. The sights and circumstances of camp life restored the old soldier's spirits, and he shaved the unsightly beard. When the young men called him General he would say, "Why, don't you boys know that Sam Houston is just a private in Company C?"

In this way passed August and September of 1861, and in October the family returned to Huntsville. The sunlit balm of Indian summer lay upon the rolling landscape. In a corner of the lawn, under a great oak, General Houston loved to sit and smoke, with a blue velvet cap on his head, soft yellow moccasins on his feet and the San Jacinto leg on a stool. Shadows played on the green hills and the melodies of Stephen Foster floated from Margaret's piano. The General's chair was the dependable rawhide bottom one that had twice served him while president of the Republic. One evening he crossed the lawn and asked Margaret to play *Come to the Bower*. . . . *Come to the Bower*. "Hold your fire men, hold your fire." Twenty-five years ago he had said it.

Thus an old man under an old tree, smoking and thinking, still on the bourne of the dream-world that had drawn into the forest a boy with a book and a rifle—half mystic, half showman; half poet, half sage.

### 4

The destiny-borne war rolled on its way. The North had not quit, but the South won most of the battles and breathed the intoxicating air of triumph. Texas regiments were with Lee in Virginia—the famous brigade of Hood. Texans were fighting in Tennessee, though not with equal success. But in New Mexico they had routed the Yanks properly and the

Stars and Bars flew over Santa Fé. The Lone Star State was taking a keener interest in the war, although an enormous concentration of butternut-clad troops remained in the camps at home. Sam Houston said they should stay there. He coached representatives in the Confederate Congress to oppose conscription and to criticize Mr. Davis's measures for financing the war.

Early in 1862 more Texas regiments were ordered to the front, among them the Second Infantry. General Houston repaired to camp. Colonel Moore asked him to review the troops. Houston put them through the evolutions. How the old drill sergeant loved to do that! Bringing the regiment into line, he commanded:

"Right about, *face!*"

The men were looking to the rear.

"Do you see anything of Judge Campbell or of Williamson S. Oldham here?" the General shouted.

"No," the regiment replied.

"Right about, *face!* Do you see anything of Judge Campbell's son here?"

"Paris at school!" yelled the soldiers.

"Eyes, *left!* Do you see anything of young Sam Houston here?"

And when the cheering subsided: "Eyes, *front!* Do you see anything of old Sam Houston here?"[8]

The regiment departed on March twelfth, General Houston describing his son as "18 years of age, 6 feet high and a rather well-made and good looking boy . . . ardently devoted to the cause in which he is engaged."[9]

At the end of the month the regiment reached the great Confederate concentration point at Corinth, Mississippi. "I am here amidst an hundred thousand men," wrote a cousin of Margaret, "Emmet & Sam are talking outside the tent—God bless & protect the boys. . . . Crazy politicians have made it necessary that we offer our Isaac's upon the altar of our country. Sam is in robust health and seems as likely to bear the fatigue of the campaign as any soldier in it. . . . A terrible struggle may be expected. . . . Present me kindly to Gener¹ & tell him they have stoned the prophets but will come to their senses."[10]

Before this letter reached Margaret the terrible struggle occurred. At Shiloh Church, on the soil of Tennessee, Albert Sidney Johnston took Grant unaware and launched a dashing assault with forty thousand men. Grant had thirty-three thousand. The Confederate leader was killed early in the fight but the fury of the southern charges rolled the Federals back. Cutting its way through the Yankee line, the Second Texas captured intact a Union battery and a reserve brigade of three thousand men. Captain Ashbel Smith was wounded. At nightfall disaster crowded the stubborn Grant. Driven back to Pittsburg Landing his left clung to the river bank until Buell arrived with a fresh army of twenty thousand, which fell on the exhausted Confederates at dawn. Again the Second Texas charged, driving a salient in the enemy front nearly half a mile deep, when, overwhelmed by flanking fire it fell back. After six hours of battle the Confederate line broke. The Second Texas deployed to cover the retreat, and Private Houston fell with a ball through the body. The Federal advance swept over him and Sam was dropped from the roll of Company C as killed in battle.

A Union medical officer, kneeling beside the wounded boy, told a blue-clad chaplain that this soldier had not long to live. Sam's knapsack had fallen off, and its contents were strewn about. The chaplain picked up a Bible. It had been shot through.

"From
Margaret Lea Houston
to her beloved son
Sam
Huntsville, Texas"

"Is General Sam Houston your father?" asked the clergyman.

This minister had been among the signers of a celebrated protest against the enactment of the Kansas-Nebraska Bill. Senator Houston was one of the few defenders of this petition.

Sam was given special care and as soon as he could travel he was exchanged.

Margaret was tending her flowers when a crippled soldier appeared at the gate. She left her work to speak to him, but he spoke first.

"Why, Ma, I don't believe you know me!"[11]

### 5

Sam recuperated at Cedar Point where the air smelled of the subtropical sea, and white clouds hung so palpable and motionless that it seemed a miracle they did not fall from the sky.

General Houston's personal popularity continued to mend. The enduring affection that Texas held for Sam Houston despite its fits of temper and his; the tradition of sovereignty of which Houston was the personification; the lynx-fox game at which the old General continued to ply his practised hand— these considerations were not to be resisted. A blunder on the part of the Confederate Government also had its effect. Richmond sent a General Hebert to command the military department of Texas. He proclaimed martial law and covered the state with provost marshals clothed in despotic power. Passports to travel on the highways were required of all citizens over seventeen years of age. One energetic guardian of the public safety took it upon himself to halt Sam Houston's top buggy.

"San Jacinto is my pass through Texas!" was the response he got.[12]

The story was repeated with relish, and the top buggy was on the roads more than ever.

In August of 1862 Houston heard that "charges have been lodged against me" with the provost marshal of Harris County, in which Houston City is located. He wrote immediately to that officer, requesting the "name of the author, or authors, who may have complained to you, or made any charges against my loyalty to the Government. . . . I claim no more than the humblest man in the community, and I am always ready to answer the Laws of my country."[13] The days of the Hebert régime were numbered.

Sam, Jr., returned to the front. "My ever precious boy," wrote his mother. "We are expecting Col. Smith this evening . . . previous to his departure for the army . . . and I almost tremble when I think of meeting one who is so intimately associated . . . with the great trial of my life. But I will not pain my darling boy by recounting the sufferings through which the Good Lord has brought me safe, but reserve it for the time . . . when we can talk together of the fearful dangers through which you have been preserved. . . . The children have given you all the news and as it is the Sabbath day I do not feel at liberty to write any secular details, so I will beg of you . . . to answer the all-important question— Have you given your heart to God? . . . My son have you sought him with your whole heart? Are you sure that you abhor your sins? . . . Once more I entreat you to flee from the wrath to come. Oh do not delay! . . . I send you a little book containing passages of scripture for every day in the year."

Sister Nannie begged to say that she had sent a pair of socks and father added a postscript in his own hand.

"My Dear Son I only send you a fond Father's tender blessing and assure you of his prayers at a Throne of Grace for your safety and salvation."[14]

All days were not gray. September sixth was the birthday of Nannie, and when she walked into the living-room there stood the handsomest rosewood piano she had ever seen. Not many people in Texas were buying pianos in 1862. While by no means a poor man, General Houston's scale of living caused people to exaggerate his wealth. A master of public economies, he was rather careless in personal matters of money. Tax receipts and other papers indicate that at the beginning of the war General Houston was worth possibly one hundred and fifty thousand dollars. Most of this was in land and mortgages. Amid the stresses of wartime debtors were unable to pay, and land was a burden. From the beginning of his retirement Houston was pressed for ready cash, though this had little effect on his open-handed style of living. When he died his estate had shrunk to eighty-nine thousand dollars.

Since leaving Austin the General had been seriously concerned about his health. Physicians prescribed in vain. The blow of repudiation by his beloved Texas had broken some vital spring. There was also an ominous cough accompanied by a loss of flesh. Out of their patient's hearing doctors whispered "consumption." Houston's eldest brother had died of it. On the other hand another brother had shot himself over a love-affair and the beautiful Mary, his favorite sister, had gone to her grave insane as the result of a tragic marriage.

In the autumn when the time came to return to Huntsville, General Houston was too ill to travel. The attending physician, a young man, having exhausted the resources of his professional skill, decided that the General was going to die. One night he rode through the rain to ask Hamilton Stewart, a neighbor, to convey the difficult message.

"Call the family and the servants," General Houston said.

In a calm voice General Houston gave his wife a summary of his personal affairs, and then bade each of his children, and the servants, good-by. He asked Nannie and Maggie to sing a hymn. The little girls broke down, and General Houston, finishing the chorus, asked every one to go back to bed. A few days later he was up and around. "Yes, tell my enemies I am not dead yet."[15]

The General gained strength and seemed on the way to better health than he had enjoyed since his retirement. Ashbel Smith, a lieutenant-colonel now, was well of his wound and about to return to the Army. With him Houston frankly discussed the separation of Texas from the Confederacy. The General's ideas had crystallized. His plan was to stop the flow of Texas troops across the Sabine and, at the right moment, declare himself the lawful magistrate of the state, unfurl the Lone Star and call Texans home from the armies of the Confederacy. Magnificent prospects spread before the grim dreamer. He foresaw in fifteen years' time steam cars running from the Brazos to Mexico City.

In November Houston was able to journey to Independence, and thence to Huntsville, making numerous stops en route. The coup d'état filled his mind. Smith returned to his regiment, and another furloughed Confederate field officer became Houston's confidant, the General writing to him from Independence under date of November 24, 1862:

"Please come and see me at Huntsville, where a warm welcome awaits, and a thousand things to speak of with a comrade who has seen other and better days in Texas. . . . We must send out no more troops, *not one man!* The Confederate Govt must agree to this, the preservation of Texas is imperative to her hopes of success. Now, I mean to preserve Texas. It is my duty. Am I not, according to the constitution, the sovereign authority of this state. . . . The people will uphold me in this and with God's help we will *save Texas*."[16]

### 6

A short half-mile by dusty road from the court-house square in Huntsville nestled the famous Steamboat House amid a bank of cedar, crêpe myrtle and fig trees. But its glory was a great oak, from the shade of which one surveyed a panorama of green-clad, orderly hills. To the south in a hollow stood the squat buildings of the state penitentiary. A small graveyard lay to the westward, across the little road. The only neighboring dwelling in view was the Rawlings mansion, a smaller Mount Vernon, half-hidden by the planting on its lovely grounds.

The Steamboat House was erected about 1860 by Dr.

Rufus W. Bailey, president of Austin College at the other end of the town. Deploring a lack of originality in the prevailing styles of architecture, Doctor Bailey determined to remedy this defect. His inspiration, the Mississippi River steamboat, was executed with alarming perfection. The long narrow structure was surrounded by a two-story gingerbread gallery. The stairways were on the outside, leading from one deck of the gallery to the other. The motif found further expression in the design of the doors and the windows with their little panes of vari-colored glass. The parlor was on the "saloon deck" up-stairs. Bedchambers bore some resemblance to staterooms.

Shortly before the war General Houston had sold both Raven Hill plantation and his town house in Huntsville, but his attachment for the placid village carried him back after surrendering the governorship. Doctor Bailey had lately died and his residence was for rent. The Houstons took it and in this bizarre pavilion, the Steamboat House, the old wanderer found his last home.

On January 1, 1863, Texas forces recaptured Galveston from the Federals, and Sam Houston congratulated Hebert's successor, Magruder, on having "introduced a new era in Texas." The Union troops and seamen taken by Magruder were confined in the Huntsville penitentiary. When General Houston learned that they were locked in cells, he got out the top buggy and lodged a vigorous protest with the authorities. More appropriate quarters were provided for the prisoners of war, and General Houston made several acquaintances among them, whom he visited in the course of his walks about the countryside during the spring of the year.

The new era moved haltingly. Ben Butler, the Federal General occupying New Orleans, was agitating Washington to make a military demonstration along the Sabine calculated to help Houston to restore the Republic. This was, of course, a form of assistance that General Houston least desired.

But as for other help, competent hands were wanting. The figures of the Revolution, the personages of the Republic, friend and foe, had passed—nearly all. The Whartons were dead. Henderson was dead. Three-legged Willie was dead. Rusk was dead—suicide. Hockley was a loyal Confederate officer. Barnard Bee had fallen at Manassas while rallying a broken brigade: "See, there stands Jackson like a stone wall!"—and History caught from the dying man's lips, "Stonewall" Jackson. Gail Borden, revolutionary editor, had returned North, perfected his process, originated in Texas, of condensing milk, and was profitably supplying Yankee quartermasters. Lamar was dead, Anson Jones was dead. His ineptitudes at the lynx-fox game had cost poor Jones dearly in popularity. To crown all he must write a book, blaming everything on Houston. Ascending the steps of the colonnaded Capitol Hotel he exclaimed, "Here I began my career in Texas, here I end it!" and applied a pistol to his temple.

And Burnet. During the summer at Cedar Point Nannie had returned from a visit with an enthusiastic account of a "charming old gentleman" she had met. "You must certainly remember him, father, for he said that he knew you in the early days of Texas, and made such kind inquiries about you." General Houston asked the name. "Judge Burnet," said Nannie. The General smiled, but told his daughter nothing of those early days with David Burnet.[17]

Penniless and alone, the ex-Provisional President was living on the bounty of friends, a broken patriarch with a white beard that might have belonged to one of those Old Testament squires he knew so well. With Houston's eventual triumph in Texas he had resumed his travels in futile search of fortune, returning to Texas to die. "In my heart dwells no bitterness towards General Houston. He is a Christian, blessed with a Christian lady and several fine children, while I am bereft and alone." The old man's all was a son, an officer in the Confederate service. He said he wished that his boy and Sam Houston's might meet and fight side to side. Ten days before the surrender of Lee, Major Burnet was killed in battle. The old adventurer turned to the Book that had been his prop for sixty years, and scrawled opposite the name of his boy. "Oh! My God! thy will be done and give me grace to submit!"

Many were the men from whom Sam Houston had parted in anger, but he hated as he loved, in hot blood, and with a few conspicuous exceptions bitterness lapsed on this side of the grave. While in the Senate a Congressman from Rhode Island told Houston he had come into possession of some notes signed by M. B. Lamar, and asked the General's advice whether to dispose of the paper for what he could get, or to hold it in the expectation of payment in full. Houston said to hold the notes. "You know what I think of Lamar, but he's honest. He pays his debts."

## 7

In Summer County, Tennessee, another Bible was brought out, and its pages turned. Under the heading "Family of John Allen, Esq," appeared this line:

"Eliza H. Allen, sister of George W. Allen, was born Saturday, Dec. 2nd, 1809."

And further down:

"Eliza H. Allen, sister of Geo. W. Allen, was married to Gov. Samuel Houston, Jan. 22nd, 1829."

On another page:

"Eliza, who first married Gov. Sam Houston and separated from him for cause unknown . . . then married Dr. Elmore Douglass."

It was now time for a last entry:

"Eliza H. Houston-Douglass (Allen) Sister of George W. Allen died March 3rd, 1862."[18]

The earth that assimilated her dust tells no more. By leave of indulgent years the worn stones have fallen into easy attitudes, which impart an air of friendliness to the Gallatin grave-yard. One may note the resting-places of Eliza Allen's parents, of her brothers and sisters and in-laws by the score, of her husband's first wife who had ten children in fifteen years and then was struck by lightning, and of two of Eliza's own children who preceded their mother in death.

No stone says where Eliza lies. The girl who changed the face of history sleeps in an unmarked grave.

## 8

The unnatural war went on. "A great many of your old friends and school-mates have died or been killed," Margaret wrote her son. "I will merely name Lem Abercrombie, Jeff Montgomery, John Garratt, Lem Hatch John Hill Proctor Porter Bill Humes John White Walter Maxey Angus Allston. Old Mrs. Thomas of our neighborhood has lost five sons."[19]

Texas had seventy-five thousand men in the field. Only Virginia, reluctant to secede but now practically sustaining the Confederacy, contributed more generously of her manhood. In the West things went badly. The imperturbable Grant, mauling at Vicksburg, wrote his wife that it made no difference to him whether the negroes were freed or not. Mrs. Grant owned slaves until the close of the war. In the East Stonewall Jackson went down. Lee, who disbelieved in slavery, carried on much alone, moving his dwindling Army of Northern Virginia by a succession of futile victories over the long road toward Appomattox.

The chances are that Mrs. Thomas, whose five sons had died for the bonny blue flag, did not own a slave. What, then, touched the instincts of these people to fight so long and so well for an institution in which they had no share? The answer is that they were fighting also for something else. "Southern rights" was more than a phrase. Like the rest of the Valley, Rockbridge County, in Virginia, where Sam Houston was born, and where he had a hundred blood relations, had staunchly opposed both slavery and secession. But when Lincoln called for troops its men went almost en masse into the Confederate regiments. Still another intangible factor supported the cause of the South—Lee's almost God-like inspiration of his armies. One asked a poor white why he fought and he would answer, "For Robert E. Lee," whom, perhaps, he had never seen. To say that Lee was the greatest soldier who has used the English tongue does not explain this devotion. Grant was a great soldier and McClellan a comparative mediocrity, yet Grant's men felt no especial love for their chief while Little Mac's adored him.

True, there was internal dissension in the South: rich-man's-fight talk; obstruction of the draft; threats by Georgia and North Carolina to secede from the Confederacy. Identical difficulties wracked the North whose swelling armies were well paid and well fed, whose people were strangers to the degree of privation that sapped the South. One must never say that the South's heart was not in this war, waged, as it was, against the protest of the great statesman, the foresight of whose prophesies became daily more apparent. Yet, in Texas, it seemed that the tide might turn in time for him.

In March of 1863 General Houston visited Houston City. He was hospitably received and invited to deliver an address. "Ladies and Fellow-Citizens," he said, "This manifestation is the highest compliment that can be paid to the citizen and patriot. As you have gathered here to listen to the sentiments of my heart, knowing that the days draw nigh unto me when all thoughts of ambition and worldly pride give place to the earnestness of age, I know you will bear with me while . . . I express those sentiments that seem natural to my mind." He spoke hopefully of the war. The North was weary. The South might find an ally in France, as a result of that nation's adventure in Mexico. Then he adroitly betrayed himself as a purveyor of dubious optimism. "I do not look with confidence to these results, nor do I advance them as more than mere probabilities. . . . Let us," however, "go forward, nerved to nobler deeds. . . . Let us bid defiance to all the hosts that our enemies can bring against us. Can Lincoln expect to subjugate a people thus resolved? No!"[20]

So cordial was the reception that General Houston thought perhaps the dawn of the new era approached. He sought the counsel of two trusted friends, E. W. Cave and Alexander W. Terrell. Major Cave had been Houston's secretary of state and the only state official to follow his chief in his refusal to take the Confederate oath. Houston spoke of the war with its wicked waste of life and the improbability of success to the southern arms. How would the people of Texas feel, he asked, about displaying the Lone Star flag, calling the Texas troops home and saying to North and South alike, "Hands off!"

Cave and Terrell were shocked. They said the stroke would fail and would ruin all concerned with it.[21]

General Houston returned to the Steamboat House and wrote his will. "To my eldest son, Sam Houston, Jr., I bequeath my sword, worn in the battle of San Jacinto, never to be drawn only in defense of the Constitution, the Laws and Liberties of his Country. If any attempt should ever be made to assail one of these, I wish it used in its vindication."[22]

Sam, Jr., was at home on furlough, preparing for a trip to Mexico with his uncle, Charles Power, who wrote the General to give his son a good horse and "decent" clothes. "When he gets to Mexico I want Sam Houston, Jr., with me, not a 'Mexican bandalho!'" Mr. Power's letter contained other observations. "I would rather be hung at a black jack than take another dollar of Confederate money." "You made the Horizon bright in your speech at Houston, and I only wish I had the same ideas. . . . I make no doubt but that the People will call you out yet for Governor. I never saw such a change in my life."[23]

On the Potomac a confidant of spies wrote a letter marked "Private" to Ben Butler at New Orleans: "The movement of Gen. Sam Houston for the restoration of the Republic, coupled with the fact that the Mexican Legation has withdrawn, has

alarmed (and not without cause) the Secretary of State. . . .
I beg of you to give this matter your serious and early consideration. . . . You can restore to the Union a State in
acreage equal to six and a half of New York."[24]

9

General Houston's popularity continued to return. He was
solicited to become a candidate for governor at the election of
August, 1863, but formally declined on grounds of uncertain
health. The fact that Sam Houston had never taken the Confederate oath was not mentioned as a disqualifying circumstance. Moreover, it appears that the disabling ailment was
somewhat diplomatic in character. In May of 1863 Houston's
health seems to have been as good, if not better, than in March
when the visit to Houston City was made with the definite
thought of reclaiming the executive power.

Since Houston was never forehanded with his plans, it is
impossible to say what was now in his mind. Had he contested for the governorship at the regular election of 1863,
the campaign would have been a strenuous one. Perhaps
Houston, who already considered himself the constitutional
chief magistrate of Texas, thought to spare himself this exertion by biding his time. Sam Houston was very good at
waiting.

In any event, instead of an electioneering tour, the General
made a trip to Sour Lake to bathe his old wounds, which were
troubling him, as they had done periodically for twenty-five
years. There was also the cough, but when the General passed
through Houston in the latter part of June the *Telegraph*
congratulated him on his hale appearance.

On the eighth of July, the day after receipt of news of the
fall of Vicksburg, Margaret wrote her husband a letter that
was more cheerful than usual. Temple, the baby, "talks a
great deal about you. He grows more and more interesting."
"Betty Sims and Della Alston spent Friday night with us, and

the young people had quite a merry time." Nannie was visiting her Aunt Emily Antoinette at Independence. Sam, Jr., after many delays, had crossed the Rio Grande in high spirits. Mrs. McGary's funeral was held yesterday "and bro. O'Brien preached a fine sermon. . . . Mr. Seat preaches tonight on the Prophesies and the Confederate government. I hope he will have better luck in predicting than he has had heretofore.

"I do hope my Love you will soon recover your health and be able to return home, but do not hurry on account of any anxiety about us. . . . I must ask you the favor to get me another supply of Jonas Whitcomb's remedy for Asthma.

"Thy devoted wife

"M. L. Houston

"P. S. Maggie sends her love to you, in which all unite. I hope soon to get a letter from you. Written with a bad pen and muddy ink."[25]

## 10

General Houston did not write a letter. He came home, quite miserable with a cold. Margaret put him to bed in the front room down-stairs and called Doctor Markham. The days were hot and the narrow couch was drawn to the center of the room to get the benefit of the circulation of air. The patient did not improve, and Doctor Kittrell, a political adversary but a personal friend, was summoned from his plantation fifteen miles from town.

The physicians told Margaret that the General had contracted pneumonia. On July twenty-fifth he fell into a drug-like sleep. The family gathered about the couch and Reverend Doctor Samuel McKinney offered a prayer.

General Houston slept through the night, with Margaret at his side. When morning dawned she asked for her Bible and began to read in a low voice.

"In my Father's house are many mansions: if it were not so, I would have told you. I go to prepare a place for you."

As these words fell from her lips General Houston stirred. It was mid-forenoon. Margaret put down the book and clasped her husband's hands. His lips moved.

"Texas—Texas!—Margaret——"

As the slanting shadows of sunset crept upon Steamboat House General Houston ceased to breathe. A life so strange and so lonely, whose finger-tips had touched stars and felt them change to dust, had slipped away.

Margaret asked God to make her children men and women worthy of their father. From her husband's finger she removed the talisman that fifty years before another mother had given a boy soldier to confront the world. Margaret held the ring so that the children might see graven on its inner surface the short creed that Elizabeth Houston said must for ever shine in the conduct of her son. It was "Honor."[26]

**THE END**